Keeping Time:
Dialogues on music and archives in honour of Linda Barwick

Indigenous Music, Language and Performing Arts

Associate Professor Myfany Turpin, Series Editor

The many forms of Australia's Indigenous music and temporal arts have ancient roots, huge diversity and global reach. The Indigenous Music, Language and Performing Arts series aims to stimulate discussion and development of the fields of Aboriginal and Torres Strait Islander music, language and performing arts, in both subject matter and approach, as well as looking beyond Australia to First Nations cultures around the world. Proposals are welcomed for studies of traditional and contemporary performing arts (including dance), popular music, art music, experimental and new media, and the importance of First Nations languages for culture and empowerment, as well as theoretical, analytical, interdisciplinary and practice-based research. Where relevant, print and ebook publications may be supplemented by online or audiovisual media.

Archival Returns: Central Australia and Beyond
Edited by Linda Barwick, Jennifer Green and Petronella Vaarzon-Morel

For the Sake of a Song: Wangga Songmen and Their Repertories
Allan Marett, Linda Barwick and Lysbeth Ford

Music, Dance and the Archive
Edited by Amanda Harris, Linda Barwick and Jakelin Troy

Recording Kastom: Alfred Haddon's Journals from the Torres Strait and New Guinea, 1888 and 1898
Edited by Anita Herle and Jude Philp

Reflections and Voices: Exploring the Music of Yothu Yindi with Mandawuy Yunupingu
Aaron Corn

Singing Bones: Ancestral Creativity and Collaboration
Samuel Curkpatrick

Songs from the Stations: Wajarra as Sung by Ronnie Wavehill Wirrpnga, Topsy Dodd Ngarnjal and Dandy Danbayarri at Kalkaringi
Myfany Turpin and Felicity Meakins

The Old Songs are Always New: Singing Traditions of the Tiwi Islands
Genevieve Campbell with Tiwi Elders and knowledge holders

Wurrurrumi Kun-Borrk: Songs from Western Arnhem Land
Kevin Djimar

Vitality and Change in Warlpiri Songs
Edited by Georgia Curran, Linda Barwick, Valerie Napaljarri Martin, Simon Japangardi Fisher and Nicolas Peterson

Keeping Time:
Dialogues on music and archives in honour of Linda Barwick

Edited by Nick Thieberger, Amanda Harris,
Sally Treloyn and Myfany Turpin

SYDNEY UNIVERSITY PRESS

First published by Sydney University Press 2024
© Individual contributors 2024
© Sydney University Press 2024

Reproduction and Communication for other purposes
Except as permitted under the Australian *Copyright Act 1968*, no part of this edition may be reproduced, stored in a retrieval system, or communicated in any form or by any means without prior written permission. All requests for reproduction or communication should be made to Sydney University Press at the address below:

Sydney University Press
Fisher Library F03
Gadigal Country
University of Sydney NSW 2006
Australia
sup.info@sydney.edu.au
sydneyuniversitypress.com

 A catalogue record for this book is available from the National Library of Australia.

ISBN 9781743329504 paperback
ISBN 9781743329511 epub
ISBN 9781743328811 pdf

We acknowledge the traditional owners of the lands on which Sydney University Press is located, the Gadigal people of the Eora Nation, and we pay our respects to the knowledge embedded forever within the Aboriginal Custodianship of Country.

Every effort has been made to obtain permission to use copyrighted images reproduced in this book. People who believe they have rights to this material are advised to contact the publisher.

Contents

Note on cultural sensitivity — viii
Note on terminology — viii
List of figures — ix
List of tables — xiii
Audio examples — xiv
Foreword — xv

Chapter 1 — 1
Dialogues on music and archives: a tribute to Linda Barwick
Sally Treloyn, Amanda Harris, Nick Thieberger and Myfany Turpin

Part I Dialogic Archiving — 21

Chapter 2 — 23
Keeping time: how the digital repatriation of western Arnhem Land song traditions deepens their meaning
Nicholas Evans

Chapter 3 — 43
Language and music recordings and the responsible researcher
Nick Thieberger

Chapter 4 — 55
The politics of repatriation: communication and consultation in Torres Strait during the "True Echoes" project
Grace Koch

Chapter 5 — 75
Researcher as facilitator: reconsidering the researcher's role in the management of archival collections
Catherine Ingram

Chapter 6 Shifting cultural protocols surrounding community-led arts and media projects in Southern Ngaliya Warlpiri region *Georgia Curran and Valerie Napaljarri Martin*	87
Chapter 7 Dispersed sound archives and diaspora communities: reconnecting with old recordings from Hula village, Papua New Guinea *Amanda Harris, Steven Gagau, Deveni Temu, Roge Kila and Gulea Kila*	101
Part II Music and Song: Knowing Through Analysis	121
Chapter 8 Endangered songs in the Kathmandu Valley: contexts, histories and meanings of *dāphā bhajan* *Richard Widdess*	123
Chapter 9 Agents of song: exploring the cultural meanings of Arandic verbs of vocal production *Jennifer Green and Myfany Turpin*	145
Chapter 10 The Hakhun Buffalo Sacrifice (*li jwe*) Song *Reis Flora, Khithong Hakhun, Stephen Morey and Jürgen Schöpf*	167
Chapter 11 Music analysed: 20th-century ethnomusicology vis-à-vis Western music theory *Marcello Sorce Keller*	187
Chapter 12 Singing Moonfish, hearing Country *Genevieve Campbell with Yikliya Eustace Tipiloura*	203
Chapter 13 Musical analysis, music sustainability and thrivance: returning to "What can one 'know' about any sort of music by means of musical analysis?" *Sally Treloyn and Tiriki Onus*	219

Contents

Part III Dialogic Futures	229
Chapter 14 Karaoke corroboree: subtitled music videos and language revitalisation *Clint Bracknell*	231
Chapter 15 *Tjendji* (Fire) and *Tjerri* (Sea Breeze): what Indigenous wisdom has to tell us about the climate emergency and the biodiversity crisis *Payi Linda Ford and Allan Marett*	245
Chapter 16 Music as formative social action *Ian Cross*	257
Chapter 17 Daluk Bininj, Ngarri-djarrk-ni/lovers, let's sit down together: popular love songs of western Arnhem Land *Jodie Kell and Tara Rostron*	271
Chapter 18 *Arrungpayarrun ta alan* "We'll follow their path" *Reuben Brown, Isabel O'Keeffe, Ruth Singer, Jenny Manmurulu, Renfred Manmurulu and Rupert Manmurulu*	293
Chapter 19 Singing from the mountains: when things really go right in Indigenous research – a story of creative collaboration and Ngarigu cultural renewal *Jakelin Troy*	313
References	325

Appendices are available online at sydneyuniversitypress.com/keepingtimeappendices

Appendix A Publications by Linda Barwick in reverse temporal order from most recent

Appendix B Sounds used in the Acoustic Recognition Task

Appendix C Morphological glosses

Appendix D Linguistic transcription with notes

Appendix E A Hakhum buffalo sacrifice song

Note on cultural sensitivity

Readers are advised that this book contains the names and images of people who have passed away.

Note on terminology

Contributions to this volume come from authors representing diverse disciplinary and cultural contexts. The language and terminology in the volume reflect this diversity. Wherever possible, terms that reference particular First Peoples groups and communities are used. But collective terms for First Nations and First Peoples vary from chapter to chapter. Collective terms include "Aboriginal", typically for First Peoples of mainland Australia, "Torres Strait Islanders" for First Peoples of the Torres Strait, "Indigenous" and "First Nations", typically used to refer to First Peoples globally, though sometimes nationally.

List of figures

Figure 0.1 Linda Barwick, April 2024.   xvi

Figure 1.1 Linda Barwick working with the late Fanny Walker Napurrurla at Alekarenge, with linguist Mary Laughren (in pink) and Napurrurla's daughters (right). Photo: Myfany Turpin, 2010.   5

Figure 1.2 Celebrating Linda Barwick at the 2021 "Hearing the Ancestors" conference at the University of Sydney. From left (in room): Nick Thieberger, Myfany Turpin, Amanda Harris, Sally Treloyn, Allan Marett, Linda Barwick, Jodie Kell and Georgia Curran; from left (on screen): Emily Tyaemaen Ford and Payi Linda Ford. Photo: PARADISEC.   7

Figure 1.3 Linda Barwick (second from right), dancing for the launch of the Research Unit for Indigenous Arts and Cultures, University of Melbourne (Southbank), with Lauren Gower (back far left), Delilah Ngarlingarli (front left), Payi Linda Ford (front centre), Ruth Singer (back left), Emily Ford (back centre) and Kathryn Marsh (front right). Photo: Jared Kuvent, University of Melbourne/Wilin Centre for Indigenous Arts and Cultural Development, 2017.   10

Figure 4.1 Vic McGrath, Senior Community Liaison Officer, Thursday Island, Torres Strait, Qld, Office, Torres Strait Regional Authority. Photo: Lara McLellan, Friday, 7 May 2021.   65

Figure 4.2 Lui Ned David, Chair, GBK. Thursday Island, Torres Strait. Photo: Lara McLellan, 17 May 2021.   67

Figure 4.3 Flora Warrior, Interviewer. Panai, Mabuiag Island, Torres Strait, Qld. Photo: Flora Warrior, 15 March 2022.   68

Figure 4.4 Vinnitta Mosby, Interviewer. Mer Island, Torres Strait, Qld. Photo: Vinnitta Mosby, 26 November 2021.   69

Figure 7.1 A Hula beach with canoe in the distance. From a collection of images taken during the Cooke–Daniels Ethnographical Expedition to British New Guinea 1903–1904. Museum number Oc,B118.45 © The Trustees of the British Museum.   104

Figure 7.2 Two Hula men engaged in a ceremonial feeding (spear feast?). From a collection of images taken during the Cooke–Daniels Ethnographical Expedition to British New Guinea 1903–1904. Museum number Oc,B121.111 © The Trustees of the British Museum. 107

Figure 7.3 A group of Hula men and women performing a dance/ceremony. From the Cooke–Daniels Ethnographical Expedition to British New Guinea 1903–1904. Museum number Oc,B120.107 © The Trustees of the British Museum. 108

Figure 7.4 "Phonograph, Hula": Charles Seligmann or Sidney Ray recording the singing of Vula'a people. From the Cambridge University Anthropological Expedition to the Torres Straits 1898–1899. Image ID N.34987.ACH20 © The Museum of Archaeology and Anthropology, Cambridge. 110

Figure 7.5 Location of stops of the Daniels Ethnographical Expedition to British New Guinea. Map created by Steven Gagau, using the historic map published in Seligman (1910, 40). 111

Figure 7.6 Portrait of a Hula woman wearing a mourning costume. From the Cooke–Daniels Ethnographical Expedition to British New Guinea 1903–1904. Museum number Oc,B119.53 © The Trustees of the British Museum. 116

Figure 7.7 Hula Lekuleku re-enactment by Roge and Gulea Kila, at Sydney Conservatorium of Music, 17 October 2020. Still from video recorded by Jodie Kell. 118

Figure 8.1 Dāphā in the community: early morning in Lākvalāche-neighbourhood, Bhaktapur, 2010. Note the small Gaṇeśa temple (centre, with clock), well (centre right), two covered platforms (left and right), dāphā group (left). Photo: Richard Widdess. 129

Figure 8.2 The dāphā song "Ganamani". *Rāg*: Āsāvarī. *Tāl*: Cvakh. As sung by the Dattātreya Temple dāphā group, Bhaktapur. Transcription: author. See Widdess 2013, 263–268. 131

Figure 8.3 The Dattātreya Temple dāphā group (Dattātreya Navadāphā Khalaḥ), Bhaktapur, 2012. Photo: Richard Widdess. 132

Figure 8.4 (a) The goddess Taleju, as represented on the Golden Gate, Darbar Square, Bhaktapur (1753). Photo: Richard Widdess. (b) The elephant-headed god Gaṇeśa. Painted book cover by Madhu Chitrakar, 2010. Photo: Richard Widdess. 134

Figure 8.5 Dāphā in the community: concluding initiation ceremony (*pidane pūjā*) of a dāphā training program. Bhaktapur, 2003. Photo: Richard Widdess. 137

Figure 8.6 Repetition pattern for first verse of "Ganamani" (see Figure 8.2). For vv. 2 and 3, repeat from *Pad*. 139

Figure 8.7 The Dattātreya Temple women's dāphā group from Bhaktapur perform for the inauguration of a training program for a new women's dāphā group in Taḥnāni tol, Kirtipur, 2021. Photo: Folk Lok Artist. 141

Figure 9.1 A segment of an Anmatyerr sand story performed by Janie Mpetyan Briscoe in 2007. 146

Figure 9.2 The approximate location of languages referred to in this chapter. Map by J. Green. 148

Figure 12.1 Yikliya Eustace Tipiloura listens to the Moonfish recordings, Wurrumiyanga, 2010. Photo: Genevieve Campbell. 206

Figure 12.2 The Tiwi Islands, showing the area these songs originate from and belong to. 211

Figure 15.1 "Wadi kan ngun pip wa!" ("Seasonal Fire" (2005)). A painting by Payi Linda Ford. Photo: Mark Ford. 248

Figure 15.2 Captain Woditj singing the "Tjendji" ("Fire") *lirrga*. Photo: Mark Ford. 250

Figure 15.3 "Tjendji" ("Fire"), composed by Dennis Nardjic: translation by Clement Tchinburrurr and Lysbeth Ford. 250

Figure 15.4 Maurice Ngulkurr points in the direction of the *Tjerri* (Sea Breeze) Dreaming site. Photo: Allan Marett. 252

Figure 15.5 "Tjerri" ("Sea Breeze") composed by Charlie Brinken. Sung by Maurice Ngulkurr. 252

Figure 17.1. Album cover for *Mayawa*, featuring "Loving and Caring", the subject of this chapter. Ripple Effect Band, 2024. 273

Figure 17.2. Authors Jodie Kell and Tara Rostron, who composed "Loving and Caring", performing as a duo in Newcastle, NSW, in 2022. Photo: Paul Dear. 286

Figure 18.1 Four generations of *Inyjalarrku manyardi* performers. Top: George Winungudj playing didjeridu for his sons, including David Manmurulu (far left in the yellow top), circa 1970s. Photographer unknown, from Manmurulu family private collection. Bottom: David Manmurulu (centre in red top) with his sons and grandsons, 2010. Photo Beth Luck, used with permission. 299

Figure 18.2 Three generations of *Yumparrparr* "giant" dancers. Top: George Winungudj, 1952. Photo: Axel Poignant (published in Poignant and Poignant 1996, 141), used with permission. Centre: David Manmurulu, 2012. Still from Gus Berger, used with permission. Bottom: Rupert Manmurulu, 2013. Still from Grubin Films, used with permission. 300

Figure 18.3 Allan Marett, Linda Barwick, Jenny Manmurulu and David Manmurulu at the Annual Indigenous Music and Dance Symposium in Darwin, 2011. Photo: Reuben Brown, used with permission. 306

Figure 18.4 Jenny Manmurulu and Linda Barwick perform *manyardi* at the Musicology Society of Australia Conference in Perth, 2018. Photo: Musicological Society of Australia collection, used with permission. 306

Figure 18.5 Reuben Brown, Rupert Manmurulu, Isabel O'Keeffe and Renfred Manmurulu prepare to perform *manyardi* for the International Council for Traditional Music World Conference in Bangkok, Thailand, 2019. Photo from Isabel O'Keeffe's private collection, used with permission. 311

List of tables

Table 3.1 Sample of language archive statistics provided by OLAC (July 2022). 48
Table 4.1 "True Echoes" Project plan, showing adjustments over time. 72
Table 9.1 Verbs of vocal production considered in the study. 150
Table 10.1 Overview of the *li jwe* event. 175
Table 18.1 *Manyardi/kun-borrk* song-sets recorded and/or discussed during the Western Arnhem Land Song Project. 295

Audio examples

Audio Example 12.1 Yikliya Eustace Tipiloura singing Moonfish
 (Recorded by G. Campbell, 2015). 217
Audio Example 15.1 "Tjendji" ("Fire"). Sung by Captain Woditj. 250
Audio Example 15.2 "Tjerri" ("Sea Breeze"). Sung by Maurice Ngulkurr. 253

Foreword

This volume honouring Linda Barwick's outstanding contributions in a number of research fields is testament not only to the quality and scope of her work but also to the respect, and indeed affection, in which she is held by her colleagues and interlocutors. Linda's work ranges over a large number of fields. She is a leader in the field of digital humanities, in particular the archiving and repatriation of ethnographic field recordings. She has published widely on Australian First Nations musics, as well as the music of immigrant communities and the oral musical traditions of the Philippines and Italy – in particular the Tuscan *maggio* tradition of oral sung theatre. Her key research focuses include: archiving practices as a site of interaction between researchers and cultural heritage communities; musical transcription and analysis of non-Western music; the language of song; musical endangerment; and the aesthetics of cross-cultural musical practice.

As Linda's life partner for more than three decades, I have been in the privileged position of witnessing and engaging with the unfolding of Linda's research career. Not only have she and I collaborated on major research projects and co-authored numerous books, articles and multimedia publications, but I have also had the benefit of being able to chew over with her many of the overlapping issues and concerns that have preoccupied us both throughout our careers. These conversations began, I suppose, in 1986 at the Musicological Society of Australia conference in Canberra, where I heard Linda give a paper that was subsequently published as "Transcription as deflowering: collection practices in Italy, pre-1939" (Barwick 1988–1989), which at a surface level examined collection practices in 19th-century Italy, but at a deeper level addressed issues such as the complex relations that researchers in the area of intercultural music research have with their "subjects", and the implications of subjecting the music of other cultures to Western techniques of transcription and analysis. Her observations in that paper spoke directly to questions that were arising for me as I embarked, in the same year, on my first fieldwork trip in an Aboriginal community. That conference was also the occasion on which a group of Chinese musicians, headed by Professor Chen Yingshi of the Shanghai Conservatory, came to Australia and performed, probably for the first time in a thousand years, music from the Chinese Tang dynasty (618–907), which I and my colleagues in the Cambridge Tang Music Project had transcribed and published (Picken, Wolpert et al. 1981; Picken, Wolpert et al. 1985). I vividly remember sitting beside Linda during this performance and feeling oddly privileged to be sharing this moment with her.

A year after "Transcription as deflowering" came out, Linda published another paper, "Central Australian women's ritual music: knowing through analysis versus knowing through performance" (Barwick 1990) that was to have a profound influence on me and many others involved in researching First Nations music in Australia, as well as on those with an interest in musical transcription and analysis more broadly. This was to be followed five years later by another equally incisive and influential paper, "Unison and 'disagreement' in a mixed women's and men's performance (Ellis Collection, Oodnadatta, 1966)" (Barwick 1995). In my 2005 book, *Songs, dreamings and ghosts: the Wangga of North Australia*, I acknowledged the importance of Linda's insights for my work as follows:

> One of the most successful integrations of elements of musical and social performance (in this case, the performance of gender roles), through a detailed analytical understanding of the processes that produce a performance, occurs in a paper by Linda Barwick (1995). Barwick focuses "on instances of gross melodic disagreement" in a mixed-sex performance of Central Australian music, in which it is clear that the men (who sing together as a group) sometimes have quite different ideas from the women (who also sing together) about how texts should be fitted onto the flexible melodic contour. Barwick argues "firstly that the *form* of the men's disagreements can be described in terms of different applications by men and women of musical principles that are operating in the inter-meshing of text and melody; and secondly, *that the degree to which the men persist* is symbolic of potentially competing claims by men and women to ritual authority in mixed-sex performances of series owned by women" (Barwick 1995, 97).

> Barwick's focus on specific details of performance, located through careful analysis and transcription, and her explanation of these as enactments of specific social agendas have had no small influence on [*Songs, dreamings and ghosts*]. In her research, she maintains a keen sense of the different perspectives derived through analysis and performance, and, like [Catherine] Ellis, insists on the inclusion of performers' perspectives in any interpretation of a performance (see Barwick 1990). (Marett 2005, 9–10)

Foreword

It is significant perhaps, given that I am now writing this Foreword for a volume of essays in honour of Linda, that our first major collaboration was the preparation of a similar volume for Catherine Ellis (Barwick, Marett and Tunstill 1995) – a scholar whom we deeply respected and who influenced us both profoundly. Catherine Ellis and Linda Barwick's work on the analysis, initially of Central Aboriginal song, and then Aboriginal song repertories more widely, not only powerfully influenced my work but also the music research work of our students, some of whom we supervised individually and some together. These include Greg Anderson, Ray Keogh, Sally Treloyn, Margaret Gummow, Reuben Brown, Myfany Turpin, Isabel O'Keeffe, Genevieve Campbell and Kathryn Marsh.

In her response to the collection of essays we prepared for her, Ellis wrote of her "anguish over correct action in intercultural research" (Ellis 1995, 202). The research environment and the politics of research are always shifting, and have shifted markedly since that time, but the question of what constitutes "correct action in intercultural research" remains a burning question for all musicologists working in intercultural research. Linda's engagements with this issue, particularly as it affects research on First Nations music, have provided insights that have illuminated the work of many other scholars. Increasingly it was community agendas, rather than abstract academic issues, that drove her work, and in the past decade she has been particularly active in mentoring and empowering Indigenous scholars, co-publishing and collaborating with a number of her Indigenous interlocutors, students and colleagues, including Kathleen Fitz Napananka, Payi Linda Ford, David and Jenny Manmurulu and their sons, Clint Bracknell, Tiriki Onus and Jakelin Troy (to name but a few).

For most of her career, Linda relied on recurrent funding to support her research, which is a precarious career path for any scholar, but in 2013 she was finally appointed to a substantive tenured university role as professor and associate dean at the University of Sydney. While continuing to produce her own groundbreaking research, she has in recent times selflessly dedicated herself to cultivating rigorous and supportive research environments and supporting the scholars who inhabit them – at the Conservatorium of Music at the University of Sydney, through her role on the Australian Research Council and through the Australian Academy of the Humanities.

This volume honouring Linda's work comes after an extraordinary year when she was also appointed a Member of the Order of Australia (AM) and received the Sir Bernard Heinze Memorial Prize for her outstanding contribution to music in Australia. It was, coincidentally, the year in which she and I celebrated our thirtieth wedding anniversary. The present volume further testifies to the rich and generous contribution that Linda has made not only across so many academic fields but also to society more broadly.

Allan Marett, February 2024

Figure 0.1 Linda Barwick, April 2024.

Chapter 1

Dialogues on music and archives: a tribute to Linda Barwick

Sally Treloyn, Amanda Harris, Nick Thieberger and Myfany Turpin

In 2021, a conference held at the University of Sydney celebrated dual achievements: the growth of the Pacific and Regional Archive for Digital Sources in Endangered Cultures (PARADISEC) archive to a collection holding 100 terabytes of language and music recordings from small languages of the world,[1] and the retirement of PARADISEC's inaugural director, Linda Barwick, after a distinguished career.[2] Key themes from the conference, "Hearing the Ancestors", resonated with Barwick's scholarship and with PARADISEC's guiding principles.[3] In this book, we bring together a collection of chapters developed out of these themes that contribute to three broad topics: dialogic archiving; knowing music and song through analysis; and dialogic futures. These topics were articulated by keynote speaker Nick Evans, whose chapter "Keeping time" also lends its title to the book. In this opening chapter to *Keeping Time*, we present a snapshot of Barwick's career, an overview of the impact of Barwick's scholarship, and a summary of the chapters. This volume was prepared by the four editors who are colleagues of Barwick's, and some of whom are former students. The editors are from the fields of music, linguistics and history, reflecting Barwick's influence across multiple disciplines.

---

1 The PARADISEC collection has more than doubled in size since then, now holding 220 terabytes.
2 Many of these presentations can be viewed at the PARADISEC YouTube channel https://tinyurl.com/2s45xvtm.
3 There are nine principles, which include findability and transparency. The set of nine principles are described at https://tinyurl.com/2e5ekpj2.

A summary of Linda Barwick's career

Having lived in various parts of regional New South Wales in her early years, from the age of 14 Linda Barwick grew up in Adelaide among a community of Italian immigrants.[4] This, as Barwick reflected in an interview with James Henry (2019), sparked an interest in the language and culture that she developed through a Bachelor of Arts (Honours) dissertation on Italian song at Flinders University, graduating with first-class honours and the University Medal in 1980. This would also lead Barwick to postgraduate study at Flinders University and research in Italy in the 1980s, producing a PhD thesis titled "Critical perspectives on oral song in performance: the case of 'Donna Lombarda'", supervised by Antonio Comin (Italian dialectology, Flinders) and Catherine Ellis (ethnomusicology, Elder Conservatorium of Music) (Barwick 1985). Barwick has continued research in Italy throughout her career, studying the *maggio* tradition in the Garfagnana region of Tuscany, with fieldwork from 1991–2007, supported by a range of project grants.[5] She also worked on the related *komedya* (popular theatre) tradition in Burgos and Vigan in the Philippines between 1993 and 1995.[6] In recent years Barwick has continued her engagement with the Garfagnana region and *maggio*, presenting on aspects of the formal structures of *maggio* sung theatrical verse,[7] and participating in several online forums, including on the sustainability and revival of the tradition.[8]

Much of Barwick's career has been dedicated to First Nations music and musicians in Australia. Needing the expertise of an ethnomusicologist to support her graduate studies in the 1980s, Barwick met Catherine Ellis and subsequently took classes at the Centre for Aboriginal Studies in Music. There Barwick undertook her first formal tertiary study in music, with Ellis and Pitjantjatjara Elders among her teachers. After graduating with a PhD from Flinders in 1986 Barwick then joined Ellis at the University of New England as a research associate and then research fellow on a project, "Style and structure in Central Australian Aboriginal Music". This resulted in three meticulous documentations of ceremonial recordings with Antikirinya, Arrernte, Pitjantjatjara, Luritja and Yankunytjatjara people

---

4   Barwick shared insight into her early experience in New South Wales and South Australia in an interview with James Henry: Henry 2019.
5   Including: "Music of the Maggio" (Australian Research Council (ARC) Large Grant (Pilot)), 1992; "Sung Popular Theatre in Tuscany and the Australasian region" (ARC Large Grant).
6   "Performance-Based Investigation of Komedya Popular Music Theatre in the Philippines" (ARC Institutional Grant), 1994–95.
7   See, for example, an abstract for a presentation on *maggio* that can be viewed at https://tinyurl.com/3z43sfw8.
8   A recording of a 2020 presentation on the sustainability of *maggio* by Linda can be viewed at https://youtu.be/y7OMZ6uDJK8.

made between 1933 and 1986: one, a documentation of Ellis's collection of field recordings (Barwick 1987b) and another, a documentation of multimodal fieldwork records from a multidisciplinary team of researchers titled "Group project on Antikirinya women, 1966–68 expeditions: secondary documentation" (1991b). This includes a 531-page document index to the primary documentation (of more than 14 ceremonies), transcripts of the language, music and dance, and a digital database using the HyperCard application. She also co-published an article on women's song knowledge (Ellis and Barwick 1989b).

During this time, Barwick identified organisational principles of First Nations music in Australia that have since been found well beyond the region of Ellis and Barwick's study. Concepts such as "text line reversal" – where a text made of two parts has the reverse order in subsequent iterations – "melodic contour" (Ellis and Barwick 1987), and "point of fit" – places in a song where the melodic and rhythmic–textual boundaries coincide – have been found to be fundamental to the musical traditions of people across much of inland Australia (Gummow 1992; Hercus and Koch 1997; Keogh 1995; Mackinlay 1998; Turpin 2015; Treloyn 2017).

From 1991 to 1995 Barwick held a Queen Elizabeth II Research Fellowship at the University of Sydney and continued research on *maggio*, *komedya* and central Australian song. These years also saw the development of an enduring and productive collaboration with Allan Marett, then senior lecturer in music at the University of Sydney, studying *wangga* and *lirrga* from the Daly region. Barwick pursued this research and teaching, with various positions and projects at the University of Sydney and University of Hong Kong. She supervised and taught students across a broad range of topics, including serving as co-supervisor of the PhD dissertations on First Nations music by Ray Keogh (1990), Greg Anderson (1993) and Margaret Gummow (1994), from three diverse parts of Australia.

Between 1997 and 2003 Barwick additionally undertook numerous research consultancies, such as with the Balkanu Cape York Development Corporation and the Goldfields Land Council. As a senior research fellow at the University of Sydney in 1997, and between 2001 and 2002, Barwick extended her focus to public performance genres in the Kimberley region,[9] while continuing work on central Australian and Daly genres.[10] It was during this time that Barwick also

---

9   "Public performance genres of the northern and eastern Kimberleys" (ARC Large Grant), 1997–1999.

10 "Kaytetye, Ngardi and Warumungu: effective representation of word meaning in Aboriginal languages" (ARC Large Grant), 2000–2002; "An ethnomusicological study of *lirrga*, a genre of public dance song from northwest Northern Territory" (ARC Large Grant), 2001–2003.

had a particular focus on setting up a digitisation pilot program, a stepping-stone towards PARADISEC (see further below).[11]

Barwick has since had an illustrious career at the University of Sydney, retiring as professor in 2020 and taking up a position as professor emerita. Additionally, Barwick is a fellow of the Australian Academy of the Humanities, a research affiliate of the Research Unit for Indigenous Language at the University of Melbourne, and also of the Rediscovering the Deep Human Past Laureate Program at the Australian National University and was previously a research affiliate of the ARC Centre of Excellence for the Dynamics of Language. In 2019 Barwick was a Leverhulme Visiting Professor at SOAS, University of London (see chapter by Widdess in this volume), and in 2020 was appointed adjunct professor at Kurongkurl Katitjin Centre for Indigenous Research and Education at Edith Cowan University. In 2022 Barwick was made a Member in the General Division of the Order of Australia for her significant service to the preservation and digitisation of cultural heritage recordings.

Across her almost 40 years of research, Barwick undertook significant field research and collaborations through much of the continent. In central Australia, she accompanied linguists David Nash and Jane Simpson to record and document Warlpiri and Warumungu songs at Alekarenge and Tennant Creek in 1996. At Alekarenge she recorded Warlpiri songs performed by a group of men led by Engineer Jack Japaljarri, with Joe Bird Jangala and Tommy Driver Jupurrula, Charlie Driver Jupurrula, Colin Rice Japaljarri, Alfie Brown Jungarrayi, Donald Thomson Jakamarra, Mundy Japaljarri, Timothy Dickenson Japangardi. She then recorded *yawulyu* performed by a group of women: Irene Driver Nungarrayi, Fanny Napurrurla, Ada Dickenson Napurrurla, Mary Napurrurla, Annabelle Nakamarra, Marjorie Limbiari Nangala-Napurrula, Lillian Napangardi, Peggy Napangardi, Jessie Rice Nungarrayi, Edna Brown Nungarrayi, Nancy Jones/Downes Nungarrayi, Gladys Nangala, Agnes Nangala and Maggie Green Nampijinpa. She has continued to work on these recordings with the community and in collaboration with linguists and anthropologists (Curran, Barwick et al. 2019; Curran, Martin et al. 2024; Walker Napurrurla, Barwick et al. 2024).

---

11 "Quadriga audio system for research archive of Asia-Pacific region sound recordings" (ARC Large Infrastructure and Equipment Funding Grant), 2003.

1 Dialogues on music and archives: a tribute to Linda Barwick

Figure 1.1 Linda Barwick working with the late Fanny Walker Napurrurla at Alekarenge, with linguist Mary Laughren (in pink) and Napurrurla's daughters (right). Photo: Myfany Turpin, 2010.

Near Tennant Creek they recorded Warumungu women's songs performed by Kathleen Fitz Napanangka, Eileen Nelson Napanangka, May Foster Napanangka, Edie Narrurlu, Edith Graham Nakamarra, Christine Narrurlu and Jean Napangarti. Barwick continued to work closely with these women and in 2000 *Yawulyu Mungamunga*, a CD and documentation of Warumungu women's songs was released by Festival Records and Papulu Apparr-kari Language and Culture Centre (Barwick 2000a). This was a groundbreaking collaborative release in having both a community and commercial publisher, where the performers directed which songs to include on the CD, where they would be recorded, and how they wished to present themselves and their songs to outsiders. The performers hold the copyright and royalty proceeds are returned to the community. Anthropologist Kimberley Christen writes that the CD:

> became a source for performative innovation, and was held up as an exemplary model of what Judy Nakkamarra, one of my Warumungu collaborators, defined as "culture work" – those daily activities that ensure the reproduction of Warumungu tradition. (Christen 2006, 416)

Since then, numerous First Nations groups have collaborated with academics furthering this model of collaborative publication of traditional music; for both outsiders and as a learning aid for younger community members (Turpin and Ross 2004; Barwick, Birch and Williams 2005; Turpin and Ross 2013; Gallagher, Napangardi et al. 2014; 2017; Campbell, Long et al. 2016; Morais, Martin et al. in press).

In all of the areas in which Barwick has worked, she has developed the next generation of researchers of Indigenous song, in the case of central Australia, supervising the PhD of Myfany Turpin (Turpin 2005), and supporting early career research by Georgia Curran. Likewise, Barwick has leveraged research to support the next generation of singers. The training of younger community members as singers has been an increasing concern for Aboriginal peoples across central Australia, as the number of people who know their traditional songs has declined (Barwick, Laughren and Turpin 2013). This led to several collaborative research projects with Indigenous organisations, some of which Linda Barwick has led,[12] and others in which she has been involved in various ways from adviser, transcriber, digitiser to mentor.[13]

Collaborating with Allan Marett, Lysbeth Ford, and others, from the early 1990s Barwick also undertook work in the Daly region including fieldwork and analytical studies in Daly musical styles *wangga*, *lirrga*, *malkarrin* and *djanba*. This early work produced significant audio collections (Marett and Barwick 1997; 1997–1999), a CD publication of *wangga* songs of Alan Maralung published by Smithsonian Folkways (Marett and Barwick 1993) and an expert report for the 1998 Kenbi Land Claim.

A range of papers elaborated on the rich musical and innovative musical heritage and practices of the Daly (e.g., Barwick 2002; 2005b; 2011; Barwick, Marett et al. 2007; Bailes and Barwick 2011). Major outputs include the Wadeye Song Database (Barwick, Walsh et al. 2009) and the massive volume with Marett and Ford, *For the Sake of a Song: Wangga Songmen and Their Repertories* (Marett, Barwick and Ford 2013), with accompanying CDs, representing 20 years of research in the region (Marett, Barwick and Ford 2016). This body of work includes attention to processes of recording (e.g., Marett and Barwick 2003) and the circulation of recordings in communities (Barwick 2017) as a topic of research. As with her work in central Australia, here Barwick also supported emerging researchers, in particular Alberto Furlan, Joe Blythe and John Mansfield.

---

12 "Vitality and Change of Warlpiri songs at Yuendumu" (ARC LP160100743), 2016; "Re-integrating Central Australian community cultural collections" (ARC LP140100806), 2014.

13 "Arrernte women's Dreaming songs" (Screen Australia grant), 2014; "Mapping the diversity of Aboriginal song: social and ecological significances for Australia" (ARC FT140100783), 2015.

1 Dialogues on music and archives: a tribute to Linda Barwick

In the Daly, Barwick's prioritisation of relationships and intergenerational knowledge transmission in research again emerged as core to the research endeavour, in the context of collaborations with Linda Payi Ford, Ford's family and Marett. Ford, Barwick and Marett reflected on how personal relationships, embedded in processes of collaboration and reciprocity, underpinned the documentation of ceremonies for Payi Linda Ford's mother (Ford, Barwick and Marett 2014). The continuation of this reciprocity underpinned ceremonies since, in 2018 at the Dharma Transmission Ceremony for Allan at the Sydney Zen Centre, and at the conference in honour of Barwick from which this volume emanates.

Figure 1.2 Celebrating Linda Barwick at the 2021 "Hearing the Ancestors" conference at the University of Sydney. From left (in room): Nick Thieberger, Myfany Turpin, Amanda Harris, Sally Treloyn, Allan Marett, Linda Barwick, Jodie Kell and Georgia Curran; from left (on screen): Emily Tyaemaen Ford and Payi Linda Ford. Photo: PARADISEC.

Related to this work, from the mid-2000s, Barwick and Marett, together with many other scholars, including Murray Garde, Nick Evans, Isabel O'Keeffe, Bruce Birch and Reuben Brown, carried out extensive research in western Arnhem Land, supported by ARC funding and a Hans Rausing Endangered Languages Documentation Programme (ELDP) Major Project Grant. This work produced recordings and documentation of numerous genres, including *jurtbirrk* (Barwick, Birch and Williams 2005), *kun-borrk* and *manyardi*. It also had as a focus the auditioning of past recordings with singers today to enrich the record and reconnect collections with living communities, and the relational status of research on song.[14] As elsewhere, Barwick supervised and supported graduate researchers through this work, supervising PhD research by Brown (2016) and O'Keeffe (2016).

Barwick also carried out extensive work in Western Australia, beginning in the later 1990s. Collaborating with Marett on the ARC project "Public performance genres of the northern and eastern Kimberleys", Barwick did fieldwork in Derby, Bijili and Maranbabidi, and further to the north-east in Kununurra and Wyndham. This work produced significant recordings of Wandjina – Wunggurr Junba, under the direction of master singers including Scotty Nyalgodi Martin (Barwick, Marett and Ngarinyin Aboriginal Corporation 1998–1999; Barwick 2003) that continue to be used in the region today. This work in part advanced that of Ray Keogh, whose research on *nurlu* from the west Kimberley Barwick supported as co-supervisor and by finalising elements of his work following his untimely death in 1993. Keogh's work on *nurlu*, which is a cyclical and isorhythmic dance-song genre, flows clearly from Barwick's analytical findings in relation to central Australian song, and provides a significant bridge in the understanding of musical process – particularly the generation of melodic contour in relation to text/rhythm – between Central Australian practice and group-performed songs of the far north-west (Keogh 1995). Always attentive to the next generation of researchers, Barwick introduced Treloyn to the field in 1999 on a fieldtrip to record *jadmi* and *jerregorl junba* with Scotty Nyalgodi Martin, and prepare liner notes for a CD in collaboration with the Ngarinyin Aboriginal Corporation (Barwick 2003; Marett and Barwick 2003). Barwick later served as co-supervisor to Treloyn's PhD dissertation on Martin's *jadmi junba* (Treloyn 2006).

Elsewhere in the continent, Barwick contributed significant knowledge and analysis to Diane Bell's study of songs of Hindmarsh Island (Bell 1998) and was a consultant working with Ngadju, Mirning, Noongar and other people in the Western Australian Goldfields in 1998 and 1999. In her *Preliminary Report on Song and Language in the Goldfields Region* (Barwick 1999), Barwick noted musical

---

14 See Brown, O'Keeffe et al. in this volume.

1 Dialogues on music and archives: a tribute to Linda Barwick

connections between peoples of the Esperance–Goldfields region and Country, the presence of the Wanji-wanji travelling song (Turpin Yeoh and Bracknell 2020) and continuing memories of singing practices. This report contributed to a number of Native Title claims in the Esperance–Goldfields region. Since then, Barwick has been a mentor and collaborator with Noongar ethnomusicologist Clint Bracknell on two ARC grants investigating the relationship between songs, Country and archival recordings pertaining to the Noongar region.[15]

Also across such diverse and expansive musical and linguistic settings, Barwick saw the need and potential for new technologies and equipment for recording, preserving recordings, and creating access to collections. As new technological tools became available, Barwick was an early adopter, becoming known among her PARADISEC colleagues as the gadget queen. She used Hypercard, an early software databasing system that allowed the linking of media and text, developed databases to track records, and saw the possibilities in new recording equipment for preservation and access.

In the early 2000s it was clear to Barwick and other colleagues that something needed to be done to preserve audiotapes made during fieldwork dating back to the 1950s. Many of these tapes were created by retired or deceased researchers and were stored in filing cabinets, homes or in university archives. The immediate task was to ascertain how many tapes could be found, and in what condition, in order that a project could be proposed to digitise them and to develop an accessible archive. Barwick assembled a group of people to support writing funding applications, and, in 2002 succeeded with an Australian Research Council Linkage, Infrastructure and Facilities grant for a one-year project to create the Pacific and Regional Archive for Digital Sources in Endangered Cultures (PARADISEC). This funded an audio specialist (Frank Davey) and an administrator (Amanda Harris) who began work on digitising what would be 500 hours of tape in that year. It was due to Barwick's skill at negotiating the university system and at pulling together an impressive list of chief investigators that this initial project succeeded and was followed by other grants that have ensured the continuation of PARADISEC, celebrating its 20th year in 2023. As can be seen from her list of publications (see Appendix A online), she also has a number of collections in PARADISEC, practising what she advocates.

Barwick was instrumental in dialogues that established the National Recording Project for Indigenous Performance in Australia (NRPIPA) in 2004. This is a

---

15 "Restoring on-Country performance: song, language and landscapes" (ARC IN200100012), 2020–2022; "Mobilising song archives to nourish an endangered Aboriginal language" (ARC IN170100022), 2017–2019.

consortium of researchers and Aboriginal and Torres Strait Islander performance groups active since 2002, conceived at a symposium convened by Marcia Langton, the late M. Yunupingu and Allan Marett, and now led by Payi Linda Ford and Aaron Corn. The NRPIPA assists Indigenous people in Australia to record, document and securely archive their music and dance traditions. Barwick also led the establishment of the Sydney University Press book series "Indigenous Music of Australia", and was the series editor until 2019. In this role, Barwick oversaw numerous recordings and monographs on Australian First Nations music to publication. The present volume is also part of this series, the title of which is now "Indigenous Music, Language and Performing Arts".

In 2017 the NRPIPA became a Study Group of the Musicological Society of Australia (MSA) and is open to community stakeholders and other professionals with interests in maintaining and revitalising First Nations music and dance. The MSA now has a dedicated student prize for the best presentation on an Indigenous music topic and the NRPIPA holds a symposium as part of the MSA conference. The book series and role of the NRPIPA with the MSA are indicative of how Linda Barwick has played a significant role in shifting the place of First Nations musics in musicology from "a fringe concern to a central touchstone of music research

Figure 1.3 Linda Barwick (second from right), dancing for the launch of the Research Unit for Indigenous Arts and Cultures, University of Melbourne (Southbank), with Lauren Gower (back far left), Delilah Ngarlingarli (front left), Payi Linda Ford (front centre), Ruth Singer (back left), Emily Ford (back centre) and Kathryn Marsh (front right). Photo: Jared Kuvent, University of Melbourne/Wilin Centre for Indigenous Arts and Cultural Development, 2017.

in Australia" (Bracknell and Barwick 2021, 75). As an adviser and contributor to workshops and the launch of the Research Unit for Indigenous Arts and Cultures at the Wilin Centre for Indigenous Arts and Cultural Development at the University of Melbourne since 2017, Barwick has further extended this reach and impact.

Overview of Barwick's scholarly impact

Barwick's scholarly contributions over close to four decades have been widely influential in ethnomusicology, field linguistics, archiving theory and practice, and adjacent fields. Her most widely cited publications continue to impact approaches to the documentation of music and languages and to shape methodological approaches to understanding music and working cross-culturally. Barwick's work broadens the reach of academic research by fostering genuine, reciprocal, long-term collaborations with communities of speakers, singers and cultural custodians in many parts of Australia, Italy and the Philippines. Barwick has continued to develop this work in recent award-winning publications that extend these fields in new directions, with a particular emphasis on collaborative work with both custodians of the musical traditions she writes about and with colleagues and former students with whom she has formed long-term collaborative working relationships (Barwick, Green, Vaarzon–Morel and Zissermann 2019; Harris, Barwick and Troy 2022b; Curran, Barwick et al. 2019). Here we discuss some of the key areas of influence of Barwick's work since her earliest publications in the 1980s, and explore directions other scholars have taken her work in recent years, before summarising the influences of her scholarship on the authors whose chapters appear in this volume.

In ethnomusicology, the transcription of music practised in oral traditions and not routinely notated was an interest of some of Barwick's earliest scholarship. Barwick published a series of articles grappling with how historical transcriptions should be interpreted and music transcription as method, including the tantalisingly titled "Transcription as deflowering" (Barwick 1988) and another that theorised different ways of "knowing song" – through analysis or through performance (Barwick 1990), drawing on her own practices of transcribing and analysing songs of central Australia (Ellis and Barwick 1987; Barwick 1989). At the heart of this work were questions about what can, and cannot, be understood about musical performance through notation. As Barwick wrote in 1988:

> Anyone concerned with what might be termed historical ethnomusicology, the application of ethnomusicological procedures to documents of now vanished musical performances, recognises that the documents do more than simply record those overtly signalled musical performances; they also embody

documentary performances by the transcribers. Both these performances need to be taken into account in assessing and understanding the document. (Barwick 1988, 35)

Present in Barwick's early theorisation of analysis is attention to questions of representation in ethnomusicology (Barwick 1989; 1990). Her attention to matters of authority and agency of First Nations singers in guiding analysis and, equally importantly, the importance of approaching analysis not as a pursuit of truth but rather as a process of listening cross-culturally, continues to be relevant and influential in the field (Knopoff 2003; see also Treloyn and Onus this volume). These themes continue in Barwick's most recent collaborative work with Ngarigu linguist Jakelin Troy, in which Troy and Barwick perform a "creative re-interpretation" of a song notated in 1834 by re-contextualising it and stripping it of the piano accompaniment added by the original transcriber (Troy and Barwick 2020).

Barwick's exploration of methods of transcription and music analysis has influenced many musicologists who have followed. The work of transcribing large corpora of songs enabled findings about song repertories that opened up understandings of the formal features of Aboriginal song practices. For example, Barwick's early work in collaboration with Catherine Ellis on understanding structural relationships of fast and slow rhythmic patterns across central Australian song cycles was brought to bear on Marri Ngarr songs from the Daly region of the far north of the continent in Barwick's work in the early 2000s. The analytical work across song traditions enabled her to make comparative findings across different songs in these distant parts of the continent in reference to the work of others in the Kimberley (Treloyn), the songs of Anbarra (Wild and Clunies Ross) and Rembarrnga (Anderson) people in central and south-central Arnhem Land and in *manikay* songs of north-east Arnhem Land (Toner and Knopoff) (Barwick 2002), as well as the Kimberley and Daly (Barwick 2011).

Other scholars have built on Barwick's theorisation of transcription and approaches to comparative analysis. Her work on rhythmic patterns has informed research in the field of text-setting, an area at the interface of music theory and phonology. Turpin (2007) and then Turpin and Laughren (2013) find that syllable quantity is encoded in rhythmic duration, and that word boundaries have a preferred alignment with metrical units (bars, or what are called "dipods" in poetics). Similarly, a recent article by Sleeper and Basurto (2022) explored the relationship of melody and linguistic tone alignment. In a 2003 article Treloyn explored the broader relevance "beyond the discipline of musical analysis" of Barwick's style of musicological analysis, suggesting it opens up possibilities for tracing "relationships between creative processes active in the moment of performance" and the "patterns and rules" of musical convention (Treloyn 2003, 208). In the same year, Knopoff drew on Barwick's early theorisations in a comparative interrogation of music analysis in understanding First Nations music and Western art music (Knopoff 2003). Katelyn Barney applied Barwick's insights on the value of transcription and analysis to developing methodologies for collaborative research with First Nations women performers of contemporary music (Barney 2004). In work on the multimodal nature of song, Turpin and Nigel Fabb (2017, 209) extended Barwick and Ellis's advocacy for both musical analysis and suspending analytical thinking in their exploration of cognitive complexity and the possibilities of accessing "the experience of Ancestral power".

Barwick's theorisations of analysis have also been extended beyond the Australian context, influencing Kirsty Gillespie's (2010) approach to transcribing the music of Duna songs from Papua New Guinea, and Tony Lewis's work (2018) on using musical analysis to become a Garamut player in Baluan, Papua New Guinea. The theoretical aspect of Barwick's contribution to assessing the ongoing value of transcription and analysis to musicology and ethnomusicology is also the subject of a section of the present volume – "Knowing through analysis", in particular in the chapters by Treloyn and Onus, and by Sorce Keller.

Combining her musicological expertise with training in linguistics, Barwick has collaborated throughout her career with linguists in work on Indigenous songs in Iwaidja (Barwick, Birch and Evans 2007), Warumungu (Barwick and Turpin 2016), Warlpiri (Curran, Barwick et al. 2019), Murrinh Patha (Barwick, Marett et al. 2007) and Mawng (Barwick, O'Keeffe and Singer 2013) languages. Beyond this collaborative work, Barwick's insistence that song is a distinctive and vital medium for studying language has influenced the practice of many linguists around the world. Her 2005 "Musicologist's Wish List" published in *Language Documentation and Description* continues to be widely cited by linguists alongside later work furthering the discussion of songs in language documentation (Barwick 2012). Linguists and musicologists have used some of Barwick's articles (2005c, 2012) as a starting point to call for language analysis attentive to song, as in Michael Walsh's 2007 "Australian Aboriginal song language: so many questions, so little to work with", Myfany Turpin and Lana Henderson's call for field linguists to record song (2015), and Lundström and Svantesson's 2022 book *In the Borderlands between Song and Speech*. Scholarship blurring the lines between musicology and linguistics has drawn on Barwick's interdisciplinary work in focusing on Noongar song (Bracknell 2017a; 2017b), Kun-barlang songs (O'Keeffe 2016), and in work further afield on Gaelic (Sparling, MacIntyre and Baker 2022), the Chicahuaxtla Triqui language of Mexico (Elliott 2020), and comparative analysis of South Indian Carnatic and Irish singing traditions (Radhakrishnan 2019). The influence of this work has even extended to studies of the relationship between tonal languages and instrumental music in Laura McPherson's argument that linguists should pay attention to the music played on the balafon (a West African xylophone) in order to understand the tonal Sambla language, and Meyer's (2011) work in the field of "talking musical instruments". Barwick's attentiveness to both music and language informed numerous contributions to the understanding of the communicative potential of music across cultural experiences. In an early article "Knowing through analysis" (1990), Barwick considered the nature of her experience of listening to and analysing central Australian women's music, finding it dynamic and innovating, as well as bringing her experience as a listener/analyser into relation to the experience of performers (Barwick 1990, 60; see Treloyn and Onus in this volume).

Reaching beyond the First Nations context in Australia, Barwick drew out Cross's notions of "semantic indeterminancy" (Cross 2009, 192) and "floating intentionality" (Cross 2007, 655) to consider the communicative and social efficacy of music in diverse and heterogeneous communities, first providing guidance to linguistics researchers (2012) and later in the context of performance and pluriculturality (2018). In the later work, Barwick considered how performers of *maggio* use performance to reference multiple identities and cultural positions (2018), allowing for an inclusive approach to difference and even tensions within and between performers and audiences:

> While Cross (2008) refers to the semantic indeterminacy of instrumental music, that is, music without words, I would argue that performance WITH words can enable a similar effect. Providing an arena for representation of intercultural tension that is displaced to familiar yet distant times and places allows for plural interpretations and responses. The frame of performance affords a broad sense of containment and resolution without specifying the tensions or rivalries. (Barwick 2018)

These themes continue to inform contemporary scholarship, as evidenced by contributions by Cross and by Treloyn and Onus, in this volume.

Marett and Barwick's (2003) article "Endangered songs and endangered languages" has informed the development of further methodological frameworks, such as parts of Ghil'ad Zuckermann's (2020) *Revivalistics*. Marett and Barwick's work has influenced these kinds of methodological considerations across the fields of language documentation, linguistics, musicology and cultural revitalisation, and importantly has also fed into discussions about processes of creating and accessing repositories for the safeguarding of song and language recordings, and involving community members in research (Treloyn and Emberly 2013; Treloyn,

1 Dialogues on music and archives: a tribute to Linda Barwick

Martin and Charles 2016; Treloyn, Charles and Nulgit 2013; Bracknell 2019a; Campbell 2012; 2017). Through Barwick's contributions, attention to the contexts of recordings when seeking to understand song has become almost standard. See, for example, work by Genevieve Campbell, whose PhD Barwick also supervised (Campbell 2014).

Barwick's field-opening scholarship in the field of archival studies re-imagined what cultural heritage repositories might look like, focusing on making primary recordings available both for the purposes of re-usable research and for speaker communities to access and use in teaching, documenting and developing their cultural heritage. Barwick's work in this field has taken both applied and theoretical forms. Her key publications are complemented by the largely unseen labour of ensuring her own recordings are well organised and thoroughly conserved in accessible archives, and in long-term collaborative work on the creation of both local and international archival infrastructure. Most notably, Barwick was co-founder of the digital language and music archive PARADISEC (Barwick 2005a; Barwick and Thieberger 2006; Thieberger and Barwick 2012; Thieberger, Harris and Barwick 2015), a world-class digital archive that has now been running for more than 20 years. She was also the inaugural president of and only Australian representative in the Digital Endangered Languages and Musics Archives Network (DELAMAN). This major international effort built on more localised work supporting communities to establish their own community-controlled archival sites, especially Wadeye Knowledge Centre (Barwick, Walsh et al. 2009; Barwick 2017).

Barwick was part of a team that digitised the audio recordings at the Wadeye Aboriginal Languages Centre (WALC). She explored new ways of making recordings available, using the free and commonly used iTunes software to present local recordings. In addition to her prodigious publication outputs, she has made substantial collections of primary records, described, organised and housed in accessible repositories: for example, the Western Arnhem Land Song Project (WALSP) data collection, housed at the Endangered Languages Documentation Program in 2012 (Barwick, Evans et al. 2012), the Philippine collection in PARADISEC (Barwick 1995) and other Italian recordings in PARADISEC.[16]

Barwick also led a project in collaboration with the Central Land Council, "Re-integrating Central Australian community cultural collections LP140100806, 2016–2019", which connected First Nations people with their cultural records, facilitated visits to archives, development of the Central Land Council Photo

---

16 https://tinyurl.com/5den55nw; https://tinyurl.com/mthkx6fy.

Database and produced 17,564 digitised files (5.92 terabytes) of analogue audio, video, image and text (Barwick, Green et al. 2019).

In her 2004 article "Turning it all upside down… Imagining a distributed digital audiovisual archive" Barwick re-imagined archives as distributed and widely accessible repositories, where cultural records would not be locked away in order to preserve them but would be both safeguarded and accessible. This has become one of her most highly cited articles, referenced by authors writing in French, Spanish, Dutch and English. It has become one of the pieces of core literature in efforts to expand thinking in music archiving and practices of return of cultural heritage, such as in Carolyn Landau and Janet Topp Fargion's 2012 special issue of the journal *Ethnomusicology*, in which contributing authors drew on Barwick's discussion of "cultural heritage communities" to call for a "more equitable ethnomusicology" across communities as diverse as London's Somali community, gospel singing communities in Los Angeles, and British Moroccan communities (Landau and Topp Fargion 2012). Barwick's work on archiving and co-authored publications on PARADISEC with Nick Thieberger also frames a number of the chapters in the recent *Oxford handbook of musical repatriation* (Gunderson, Lancefield and Woods 2018).

Outline of this volume

The chapters in this book are divided into three themes. The first, Dialogic archiving, focuses on multidirectional ongoing dialogue between archives, communities and researchers. The second theme, Music and song: knowing through analysis, explores the role of analysis in understanding performance practices. The third theme, Dialogic futures, explores contemporary uses of recordings in social action and new creative work.

Dialogic archiving begins with Nick Evans's chapter, which describes how practices of dialogic archiving keep archival materials safe across time, allowing us to interrogate, understand and value musical time, and to keep archival materials in circulation by bringing them back into relationship with speaker communities, thus informing music making in the present time. Next, Nick Thieberger asks what it means to be a responsible researcher in the digital age. Thieberger outlines the scope of language and musicological fieldwork materials that should be available in archives, but are generally not, and so he emphasises the ongoing need to find, digitise and make these materials accessible. An extreme example of recordings that have been inaccessible for some time are wax cylinder recordings made in the early 20th century. In a project led by the British Library, digital versions of some of these recordings were returned to various parts of Melanesia, as described in Grace Koch's chapter. Continuing the theme of access to archival materials, and developing the dialogue between the archive and the current community, Catherine Ingram notes the importance of community engagement with archival materials, perhaps facilitated by the researcher, but recognising that the dialogue between members of the source community and the archival collections enriches both. As the connection between the community and the archive grows, so does the community's ability to control and inform the use of the archival materials.

While archival materials locate performance in a past that can be construed as "true" or "authentic", there is clearly a need to interpret that past and to make allowances for change over time, as discussed in Curran and Martin's chapter, where they observe how traditional protocols surrounding Warlpiri cultural knowledge are reconsidered and renegotiated in new contexts. These contexts can also extend to diaspora populations, no longer living in the community's heartland; Harris, Gagau, Temu, Kila and Kila show that speaker communities are constituted not just by those present in a village of origin, but by a larger group of interconnected members of the diaspora. Just as historical records have been dispersed across the world, so have community members joined an international diaspora that remains engaged in cultural practices of the past.

Changing contexts for songs linked to place is also the topic of the second section of the volume, Music and song: knowing through analysis. The first chapter by Richard Widdess takes us to the Newar people of Nepal and their dāphā song tradition. He traces the history of the tradition and shows the novel uses of songs as part of, quoting Barwick, the "never-ending flow of knowledge, forms and practices into new contexts".

The multidisciplinary analysis of the Buffalo Sacrifice Song of the Hakhun, a minority group of North India, by Reis Flora, Khithong Hakhun, Stephen Morey and Jürgen Schöpf is a compelling example of the complex interlocking of dance, singing and percussion laid out through musical and linguistic analysis. The combination of singing and percussion is unusual in this region; although no longer performed, the Buffalo Sacrifice Song is regarded by the community as a once culturally important event. Moving back to Australia, Jennifer Green and Myfany Turpin, drawing on musical, linguistic and ethnographic analysis, argue that in the Arandic languages of central Australia, what constitutes "singing" in contrast to other forms of vocal practices such as "talking" and "humming", is markedly different from what it is in English.

Marcello Sorce Keller surveys the receding role of musical transcription in ethnomusicology and interrogates what exactly transcription is, its various methods (notation), what it can and cannot do, and its relevance in an era when audiovisual recording is commonplace. Genevieve Campbell with Yikliya Eustace Tipiloura work with archival recordings from the Tiwi Islands in the 1960s and then add to that collection with contemporary performance, further enriching the archival record. The allusive nature of much song text requires interpretation, and archival song is full of potential, waiting for the right listener, in this case the late Yikliya Eustace Tipiloura.

Bringing the themes of this section together, Sally Treloyn and Tiriki Onus consider the question asked by Barwick 34 years ago: "What can one 'know' about any sort of music by means of musical analysis?" (Barwick 1990). They consider the vexed role transcription and analysis have played in ethnomusicology, where they "operate in the shadows of colonialism", and yet can also be tools of a constantly evolving "way of relating to the music". They suggest that a focus on the artists, their musical systems, and relationships, as has been demonstrated by Barwick, can resist a discourse of loss and endangerment and assist in music sustainability.

The final theme, Dialogic futures, has six chapters that focus on performance and uses of recordings as social action. Bracknell shows how subtitled Noongar karaoke mobilises new instruments and technologies to support the circulation of endangered language and song practices and encourage community engagement. This puts language use back in the hands of the community building towards self-determination in revitalisation efforts.

In their chapter on Tjendji (Fire) and Tjerri (Sea Breeze), Payi Linda Ford and Allan Marett draw out the reciprocal relationship between all beings and the world more broadly, and the role of performance in reminding us of that relationship. They make a plea for this view that sentience exists beyond humans to inform mainstream society in order to develop a deeper ecological sense, especially important in the climate emergency we now face.

Bringing an international and new disciplinary lens to Barwick's contributions to our understanding of the potential of music, including dance and other modes of expression, for communication across cultural experience and for social cohesion, Ian Cross describes song as social action, recording associations with Country, and forming bonds. He explores music's key status as both emblem and engine of First Nations cultural identity in Australia. In this context, music establishes social relations and is the warrant for action, land holding and inheritance.

Jodie Kell and Tara Rostron show how, in West Arnhem Land, a women's rock band is using the intercultural space of popular music to compose, record and perform its members' perspectives on cultural and social issues. They analyse two of the band's love songs, arguing that the inspiration and intention of these songs is to influence perceptions of the role of women in relationships and negotiate greater agency for women. Brown, O'Keeffe, Singer, Manmurulu, Manmurulu and Manmurulu describe practices of intergenerational transmission of song and dance through the Mawng expression *arrungpayarrun ta alan* (we'll follow their path). The authors reflect on their collaborations over a 15-year period in fostering intergenerational *manyardi* performance and research, following the paths of senior ceremony leader for *Inyjalarrku* – the late Nawamut David Manmurulu – and of collaborator, scholar and friend, Linda Barwick. Finally, Jaky Troy's chapter takes us into the dialogic future by working through a record of a song written for parlour piano performance in 1834, capturing a local song from the "Menero". Working with Linda Barwick to recover what the original song may have been, in a kind of musicological archaeology, the song now has a new life.

Part I

Dialogic Archiving

Chapter 2

Keeping time: how the digital repatriation of western Arnhem Land song traditions deepens their meaning

Nicholas Evans

Introduction

The title of this tribute to Linda Barwick is triply ambiguous, reflecting the flexibility and range with which she has approached the manifold problems of "keeping time". Besides the rhythmic complexities of "keeping time" in music, which Barwick and her collaborators have explored in many publications (e.g. Bailes and Barwick 2008; 2011; Barwick 2002; Ellis and Barwick 1989) she and her comrade-in-archiving Nick Thieberger were among the first to recognise that it was "keeping time" – in other words, *time to keep* – and to found the visionary project that PARADISEC has proven to be (see e.g. Barwick and Thieberger 2006 for an early statement). But she has also long been committed to "digital repatriation", of music and language, and their meeting place: song. In this third twist to the phrase, the idea is that we can *keep time at bay*, by bringing voices from the past back from the archive and into renewed conversation with, and interpretation by, their descendants.

It is particularly on this third sense of keeping time that this tribute will focus. I concentrate on two song traditions: the Milyarryarr songs of Croker Island,

Goulburn Island and the Cobourg Peninsula,[1] and the Bongolinj-bongolinj songs closely associated with Dalabon/Mayali songman Djorli (Jolly) Laywanga.[2] In both cases I had the privilege of working with Linda on recording, analysing and interpreting these traditions, working closely with singers and speakers who generously shared their deep knowledge with us. I hadn't really known Linda before we began work together on the Iwaidja project[3] in 2003, but as soon as we got to the field I was blown away by her speed in picking up complex musical structures and her sensitivity to how discussing music and language come together.

An early example was in our explorations of Iwaidja musical vocabulary with David Minyumak and Archie Brown: one way of "keeping time" with clapsticks (*arrilil*) in this musical tradition would appear at first sight to involve beating the first three beats of a four-beat sequence, then leaving the fourth beat silent: I I I Z. But the Iwaidja term for this beat, *burruldakuku arrilil*, literally "half-half" beat, reveals a different musical conception of how this rhythm is understood and executed: one song man claps I I Z Z and the other claps I Z I Z. Each is clapping "half-half": in other words, their half of a polyrhythmic beat where two different rhythms are played together at the same tempo. Their overlaid rhythms generate the I I I Z beat, but with a slightly ragged emphasis on the first beat that could be shown as II I I Z. As we talked about that way of keeping time, it made me think of how ingrained it is in Barwick's style to get different people's contributions to link together into something that transcends what any one of them would do on their own.

I was equally in awe of Barwick's way of organising and pushing along efficient workflows, and especially in the rapport she established with people we worked with – and in ways of making sure that recordings got back to communities (see e.g. Barwick, Marett et al. 2005), which in those days involved burning lots of

---

1 The Croker Island work was part of the project "Yiwarruj, yinyman, radbiyi lda mali: Iwaidja and other Endangered languages of the Cobourg Peninsula in their Cultural Context", supported by the Volkswagenstiftung through its DoBeS program ("Dokumentation bedrohter Sprachen"). A key further fieldtrip, which enabled us to record Johnny Namayiwa, was supported by David Grubin's documentary project "Language Matters", with further input from Bob Holman.
2 The Bongolinj-bongolinj work was part of the Western Arnhem Land Song Project, funded by the Endangered Languages Documentation Project of the Hans Rausing Endangered Languages Project.
3 I use "the Iwaidja project" as a shorthand way of referring to the DoBeS project mentioned above, which in addition to Iwaidja also documented, in a more limited way, material from Garig, Ilgar and Marrku. Other researchers in this project were Kim Akerman (material culture), Bruce Birch (Iwaidja phonology), and Murray Garde (anthropology) in addition to Linda and myself.

CD copies in the evening hours, and a bit further down the track producing the prize-winning CD that brought *jurtbirrk* songs to wider attention.[4] Later on, in the Bongolinj-bongolinj project, long conversations about musicology with her and Allan Marett as we drove down the dusty road to Bulman opened my ears to a whole new way of understanding music. It is a pleasure to dedicate this chapter to her: on the one hand paying equal respect to the scope, timeliness and originality of her contributions to archiving, and on the other to her many accomplishments as a musicologist.

Hearing the ancestors

Barwick's far-sighted contribution to the design and growth of digital archives, in partnership with Nick Thieberger and others, is well known, and detailed elsewhere in this volume. While the "Paradisec@100" event measured the runaway success of PARADISEC in terms of terabytes of material, there are other ways of measuring its success: the streamlined efficiency of its deposit procedures has played an important role in speeding archiving contributions; the appeals to speech communities to help identify deposits, by Steven Gagau, have raised public awareness of its value; and the many local workshops and imaginative methods of digital repatriation, creatively pursued by Nick Thieberger, have ensured that it is known in many parts of the world where internet access remains limited.

But in this chapter, I want to focus on another consequence of Barwick's activities: the way that digital repatriation of archives (cf. Barwick, Green and Vaarzon-Morel 2019) can establish a "dialogue with the ancestors" whose voices the archives keep through time. In the first case, "the mystery of Manbam", earlier archives made by Barwick mention the existence of song genres whose full recording and musical exploration needed to wait for later. In the second, "receiving Bongolinj-Bongolinj", earlier recordings of this song genre, by Allan Marett and others, stimulated fascinating commentaries about how these songs were composed/received when our Western Arnhem Land Song Project (WALSP) team took recordings of these songs to Dalabon speakers in a number of communities. In both cases, digital repatriation enabled descendants not just to listen but also talk and sing back, adding their own voices back into the archive.

---

4   See Barwick, Birch and Williams 2005. A further outgrowth of this project was a similar CD on Nginji songs: Birch and Brown 2006.

The mystery of Manbam

Barwick's work on music of the north-western Arnhem Land coast, initially within the auspices of the Iwaidja project, established the striking number of named musical genres in the region, at least one per language in an area already famed for its linguistic diversity.

For staggering as the linguistic diversity is, the multiplicity of song styles in western Arnhem Land is even greater. An initial stocktake of the Cobourg area revealed that the number of named and musically distinct song-sets exceeds the number of identifiable languages. A song-set is always associated with a particular language: *Manbam* with Marrku, *Milyarryarr* with Ilgar, *Yanajanak* with Amurdak, *Ngarnarru* with Manangkardi, *Inyjalarrku* with Mawng, and so on. Each language is associated with at least one distinct song-set, even languages that no longer have fluent speakers. This is the case, for example, for the Ilgar *Milyarryarr* songs and the Manangkardi *Ulurrunbu, Mirrijpu* and *Ngarnarru* songs (Barwick, Birch and Evans 2007, 8–9). To fully appreciate the significance of this finding, we need to remember that many of these languages – Ilgar/Garig and Manangkardi, for example – had speaker populations of less than 100 for as far back as we can reconstruct their demography. Quite clearly, the full musicological documentation of this rich tapestry of musical traditions would be a major project, and in the years following the above article Barwick would oversee two doctoral dissertations that carried out detailed investigations on some of the song traditions of the region (Brown 2016; O'Keeffe 2016).

One barrier to this massive task was the fact that, due to the deaths of senior singers, certain song series had been "closed off" for performance at the very moment that their existence was talked about. Just before our Iwaidja project began in 2003, senior Ilgar songman Charlie Wardaga passed away, and the Milyarryarr song cycle of which he was the acknowledged master performer was "closed off" for a number of years – it would have been inappropriate for anyone to sing it, let alone for it to be recorded. At the same time, another song type associated with the Marrku language, known as Manbam, was mentioned by several living songmen on Croker Island – Charlie Brown, David Minyumak and Andrew Yarmirr. Though we obtained some partial recordings, none of these men was confident enough about the songs to help make proper transcriptions. Two important song genres thus had their existence noted in relevant archival materials (in this case, in the DoBeS archive), but it was not possible to investigate them further at that time. Barwick, patient and respectful as always, was happy to wait for the right moment to come; in 2007, she made further recordings of the Milyarryarr song genre with Wardaga's son Henry Guyiwul, Johnny Namayiwa and Jason Mayinaj. Guyiwul and Namayiwa had received the Milyarryarr songs from Charlie Wardaga before the latter's death, culminating a long musical relationship in which they had been Wardaga's backup singers: "Towards the end of his life Wardaga passed on the responsibility for leading the performance of his Milyarryarr songset in public ceremony to both his son Henry Guyiwul and to Namayiwa. This handover was formalised in a ceremony in which Wardaga gave his clapsticks to Namayiwa" (Brown and Evans 2017, 289).

In late 2013 I was visiting Warruwi on Goulburn Island with an American film crew, gathering materials for David Grubin's documentary *Language Matters with Bob Holman*.[5] That part of the film focused on the phenomenally dense and stable multilingual situation in Warruwi (Singer and Harris 2016), and involved interviewing Namayiwa, whose main language was Mawng but who spoke a number of other languages of the area (Iwaidja, Kunwinjku and Kun-barlang), and incorporated songs from a number of languages into his performances. Ruth Singer, a linguist with longstanding connections to the Warruwi community, and Reuben Brown, then a PhD student in musicology with Barwick, helped set up the interviews with Namayiwa. These led us to listen over the Milyarryarr recordings that Barwick had made in 2007. Namayiwa was a clear and patient teacher and, with his help, Reuben and I were able to make a reasonable transcription of one of the songs.[6]

The fascinating discussion that ensued helped unlock some of the mysteries that had been lying in the archive since our first recordings of Manbam in 2003, and Barwick's subsequent recordings of Milyarryarr songs in 2007. Early in our discussion with Namayiwa, he had indicated that "the only [song that I can translate] is that Marrku one" – already a cue that the language of the song is Marrku. Even though Namayiwa did not include Marrku in his language portfolio, and did not know the meanings of individual words, he would have had the meaning of the overall song explained to him by Charlie Wardaga, who did know Marrku (and indeed had been one of my Marrku teachers before his death). Importantly, Namayiwa was able to pull individual words out of the flow of song, articulating them clearly so that I could recognise many Marrku words among them, some reduced to fit to the song's rhythm: *ngarta* "I, me, my", *ngiro* (from *nginiru* "(an)other, different", *mangurtyi* "I have come, arrived", *kunhi* (from *mukunhi*) "there", *mirakuny* (from *mirangkuny*) "they went, they had gone", and *yakunhi* "not". There was also an Ilgar word (*yi*)*mardba* "different", a previously

---

5   *Language Matters with Bob Holman* 2014.
6   WALSP song ID MR07, Milyarryarr (Black heron), archived as 20070427MRMP-30-MR07. For a full analysis, see Brown and Evans 2017, 291–293.

unidentified placename Bakarnalinya (identified as a placename by Namayiwa), and the word *manbam* itself, which the reader will recall as the name of one of the Marrku song genres we recorded in 2003, and which Namayiwa explained is a reduced form of *warramanbam*, referring to "a little dwarf". Putting this all together, we can venture a translation for the song: "I have come from another place, they have gone somewhere else to Bakarlinya, oh no . . . I have come, I am a little *manbam* [ancestor]".

Keeping patient time, moving between performers, the archive, performers again, further digital repatriation and discussion, and back into the archive, an unapproachable genre has been first given the permanency its musical inspiration deserves, resuscitated by other singers, then transcription and translation to unlock its secrets. This has been Barwick's own commitment over many decades, as she has moved between the roles of field musicologist, archive builder, and advocate and practitioner of digital repatriation (Barwick and Thieberger 2018; Barwick, Green and Vaarzon-Morel 2019; O'Keeffe et al. 2018). In this way, the archival dialogue moves along.

Receiving Bongolinj-bongolinj

Between 2007 and 2009 I had the good fortune to work on a project led by Linda Barwick, also involving Allan Marett and Murray Garde, on endangered song language traditions of western Arnhem Land. One of the song styles we looked at in that project, Bongolinj-bongolinj, is among the most passionate, beautiful and musically complex song styles to be found anywhere in the rich musical traditions of this continent. Its most famous exponent, Djorli Laywanga (whose name is also spelled Jolly or Djoli Laiwonga), was an accomplished songman, a speaker of Dalabon and Mayali from around Beswick (now Wugularr). Along with David Blanasi, the famed player of didjeridu (called *mako* in Mayali and *morlû* in Dalabon), he took his songs on tour in a range of contexts – to ceremonies as far west as the Daly River, to the Darwin Eisteddfod and, famously, on tour with Rolf Harris to the United Kingdom, where he performed for and met the Queen.[7]

---

7 The interview with Maggie Tukumba from which this is excerpted also mentions travels to Fiji, Papua New Guinea, China, India and Singapore, as well as other Australian destinations.

2 Keeping time: digital repatriation of western Arnhem Land song

Example 2.1

kanh lambarrano barrahdjadrablingranhminj yow	He (Maggie Tukumba's late husband, as son-in-law) and Djorli travelled around
yeah hat bulahyedudjminj kanh Mexicanwalûng,	they brought back a hat from Mexico
Paris, Queen bulahmidimhminj	(went to) Paris, and they met the queen,
nahda balahbong Queen Elizabeth bulahmidimhminj kanihdja	They went and met Queen Elizabeth and they met her over there
duluno bulahyunj	They put on a corroboree there.
nahda balahdjabong Rolf Harris	They went there, with Rolf Harris[8]

Recordings of Laywanga, Blanasi and their group had been made by many people, including by American anthropologist LaMont West in 1961–62,[9] in 1976 (Blanatji 1976) and in recordings made by Allan Marett at Barunga in 1986. Producing a full musical analysis of this rich musical heritage, scattered across this and other sources, is a vast, ongoing project, against the background of which I want to offer a small snippet here of how the work Barwick and I were involved in has begun to enrich our understanding of the genre and its origins. I particularly want to illustrate how, by bringing archived material recorded from deceased singers into conversation with living members of the tradition, it is possible to greatly enrich our understanding. Here I focus on the song words, and on our knowledge of how the songs were composed by the songman.

By the time we began the Western Arnhem Land Song Project, both Laywanga and Blanasi were deceased, though Laywanga's younger brother Jimmy Wesan was still alive and in May 2007 we were able to record him performing a number of Bongolinj-bongolinj songs, accompanied by *morlû* player Brett Cameron. Allan Marett had begun the task of transcribing some Bongolinj-bongolinj songs with Laywanga in the late 1980s, but there were no existing musical transcriptions of this oeuvre of at least 16 songs. The songs are sung in a range of languages – Mayali, Dalabon, "spirit language" and various mixtures of these – and, as in many Australian song traditions, they contain various archaic or little-known words as well as lines whose relaxed articulation allows for multiple interpretations by

---

8   Source: https://dx.doi.org/10.26278/7DCP-WS47 (Maggie Tukumba, recorded by Linda Barwick at Weemol in discussions with Margaret Katherine, Marie Brennan, Linda Barwick and the author, transcribed by the present author and Manuel Pamkal in March 2022, in PARADISEC)
9   Released as a vinyl EP, *Arnhem Land Popular Classics*, in 1963.

different listeners. On our fieldtrips, by interviewing Dalabon and Mayali speakers with whom we listened closely to the songs and discussed them intently, we tried to accurately identify, transcribe and translate as many of these linguistic elements as possible.

We can illustrate the difficulties of coming up with a clear linguistic transcription of archived song materials with two lines from one Bongolinj-bongolinj song,[10] all the words of which are attributed to Mayali rather than Dalabon. For this song we have interpretive notes from four separate discussions with speakers of Dalabon, Mayali[11] and other Bininj Kunwok varieties. I first give the four transcriptions without analysis or context, to show that they are roughly similar, but then pass to an analysis, through glosses, which shows that these apparent similarities conceal a wide range of interpretations once the effect of slight differences in phonemic rendition, as they affect the words *kungol/kunngorl/kangurl*,[12] *djare/djarre* and *wakwam/wakwan/wakba*, are taken into account.

Example 2.2

(2a) *kungol djarre kungol wakwam / ngale! kungol djarre ngale kungol wakwam yidi yidi*
(2b) *kangurl djarre kangurl wakwam / ngale! kangurl djarre ngale kangurl wakwam yidi yidi*
(2c) *kunngorl djare, kunngorl wakwan / ngale! kunngorl djare, kunngurl wakwan yidi yidi.*
(2d) *kangurl djarre kangurl wakba / ngale! kangurl djarre, kangurl wakba yidi yidi*

The phonetic differences between these four renditions seem slight. Though I have been working on the language for several decades and am used to a range of ways of speaking it, at one point or another, as I consulted with living Mayali and Dalabon speakers, each of the four transcriptions above seemed reasonably

---

10 #5 in the song-set cataloguing used by Marett and Barwick (Barwick et al. 2011–2015).
11 Mayali is a variety of the dialect chain known collectively as Bininj Gun-wok (Evans 2003), now usually spelled Bininj Kunwok: Bininj Kunwok Regional Language and Culture Centre n.d. At the southern end of this dialect chain (e.g. at Barunga and Beswick) the term Mayali is used as a term for the whole dialect chain, but when used by speakers from further north it usually refers to the variety spoken around Manyallaluk, Barunga and Beswick. In terms of key shibboleths it is closest to the Kundjeyhmi and Kundedjnjenghmi varieties, spoken by Lofty Nadjimerrek; all other speakers mentioned here self-identified as speakers of both Mayali and Dalabon. Dalabon (Evans 2017b; Evans, Merlan and Tukumba 2004) belongs to the same language family as Bininj Kunwok, the Gunwinyguan family, and the two are about as different as Spanish and Italian.
12 In the orthography used here (see Evans 2003 and Bininj Kunwok Regional Language and Culture Centre n.d. for details), r is a retroflex continuant, rr is a tap/trill, r before other consonants indicates retroflexion, ng is the velar nasal, and dj is a lamino-palatal stop.

plausible (with one exception to be discussed), particularly bearing in mind that Djorli Layawanga's singing style favoured relaxed pronunciations of consonants to bring out the much more resonant vowels they flanked. But in each discussion session, the speakers we consulted with were quite adamant about their own version, and the interpretation it brought. Let us now look at these closely.

The first transcription was one that Allan Marett and I had worked up, based on Marett's rough and preliminary field notes made with Djorli Laywanga himself, in discussions between Allan Marett, Jimmy Wesan and myself in Beswick in 2008.

(2a) *kungol djarre kungol wakwam, ngale! kungol djarre ngale kungol wakwam yidi yidi*

ku-ngol	*djarre ku-ngol*	*wakwam*	*ngale!*	
in-cloud	far in-cloud	it.lost.it	hey!	

ku-ngol	*djarre ngale*	*ku-ngol*	*wakwam*	*yidi yidi*
in-cloud	far hey	in-cloud	it.lost.it	[vocable]

"In the clouds far away, it got lost in the clouds /
Hey! in the clouds far away, it got lost in the clouds!"

The crucial words for this interpretation are *kungol* [guŋol] "in the clouds", *djarre* [care] "far" and *wakwam* "(s)he lost it".[13] It is a plausible interpretation, especially when one considers the haiku-like compression of so much song language in northern Australia.

A somewhat different transcription, and translation, was given to me in discussions with Maggie Tukumba and her husband George ("Left-Hand") Jungunwanga at Weemol in July 2008. Jungunwanga had travelled widely with Djorli and David Blanasi in the heyday of their musical performances, so was familiar with the song as a performer. Here is their interpretation (from now on I restrict the transcription and interlinearisation to the first four words, since the remainder are either the same through all four versions, or simply recapitulate differences already present in the first four words). The bracketed explanation about the Mimih spirit is not part of the words but was given by Jungunwanga as part of the background.

(2b) *kangurl djarre kangurl wakwam*

ka-ngurl	*djarre ka-ngurl*	*ø-wakwa-m*
3sgS-loom.darkly	far 3sgS-loom.darkly	3sgS>3sgO.Pst-lose-PP

---

13 *Wakwam* is also used in talking about deceased people, as "lost", and about forgetting, so there are a number of resonances to this word.

"The clouds loom up dark, far away, he [the *mimih*] lost them [they were tied up outside the cave where he was sleeping],
Hey! it's dark far away, they are looming darkly, he lost them."

A third transcription, and translation, was given by Queenie Brennan in discussions with Barwick and me in Barunga, in July 2008. There are two small but meaning-altering phonetic differences – *kunngorl* [gunŋol] "heart" versus *ku-ngol* [guŋol] "in the clouds", and *djare* [caɟe] "I want you" rather than *djarre* [care] "far". These changes combine with the polyvalence of the "zero prefix" on transitive verbs in Mayali, and the fact that the non-past form *wakwan* means "not know" as opposed to the past perfective *wakwam* "forget"[14] (it can mean either "(s)he acting upon him/her", or "I acting upon you") to turn this into a love song rather than a song about clouds and their spiritual significance.

(2c) *kunngorl*   *djare,*   *kunngorl*   *ø-wakwa-n*
      heart   I-want_you   heart   I.don't.know.you

"I want your heart, I don't know your heart /
Hey! I want your heart, I don't know your heart."

Though each of these three transcriptions, and translations, seemed plausible, one small but nagging phonetic discrepancy bothered me: though all three of the above interpretations proposed the verb *wakwam* / *wakwan* "not know, forget, be lost" (the final nasal is a tense/aspect inflection), the middle part definitely sounded more like *akba* to me, suggesting a word *wakba(n)*. At the time, the only word I know that sounded anything like this was the word *wakbah* "eel-tailed catfish", but everyone I spoke with rightly rejected this as nonsensical. My doubts remained. Then, a bit later on the same fieldtrip (July 2008, in Kunbarlanja), we[15] had the great privilege of speaking to Lofty Bardayal Nadjimerrek, legendary across western Arnhem Land for his deep knowledge of language and lore. He proposed this fourth version, in which there is, after all, a word *wakba*, which nobody else present had heard before, dropped into version (b) above:

---

14 That is, forgetting is treated, grammatically, as the inception of not knowing: see Evans 2003, 372. The past imperfective *wakwani* means "used to be ignorant of" (e.g. in talking about old people's ignorance of tobacco before they were introduced to it).

15 Linda, Murray Garde and Allan Marett were all present for this discussion. That trip was memorable for many other reasons as well, one of them being that members of the Nabarlek band (Birribob Dangbungala Watson and Stuart Guymala) were also there – a rock band tracing many of its musical origins to the Bongolinj-bongolinj style. Re-tooling some of their songs on 5 June 2007, in the demanding presence of Lofty and Jimmy Kalarriya, they gradually transformed them back to something like the original Bongolinj-bongolinj style, necessitating a lot of complex musical reshapings. But that is a story for another time.

(2d) *kangurl djarre kangurl wakba*

ka-ngurl	*djarre*	*ka-ngurl*	*wakba*
3sgS-loom.darkly	far	3sgS-loom.darkly	billowing.spinifex.smoke

"Far off it looms darkly, the billowing black spinifex smoke /
Hey! Far off it looms darkly, the billowing black spinifex smoke."

Now it would be naive to call this the "right" version of the transcription, and translation. Songs, everywhere, take on lives of their own, and different people internalise different versions, each plausible in their own way. Indeed, Djorli was such a masterful composer that he may have deliberately cultivated these multiple readings. Nonetheless, Lofty's version has several interpretive advantages. It is closer to what, phonetically, definitely sounds like a *kb* rather than *kw* cluster in *wakba*. The "billowing black spinifex smoke" is thematically more coherent with the first two words – watching the distant horizon for the characteristic dark smoke produced when spinifex catches fire is a common practice in western Arnhem Land. And, as happens so often in verbal art, it uses a lexical item only known to the most masterly of speakers, to powerful effect.

Discussions in the context of repatriating archival recordings were not confined to elucidating the words of the songs. They also provided a fascinating series of accounts of how the Bongolinj-bongolinj song series came into being. This relates to important wider debates about how music is created across Indigenous Australian traditions. Is knowledge of song simply transmitted: for example, from father to son in a clan, back from time immemorial? Is it presented in dreams? Is it actively composed? Or can it come by some other route? The stories that arose in the context of playing back archived recordings of Djorli Layawanga singing provide fascinating, if inconsistent, answers to these questions, at least as they pertain to the Bongolinj-bongolinj tradition.

In the course of these "dialogues with the archives", we recorded many people who had known Djorli telling us vivid stories about how he received these songs. (I use "received the songs" as a neutral translation of Dalabon *dulumang* "get song(s)", which encompasses composing, hearing songs from spirits and learning them from others – the exact nuance will shift according to the stories we examine below).

One pair of versions (a first version in English, then a subsequent version in Dalabon) was told to us by Djorli's half-brother Jimmy Wesan in May 2007.[16] The Kriol version begins by talking about Djorli's wish to get his own song-set. Starting off as someone who is known not to have previously possessed any songs, he goes to the cemetery and lies down next to the grave of a recently buried woman so as to listen in on the spirits who have come to fetch her, and learns the Bongolinj-bongolinj set in this way.

Example 2.3

and one time he come back he start think about, you know
he was worrying about
brother, my brother, he was worrying
I like to getti[17] song, you know, somewhere
I'm try to getti song corroboree song, you know

It turns out that a woman from Maningrida[18] had recently been buried in a nearby graveyard, apparently having been killed for a ceremonial infringement. As the story continues, Djorli decides he should go and lie down next to her in the graveyard, so as to listen to the songs that will be sung by the spirits of the dead as they come to fetch the woman's spirit:

---

16 The English/Kriol version was recorded at Burrih (a bore outside Beswick) on 30 May 2007, from Jimmy Wesan (Kodjok) with some additional remarks by Brett Cameron (Bulanj), after a session where the two of them had performed some Bongolinj-bongolinj songs. See 20070530AM02.wav for the original recording. First transcription of file by the author, July 14-15 2008; then checked with Queenie Brennan, Barunga, 17 July 2008. Discussions with Queenie emphasised the way that Djorli had found it hard to get hold of the music he heard, with its alien beats different from the *darh-darh* style of clapstick beating he was used to.

17 There are inevitable transcriptional challenges in dealing with speech such as this, somewhere on the spectrum between Aboriginal English and (Roper River) Kriol, as well as in how far to accommodate the transcription to individual idiosyncracies. In this particular case, Jimmy Wesan pronounces this word [gedi] rather than the /gedim/ more typical of Kriol.

18 There is a fascinating musical twist here: according to Allan Marett (personal communication), there are important musical features of the Bongolinj-bongolinj songs that show interesting resemblances to song styles from the Arafura coast, so linking these songs to a deceased woman from Maningrida would have some basis. Another intriguing clue is that the word *(ba)karnalinja* – mentioned as a placename in the discussion above of the Mirrijbu song – crops up as a "spirit word" in a number of Bongolinj-bongolinj songs. The musical evidence for these links is something we plan to pursue in a more elaborated discussion than can be given here.

Example 2.4

> *he seen that, ground*
> *there's this grass and, that groun', you know*
> *they just buried that girl that old lady, they bin buryim*
> *first time before he come in before he comin up*
> *they bin bury him and, all bin go way now, that people*
> *when they buried that old lady*
> *they bin all go back, to camp and my brother*
>   *he saw that ground that lady was buried up there and*
> *he bin see*[19] *"oh, new, fresh track, this one new one"*
> *"somebody bin die here. They bury him, they bin bury him.*
> *anyway, never talk that way now", he bin just*
> *he just start thinkabout you know, he bin think*
> *"I better sleep here, I better bin camp"*
> *he was tired now, "little bit I camped", he was sleep early*
> *that graveyard bin like that, he was sleep there one side*
> *that graveyard till he too listen bin dark*
> *you know when sun he go down, 'bout eight o'clock or*
>   *something like that*
> *eight or nine eight or nine*
> *that devil bin come out, you know, singing la graveyard*
> *he was sleep – my brother was sleep now*
> *and one devil he touch touch body to him*
> *him oldei*[20] *keep movin you know*
> *and that, all the devil sing you know they singin that*
> *this man might be still live*
> *but that really live one now, he was sleepin*
> *and that dead one he was underground inside*
> *anyway he was sleep, he didn't worry about them people*
> *he was sleep, sleep there to find that song now*
> *corroboree they make corroboree, big play now*
> *make a noise, and he keep listening, my brother he keep*
>   *listening that song*

---

19 This use of "see" to introduce a direct quote, with the meaning "saw and said to himself", is typical of Dalabon, as in a number of other Australian languages, and carries over to Jimmy Wesan's Kriol / Aboriginal English. See Evans 2021, 77, ex. 80, for a glossed Dalabon example, corresponding to lines 5–6 of example (5) below.

20 The word *oldei* in Kriol and many varieties of Aboriginal English comes from "all-day" but has changed its meaning to 'keep, habitually do'.

I grab this song now
when I get up, he said
and keep singim, singim, singim, other race[21]
nother song he didn't worry about, he bin only worry about that kun-borrk
that's the song now he bin worry about
"I grab this song now" he said. Everybody was know him
he didn't have any song he didn't have any song
yeah, that my brother now he didn't have any song
him never savvy, he not know
anyway, they keep teachim[22] *him*
you know, that dead man
people want, they was singin you know
they keep teachim till, you know, they learnim
so they can singim properly anyway
that bin morning now, that was morning
he bin morning just get up, and go
he bin go to Barunga now go to Barunga, come out
come out, and I'll talk to my, our father
and that man now, my brother
our father was there too, he was still alive
and I talked to my dad, you know
"Hey daddy, my brother comin up here"

A couple of days later Wesan gave us the same story, this time in Dalabon (left column; my English translation on right), which adds in a few extra details, including an interesting comment on how much more difficult it was for Djorli to get hold of the musically complex Bongolinj-bongolinj songs than it was with songs in the Walakka style:

---

21 By "other race" he here means "another type" of song – i.e. disco songs (as now practised by more recent bands) as opposed to the Bongolinj-bongolinj *kun-borrk* songs he was concentrating on.

22 Pronounced /tisim/, Kriol-style, in the transcript.

2 Keeping time: digital repatriation of western Arnhem Land song

Example 2.5

kirdikird wanjing kahdonj	An woman had died before
yongkihyongkih	An old woman
wurrhwurrungu kahdonj	So he went there (to the graveyard)
kahlngbong bûkahnang yulu-kah	and looked at the earth, freshly dug.
yulu_djerrngû	"Hey, I'll sleep here to get hold of
yulu-djerrngû kah-nang	corroboree music" he said.
"Ngale! Ngahyongiyan djarra, kunborrk	He spent the night there, he stretched
ngahmiyankûn" kahyininj	himself out.
kahyo, kahyurrinj	The sun was about there, like where
mudda kahyinhyininjkûno	it is when we say five o'clock or six
the sun was like that, round about that	o'clock
time	That's when he saw that graveyard, he
wanjh ngarreyeyin five o'clock like we	looked at it
say	
five o'clock or six o'clock ngarreyeyin	
kanhkuno kahnang	
that graveyard, kahnang kanihdja	"Well, this is where I'll spend the
"Ngale djarra ngahyongiyan" kahyinj	night" he said, "so that I can get hold
"ngahdulumiyankûn	of those *kun-borrk* songs".
kunborrk" kahyinj	He spent the night, and stretched
kah … kahyo	himself out.
kahyurrinj na	He made a fire and slept the night
kahworrhminj kahyo	there by the grave
nûnda kanh bulno	He lay down a bit to one side
wansaid kadjawohmarnûyo redjnokah	
kahyo	
kahyurrinj kanh warhdû balahlng-	He laid himself down and the spirits of
burluburlhminj	the dead came out around the grave,
kanh bulnokah	they were singing,
kahlngwayininj, balahwayininj	singing *kun-borrk* songs
kunborrk balahwayininj	"It's really different from Walakka
"KahwirriHminj[23] *walakka, mak*	songs, I can't get hold of the way they
ngamiyan,	are beating the sticks, I can't get it" he
bungkurl balahdarhdarhminj mak	said. "I'm going to get the *kun-borrk*"
ngamiyan kahyininj	he said.[24]
kunborrk ngahmiyan kahyin"	

---

23 The letter H here represents an h-like sound, with air flowing through the nose at the same time.
24 Original recording by Allan Marett 20070602AM03.wav. First transcription by NE 14–15/7/2008, checked with Queenie Brennan 17 July 2008, then finally checked with Manuel Pamkal March 2022.

In terms of the central question of how Djorli received the songs, both these versions are quite clear: before going to the graveyard to hear the songs from the spirits he was known not to have possessed knowledge of his own song-sets; he deliberately goes to the graveyard to hear them from the spirits, learns them there despite the complexity of the music, and returns to his family to teach them to his brother and others, who then begin taking the music around to perform it in various places. (The Dalabon verb *wowan* means "to [go on] tour", "to take a music performance or corroboree around to perform it in various places").

Another version we recorded in Dalabon, from Maggie Tukumba,[25] presents a very different picture. On her account, Djorli's father already knew Bongolinj-bongolinj – *kardu mawahmawah ngayin, ngaldjun mawahmawah kanh, mawahnjerrng Djun kanh kayedulunanHnaninj*[26] *Bongolinj-bongolinj* "maybe my (paternal) grandfather, the grandfather of me and June (and father of Djorli, since we call Djorli father), he was a Bongolinj-bongolinj songman. Djorli still goes to the graveyard, on this version of the story, but it is in order to get songs that he had not learned from his father. When he lies down next to the grave and falls asleep, two birds (*korrdjdjork* the boobook owl and *kuluyhkuluy* the tawny frogmouth) land one on each side of him, and lift up his spirit, singing to him and taking him to another part of the graveyard, where he gets songs given to him by the spirits of others from his lineage who are buried there. On this interpretation, learning songs back from the spirits is more like an intensified, delayed way of reclaiming musical traditions that were already part of his clan heritage.

---

25 We recorded two discussions of Bongolinj-bongolinj music from Maggie Tukumba, on 22 July 2008. This transcription is from 20080722NE02.wav; elan filename 20080722.MT2OnBongolinjbongolinj.eaf, transcribed by the author and Manuel Pamkal in March 2022. In the second recording, which deals with a series of "intellectual property" disputes between Djorli Laywanga and another Bongolinj-bongolinj performer, Les Mirrikkurrya, Layawanga is angry with Mirrikkurrya because he believes he has stolen the songs from him without authorisation, whereas another view advanced in the story is that Les had learned them from Namorrorddo spirits; mention is also made of a third, related series, received by David Karlbuma from the spirits of Nabarlek rock possums. The theme of how source of musical knowledge interacts with culturally defined intellectual property to determine performance rights is central to this text, which we plan to discuss in detail in a forthcoming joint publication.

26 In discussing these various songmen, Maggie Tukumba uses the Dalabon verb *dulunanHnan*, lit. "see and see the song", with a meaning which according to Manuel Pamkal can range from "be a practising songman" to "rehearse / be a performer of (the relevant style of) songs".

2 Keeping time: digital repatriation of western Arnhem Land song

Example 2.6

korrdjdjork kuluyhkuluy barrahboninj,	Boobook owl and tawny frogmouth,
barrahboninj bûrrah-wayhkanj	The two of them went there at night
kodjnokah kahnjenguyo barrahboninj	and lifted up his spirit (from the
burrahmarnûyenjdjunginj	graveyard); the two birds landed, one
burrahmarnûyenjdjunginj kodjnokah	on either side of his head, and sang the
munano	song to him that way.
bûrrahkaninj nahda, bulnokah wanjh	With his head laid there, as he was
balebuldikah wahdu	sleeping, the two of them went and
kardu mawah kardu ngayin mamamh	called out to him.
kardu ngayin, djongok	The two of them called out to him, to
kardu ngayin mimi kardu ngayin kardu	his mind, in the night time
*bulah**dulungabbuninj**, kanihdja*	they lifted up his spirit, they took him
bulnowalung	away there, to another graveyard where
*kah**dulumanginj** bulah**dulungabbuninj***	[others] were buried
*kah**duluyedudjminj***	to where my grandfather [Layawanga's
bulkadehmarnûyenjdjunginj,	father] and my mother's father are, and
kadehbarrhbuninj	my aunty,
"nûnda duluno yimba kahnunda,	Maybe they gave him the songs, maybe
ngahdulumakniyan ngahwayiningiyan"	they gave him the song there in the
	graveyard,
	He got the song, they gave him the
	song,
	He took the songs back home [after
	learning them]
	He spoke to them [the others in his
	family] about it in the morning time,
	when the sun came up.
	"this song I got from the graveyard, I
	might try it out, and let all the family
	start dancing and singing".

A key question in the study of music is how composers of song styles like Bongolinj-bongolinj obtain their musical ideas and develop their performance styles. The term "receive" is sometimes used, or sometimes people are said to "dream" them, but either way it's often presented as just a single event. Going over these and other musical discussions from the Dalabon archives, by a range of speakers, about how singers of Bongolinj-bongolinj and related styles got their songs or *dulû-no* (also pronounced *dulu-no*, and the *-no* drops when the noun is incorporated into a verb), a range of relevant words come up, all exemplified in the above texts (I cite them here without their pronominal prefixes).

These include *dulû-manginj* [song-get] "got, received, obtained [the] song(s) (in the graveyard)" and *dulumangiyankûn* "so as to get hold of the songs, catch on to the songs'", *dulû-ngabbuninj* [song-gave] "[the spirits] gave/taught [him] [the] song(s) (in the graveyard)", *dulu-makniyan* "will rehearse/try out the song". In describing Djorli, Maggie Tukumba regularly used the combination *dulunanHnaninj* "saw songs, rehearsed songs, was a practising songman". What is interesting here, from a linguistic point of view, is how two form changes are applied to the basic verb *nan* "see" to give *nanHnaninj*. The imperfective suffix *-ninj* marks this as a repeated event, used for repeated or drawn-out actions in the past. And the left-reduplication of basic *naninj* (lit. "he kept seeing') to *nanH-naninj* "he kept starting to see" indicates that the repetition applied to the process of "seeing" – or mastering – the song properly, something that could be rendered as "keep trying to master the song". In fact, Manuel Pamkal, with whom I worked on the transcription and translation of this text in March 2022, was insistent that *dulunanHnaninj* is closer to the word "rehearsed" in English, like a band. This is just one tiny piece in the puzzle of using recorded discussions to understand the beautiful Dalabon musical tradition, and of how these songs come into being through complex interplays of human agency, circumstance and the inspiration of music-giving spirits. The transcription and notes on these discussions – still ongoing – will then find their way back to the archive, as an enriched transcription of the media files that are already there.

Barwick has long been a powerful advocate of the need to link the study of endangered languages with the study of endangered musical traditions.[27] These two case studies show how the back-and-forth of dialogic repatriation creates many opportunities for discussions of music to enrich our understanding of language both in terms of esoteric vocabulary (*wakba* "billowing spinifex smoke"[28]) and as it pertains to musical traditions (conceptualisations of composing and receiving). These discussions also enrich our understanding of the culture of music making in the communities that hear and appreciate these songs – whether it be in how different speakers position their own differing interpretations of a particular song, or how they locate (and validate) a composer and songman like Djorli Laywanga and other Bongolinj-bongolinj in the contested borderlands between innovation, inheritance and overhearing from the spirit world, while maintaining his reputation

---

27 See e.g. Marett and Barwick 2003; 2007; Walsh, Barwick and Marett 2011; Marett and Barwick 2003; 2007.
28 See further examples in the realm of emotional vocabulary in Barwick, Birch and Evans 2007.

against possible charges of unauthorised musical appropriation.[29] Through these examples I hope to have given a glimpse of how ongoing digital repatriations can create an evolving dialogue that enriches our understanding not just of music and of language, but of the social context in which both are situated.

Conclusion

To conclude this tribute to Barwick's unique contributions across musicology, archiving and dialogic repatriation of both music and language, it is fitting to briefly revisit the triple readings of "keeping time" with which I began the piece, so as to bring out, through its ternary form, two conceptions of how we keep – or mark – time, which I have wrapped around the middle sense of "time to keep" – of the need to archive fragile knowledge of music, language and other cultural forms.

Musical notation is indifferent to whether the timing of a beat – say 4/4 time – is kept by a metronome or a conductor. And in an ever more quantitative and digital age, we are constantly tempted to measure worth in terms of seconds, hours, terabytes – or numbers of song styles, or bars.

But the difference between a metronome and a conductor lies in the human interaction breathed by the latter – watching the musicians, or dancers, and subtly or even imperceptibly accommodating the flow of human action into the advancing beat. As someone who loves music without ever having studied musicology, and who was puzzled by the devilish unpredictability of some of Djorli's rhythms, I remember having the scales fall from my eyes along that dusty road to Bulman when Linda and Allan explained to me that Arnhem Land songmen watch the dancers moving towards them and adjust their rhythm in the instrumental sections that signal when the dancers should advance or retreat (Marett 2005, 100–101; Marett, Barwick and Ford 2013, 45–47; Brown 2016, 151). The potentialities of digital repatriation, of conversations with the archives, that Barwick has pioneered through her own work and the possibilities she has created for others, are more directly akin to this interactive keeping of time. The open-ended "dialogues with the dead"[30] that this conception allows for make archives anything but a dead, fixed resource – they can be constantly enriched, freshly interpreted and elaborated by the conversations they bring out with the living.

---

29 Another series of discussions that was stimulated by playing back these songs concerned what were effectively intellectual property disputes between Djorli and another singer of a similar genre, with Djorli accusing the other singer of stealing his songs. See Evans 2021, 38–39 for transcripts of the relevant lines.

30 I borrow this phrase from Piers Vitebsky's (1993) splendid ethnography of Sora culture and the conversations it sets up with ancestral spirits.

In this chapter I have tried to capture this unfolding process by weaving two Arnhem Land songs into a time line of performing and recording, archiving, repatriating, discussing, transcribing and understanding. For each song, Barwick's involvement was crucial at vital stages: for conceiving an ambitious project of recording western Arnhem Land music through two large projects when there was still time to keep, by recording the first (and still seemingly linguistically indecipherable) songs in the Manbam style, and by her listener's art of bringing out discussions of Djorli Laywanga's musical production (in this case originally recorded by Allan Marett) with Queenie Brennan, Jimmy Wesan and Maggie Tukumba. I was fortunate enough to be present with her at those various stages, and then to continue the investigation of these haunting songs through the unexpected new performance and explication of a Manbam song by Johnny Namayiwa (with Reuben Brown doing the musicological analysis) and by transcriptions and translations of the Dalabon discussions over the ensuing years with Maggie Tukumba and Manuel Pamkal. I hope that these enrichments to our archival record will play a small role at keeping time at bay as these rich musical traditions are threatened with forgetting, not just of what they sound like, but of what they mean to singers and their listeners.

Acknowledgements

In addition to the Volkswagen Foundation's DoBeS program, David Grubin Productions' and Arcadia's Endangered Languages Documentation Project, I would like to thank the ARC Centre of Excellence for the Dynamics of Language (CoEDL) for supporting more recent work that allowed the transcription and translation of Dalabon material presented here. I especially thank the speakers and singers of the song traditions discussed here – Archie Brown, Henry Guwiyul, Johnny Namayiwa, Charlie Wardaga, Brian Yambikbik, Andrew Yarmirr (Croker/Goulburn Islands), and Manuel Pamkal, Maggie Tukumba, Jimmy Wesan (Dalabon/Mayali traditions). I would also like to thank the following people who participated in various fieldtrips in these projects and helped advance our understanding of this fascinating music: Isabel O'Keeffe, Bruce Birch, Reuben Brown, Murray Garde, Allan Marett and Ruth Singer, as well as Nick Thieberger and an anonymous referee for their useful critical comments on an earlier version of this chapter. Finally I would like to thank Linda Barwick herself for her friendship, her inspiration, and for her help and encouragement in entering the challenging musical worlds of Arnhem Land song.

Chapter 3

Language and music recordings and the responsible researcher

Nick Thieberger

"Indigenous knowledges, cultures and languages, and the remnants of indigenous territories, remain as sites of struggle."

Linda Tuhiwai Smith, *Decolonizing Methodologies* (1999)

Introduction

Archiving of music and language materials has come a long way in the past 20 years. Curated primary data in an archive, and the practices that go into creating that data, have the potential to radically change the way we conduct fieldwork, cite our data and access records made by others. The apparently simple fact of being able to cite primary data to any level (text, sentence, word, phoneme, song, stanza, line) allows verification of analyses that was not previously possible. Archived recordings also ensure that the records are available for re-use in the future, by both researchers and the broader community. The acts of making re-usable primary records in collaboration with the speakers, their consent in how the records can be shared and the creation of suitable repositories all support significant changes in methodology.

While it seems that many academics find it difficult to archive their recordings, Linda Barwick is an exemplar in having done just that, as well as creating an outstanding output of descriptive and theoretical papers (as can be seen in the list of her output provided with this volume). Here, I will take Barwick's practice as the starting point for a discussion of the central role of archiving in language and music documentation.

Accessible primary data are part of the exchange relationship we (as researchers) enter into in the field. We make recordings initially for the purpose of academic analysis, but have, until recently, ignored their value for the community we work with. This is evident because we have either not made re-usable records, or have kept them in inaccessible locations. Making recordings available via an archive relieves us of the need to keep track of our records into the future and of the need to deal with occasional requests for copies of their records that require finding the records and then sending them to the requester. This is a positive post-colonial aspect to archiving of language materials, especially in contrast to the prevailing past practice in which no material was made publicly available.

Why then is it that records arising from fieldwork can be so hard to find, especially for the speakers and their communities? A certain amount of detective work can be required to even know that these materials exist. When the records were analogue (reels of audiotape, audiocassettes or papers), a concerted effort was required to find them, first, based on an expectation that there were recordings made to support a piece of research reported in a publication, and, second, requiring travel to a single location to consult the materials. While there are individual catalogues of collections in each particular holding institution, there is no unified catalogue of all of these kinds of collections that would provide, for example, a list of all known material in a given language or musical style. To make it even harder, the only copies of analogue tapes were held by the researcher, and access became harder still if they had retired or died. Getting access in these cases required the good graces of the new custodian (the executors of the estate).

Digital records should, in principle, be easier to locate. After all, they can be copied to various locations in a manner similar to the taper light famously observed by Thomas Jefferson: "he who lights his taper at mine, receives light without darkening me".[1] In fact, digital records are at risk, to extend the taper analogy, of being snuffed out so that no further light can be received from them, especially if they are held on a computer or hard disk as inaccessibly as the analogue files discussed earlier.

Tuzin noted:

> If it is true that one of ethnography's distinguishing features is the moral cloak with which it wraps itself, then it is all the more surprising and ironic that the record of ethnographic conduct is abysmal concerning the preservation and dissemination of its findings. (Tuzin 1995, 24)

---

1 Letter to Isaac McPherson, 13 August 1813. https://tinyurl.com/376ray2n.

3 Language and music recordings and the responsible researcher

Sadly, despite the passing of nearly 30 years, and the rise of digital preservation strategies, Tuzin's observations largely hold true today. This chapter outlines the gains made by archiving and then assesses the costs of not archiving language records. It charts the growth of archives over the past two decades and argues for the need for new archives to serve the anticipated future uptake of archiving habits by musicologists and documentary linguists.

Grammars but not records

As an example of how much acceptance there is among researchers of archiving outputs of fieldwork, let us take the example of linguistic fieldwork and grammar writing. In earlier work (Thieberger 2017) I noted the large number of languages for which grammars have been written but for which there are no primary records archived. Some 683 grammars are listed in Glottolog[2] as appearing since the beginning of 2000. Of the languages represented by those grammars, 555 have 40 or fewer items in a digital language archive. So, even in the now 26 years since Himmelmann's 1998 framing of the field of language documentation (which focuses on the creation of primary records, re-usable by others, in addition to the analysis traditionally expected of academic research), it seems that the majority of linguists are either not creating records or, if they are, are not prepared to archive them in a relevant digital language archive. We are not alone in this; Piwowar (2011, 5) finds that, even in biological science, only "25% of studies that performed gene expression microarray experiments have deposited their raw research data in a primary public repository". She did also report an improvement in the use of shared datasets over time from "less than 5% in early years, before mature standards and repositories, to 30–35% in 2007–2009". Perhaps we can also look forward to an increase in archival deposits with a new generation of researchers, and my impression is that those working in Australia have learned the importance of archiving from role models like Barwick (e.g., Barwick 2004; Barwick and Thieberger 2006; Barwick, Green and Vaarzon-Morel 2019). Of course, it may be that language records are archived, for example, in a state library or university repository. But because these kinds of archives are not part of linguistic search mechanisms like the Open Language Archives Community (OLAC, discussed further below), the items are difficult to locate and do not feature in the metrics presented here.

---

2   Glottolog is a service that lists resources available for each of the world's languages (https://glottolog.org).

Language identifiers are an internationally recognised system that avoids problems of variant language name spellings and forms. Each language will have different names in different languages (français, French, Francese, Französisch) so which one do you search for? There are languages whose names are also common words (e.g., Maria, Mono, Mum, Noone, Karen, Kola, Titan). Assigning a code to each language avoids this problem and there are two main systems of codes available: notably ISO-639–3 (the three-letter codes) and Glottolog. In order to take advantage of these codes, there needs to be a system in place that identifies what language an item is in, and publishes that information to make the item findable on the web. This is what language archives do.

As has been observed by Moyse-Faurie:

> the basic description of languages with an oral tradition . . . contributes, with the transition to the written word, to the revitalization of a language, if it is in danger, or to ensuring its documentation in the form of archives which will remain available for any other future use, whether for research in the strict sense or for applied linguistics. (Moyse-Faurie 2014, 140)

This applies equally to musical records and recognises other possible uses of archival records beyond foreseeable issues in research and cultural revitalisation, including cultural heritage and personal histories of the people recorded.

I first met Linda in Perth in the 1980s and discussions with her about fieldwork later inspired my own work on a corpus of Nafsan (South Efate) based in my research in Vanuatu in the 1990s, linked to media using SoundIndex (Thieberger 2004; Thieberger and Jacobson 2010), and the development of the online system EOPAS (Schroeter and Thieberger 2006) for presenting interlinear text and media. All of this work demonstrates the utility of creating time-aligned transcripts of field recordings from the beginning with the primary goal of creating a corpus in which transcripts are always verifiable. As the analysis of the language improves, the ability to re-listen to the source will support re-analysis, especially if it relates to prosodic aspects of the language that are only apparent because of the ability to hear linked media. Examples given as evidence of linguistic phenomena can be checked by the readers, together with the context from which they are extracted.

A major motivation for archiving, from an academic disciplinary perspective, is the ability to cite primary sources (Berez-Kroeker et al. 2018) and so to allow verification of examples and the context in which they occur, potentially leading to new analyses. Barwick's work in establishing PARADISEC helps popularise what Nick Evans (this volume) calls "dialogic repatriation", the ability to take archival records, interpret them, and enrich the archival collection, while also using them to support relearning of traditions that may have been lost. While I am mainly discussing language records here, the same issues are applicable to music records, especially where the two are combined in single archival collections. Linguists have the advantage of shared tools and infrastructure and a consensus about metadata terms, largely provided by two sources, OLAC (mentioned earlier) and The Language Archive (TLA).[3] This is the basis for the kinds of search mechanisms discussed in this chapter.

Archiving language material, the successes

Online digital archives have the potential to be dynamic centres of activity (Holton 2012), and to support revitalisation of heritage knowledge of performance and language by providing a link between generations in places where little else was recorded in the past. In many cases, the archival recording is the only online reflection of performances from a village or family member. Success for an archive can be measured in several ways, but a critical success is the number of times people unexpectedly find recordings related to their families or languages. Another is the re-use of archival recordings for new research purposes. In both cases, access to the primary records can result in enriching existing materials with transcriptions or additional metadata. Of course, another side to the ubiquity of digital material is the need to ensure appropriate access, with licences in place that indicate how material can be used, as specified by the depositor. There is always a risk that material will be misused, but that risk needs to be weighed against the risk that speakers will not find recordings of performances that may inform current practice, or whose records they may be able to enrich with current knowledge.

Digital language archive catalogues can provide a feed to a service provided by OLAC. It aggregates each archive's catalogue and lists all resources available per language with the URL http://www.language-archives.org/language/ followed by a language code.

OLAC lists 373,197 items in 60 archives (in 2023) compared to 223,664 items listed in 58 archives in 2008, a 66 per cent increase in fifteen years. But, if we set an arbitrary goal of at least 200 archival items for each of the world's languages (see below for more hypothesising about future records of languages), we would expect there to be in the order of 1,400,000 archival sources.

Table 3.1 shows the number of resources (bundles or items, which contain files) and languages represented by ten selected archives.

---

3 https://archive.mpi.nl/tla, formerly funded by the DoBeS program of the Volkswagen Stiftung (*Documentation of Endangered Languages*, https://dobes.mpi.nl).

Table 3.1 Sample of language archive statistics provided by OLAC (July 2022).

Archive	Number of Resources	Distinct Languages
Archive of the Indigenous Languages of Latin America (AILLA) (USA)	289	257
C'ek'aedi Hwnax Ahtna Regional Linguistic and Ethnographic Archive (USA)	1,474	3
California Language Archive (USA)	14,959	295
COllections de COrpus Oraux Numeriques (CoCoON ex-CRDO) (France)	17,495	273
Endangered Languages Archive (UK)	93,687	594
Kaipuleohone (USA)	5,621	226
The Language Archive (Nijmegen, Netherlands)	167,996	460
Living Archive of Aboriginal Languages (Australia)	3,738	41
Pacific And Regional Archive for Digital Sources in Endangered Cultures (PARADISEC) (Australia)	27,219	1,360
Pacific Collection at the University of Hawai'i at Mānoa Hamilton Library (USA)	5,292	749

A further important development in the recent past was the formation, in 2003, of the network of archives known as the Digital Endangered Languages and Musics Archives Network (DELAMAN) of which Barwick was the inaugural president. With 14 current member archives, DELAMAN agrees on archival standards and helps with referring users to appropriate archives.

An ongoing challenge for academic repositories is how to make the materials they hold more accessible. Directories like OLAC increase the exposure of archive catalogues and make them available via other online services (e.g. the Virtual Language Observatory, or WorldCat, and also through Google). The webpages they present are, in general, not particularly attractive or intuitive to navigate as their effort is typically directed to building and maintaining collections with little funding. As most archives include information from a number of languages it is not possible to localise their interfaces, with a notable exception being the Archive of the Indigenous Languages of Latin America, which has both an English and Spanish (and soon also Portuguese) version of its catalogue and webpages.

More archives needed!

The extent of the task ahead can be daunting. Consider the many millions of words, sentences, recordings and movies in languages with many speakers (English, Spanish, French, Russian, Hindi, Mandarin to pick just six) that will provide an enduring record. To create comprehensive records of performance in each of the world's languages would mean extending the sort of records linguists and musicologists currently produce. Evans observed that "it is becoming feasible to record around 500 hours of linguistic material in the course of a year or two's fieldwork, thanks to the miniaturisation, fidelity and portability of our recording devices" (Evans 2017a, 41). As new technologies allow more recording, so increases the need for careful management of this wealth of material. As an impressionistic measure of the current scale of such outputs of fieldwork, let us assume there are 100 language documentation projects underway around the world at the moment and that they have a life of around five years each. Ideally, each modern fieldwork-based documentation project would create audio and video recordings, images, transcripts, and a dictionary. Looking at deposits in PARADISEC, an average modern collection would include something like 30 hours of audio, 10 hours of video, with transcripts, and associated files, in 300 files totalling around 100 gigabytes of data (nowhere near the ideal that Evans hoped for above). Of course some collections are much larger than this but for present purposes this will do. Over the next 20 years there would, on this artificial and probably conservative estimate, be four such sets of 100 projects, creating 40 terabytes of material that needs to be described, accessioned and curated over time by language archives. Additionally, if Evans's ambitious forecast eventuates, there will be 500 hours of recordings per language, a mix of video and audio that would amount to about a terabyte per language, and thus a requirement of 400 terabytes of storage. It can be envisaged that, in future, such volumes will not be problematic to obtain or as expensive as they are today.

It is important to distinguish between storage and archiving of these kinds of records. Most academics are provided with storage by their universities, and that is a necessary first step towards ensuring files survive into the future. But storage on its own does not include a catalogue of the contents, with controlled metadata terms, or licences for use of the material. Storage is often restricted to those within the institution and so is not a public-facing resource. Storage does not allow for differential or restricted access based on a user's characteristics. Storage does not enforce file-naming conventions, or convert formats over time as is necessary, or produce compressed formats of files for web delivery.

There is a backlog of legacy records yet to be accessioned and in some cases yet to be found. Legacy records include analogue tape collections made by linguists, musicologists and anthropologists. PARADISEC conducts an ongoing survey[4] to find these collections and has so far digitised most of those found. A recent example is the collection of 240 tapes made by Ian Frazer in the To'aba'ita language in northern Malaita (Solomon Islands) between 1971 and 1985. These tapes, together with a large set of notes, are kept in his house in Dunedin and appear to be the only known recordings in this language. In 2018 PARADISEC was granted funds by the ELDP's Legacy Materials Grants to digitise and accession this collection. There are many more similar collections yet to be located.

Cultural agencies involved in collecting oral tradition, like local cultural centres in Pacific nations, often have a backlog of recordings that need to be digitised, catalogued and archived. They need advice and help with choosing software to keep track of their collections, and ultimately they need an archive that they can trust to look after this material. PARADISEC, under Barwick's leadership, has worked to obtain the necessary funds and then to digitise tape collection from agencies including the Solomon Islands National Museum and the Vanuatu Cultural Centre, and, in 2022, the Yap National Archives.

The use of mobile phones as portable recorders is also increasing the amount of documentation that can be made by speakers themselves. Websites, online video, Facebook pages and so on all present a dynamic and often heterogeneous set of linguistic performances, with variation in spelling and mixing of language varieties. The challenge is to capture this record ethically and efficiently so that it is part of the long-term record for all small languages.

There is therefore a great need for more archives to deal with this foreseeable proliferation of language records. As was noted above, there have only been two new archives added to OLAC since 2008. While digital archives do not, in theory, need to be located in any particular place, it still makes sense for archives to be close to the speakers of the languages they represent. So, for example there is no general language archive in Canada but there have been discussions about setting one up there. In the United States of America, there are several archives that each focus on a particular region (Alaska, Hawaii, Latin America, California, Oklahoma) and recently the American Philosophical Society has emerged as a more general archive, but still only dealing with American languages. For Americans conducting research in other parts of the world there is no American archive. In the Francophone Pacific, the LACITO archive (Pangloss/CoCoON) in Paris serves local needs, and

---

4   "Project Lost and Found", *DELAMAN*, https://www.delaman.org/project-lost-found.

3 Language and music recordings and the responsible researcher

there is a new archive based in French Polynesia (Anavevo[5]). In India, there is the CORSAL[6] repository (based in Texas but focused on north-east India). Japan has the resources and the research and recording tradition to build an archive but has yet to do so. An archive devoted to a single linguist has been established in the Philippines (Or and Estrellado 2023). Elsewhere in Asia there could be several digital archives, potentially in Singapore and Thailand. Similarly, in Cameroon, there was an archive operating with systems supplied by The Language Archive (TLA) in Nijmegen, but that no longer seems to be the case (the website of the Archive of Languages and Oral Resources of Africa – ALORA – is not accessible at the time of writing[7]). There does not seem to be another language archive specifically serving African languages.

The cost of not archiving

There is a clear social benefit to making cultural recordings safe and available over time. As noted elsewhere in this chapter, it should be a normal part of research practice to create records of the language we are working on in ways that can be accessed and used by the speakers and by their descendants. To fail to do this risks the trust we have established, which, besides being an act of bad faith in itself, can then make it more difficult for future researchers to work in the same area. In a science discipline it may be possible to re-create lost data, but, even then, notorious examples can be found of unique data being put at risk. In a (possibly apocryphal) story that resonates with my experience in searching for audiotape collections, experimental data from the moon landings was stored on data tapes that had apparently been overwritten to save costs, and no copies could be located in the archives.[8] After 35 years, determined researchers hunted down a copy in a basement storeroom, and the data was eventually copied for future use. Without this dedicated sleuthing, it would have been lost.

There is a real financial cost in not securing outputs of linguistic research. Typical fieldwork is an expensive project, requiring years of researcher training, then sometimes considerable travel to meet the speakers. Great care is taken to have good recording equipment and to make backups of recordings for use in research. There is the labour of the researcher analysing the recordings, organising them and

---

5 "About us", *Anavevo*, https://v-anavevo.upf.pf/apropos.
6 "CoRSAL: the computational resource for South Asian Languages", *University of North Texas*, https://corsal.unt.edu.
7 https://www.delaman.org/members/alora/ [ALORA's link was not working when tested in September 2023].
8 https://en.wikipedia.org/wiki/Apollo_11_missing_tapes.

making them accessible. There is an imposition on the language speaker's time and a possible expectation on their part that they are contributing to a long-term record of their culture and language. A major part of the investment, both financial and emotional, in the creation of fieldwork records will be lost if there is no service that takes the output of research and safeguards it for future use.

In a study of the cost of data centres or archives, Beagrie and Houghton (2014) found that their use resulted in very significant increases in research, teaching and studying efficiency. They noted that the "value to users exceeds the investment made in data sharing and curation via the centres".[9] Critically, they found that it is the ability to re-use existing data that increases "measurable returns on investment" (Beagrie and Houghton 2014, 16). In the specific case of the Archaeology Data Service, they calculated a benefit to users that is "5 times the costs of operation, data deposit and use" (Beagrie and Houghton 2013, 7). They also "identified a potential increase in return on investment in data creation/collection resulting from the additional use that was facilitated by ADS that may be worth between £2.4 million and £9.7 million over thirty years in net present value from one-year's investment – a 2-fold to 8-fold return on investment" (Beagrie and Houghton 2013, 7). The benefit of data curation, abstruse though it may appear, should therefore be apparent to even the most neoliberal and output-oriented administrator, of the kind who are making many decisions about research funding today.

There is also a great personal relief in archiving one's research materials. Many researchers only organise their materials when they come to archive their collection, so there is a benefit for them in then being able to retrieve their own materials over time, providing the crucially needed backup of a file long since lost from their laptop. Archiving is not so onerous if researchers are trained in data management methods (and practise what they have learned!). As Corti and colleagues noted, data management "reduces time and financial costs and greatly enhances the quality of the data you use" (Corti, Van den Eynden et al. 2014, 10). It also relieves the stress of knowing that the records in your care deserve to be made available but, at the same time, not knowing what to do with them.

From the perspective of funding agencies, the creation of primary research data is one of the outcomes they have supported. Some agencies already ask that primary data be made available and this will increasingly become the case (Tenopir et al. 2011). As an example of the scope of work that needs to be done, PARADISEC, in 2023 in its 20th year of operation, has archived 16,500 hours of audio recordings, representing over 1,360 languages, about half of it digitised from analogue tapes

---

9   Beagrie and Houghton 2014, 4.

recorded in the mid-20th century. Typically, these older collections come from retired or deceased academic linguists and musicologists and are limited to audio and some paper notes. New digital collections are large and can contain many video files, in addition to transcripts and image files, all of which require more management than the earlier analogue collections.

The post-colonial archive

While archiving is often and easily considered to be an extension of the colonial enterprise, a major motivation for digital language archives is making records available to the people recorded and their families. I suggest this is a post-colonial activity.[10] In the past, for example, linguists were criticised for taking materials from communities with nothing being returned. For example, Paulina Yourupi, from Chuuk in Micronesia, asked:

> Whatever happens to the previous research? What benefits were they to our community? Were researchers who seek to get their PhDs merely exploiting us or was it for a greater good? When do we see products and results and not more study?[11]

Similarly, Smith (1999) critiques the role of academia in dividing indigenous cultures into discipline areas, "disconnecting them from their histories, their landscapes, their languages, their social relations and their own ways of thinking, feeling and interacting with the world" (Smith 1999, 28, and see also the opening quote above). Errington's (2001, 34) critique of a "colonial linguistics" is at a more abstract level than the issues discussed here, but his observation resonates with the argument put in this chapter that linguistic texts can be "more meaningful than their authors knew, moving beyond while also incorporating knowledge they provide – in some case, the only knowledge available".

What is to be done?

It should be clear that documentation created in the course of research requires archives, and it requires records to be deposited in archives. Keeping records in one place is no longer tenable – recall the disastrous fire that destroyed the national museum of Brazil in September 2018 (Solly 2019), taking with it countless unique language records. We can no longer do nothing and hope it will all work:

---

10 See also Thieberger 2020.
11 Paulina Yourupi, 2008, class paper, U. Hawai'i Mānoa Linguistics Department.

> [doing nothing] is actually a choice too . . . Thoughtful repatriation of ethnographic materials can assist not only in the decolonisation of anthropology, but in empowering both communities and the people who comprise them by allowing easier access to a greater range of ethnographic information. (Chambers et al. 2002, 213–214)

As an established researcher who has embraced the possibilities offered by new technologies, Barwick offers a fine example to the next generation of researchers of the decolonising possibilities offered by repatriation of musicological and linguistic records and the possibilities of building networks and infrastructure within academia that also serve the needs of speakers, performers and the general community.

Acknowledgements

Thanks to two anonymous reviewers for constructive comments that have improved this chapter.

Chapter 4

The politics of repatriation: communication and consultation in Torres Strait during the "True Echoes" project

Grace Koch

Introduction

> Human and archival histories are mutually informative, and as such, moments when people bring the two modes together can also become moments of new memory creation. Repatriation, understood as a meeting point of human and archival memory, can be deeply meaningful because archives are extensions of humanity. When the two modes of memory, archival and human, are brought into conversation, the result can be powerful, augmenting the potency and value of each. (Reed 2019, 23)

These words, written by Daniel Reed, former director of the Indiana University Archive of Traditional Music, sum up the objectives of the "True Echoes" project that sought to bring together Torres Strait Islanders and recordings of their ancestors made by the Cambridge Anthropological Expedition to Torres Straits (the "Cambridge Expedition") in 1898. The success of True Echoes depended upon effective human interactions among staff from the British Library, the Australian Institute of Aboriginal and Torres Strait Islander Studies (AIATSIS) and Torres Strait organisations and researchers, as they connect with individual Islanders, most of whom are direct descendants of people recorded in 1898. "True Echoes" aimed to balance the *process* of personal interactions and connecting with Islanders with the planning for *products*, such as catalogue records, new recordings, a website and reports (Barwick, Green, Vaarzon-Morel and Zissermann 2019, 2). After describing the "True Echoes" project, this chapter will give a brief background on the Cambridge Expedition and the rediscovery of the recordings, the importance of the expedition to Torres Strait Islanders, my own personal reflections based upon a description of the connections formed and the progress of the project up to its conclusion in 2022.

The "True Echoes" project

In 2019, Isobel Clouter, a curator in the World and Traditional Music section of the British Library, was awarded a three-year grant from the Leverhulme Trust in the United Kingdom to connect early sound recordings from the Pacific held by the British Library with their communities of origin. Additional funding for the "True Echoes" project was provided by the UK Government's Department for Business, Energy and Industrial Strategy to support placement of an early career archivist from Torres Strait to learn the British Library cataloguing scheme and use it to catalogue audio material generated by the Torres Strait part of "True Echoes", to prepare blogs for the British Library website, and to add to catalogue records on the Torres Strait collections held at AIATSIS.

The recordings were made on wax cylinders in the late 19th and early 20th centuries, and were catalogued and digitised by the British Library in the early 2000s. The earliest of these, recorded by the Cambridge Expedition in 1898, is the focus of this chapter. Other cylinders in the British Library collections originated from Papua New Guinea, the Trobriand Islands, Vanuatu, the Solomon Islands and New Caledonia. "True Echoes" had nine institutional partners based in the United Kingdom and the Pacific, including the Pacific and Regional Archives for Digital Sources in Endangered Cultures (PARADISEC), which had been co-founded by Linda Barwick.[1]

---

1   British partners for "True Echoes" were the British Museum and the Museum of Archaeology and Anthropology in Cambridge, UK. Pacific partners were the Institute of Papua New Guinea Studies, PARADISEC, Vanuatu Kaljoral Senta, Solomon Islands National Museum and Archives, Tjibaou Cultural Centre in New Caledonia, and AIATSIS. An International Project Board and a True Echoes Advisory Board met periodically, and presentations about progress on historical discoveries and fieldwork were given to various professional organisations, such as the Pacific History Association and the Pacific Regional Branch of the International Council of Archives.

A website was compiled including historical research, metadata for the cylinder recordings, and photographs mapped from related UK and international sources.[2] Participatory research involved meeting descendants, working with knowledgeable Elders to design a research plan, and arranging interviews with descendants of people recorded on the wax cylinders. The interviews provided more information about the historic recordings and traced their importance to Torres Strait Islanders today (Clouter 2020). Two British Library research fellows conducted historical research on the collections: Vicky Barnecutt's work centred on Papua New Guinea, Vanuatu, the Solomon Islands and New Caledonia; and Rebekah Hayes did extensive research on the Torres Strait material.

Seeing afresh – a brief history of the recordings of the 1898 Cambridge Expedition to the Torres Strait

Rebekah Hayes compiled a comprehensive history of the Cambridge Expedition for the True Echoes website,[3] and this section will give a short background based upon her work.

In 1888, Alfred Cort Haddon, an anatomist and zoologist educated at Christ's College, Cambridge, went to Torres Strait to study marine biology. Although he produced many papers on that topic, he found that his real interests lay with the people and societies of the area.[4] In 1898, he assembled a group of researchers from various disciplines to document the culture of Torres Strait. Six extensive volumes of reports were published between 1901 and 1935 on anthropology, linguistics, physiology, photography, arts and religion. In addition, the Cambridge Expedition took back to England a large collection of artefacts and art objects, including several items from Maino, an important leader from Central Torres Strait who had befriended Haddon on his trip in 1888. Maino gave him the artefacts so that people on the other side of the world could know about Torres Strait culture.[5]

The Cambridge Expedition had a major impact on the development of the field of anthropology, setting a benchmark for professionalism of the discipline. It used new technologies, such as sound recordings and films, to document aspects of Torres Strait society, and produced the earliest ethnographic audiovisual records of the area. Several Torres Strait Islanders mentioned in this chapter had visited the British Museum and the Pitt Rivers Museum in Britain where the objects were

---

2   See https://www.true-echoes.com.
3   https://www.true-echoes.com/1898-torres-strait-and-new-guinea/.
4   Britannica, The Editors of the Encyclopaedia n.d.
5   See https://www.youtube.com/watch?v=uoOW_cm-MRo.

held. When they saw the items, they experienced great power emanating from some of them, especially a tortoise shell mask from Mer.[6]

The collection of wax cylinder recordings from the Cambridge Expedition held by the British Library consists of 101 recordings made in Torres Strait and 39 made in what is today Papua New Guinea. They are the earliest recordings held in the British Library's Sound Archive (Hayes 2021a). The story of the Cambridge recordings, their rediscovery and connections with AIATSIS follows.

AIATSIS, Alice Moyle and rediscovery of the 1898 recordings

In 1975, I (the author) was appointed research assistant to Alice Moyle at the Australian Institute of Aboriginal Studies (AIAS) in Canberra. Moyle, an eminent ethnomusicologist, had spent many years locating early recordings of Australian Indigenous music as well as advising AIAS grantees on ethnomusicological research. One collection, recorded by Wolfgang Laade, who had worked in North Queensland and the Torres Strait in the early 1960s, intrigued me and led to my interest in Torres Strait and Cape York island style music. Later, my own research was diverted to the music of Central Australia when my husband received grants to work on the Kaytetye language of Barrow Creek in the Northern Territory, but Torres Strait music and culture still fascinated me.

For the following background information, I thank my fellow "True Echoes" history researcher, Rebekah Hayes, for much of the work done on the historical background of the Cambridge Expedition and the various movements of the cylinder recordings (Hayes 2021, 23–25). I was able to research the relevant correspondence, files and other documents held at the Australian Institute of Aboriginal and Torres Strait Islander Studies (AIATSIS – the successor to AIAS) to add to her research.[7]

As early as 1968, J.S. Boydell, secretary of the AIAS, had corresponded with Patrick Saul, director of the British Institute of Recorded Sound, about the "C.S. Myers

---

6   Personal communication, Ron Day, 14 June 2021.
7   In 1989, the Act that established the Australian Institute of Aboriginal Studies was changed to include Torres Straits Islander in its title. The organisation became the Australian Institute of Aboriginal and Torres Strait Islander Studies (AIATSIS).

collection" held in London.[8] In 1969, Saul mentioned the C.S. Myers Torres Strait recordings to Moyle, ethnomusicology research officer at AIAS, and that plans were being made to transfer the recordings to audiotape. Moyle advised him of the work being done on transfers of wax cylinder recordings to magnetic tape by Wilfried Zahn at the Deutsches Rundfunk in Frankfurt, West Germany. She suggested that similar work could be done in Australia if the cylinders could be dispatched to AIAS. Unfortunately, they could not be posted due to their fragility and unique value.

In 1978, the British Institute of Recorded Sound ethnomusicologist, Lucy Durán, informed Jane Forge, director of the Resource Centre at AIAS, that the cylinders were still being traced and it was unclear whether they were "extant".

Moyle retired from AIAS in 1978 but maintained an office next to mine as an honorary research fellow. At her own expense, she travelled to the United Kingdom, spending two weeks (8–22 September) at the British Institute of Recorded Sound.[9] She wrote about "scaling ladders and investigating the dusty corners" (Moyle 1986) of the institute in search of the Australian cylinders, which she found lodged within the wax cylinder collection of Sir James Frazer. These were housed in two specially made boxes and individual cartons and tins, some of which bore the trademark of "van Houten cocoa" (Moyle 1983, 80). Anthony King, the British Institute of Recorded Sound director designate, noted that Moyle had located, sorted and listed the Australian cylinders on her visit, and he agreed that the institute would send free tape copies of the Australian and Torres Strait material to AIAS. The transfers arrived at the AIAS in 1983 and were auditioned and catalogued by Moyle, who graciously allowed me to do some work on them as well. Subsequent dubbings on superior equipment were made in 1990 and sent to AIATSIS,[10] where I auditioned them. The 1898 recordings held a special place at AIATSIS as the earliest ones held in the archive. Later it became known that they were the first ethnographic recordings held from the Pacific. Copies of other research documents from the expedition, such as the photographs, films and the six volumes of reports, had been obtained by AIATSIS several years before the recordings arrived.

---

8   Myers, a researcher on the Cambridge Expedition, had a special interest in music. After he returned to England, we know that he may have started to search for the cylinders. There is evidence that the cylinders then became part of the Sir James Frazer collection of anthropological and ethnographic recordings. This was corroborated later by Moyle.
9   After her trip, Moyle was paid a small sum by AIAS for travel expenses.
10 Although the AIAS had been collecting research material from Torres Strait, the region was not recognised in its title until 1989.

In 1993, Alan Ward, archives administrator of the (British) National Sound Archive, where the originals had been transferred after the closure of the British Institute of Recorded Sound, allowed that copies held at AIATSIS could be made for the purpose of private study, educational and research purposes, but he wanted to be notified of all requests so that the organisation could keep track of the use of the collection. When the British National Sound Archive changed its administrative structure to become part of the British Library as the British Library Sound Archive, the 1898 collection was digitised and put into the Collect Britain project after permission was obtained from Elders at Murray Island (Mer) in 2004. A selection of the cylinders is now available online.[11] AIATSIS has put the copies that it holds under open access in order to align its collection with access conditions at the British Library.

My positions within the audiovisual collections held at AIATSIS changed through the years, but an important part of my duties remained working with external clients to locate and, where possible, obtain copies of requested material. When it became known that AIATSIS held the 1898 recordings, clients began to request copies. One was James Rice, a Murray Islander who had been a plaintiff for the Mabo case (see following section). After the recordings had been digitised at the British Library and put on its website in 2004, clients could be directed to the digital versions online.

Importance of the Cambridge Expedition to Torres Strait Islanders

Most Islanders know about the Cambridge Expedition and see its value as an important historical event that contributes to the continuation of their culture but only recently have the volumes of the Cambridge Expedition reports been available to them. In 2001, the Aboriginal and Torres Strait Islander Commission (ATSIC) funded a two-year pilot digitisation program with the aim of creating, managing and delivering electronic information resources and services to clients via the AIATSIS website and the AIATSIS collections catalogue (Mura) (Lewincamp and Faulkner 2003, 239). The AIATSIS library director, Barbara Lewincamp, prioritised 10 collections for digitisation, one of which was the set of six reports of the Cambridge Anthropological Expedition to Torres Strait. Lewincamp contacted the Torres Strait Regional Authority, obtaining enthusiastic support for digitisation of the reports from the chair of the authority at that time, Terry Waia. Cambridge University Press, who held copyright of the volumes, was willing

---

11 At https://sounds.bl.uk.

to provide a licence to AIATSIS to digitise the volumes and to provide access electronically, both online and in CD-ROM format (Lewincamp and Faulkner 2003, 244). Digitisation of the volumes was completed in late 2003 (AIATSIS 2002–2003, 65–66), and a set of the CD-ROMs was presented later to the Torres Strait Regional Authority.

Some of the most important sections to Islanders from the reports are the genealogies from Badu, Mabuiag and Mer collected by expedition member W.H.R. Rivers. Some of the family trees extend to six generations and give the names of the villages where the information was gathered and, often, clan affiliations for individuals. Copies of the genealogies had been distributed to Islanders and are among their most treasured documents. Many of the people recorded in 1898 are listed in the genealogies.

One of the most crucial uses of the reports occurred during the series of court cases that led up to the recognition of a system of land rights, known as native title, for Indigenous peoples of Australia. In 1982, Eddie Mabo, originally from Murray Island, Torres Strait, pursued a claim for rights to his land, stating that his people had lived there before the Federation of Australia. Part of the evidence for that case came from the volumes of the Cambridge Expedition.[12] The High Court of Australia found this claim to be valid and established a process whereby both Torres Strait Islanders and Aboriginal people could claim their rights to land. In 2013, the amalgamated Torres Strait Land and Sea Claim, encompassing all islands of the Torres Strait, was accepted by the High Court. Since then, the Torres Strait Regional Authority has become the government agency coordinating regional councils, and native title representative bodies for each island were established under the umbrella agency of Gur A Baradharaw Kod Torres Strait Sea and Land Council (GBK).

As for all Pacific nations, there is great concern for rising sea levels brought about by global warming. Torres Strait Islanders treasure the reports as historical documents that preserve knowledge of their culture, even as the islands themselves are in danger of disappearing beneath the sea. On 23 September 2022 the United Nations Human Rights Committee found that Australia had failed to protect individual Torres Strait Islanders against the adverse effects of climate change.[13]

Islanders value the reports highly, but the emotional and spiritual experience of listening to the voices of their ancestors allows them to relate directly to their

---

12 See Koch 2013, 14–17 for further information on the Mabo claims.
13 United Nations, Office of the High Commissioner for Human Rights 2022. https://tinyurl.com/4c3xr747.

relatives. Listening to recorded voices can bring people together in laughter and tears through shared memories and past experiences. Hearing the recorded voice of a family member who has passed, no matter how long ago, can transport the person who has been recorded from the internal to the external, to the here and now (Diettrich 2019, 163–164).

The following part of this chapter traces how AIATSIS became part of "True Echoes".

"True Echoes" – an invitation to AIATSIS

On 27 June 2019, Janet Topp Fargion, head of Sound and Vision at the British Library, sent me an email informing me that she was applying for funding to conduct a project on the early wax cylinder collections held in the British Library from the Pacific. One of the earliest of these collections had been recorded by the Cambridge Expedition, and she knew about my work with Moyle in locating and cataloguing the recordings. Although AIATSIS was not cited as a partner to the project, she asked my advice on whom to contact about arranging a visit for the lead researcher, Isobel Clouter, to discuss the project and to make connections with relevant staff there. I suggested Jonathan Wraith, director, Collection Development and Management. Clouter contacted him almost immediately and made plans to travel to Canberra from Sydney, where she had been liaising with project partner PARADISEC. As a visiting researcher at AIATSIS, I had just completed a project with GBK, the organisation coordinating the native title representative bodies throughout Torres Strait, so had a keen interest in Clouter's visit. Wraith requested that Lara McLellan, the collection manager, and I meet with Clouter to brief her on AIATSIS holdings on Torres Strait and to offer her any assistance that she might require.

After our meeting it became obvious that AIATSIS, with its extensive Torres Strait collections, should become a partner in "True Echoes". Clouter asked if AIATSIS could provide a history researcher to examine AIATSIS connections with the Cambridge Expedition recordings and to provide documentation about the work of Moyle in locating and listing them. She also needed someone to establish connections with Torres Strait organisations and Elders. Because of my work with Moyle, knowledge of the Torres Strait collections and prior experience in Torres Strait, I was nominated for the role. McLellan became the liaison person with AIATSIS and was tasked with the management of administrative details. Clouter returned to Sydney where she was working with PARADISEC to plan a workshop with all project partners to discuss the best ways to proceed with the project. McLellan and I attended part of the workshop in Sydney in December 2019.

Connections with Torres Strait people and organisations

Once AIATSIS had formally become a project partner, McLellan and I worked with Clouter to create a plan detailing jobs to be done, a time schedule, travel, payments, documentation needed and connections to be established.

"True Echoes" came at a favourable time for AIATSIS, as it was in the process of establishing closer links with both the Torres Strait Regional Authority, which, since it is named in the *Australian Institute of Aboriginal and Torres Strait Islander Studies Act 1989*, was formally recognised by the federal government, along with other organisations in Torres Strait. Our aim for "True Echoes" was to ensure that we informed the right people and organisations about the project so that we could establish the correct lines of communication. I had no idea of the complexities involved.

Lisa Strelein, director of research at AIATSIS, had written a most informative, if daunting, chapter in the book *Living with Native Title*, that detailed the complexities of Torres Strait governance. There are seven levels of governance for around 8000 people. She quoted Getano Lui, then chair of the Torres Strait Regional Authority, as saying that, as Torres Strait Islanders, "we are probably the most over consulted, over researched group of people in Australia . . . we are also over-governed" (Strelein 2013, 68).

From the earliest sources available, we learned that each island had maintained a strong identity with separate cultural practices. When the Queensland government annexed the Torres Strait between 1872 and 1879, it established systems of local government that recognised local chiefs, elected councils and island courts, a system that differed substantially from that existing on the Australian mainland for Aboriginal peoples. This distinction was enshrined by law through the *Torres Strait Islanders Act 1939*, which had arisen from a meeting of local Torres Strait Councils on York Island (Masig) in 1937 (Strelein 2013, 69).

Connections: AIATSIS, repatriation and the "Reconcile, Return and Renew" Australian Research Council project

As mentioned earlier in this chapter, from the time I began working with the AIATSIS collections, I had been fascinated with the music and culture of the Torres Strait, especially as I had auditioned and catalogued most of the audio collections from the area. When I moved to the position of native title research and access officer, I was able to advise Aboriginal peoples and Torres Strait Islanders about relevant holdings in the AIATSIS library and archive collections.

In 2014, Associate Professor Cressida Fforde at the Australian National University approached me about participating as a Chief Investigator in an Australian Research Council grant, "Return, Reconcile, Renew", that would work with three Indigenous community groups (Fitzroy Crossing, in Western Australia; the Coorong, in South Australia; and Torres Strait) to advance research into repatriation of human remains, to explore the effects of repatriation, especially through conducting interviews with members of communities affected by removal of remains of their ancestors, and to create a database of collections of remains. One of the community consultants was Lui Ned David, who later became the chair of GBK. Also, during one of our team meetings in Melbourne, I met Vic McGrath, senior community liaison officer for the Torres Strait Regional Authority. Towards the end of the "Return, Reconcile, Renew" project, Michael Peters, an Islander living on Thursday Island, was brought to Canberra to meet with the team and to explore how he could contribute to the project.

In 2019, GBK approached me about mentoring Michael Peters as he prepared to speak with Elders from Mer and Erub about the "Reconcile, Return and Renew" project. We travelled to those islands and were met on Mer by Aven Noah Senior, a direct descendant of Ulai, one of the main Torres Strait Islanders recorded by the Cambridge Expedition. In turn, he introduced me to one of the local councillors, Robert Kaigey, whose ancestor had also been recorded in 1898. I had met Noah in 1992 at the International Association of Sound and Audiovisual Archives conference in Canberra when he gave a Welcome to Country (for Torres Strait) and participated in several panels on Indigenous broadcasting. These personal connections were key to establishing the groundwork for my part in "True Echoes".

Setting us straight: learning from Vic McGrath

Figure 4.1 Vic McGrath, Senior Community Liaison Officer, Thursday Island, Torres Strait, Qld, Office, Torres Strait Regional Authority. Photo: Lara McLellan, Friday, 7 May 2021.

McLellan and I travelled to Thursday Island (Waiben), Torres Strait, to explain "True Echoes", to make contacts with relevant people and organisations, and to learn the best ways of observing cultural protocols for returning copies of the 1898 recordings and for arranging interviews with relevant people. I had assumed that I would conduct the interviews and would engage a local film crew to record the reactions of people when they heard the recordings for the first time. We also wanted to ensure that the participants would control access restrictions to the recordings of the interviews and would be joint owners of the project. All these elements would require a careful balancing act among the requirements of the British Library, AIATSIS and local protocols. We brought folders containing information about the project, the research documents about the Cambridge Expedition compiled by Rebekah Hayes, listings of the people recorded in 1898, a comprehensive list of all Torres Strait material held in the AIATSIS collections, digitised copies of the 1898 recordings, and a time line for each step of the project. These were distributed to council members from Mabuiag and Mer, and the CEO and relevant staff members of the Torres Strait Regional Authority, and GBK.

Vic McGrath, my colleague from the "Reconcile, Return and Renew" project, graciously agreed to meet with us the day after we arrived at Waiben. We could not have had a better guide to give us an unvarnished account of the challenges facing us. I knew that he was a very straight talker who would not soften any descriptions of the difficulties we might encounter and that he was comfortable in communicating with me.

The first change came with the interview procedures. McGrath said that,[14] although I should be in a guiding role, Islanders needed to interview Islanders because the

---

14 I will refer to my Torres Strait Islander colleagues by their last names from here on.

recordings were very personal and could evoke deep emotions. It also became clear that we needed to limit the interviews to descendants of people recorded in 1898.[15] He narrowed this down further to family interviewing family members. The film crew specified in the original plan would probably be seen as intrusive.

He strongly advised against our getting involved in Island politics, but we should know "who is in and who is out" whenever we would schedule a meeting. The most important guideline for us would be "right people for right knowledge". Finally, although we were required by the *AIATSIS Act* to liaise with the Torres Strait Regional Authority, we would really need to work mostly with GBK, as they had representatives on the ground on Mer, Mabuiag, Yam, Tudu and Saibai where the 1898 recordings had been made. McGrath gave us a list of people to contact, both inside the authority and from the wider Torres Strait area. We found ourselves being "on call" during our time at Waiben to arrange meetings with relevant people and to interrupt whatever we were doing to seize the moment with important people. True to form, his parting words to us were that we were going to trip up (but expressed in more colourful language) but that he would be glad to help us if we needed him.

After our meeting, we held several sessions with the Torres Strait Regional Authority, including an explanation of their traditional ecological knowledge database that had a sophisticated access system based on cultural norms of Torres Strait society. It became obvious that GBK would be our main contact for further engagement, especially as their offices on all inhabited islands had the database on which we could lodge copies of the recordings and the Torres Strait part of the website being constructed by Rebekah Hayes. Almost every Islander has relatives on several islands as well as the mainland, so, according to cultural protocols as set by interviewees through the database, all Islanders will be able to access the cylinder recordings and the research information compiled by Hayes.

---

15 The project called for 10 interviews. In 2020, I had interviewed Jeremy Beckett at his home in Sydney.

Further changes in plans

Figure 4.2 Lui Ned David, Chair, GBK. Thursday Island, Torres Strait. Photo: Lara McLellan, 17 May 2021.

After our various meetings, it became obvious that the interview I had hoped to arrange with Lui Ned David, chair of GBK, would have to be put on hold because we needed to work with Islanders to workshop the questions to be asked and to determine the proper protocols and permission forms for the interviews. Ned advised us to inform the GBK chairs on Mer (Falen Doug Passi), Mabuiag (Johnny Kris), Saibai (Herbert Warusam) and Yama/Tudu (David himself) of our activities regularly, preferably by telephone but also by email. During our second trip, McLellan and I gave a presentation about "True Echoes" to all the GBK chairs at a conference in Cairns. David gave us more names of people to speak to, and our web of contacts grew exponentially. Two of these, Flora Warrior (Mabuiag) and Vinnitta Mosby (Mer), actively shaped how we should proceed, giving us further contacts and advice for how the interviews and permission forms should be structured.

Early career archives placement

Figure 4.3 Flora Warrior, Interviewer. Panai, Mabuiag Island, Torres Strait, Qld. Photo: Flora Warrior, 15 March 2022.

The British Library included funding for a short training position so that an early career archivist from Torres Strait could learn the cataloguing system used by the library and use it to catalogue the new recordings made by the interviewers in Torres Strait. They would also prepare several blogs about their part in "True Echoes" and would familiarise themselves with audiovisual collections at AIATSIS and Torres Strait artefacts held in the British Museum and the British Library. Finally, they would make a presentation to a conference to be held with all project partners where research findings and future directions for the project would be explored. GBK chose Mary Bani, who was its chief operating officer, for the position.

Seeger (2019, 145) raises several questions in relation to the return of recordings, such as how does the return impact upon people's lives, and how does it improve the relationship between those who return and those who receive them. For me, the return involved meeting Islanders whom I had never met before and to whom I needed to demonstrate my own trustworthiness and respect for their culture. Because I had worked with McGrath and David on the "Reconcile, Return and Renew" project, they both knew me and were free to express their opinions and criticisms. As I had not met Warrior or Mosby, I needed to prove myself to them. During our first fieldtrip to Waiben, Warrior, a descendant of Ned Waria, and I spoke over the phone for approximately an hour. My purpose was to explain "True Echoes" to her and hers was to test my trustworthiness as a possible colleague. Fortunately, she had arranged travel from Mabuiag to Waiben on business the day after our conversation and was happy to meet with us. To our delight, she expressed her willingness to be a "champion" and the lead interviewer for "True Echoes" on Mabuiag. A similar process occurred with Mosby, who met with us during the second fieldtrip accompanied by Reverend Ron Day, her eldest cousin and descendant of Jimmy Dei from Mer. Both women emphasised how the cylinder recordings would strengthen the identity of Islanders with their culture and their history. In turn, one of our aims was to create an ongoing relationship among the

British Library, AIATSIS and Islanders. Throughout the project, McLellan and I kept in close touch with Mosby and Warrior through Zoom meetings, phone and email.

Learning from Mosby and Warrior

Figure 4.4 Vinnitta Mosby, Interviewer. Mer Island, Torres Strait, Qld. Photo: Vinnitta Mosby, 26 November 2021.

As a lecturer at the School of Social Work and Human Services at James Cook University with extensive experience in fieldwork, Mosby understood about negotiating issues that arise from bringing together various cultural viewpoints, such as requirements of the British Library, AIATSIS and Islanders. Like Vic McGrath, she was very direct in instructing us about how she thought we should proceed and how much she was prepared to do. With her kinship ties and cultural knowledge of Mer society, she became our lead interviewer for Mer, where Haddon had made most of his recordings. She also helped us to formulate an information page and a consent form that was culturally acceptable and would meet with the requirements of the British Library.

Mosby requested that we write a step-by-step guide for interviewers, which both she and the British Library approved. All Pacific partners in "True Echoes" have used the guide and the other forms as templates, adapting them for their own use.

Clouter had created a tool kit consisting of a Samsung tablet, microphone, solar battery with power bank and LED lights, a 1-terabyte hard drive, a tripod and a micro SD card (a type of memory card) In addition, we provided a Zoom digital recorder, which we chose for archival quality recording. After several discussions, Mosby agreed to use the Zoom recorder for the interviews and the tablet for photos and video documentation of the reactions to the playback of the cylinders. She completed three interviews by the first week in December along with transcriptions and translations of each interview. Only one of the interviewees, Adimabo Noah, chose to speak in the Meriam Mer language.

McLellan and I had been waiting to hear from Mosby about how the equipment and general procedures worked for her before finalising the project design with Warrior. We had sent Warrior all the information about what we expected of her, payment details and so on, but were not aware of her tight time frame. Warrior, as a proprietor of her own business, Saltwater Blue Consultancy Services, required earlier payment for travel than Mosby because she had a narrower window of time to do the interviews, mainly the last week in January. A Zoom meeting with Warrior outlined her needs, so McLellan was able to contact Mary Bani at GBK to arrange for the recording equipment to be sent to Mabuiag and for payment for travel to be supplied.

When Warrior began conducting interviews, other descendants came forward wanting to be recorded. She submitted 16 videos made on the tablet along with transcriptions and translations of two interviews given in Kala Lagaw Ya.

All interviewees were deeply moved by hearing the recordings of their ancestors, and some came close to tears. The melodies of some of the songs were familiar, even though they have changed during the intervening years. Ron Day recounted a number of stories about his ancestor, Jimmy Dei, and Adimabo Noah sang parts of the songs that had been recorded by Ulai in 1898. Several interviewees gave detailed genealogical information about their relationship with their ancestors. Ned David had travelled to the United Kingdom to see Torres Strait artefacts held by various museums and spoke of the important connections between Maino and Haddon. Mosby, Warrior and Charlie Kaddy recorded more interviews than we expected, due to interest shown by descendants.

Completion of research for "True Echoes"

Mosby and Warrior had different ideas about the use of the videos and recordings that they made. Mosby did not give blanket permission for her work to be put on the web whereas Warrior was agreeable for the project to use her recordings. Because Mer was so important to the Cambridge Expedition, I wanted to ensure that at least part of Mosby's videos could be put on the web. I created edited clips from the Mer videos and sent them to Mosby, who agreed that they could appear on the site.

Ned David, who had been so helpful to McLellan and me earlier, is a direct descendant of Maino, one of the main contacts for Haddon on Yam and Tudu Islands. Although David was more than willing for me to interview him, I was unable to travel due to Covid-19 and unsuitable time frames for both of us. As the tablet used for the other interviews was in the GBK office in Cairns, we decided that someone there would be best placed to conduct the interview with him. Charlie Kaddy, acting CEO of GBK (Figure 4.5), kindly offered to do the interview and did it almost immediately as David was in the Cairns office at that time. David gave two interviews, one about his ancestor and the other about the proper protocols to follow for anyone seeking to use traditional knowledge of Torres Strait culture.[16]

---

16 See https://www.true-echoes.com/community-voices/ for interviews from the project.

Transformation of the Torres Strait section of the "True Echoes" project

The importance of flexibility cannot be over-emphasised. Grants obtained through institutions, governmental bodies, and private foundations require timetables, firm budgetary allocations, timely reporting and products associated with milestones. "True Echoes" has suffered through the Covid-19 pandemic, travel restrictions, political upheavals (in the case of the Solomon Islands) and institutional reorganisations. Also, during the last year of project work, Mary Bani resigned from GBK and ended her traineeship with "True Echoes". Preparation of blogs, reports and presentations fell to Hayes and to me. I became a surrogate "trainee" and learned from Hayes proper British Library cataloguing techniques. I then catalogued all the recordings and other material generated by the project. The success of the project has been nothing short of miraculous during these challenges, and the following table shows some of the major changes in plans.

Table 4.1 "True Echoes" Project plan, showing adjustments over time.

Original plan	Modified plan
Interviews to be conducted by Grace Koch with relevant Islanders	Direct descendants of people recorded by Haddon to be interviewed by family members
Appointment of a single "fixer" in Torres Strait to arrange meetings and connections	Meetings and connections arranged by Lara McLellan and Grace Koch with help from GBK
Researchers to attend important Island festivals and arrange filming	Covid-19 delayed or changed the scope of some festivals; attendance by researchers not possible
Early career archivist to be trained in London by British Library staff	Archivist, Mary Bani, chosen by GBK to be trained using video conferencing by British Library staff from London to the GBK office in Cairns; later removing herself from the project
Creation of blogs by early career archivist for British Library website about their part in "True Echoes" and presentation to a conference	Blogs written by Rebekah Hayes; no conference was held

Original plan	Modified plan
Cataloguing of recordings generated by the project to be catalogued in format used by British Library by early career archivist	Cataloguing done by Grace Koch and Rebekah Hayes
Local Islander film crew to be engaged	Islander interviewers to film initial reactions to playback on tablet
Translations and transcriptions of interviews to be outsourced	Translations and transcriptions to be done by interviewer, with some transcriptions of interviews in English completed by Koch
Use of Samsung tablet, microphone, solar battery with power bank and LED lights, a 1-terabyte hard drive, a tripod and a micro SD card.	Purchase of a Zoom recorder; interviewers used the tablet and recorder
Progress reports to be submitted to British Library, AIATSIS and the Torres Strait Islander Authority	Reports also to be sent to GBK chairs on Mer, Mabuiag, Yam and Saibai
Final conference to be held at British Library in London	No conference was held but a launch of the website held via Zoom among all partners and comments given by Ned David

Although the project funding went until the end of August 2022, the British Library wants to establish an enduring relationship with Torres Strait Islanders so that effective two-way channels of information can be established. The material gathered by "True Echoes" will fit in with cultural maintenance and education projects already being conducted by Torres Strait Islander organisations (Torres Strait Regional Authority n.d.).

Conclusion

The Land and Sea Management Strategy for Torres Strait 2016–2036 lists the following strategy under Management Directions: "Collaborate with communities to ensure cultural heritage records, including sites, artefacts, stories and histories, are owned and securely accessible by Torres Strait Islanders and Aboriginal Peoples" (TSRA 2016, 37).

"True Echoes" meets these aims by returning copies of the recordings of the Cambridge Expedition to Torres Strait, providing a template for continuing the interview process as well as providing recording equipment, creating a website, and making important connections between the past, present and future by creating links between collecting institutions and Torres Strait organisations.

Acknowledgements

I would like to extend my thanks to Dr Harold Koch, Lara McLellan, Rebekah Hayes and anonymous reviewers for taking the time to offer comments and suggestions for this paper.

Chapter 5

Researcher as facilitator: reconsidering the researcher's role in the management of archival collections

Catherine Ingram

Introduction

> When I was training as a researcher . . . the sound archives' primary relationship was with the individual collector, who typically travelled to remote places to collect the recordings for deposit in the archive. Relationships between the archives and the individuals whose speech or performances were recorded were typically limited by geography, technological differentials, and sometimes language barriers. (Barwick 2004, 253–254)

As Linda Barwick described, until just recent decades the researcher's central role in relation to creation and management of archival collections was widely accepted. Barwick's paper, published 20 years ago, was already offering innovative solutions to this and associated archival management issues, and the approaches she proposed have influenced the work of many researchers and archivists of my generation and those following. Yet these tacit expectations of researchers to assume a central role at various junctures of collection management often – for a variety of historical, conceptual, practical and other reasons – remain in archival work to some degree.

This chapter focuses on how the researcher's role in archive management might be reconsidered in light of the changing relationships between archives and custodian communities. More specifically, I explore the actions in relation to archival management that the archives, the custodian communities and the researchers themselves see as part of the researcher's role in the processes of collection creation and management, proposing that facilitation of dialogue and other forms of engagement between archives and communities should be the researcher's central activity within archiving. At present, the extent and nature of the researcher's archival management role is rarely discussed explicitly, and in teaching the next generation of researchers we do not always focus in much detail on exactly how facilitation might form an important part of our roles as researchers or in the projects we, our collaborative teams, and our students, design. Nevertheless, there are many advantages to more carefully interrogating the researcher's role in the management of archival collections, and explicitly evaluating what that role should be and how it should be carried out – including greater community engagement with and benefits from research projects, reduced ethical concerns around archival access, and better alignment between archive development and community desires or requirements.

A greater focus on facilitation of dialogue within the researcher's role can be especially important for those archival collections that include music, since the management of possible access to musical recordings from people who are not members of the custodian community leads an additional series of ethical concerns to arise. Within the published research on this issue, several different perspectives on ethics and archive access seem to have emerged. One body of research has revealed many instances of the detrimental cultural, social and economic impact of the usage of musical recordings, including those from archives, beyond their intended scope (see, for example, Feld 1996; Lancefield [1998] 2019; Guy 2002; Seeger 2004; Hilder 2015; Moyle 2019). Another discussion suggests that wider availability of archived musical recordings can produce only limited benefits, aside from benefits in some instances through commercially available recordings (Feld 1992; Neuenfeldt 2001; Christen 2005; Levin and Süzükei 2006, 41–44).

A third perspective from a more recent body of research discusses the many different ways in which historical archived musical recordings have been practically useful to descendants of the original singers. Many chapters in *The Oxford handbook of musical repatriation* (Gunderson and Woods 2019) provide key contributions to support this perspective, as do a number of other sources (including Bracknell 2017b; Campbell 2017; Treloyn 2017; Bracknell and Scott 2020; Gibson 2020). Some of the discussion from this third perspective emerges from the use of historic musical recordings where performers and recordists/archivists are no longer alive, and where the recordings have not previously been widely available; in these cases, discussion around use of these recordings attends less to archival processes and more to the appropriate methods of access and distribution. But some work on contemporary archiving of musical recordings (such as Barwick 2004; Turpin 2018; Vaarzon-Morel, Barwick and Green 2021), provides a complementary position to that outlined in the first perspective above, but one which is highly attentive to the need for care in how archives are created and controlled.

In this chapter, I focus on the role of the researcher/depositor in contemporary archival processes and speak primarily to the situation where a researcher is not a member of the custodian community – since to date that position is most familiar to me through my own experiences (see Ingram et al. 2011; Ingram 2019 and below) and in guiding my graduate research students. But I look to learn from ways that custodian member researchers often engage in dialogue about their roles in research with other community members, and how their actions may respond to responsibilities and/or demands to clarify or share their role in archival management. From my vantage point, these discussions seem to deal more explicitly with the details of the researcher role in the research and archiving process than might be the case for non-custodian researchers, and reveal concepts of the role that are much more integrated into the consultation and research process. They also seem to be one important factor leading to greater community satisfaction with and support for research. I hope custodian researchers might feel encouraged to further share their advice and experiences, and to identify errors in or improvements to the arguments and suggestions presented.

Changing aims in archival collection and management

The aims and management of archival collections of musical expression directly correlate with requirements of those performing the role of researchers, and a brief survey of some of the major developments offers insights into the issues I explore. The aims and management of audio (and later, video) recordings of cultural expression have altered greatly from those typical in the early 20th century, following Edison's invention of the phonograph in 1877 (Vallier 2012) and the establishment of the first European and North American archives from 1899 onwards (Ames 2003; Landau and Topp Fargion 2012, 131–132). As Ames explained, for European archivists and researchers in the early 20th century, the phonograph assumed a role as a scientific instrument to permit study of human evolution through culture. This was particularly so for scholars associated with the Berlin Phonogram Archive (das Berliner Phonogramm-Archiv), which was established by Stumpf in 1900 and which distinguished itself from the archive established a year previously in Vienna (das Phonogrammarchiv der Österreichischen Akademie der Wissenschaften) by focusing on the collection of recordings of non-European musics (Ames 2003, 300). The Berlin archive directly enabled the development of comparative musicology, a field of study considered one major forerunner to the discipline of ethnomusicology (Toner 2007, 89–92). The types of recordings it held during its early years are outlined by Stumpf himself in a 1908 publication as deriving from occasional recordings made in Berlin, recordings obtained from travelling researchers, recordings provided by exchange with other archives and recordings from "donations by the large [commercial] phonographic companies" (Stumpf 1908, cited in Ames 2003, 300).

It is clear that the Berlin Phonogram Archive, like others, was established by researchers for researchers' own purposes in scientific investigation, and without an apparent need to connect with or fulfil requirements of the communities from which the cultural practices originated. Archives established in other places have initially had some similar aims, albeit with changes in recent times that parallel those for archives in English-speaking regions (as discussed further below). For instance, in a detailed study of diverse audiovisual archives in mainland China, Wei Xiaoshi (2018) explained how during the 20th century these were particularly for the purposes of research organisations, and sometimes also had a political function. He noted that concerns about a loss of traditional practices during the first two decades of the 21st century have been instrumental in enhancing general public interest and wider utilisation of archival materials. Shuba Chaudhuri described the 1982 creation and subsequent development of the Archives and Research Centre for Ethnomusicology (ARCE) in India, noting that:

> The ARCE started out as an archive by scholars, for scholars. As we carried out fieldwork projects and came into contact with communities and performers, the relationship changed from regarding performers and communities as stakeholders to active participants in the archive. (Chaudhuri 2021, 100)

In observing the contrast between original aims of the ARCE and the changing relationships between communities and archives in more recent times, as well as commenting on the shift towards digital recording and file sharing, Chaudhuri identified an important change that seems to underpin changing requirements in the role of the researcher. Such change has also led to many issues for archives and archivists too – as Barwick and co-authors pointed out: "For archivists, balancing the equation of curation, care, and distribution or access is a difficult task . . . Archives may inherit impossible conundrums in their collections . . . the time and resources it would take to resolve all these problems is inestimable" (Barwick, Vaarzon-Morel and Zissermann 2019, 4).

The establishment of the Australian Institute of Aboriginal Studies (AIAS, now AIATSIS) during the 1960s, and the focus of its collections, has followed largely similar recent trajectories in moving from an initial aim of outsiders collecting cultural records of Australian First Nations peoples for the nation's historical record to involving those peoples and recognising responsibilities towards them at every level in management of archival resources (AIATSIS 2022). Likewise, PARADISEC focuses on fulfilling aims of and responsibilities towards custodian communities; in an interview with national broadcaster ABC, Nicholas Evans explained:

> The goal of PARADISEC is to create a special, enduring, digital archive for the languages and cultures of our region – and that includes music, it includes storytelling, it includes a lot of things other than just language itself. [It] will be a secure repository that will hold things and which ultimately can be accessed by anyone. (Evans 2013, as cited in Arnott 2013)

It is beyond the scope of this study to trace these changing aims of archival collections over the past century in greater detail. But the combination of changing aims and other sociocultural and technological changes have also occasioned changed perceptions of archives within custodian communities as well, further illustrating the existence of this shift. Vaarzon-Morel, Barwick and Green noted an example of the extent to which archiving has become considered an important activity for members of one central Australian First Nations community in one recent publication:

> The [unintentional] erasure of cultural and archival material from Willowra Learning Centre computers provoked much community discussion about short-term access and long-term preservation in distant archives. Despite having limited understanding of institutional archives and how they functioned, people wanted to be responsible for holding and managing access to their cultural material in both the present and the future. (Vaarzon-Morel, Barwick and Green 2021, 703)

In an earlier publication, I have noted similar views about the importance of cultural preservation held by my Kam (in Chinese, Dong) collaborators, observing that "the appearance in the videos [that I was asked to make and distribute on VCDs (video compact disk) and DVDs (digital video disk)] of singers who have since passed away has also proved to be a great stimulus for making recordings, and for appreciating their long-term value" (Ingram 2019, 305). During a 2017 visit to Sydney by six Kam singers for the "Songs of Home" project (see Turpin, Campbell et al. 2017), I was very appreciative of then-PARADISEC directors Linda Barwick and Nick Thieberger kindly agreeing to speak with my Kam friends and answer questions about the archive. To enable this interaction I provided translation between English and Kam, a Tai-Kadai language spoken by my collaborators as their first language and one with no widely used written form.

An energetic and wide-ranging discussion ensued that began from understandings of the processes of preservation of material in the archive. It then continued to cover issues such as the maintenance of culture, who had the right to make decisions about the archive, the management of it, the material, and whether the archive had the capacity to permit some items be open for wider access while access to some others could be kept for community only. As the conversation moved between the two languages, I was permitted a powerful lived experience of one way that the researcher-facilitator's role could exist. In this instance, I was able to facilitate the interaction by translating ideas from each person into a language that others could understand and, equally importantly, translating cultural concepts from one group to the other by drawing on my experiences in working with both groups of people. On previous occasions in both China and Australia, I had attempted to enact a similar facilitator's role, but without the other party present it was much more difficult to be seen in and to act in that position. But, on this occasion, with my China-based collaborators and my Australia-based colleagues in the room together, and with everyone able to approach our dialogue with a sense of openness and interest in learning from (and not judging) the other's perspectives, it felt to me that my Kam collaborators gained a much clearer idea of the archiving process. I think it also gave them a clearer perspective on potential ways in which they could control and guide my actions and those of my Australia-based colleagues in relation to Kam materials. It also seemed to be a valuable opportunity for my Australia-based colleagues to better understand the aspects of archiving that were of greatest concern to my Kam collaborators.

Researcher roles in recent times

As both custodian and archivist perspectives on the appropriate aims for archives have altered over time, so too have the actions that are expected to be undertaken by those acting as depositors and/or managers of archival collections. These are the actions usually undertaken by a researcher, and which comprise the researcher role within the archiving and management process that is the focus of this chapter. Yet even into this third decade of the 21st century, the three limitations on relationships that can exist between communities and archives and were highlighted in Barwick's opening quote – geography, technological differentials and language barriers – can remain difficult to overcome. In reflecting on my own research in rural south-western China, it seems that, while these limitations may remain, we do have more tools at our disposal to try to overcome or work around them. Where suitable technology is accessible, it can offer connections across language and geographical boundaries, changing approaches to research methodologies that emphasise collaboration with custodians present other useful possibilities.

The 21st century has brought an increase in diversity of perspectives regarding the fieldworker-archivist role, and not only among archives and custodians. Fieldworkers ourselves have our own individual perspectives on what our roles should entail, and these may not always entirely overlap with the perspectives of our colleagues, our collaborators or the archives where we deposit materials. (see also Ingram 2019, 309–311). In addition, a researcher's role in each archiving process is necessarily influenced by the distinctive characteristics of the field sites or communities involved. For example, my understandings of the archiving wishes of Kam community members initially focused on access to the physical items (VCDs and DVDs) that I was requested to produce. We discussed how these should be handled within communities, and who should have access to what. This proved a useful beginning and very instructive for me in terms of understanding the cultural context of access, and of dialogue around recordings in general, before we started to move into more complex discussions around management of the archive and access to the digital archival collection. When I began my research in China in 2004 there was no internet in the main villages where I worked, many people had never seen a computer and most had not had experience with universities, researchers or archives. I also had to develop language skills in Kam. As it was very hard to facilitate dialogue around the concept of management of archives in such a context, and to make sure that it was informed, this context necessarily influenced the ways in which my role as researcher has evolved in processes of creation and management of Kam archival materials.

Insights from the work of custodian member researchers

Custodian member researchers' published reflections on their experiences in the fieldworker/archivist role frequently feature deeper reflection on the nature of the researcher role, and careful inclusion of specific forms of community consultation regarding management of archives and their repatriated materials. These descriptions offer further insights into how facilitation of different types of dialogue and engagement necessarily form part of the custodian member researcher's role in handling and managing archival materials. Two recent examples of these – provided in publications by Robin Gray (2019) and Clint Bracknell (2019a) – permit insights into two different contexts where the researcher has explicitly facilitated extensive consultation and discussion within their communities (in Canada and Australia, respectively).

Robin Gray described a project that, at the time of writing, she had been undertaking for almost seven years. At that point she had been working with nearly 300 people who identified as members of her Ts'msyen community in three different sites. Her discussion reveals an extremely extensive, wide-ranging project in order to obtain the type of dialogue she felt necessary to deal with repatriation of musical recordings:

> With consultation and guidance from Ts'msyen people, I began to implement a comprehensive, community-based Indigenous research paradigm to explore the motivations, possibilities, and obstacles associated with repatriating Ts'msyen songs from archives. Since 2012 I have engaged nearly three hundred Ts'msyen from infants to elders in a multisited, ethnographic research project [in three different sites]. (Gray 2019, 724)

Such extensive consultation across her community indicates that Gray has a particular idea of the researcher's role. To my reading, Gray envisions the researcher not as someone with individual responsibility for making decisions about archived material on behalf of the community, but as someone assuming a role enmeshed within and responsive to community direction. Another way of understanding this role would be to conceptualise the researcher as a facilitator of both eliciting and enacting community instruction regarding archival materials.

Clint Bracknell, in a discussion of his work in southern Western Australia with his Noongar community, talks about connecting older recordings of songs with community while receiving advice from specially established cultural reference groups comprised of particular community members. His observations on the length of time, the ongoing nature of dialogue, and the many ways in which community members can be involved in that dialogue are very instructive for others:

> Based on the Wirlomin model for working with archival material in the south coast Noongar community, the first step in the continuing process of recirculating archival Noongar song from the south coast of WA as part of the project *Mobilising song archives to nourish an endangered Aboriginal language* involved identifying individuals who could act as contemporary custodians for songs performed on archival recordings by now-deceased singers. This process – and the initial decision to begin working with the Dabb and Roberts songs – was guided by the Wirlomin cultural reference group. (Bracknell 2019a, 6–7)

From the regular mentions of these groups in his descriptions of various stages in the project, it is clear that discussions among all parties occurred in an ongoing manner at different points during the handling of the recorded materials. Although

Bracknell is not specifically discussing how he envisages the researcher's role, I suggest that, as with my reading of Gray's work, these comments indicate a very particular idea of how individuals such as he who are handling his community's archival materials should understand and undertake their role. Bracknell described a networked process of engagement where the researcher plays a central role not in determining and directing archival management, but in creating and promoting space for the researcher's role to emerge in response to broader community standpoints.

Challenges and future approaches

According to current archival aims and management models, both researchers and archives should be aiming to support custodian communities in their dialogue and engagement with archives. Communities should be involved in decisions around the management of their archival collections, thereby promoting custodian communities' self-determination in the maintenance of their own cultural heritage. Yet while all parties may advocate this model, the daily realities and pressures of collection management and the ongoing issues around connecting with members of custodian communities, including those identified previously by Barwick, may impede this model becoming a reality. Indeed, as I have discussed elsewhere:

> The often differing perspectives and pressures of communities and archives may make it difficult for the fieldworker/archivist to act in a manner that entirely satisfies one or both parties. Part of this difficulty is also due to both archives and custodian communities developing a range of different concepts of the role of the fieldworker/archivist – none of which may entirely concur with the researcher's own perspective on the scope of his or her role in the archiving process . . . Where possible, I strove to remain silent in decisions or actions regarding Kam cultural matters and to defer the decision-making to my Kam friends and colleagues. Through this method, people began to feel comfortable expressing their opinions to me. They also gained a clear sense that I was interested in helping them to promote Kam culture in the way they saw best, rather than dictating to them how it should be done. (Ingram 2019, 310)

The fact that expressing opinions regarding important community decisions was an uncommon experience for many people I worked with, and something that took them some time to come to terms with, seemed indicative of the rather minimal degree of control that many of them felt over how their own cultural heritage was used in many other contexts. It highlights one challenge and possible approach that might support dialogue around archival management. It also illustrates the crucial importance of understanding the particular issues of each individual context of cultural engagement, a skill that both community members and researchers, more than archivists in a distant location, could reasonably be expected to possess.

One final perspective that can help reassess challenges and future approaches involves awareness of how archives themselves can be considered to take a form that is not limited to a static collection of materials, but that can also be a space for action or doing (see see Harris, Gagau et al., this volume). In the work of Gray and Bracknell, the existence of archival materials is a starting point for activities that bring people together to do things that give rise to significant and positive cultural effects. In my work in Kam communities, the creation of a collaboratively managed archival collection has seen the creation of several parallel activities. At times, it has brought together large groups of villagers to sing and to re-enact cultural practices that had not been regularly performed for some time. It has also led to specifically organised, detailed discussions with expert singers of community wishes regarding musical recordings. Yet on other occasions I have felt that the "doing" extending from archival processes – as, for example, in decisions concerning the form of singing for recordings, as described above – required me in my researcher-facilitator role to maintain silence and step back, leaving the space for community members alone. This broader perspective on archives seems to have parallels with aspects of the decolonisation of archives described by Lee Watkins, Elijah Madiba and Bonnie McConnachie of the International Library of African Music as they wrestle with managing Hugh Tracey's archival legacy:

> Decolonization takes shape more profoundly as and in practice, in the *doing* of an archive as a space for radical engagements. By radical, I refer to opening the doors of the archive to everyone, taking the holdings of the archive to remote communities, and through developing partnerships with organizations which have previously deemed the archive a mysterious domain. (Watkins, Madiba and McConnachie 2021, 24)

Although a reconsideration of the researcher's role in the process of creating effective relationships between communities and archives seems to be an important step, future approaches to successful engagement between archives and communities will depend upon many other factors as well. These include the nature of all kinds of relationships and cultural understandings among parties involved in the archiving process, and the availability of sufficient time and funds (including for activities, travel and meetings). Community trust in the researcher is also crucial, and the researcher's own awareness of the value and nature of this role (as an ongoing, open-ended and possibly lifelong process) will also have an important impact. It is essential that spaces are created for community-led discussion. Finally, in an era of globalised digital music distribution and access, all parties involved in the creation of and access to music recordings need to develop specialised knowledge and sensitivity to the kinds of issues discussed here (as, for example, described in Levin and Süzükei 2006, 41–44).

Conclusion

In this chapter I have traced some of the changes to the role of the researcher in the creation and management of archival collections, explaining how these are connected with changing aims for archives. I have described insights for more effective reconsideration of this role that involve a focus on facilitation that can be observed from various examples – particularly the work of custodian member researchers. Together with the exploration of the ways that the concept of an archive can be extended beyond the curation of a set of materials, these ideas propel the discussion around the concept of researcher-as-facilitator beyond consideration of the emerging features of researcher roles and into exploring whether it might signal a re-conceptualisation of the research approach as a whole.

Such possible re-conceptualisation has interesting resonance with a relatively recently reformulated mode of research referred to as "rematriation". Monique Giroux offered an extensive outline of this new approach, worth quoting at some length:

> I propose that rematriation might be understood as a mode of research that emerges in direct response to the legacy and ongoing practice of collection-oriented research within ethnomusicology, its sister disciplines, and their academic ancestors; it is a research mode that acknowledges the deeply embedded practice of extraction on which our discipline was built (for which we have an inherited obligation to address), and under which it still functions (for which we are personally responsible for acknowledging and changing through the years of hard work it will require). Beyond using collection-oriented research as an opportunity to "dissemble and undo", rematriation is a mode of research that centres community understandings of musical knowledge; that prioritises the flourishment of the music cultures with which we work . . . rematriation as a research orientation can move beyond individual, bounded projects, and be integrated into our everyday research practices. (Giroux 2021, 122)

Here, Giroux explicitly avoids providing a prescriptive method for a rematriation process. Her avoidance seems apposite given that the aims and processes surrounding recording (and any ensuing archiving and repatriation) are the elements that rematriation encourages us to consider and explore as the archival process moves away from being transactional and project-focused towards a comprehensive ambit that sees action as a product of structural and other societal norms (see also Tuck and Gaztambide-Fernández 2013). It is not difficult to imagine some of the ways that a facilitation role for a researcher-archivist overlaps with the approach she advocates – perhaps through researchers reflecting on their aims and role from the very outset of the project, or by work in research education that partners with custodian communities to train new generations of researchers in revised archival approaches. Yet by proscribing the role any more explicitly it risks losing its usefulness. If, as researchers, we are willing to think a little more explicitly about taking on this facilitation role, and can see, explore and work towards articulating its form and value for all involved, it may well provide a practical and useful first step in finding more appropriate approaches to guide our entire research endeavour.

Chapter 6

Shifting cultural protocols surrounding community-led arts and media projects in Southern Ngaliya Warlpiri region

Georgia Curran and Valerie Napaljarri Martin

Linda Barwick has long been a passionate advocate for community-based archiving, recording and documentation of ceremonial songs, as well as community-led music and arts projects.[1] Her active mentoring of many researchers and community members across Indigenous Australia and beyond has led to significant return of and access to archival collections of photographic and audiovisual materials, many of which have inspired creative initiatives in contemporary contexts.[2] Within the southern part of Warlpiri country, a recent ARC Linkage project "Vitality and change in Warlpiri songs" (2016–2020), which was led by Barwick, has seen significant community engagement with older documentation of cultural heritage and opened up discussions on how present-day Warlpiri people may

---

1   Projects which Barwick has driven and been part of include ARC Linkage projects: the National Recording Project for Indigenous Performance in Australia (LP0560530), the Sustainable Futures for Music Cultures Project (LP0989243), Re-integrating Central Australian community cultural collections (LP140100806) and Vitality and change in Warlpiri songs (LP160100743) and Discovery Project: Reclaiming performance in southeastern Australia (DP 180100938) as well as the work of her past PhD students Myfany Turpin, Sally Treloyn, Genevieve Campbell, Reuben Brown and Isabel O'Keeffe. Barwick has also worked with communities in southern Italy on endangered *maggio* traditions.
2   See Barwick, Green and Vaarzon-Morel 2019.

choose to engage with these materials.[3] Many music and arts projects have been initiated entailing new, and often innovative modes for representing traditional ceremonial knowledge and practices. Unlike in parts of northern Australia where this kind of innovation is inherent in song traditions (see, for example, Campbell 2013; Clunies Ross and Wild 1987; Corn and Gumbula 2007; Stubington 1978), central Australian musical traditions hold on to a high degree of conservatism and custodians reflect this in their views, which emphasise the importance of carrying forward *jukurrpa* and knowledge of Country as it has been given to them from their ancestors. The late Warlpiri elder, Rex Japanangka Granites, explained this viewpoint in saying: "We can't change it because it's there all the time, you know the country never changes. *Kuruwarri* tracks are always there. I mean, the songs don't change, it's there because we still sing the tracks of how it is" (Curran, Barwick et al. 2024, 5).

Enid Nangala Gallagher also expressed a similar view, in saying:

> [They] sing altogether. It's those same places, they don't change where they are about. Our yawulyu (women's songs) are always like that forevermore. We always sing them like that. It's the same for the men, the men sing like that too. It's the jukurrpa (Dreamings) that they sing. (In Curran and Gallagher 2023, 719)

But it is apparent in the contemporary contexts in which Ngaliya Warlpiri engage with new media and technology that these traditionalist ideas can often sit at odds with the kinds of new productions and music which are nowadays being created and shared in efforts to carry forward this cultural heritage, although Warlpiri views regarding the fixed passing down of songs do consider the varying ways in which they will manifest in contemporary performance – a view also in keeping with the creative power of the *jukurrpa* with its eternal capacity for creation. Warlpiri manager for the Warlpiri Media Archive at Yuendumu, Simon Japangardi Fisher, explains: "We need to [keep] initiat[ing] new ways for our community to ensure the passing on of this [cultural] knowledge to younger generations" (Curran, Barwick et al. 2024, 15). Barwick has sat sensitively, throughout her career, in a space that respects the legacy and cultural importance of these established protocols, while also empowering individuals and communities to manage their own cultural forms

---

3   This project was a collaboration between PAW Media and Communications, University of Sydney, Australian National University and Kurra Aboriginal Corporation. Author Martin was a partner investigator from PAW Media and Communications; Curran worked as research associate, leading much of the Yuendumu-based fieldwork. Simon Japangardi Fisher was also a PAW Media partner investigator, Linda Barwick was lead chief investigator, and Nicolas Peterson and Myfany Turpin were chief investigators.

of authority and representations of their cultural material in the contemporary contexts often marked by rapid social change.

This chapter considers some of the ways in which traditional protocols surrounding Warlpiri cultural knowledge are reconsidered and renegotiated in these contexts. We discuss some collaborative music and arts projects developed by Warlpiri people in Yuendumu, the heart of Southern Ngaliya Warlpiri country. Yuendumu is also home to the central office of Pintupi Anmatjere Warlpiri (PAW) Media and Communications, which has since the mid-1980s driven many music and film productions, supported research projects and maintained an on-Country archive (see Curran, Martin et al. 2024; Hinkson 2002; Michaels 1994). We document some of the negotiations that have occurred around these projects with respect to the emergent representations of ceremonial knowledge. We illustrate the importance of these negotiations for collective community comfort around these projects and for their current and future value. Von Sturmer framed these kinds of processes as the "politics of representation": "a driving force in an amorphous and shifting field of persons, things, concerns, issues, actions, events" (1989, 130). We acknowledge that these issues are sensitive in Indigenous communities and do not enter into this discussion lightly, nor do we claim to be any kind of authority on this topic. We speak from our respective positions: Martin as a senior Warlpiri woman and chairperson for PAW Media and Communications, and Curran as a non-Indigenous researcher with long-term research collaborations with Yuendumu community members. We share our experiences of the negotiations that have been necessary surrounding some recent films, performances and music productions that involve representations of Warlpiri ceremonies and traditional songs. To begin, we set out some of the accepted protocols surrounding traditional Law for Warlpiri people, particularly focused around songs and their ceremonial manifestations. The examples we discuss are produced by Warlpiri people through PAW Media and other collaborations with researchers and arts organisations. Throughout this chapter, we emphasise the importance of open and inclusive communication among the custodians (often a collective) of these cultural traditions who assume the ultimate authority for the in-context choices that need to be made around how these traditions are represented.

Cultural protocols surrounding Southern Ngaliya Warlpiri cultural knowledge

Protocols surrounding the representation of ceremonial knowledge in central Australia have been widely documented as structured according to strict Laws, which have been passed on through generations. These are often described by

Aboriginal leaders, policy makers and in academic literature as being relatively fixed and having clear determinations between male and female domains of knowledge, as well as clear separations according to whether they are restricted (sometimes also by gender) or publicly accessible. Based on fieldwork in the Kimberley, Phyllis Kaberry (1939) began to break down some of these dichotomies in her early work, which highlighted the important ritual worlds of Aboriginal women, and Françoise Dussart (2000) has illustrated through case studies of ritual leaders that there has long been significant inter-gender sharing of knowledge, particularly between husbands and their wives. Thomas Jangala Rice also emphasised that he remembered female ritual knowledge from the period before he went through "men's business" when he largely spent his days with his mother and female relatives (Curran 2013). It is certainly the case that most large-scale ceremonies involve men and women, and that the sections "restricted" to men are in many instances audible, and sometimes also visible, to women, although never publicly presented (see Curran 2020, 92–94). It is evident that even in the stricter contexts of past eras that a much more blurred kind of dichotomy existed, and that most of the "restrictions" surrounding ceremonial forms are not predetermined but rather are negotiated in specific contexts and according to the contingencies that surround those moments and events.

As has been well documented, Warlpiri ceremonial knowledge and practices are owned through patrilineal inheritance: that is Warlpiri people are *kirda* for the *jukurrpa*, Country, songlines and ceremonies of their father(s), and are *kurdungurlu* – that is, have management responsibilities – for those for which their mother(s) is/are *kirda*. (see Nash 1982; Dussart 2000; Curran 2020). In recent decades the land claim and native title processes across central Australia, with their listings of "traditional owners" for particular Countries as key points of authority and contact, has tended to emphasise the importance of the *kirda* patrilineal connections.[4] As Ned Jampijinpa Hargreaves explained:

> We have *kirda* AND *kurdungurlu* and they are both important, both necessary to looking after the *jukurrpa,* [and] the Country. The *kurdungurlu* need to be there to watch that the *kirda* are doing the right thing . . . people need to realise this . . . they are both necessary to make decisions. (Pers. comm. May 2022)

---

4 With respect to Warlpiri land ownership, extensive literature since the early 1980s has recognised and demonstrated the complementary roles of *kirda* and *kurdungurlu*: see e.g. Bell 1988; Hale 1986; Maddock 1981; Nash 1982; Office of the Aboriginal Land Commissioner 1981.

6 Shifting cultural protocols

In recent decades, with the many Warlpiri initiatives to create resources that represent cultural knowledge, the *kirda* and *kurdungurlu* roles and responsibilities have been reconsidered to properly support the creation of representations of ceremonial knowledge that appear in publicly available productions. Eric Michaels described in the 1980s how these kinds of fixed representations sat at odds with Warlpiri storytelling in the early days of media production (1994, 107), noting:

> The Law, in its characteristic story forms, is differentially distributed across the population. Age, gender, kinship category, and "country" determine who might have access to which aspects of the knowledge, which parts of the songs, what designs or dance steps. "Country", a critical qualification for access to knowledge, is reckoned in terms of place of conception/birth, death of (ascendants), and residence. One speaks for, and from, one's particular place . . . No one will have total access or privileged authority . . . A longer story, a full myth, a major decision, requires many people, enmeshes many communities, in its enactment. (Michaels 1994, 107)

Martin explains how these kinds of decisions are made:

> *Kurdungurlu* talk to the *kirda* about how it's done, the right way. It could be a man or a woman. *Kurdungurlu* talks to the boss, to the *kirda* about how to do it, to do it the right way and how to sing the song and dance to it. You must work with *kirda* and *kurdungurlu* to choose how it is going to be done, how they want it done, the right way. [Across Central Australia] . . . they all follow that line where *kirda* and *kurdungurlu* work together on how it's going to be done and talk amongst themselves. Women usually wait for men *kirda* and *kurdungurlu* about how it's going to be done and then they have to do the same. If it's a restricted one they don't show it . . . but it's up to the *kurdungurlu* . . . the *kirda* to stop because they make the decisions: They invite the other *kurdungurlu* as well and they make a decision. But the main one they need to listen to is the main first *kurdungurlu* about how it's going to be done and what needs to be done. In the old days they were VERY strict! They are still strict about the sacred ones, the forbidden ones and the sensitive ones.

These kinds of shifts or adaptations made to traditional systems of cultural management, as well as the importance of continued renegotiation around cultural protocols, have also been noted elsewhere (see Thorner, Rive et al. 2019; Vaarzon-Morel, Barwick et al. 2021). Additionally, adaptations have been made surrounding the representation of authority, and rights to speak for cultural materials have been required so that categories, including those of author or producer, can now be associated with individual roles in the productions rather than, or as well as, acknowledging rights in the cultural materials.[5]

On top of the blurred categories of gendered and public access, and the complex negotiations between various kinship and extended networks are significant contemporary changes around attitudes to photography and filming. Where there once was a strong taboo against looking at images or hearing the voices of the deceased (see Michaels 1994; Lydon 2010), it is nowadays common at Warlpiri funerals to have a large close-up portrait photo of the deceased on a screen and sometimes even a portrait photo on their grave.[6] At a recent large-scale funeral for a very senior and widely respected Warlpiri man with many attendees from across Australia, a video collage production featuring the deceased's voice and name was screened. Although this production was met by wails from the deceased's two widows, they were quickly told to be quiet by their sister-in-law who stated as reason for the screening that "we are all Christians now". Although controversial among the family members, the screening was allowed to proceed, indicating the significance of these shifts in attitudes, even if too rapid for wider agreement in this instance.[7]

Martin indicates the significance and rationale behind these shifts in attitudes:

> Nowadays, families want memories. They want other people to see their families . . . which is great. Like before we weren't allowed to see in-laws, like for example I wouldn't see my in-laws or my son or my daughter after they passed away. Now it's okay as we want memories of who they were. Back in the old days it was strict – we also couldn't hear the voice of someone who passed away. This has changed very slowly over about 10 years, less than that probably . . . 10–15 years ago this started to slowly change. We all attend funerals now too and people welcome that. Way back, we weren't allowed to go to certain funerals. We'd have to go into the bush instead, especially for our in-laws, for those through marriage. We weren't allowed to go to the funerals but now anyone can go. We are trying to keep their memory alive and to celebrate them.

---

5   See Kelly in Michaels 1994 for a broader discussion of the emergence of some of the tensions with early representations of ceremonial and religious knowledge.
6   See Deger 2016 for a discussion of shifts in photographic practice in northern Australia.
7   The Baptist Church has had a presence in Southern Warlpiri settlements since their beginning in the mid-1940s and as such most residents have a moral commitment to Christian beliefs, particularly surrounding death. The deceased at this particular funeral was also an ordained pastor and therefore this was particularly sensitive for families.

Elsewhere we have documented the processes of working in collaborative intercultural teams for the production of two songbooks of Warlpiri women's *yawulyu* (Warlpiri women from Yuendumu 2017; Gallagher et al. 2014). Writing down, recording or fixing what are more usually orally passed-down song traditions raised many challenges, which were negotiated in the workshops through which these books were produced (see Curran, Carew and Martin 2019 for a broader discussion). As Ken Hale has described, there are in-built mechanisms in central Australian song traditions which undergo subtle change over time through a process of slight "slippage" (Hale 1984). The creation of these resources and the documentation of song traditions in fixed forms risks losing these specialised mechanisms for passing on song. But, as we have illustrated, "These books not only represent forms of Warlpiri cultural knowledge but also contribute to the dynamic forms of cultural reproduction that ensure continued engagement with the song traditions into the future" (Curran, Carew and Martin 2019, 68). Many of the media projects that we discuss in this chapter have similar intent and face many of the same challenges.[8]

Films of Warlpiri ceremonies

A Warlpiri history of filming ceremonial content reaches back decades with some of the first ethnographic films made in Warlpiri country in the late 1960s as part of the AIAS (now AIATSIS) initiatives in which film-makers were sent into Warlpiri country to film larger ceremonies. These films include, for example, the today-loved film *A Warlbiri Fire Ceremony – Ngatjakula* (filmed in 1967 by Roger Sandhall with Nicolas Peterson, and released in 1977). As has been documented elsewhere, the establishment of Warlpiri Media Association in Yuendumu in the mid-1980s was partially a response to the establishment of a satellite in the community that would broadcast mainstream Australian television content for the first time.[9] This significantly changed the ways in which Warlpiri people engaged with filming, with a number of community members who were involved in the establishment of Warlpiri Media Association taking on a role behind the camera rather than in front of it, as was the case for the ethnographic films of a prior era. While the impacts of these filmed representations of ceremony have been discussed elsewhere (Ginsburg 1995b; Curran 2019), it is important to note for this chapter that this was the beginning of an era where Warlpiri people had to consider, perhaps for the first time, the kinds of representations of Warlpiri ceremonial life that were being projected both to the outside world, and more importantly for most Warlpiri

---

8 See another account in Treloyn, Martin and Charles 2019.
9 See Michaels 1994 and Curran 2019 for an overview of Warlpiri attitudes during this time.

people to their children, grandchildren and future generations who would be able to view the filmed content.[10]

As Eric Michaels described of Francis Jupurrurla Kelly, one of the first Warlpiri filmmakers: "[he is] indisputably a sophisticated cultural broker who employs videotape and electronic technology to express and resolve political, theological, and aesthetic contradictions that arise in uniquely contemporary circumstances" (Michaels 1994, 104–5). The productions that come out of PAW and Yuendumu today continue to grapple with these issues as they occur in their specific contemporary contexts. Where once there was a focus on "capturing" ceremonies that were already being held, many ceremonies have since been staged for the purpose of filming.[11] This has allowed large groups of Warlpiri people to be involved, recompensed, and to work together to make sure that the proper kinship networks are involved to make the right collective decisions and engage in appropriate discussions.[12]

Martin explains:

> Those old films of Ngajakula and Jardiwanpa *(1967 film of Ngajakula and the 1993 film of Jardiwanpa)* – they were a really big effort. They got the sensitive [material] out. They had to work closely with people who knew the Dreaming well and talk about which parts were sensitive and which were not [to figure out what they could] show. They did a really good job. They talked to the right people about what to put on and what to sing. And everyone loves watching it now – watching how it was done in the old days. They love watching it you know. Some [of the Elders] knew the sacred ones, the sensitive ones . . . and they kept it out, which is good. They couldn't put it in because it was too sensitive and it wasn't meant to be public. It's for them to know it's there. They know the full story but they cut it [for the public]. They made good decisions. And not only that, they had to talk to the people from where [the songline] starts.[13] They had a meeting and talked about who it belongs to and who had to dance in the film, like that.

---

10 See also Dussart 1997 for discussion of similar issues surrounding representation of ceremonial designs on painted canvas.

11 See, e.g. Lander and Perkins 1993; see Curran 2019 for an overview of Warlpiri efforts to film counterpart ceremonies Jardiwanpa and Ngajakula, which represent opposing patrimoieties and even out representations of these ceremonies in films across all Warlpiri kin groups.

12 See further discussion in Langton 1993.

13 The Jardiwanpa songline for example begins in Luritja lands in the region near to Haast Bluff with varying other connections to different Dreamings owned by other groups. As such it is important that the traditional owners from this region were also consulted about the film productions, as was the case for *Yarripiri's Journey* (2018).

In the making of the most recent film of the Jardiwanpa ceremony, *Yarripiri's Journey* (2018), directed by a 24-year-old Warlpiri man, Simon Japanangka Fisher Jnr, many of the issues of the representation of this *jukurrpa* story for a wider, public audience arose again. The senior group of Warlpiri men and women who were in charge of leading the telling of the storyline chose to take the viewers through the series of named places along the Jardiwanpa songline, but in-the-moment tensions emerged around which were appropriate parts of the story to tell. The producers' desire for a coherent narrative storyline to project to a wider audience and the Warlpiri desire to leave out the significant sexualised (and hence gendered) content of this story became problematic, highlighting the ongoing tensions for Warlpiri people in fixing representations of their cultural knowledge. Jardiwanpa is renowned for being a widely shared public ceremony, but in this context where the storyline was instead centralised, rather than its ceremonial manifestation as in earlier films (Sandhall 1969; Lander and Perkins 1993) it emerged that there were many aspects that were deemed inappropriate for public viewing. Barbara Napanangka Martin explains that these decisions around content to be included in publicly viewed resources is more a contextual decision, noting: "this knowledge is not really sacred or restricted, it's just considered rude [shameful] and [therefore] people don't want to sing about it in public contexts".[14] The late Harry Jakamarra Nelson led the collective decision making within the senior Warlpiri group involved in *Yarripiri's Journey* and the film's narrative became focused on the journey of *Yarripiri*, an ancestral inland taipan snake, across Warlpiri country. Archival footage from the earlier film, *Jardiwanpa – a Warlpiri Fire Ceremony* (Lander and Perkins 1993) was used against some of the footage of this Country to enliven the places and indicate the particular songs to Warlpiri people without the need to articulate the story content.

Community arts events

Across Warlpiri communities there are a number of community arts events in which Warlpiri groups participate. As described above, there are some key differences in the ways in which Southern Ngaliya Warlpiri from communities including Yuendumu and Nyirrpi and Warnayaka Warlpiri, from Lajamanu, engage with these events. Here we will describe two community arts events and the different approaches and tensions surrounding the sharing of ceremonial materials in public spaces.

---

14 Personal communication, April 2022.

At a community arts event called Unbroken Land, in which Warlpiri women from Yuendumu were invited to participate in 2018, a group of dancers performed Ngapa "Rain" *yawulyu* with a large group of singers including important *kirda* and *kurdungurlu*. Additionally these same singers gave permission for the use of an older recording of Ngapa *yawulyu* to be used as the background music for a contemporary dance.[15] As will be discussed in the next section, Warlpiri women are often reluctant to "mix" *yawulyu* with more contemporary music styles but in this instance they felt they had strong agency over the representation depicted in the performance and were supporting younger non-Warlpiri but Indigenous dancers to be part of the *yawulyu* event on their own terms.

Another arts event held biannually in Lajamanu is Milpirri, an event supported by Tracks Dance Company who come to the community for several weeks surrounding these events (see Patrick and Biddle 2018; Biddle 2019). A space is set up in which different skin groups perform traditional genres of ceremonial song, including *yawulyu* and *purlapa*, and younger school-aged children are taught and perform choreographed hip-hop dances. These performances are interspersed in a one-night event on a centralised ceremonial area but the styles are never mixed. Steven Patrick Jampijinpa, the creative director and founder of Milpirri, has commented that "Milpirri was always intended to be for communities across the Warlpiri region, rather than centred in Lajamanu, but the Yuendumu side just didn't like it".[16] Ngaliya Warlpiri people do not participate in Milpirri, though some do travel for the spectacle of the event, and many have deep objections to the public format in which many of the ceremonial songs are presented.

Tim Newth, artistic director of Tracks Dance Company, explained the important role that senior man and father of Steven Patrick, Jerry Jangala Patrick, had in legitimising Milpirri for the older men in Lajamanu:

> Jangala was really crucial was that for most older men in Lajamanu . . . their thoughts of those ceremonies were those that happened out bush that took 3 months to happen – Milpirri takes 2 hours at the most to happen. So he had the job of convincing . . . at that stage I think there were about 40 older senior men in the community and he had to say . . . he's had the responsibility . . . of getting everybody to understand, particularly the older people about . . . how it could possibly, possibly work with those things that could take 3 months and just do it in a couple of hours. (Tasman and O'Shannessy 2020)

---

15 See Curran 2019 for a fuller description of this event.
16 Personal communication, 2022.

Perhaps due to the more flexible northern influences, Lajamanu community has grown to love Milpirri and anticipate these events with excitement every two years. The whole community participates, though sadly Jerry Jangala is the only senior man still alive to sing the songs.

Tensions surrounding old and new music

Across northern Australia, the mixing of musical genres is common. As East Arnhem Land music producer Arian Pearson explained: "Bands like Yothu Yindi were really influential and inspired so many of the bands that exist today" (White-Radhakrishnan, Curran and Pearson 2021). The flexibility of northern Australian music and openness to innovation allow for this to be an accepted part of Aboriginal song traditions (Corn and Gumbula 2007). Stephen Wild has described how these northern influences, with more improvisation and individual assertiveness, can be seen in the Warlpiri musical styles in Lajamanu despite structural similarities to central Australia musical traditions (Wild 1984). Ngaliya Warlpiri are typically known for being more conservative in this respect, a tendency enhanced by increased ceremonial gathering with women from Anangu Pitjantjatjara Yankunytjatjara (APY) lands and other areas of central Australia who have again stricter Laws surrounding ceremonial singing, particularly around preventing gendered sharing. As Ngaliya Warlpiri senior singer Lynette Nampijinpa Granites explained when questioned on why central Australian groups do not incorporate traditional song genres into contemporary music: "*Yawulyu* is just not like that. It's just not the way it can be done – the old songs and the new music need to be kept separate".[17] Another important senior female singer, Lorraine Nungarrayi Granites, reiterated this attitude: "*Yawulyu* is different. It needs to be sung in a straight way like it has been sung for a long time".[18]

But, in the north-eastern part of Warlpiri country, the following story is told by Neil Murray (of Warrumpi Band fame) about the recording of the track "Jipuranpa" by young Warlpiri man, Brian Murphy, in Tennant Creek:

> an occasion at Winanjjikari Studio when Brian turned up unannounced in a taxi with a bunch of elderly grandmothers and said, "We're recording now." Jeff barely had time to get the leads plugged in. Brian launched into

---

17 Personal communication, 2021. This was stated after viewing a video of the all-female band Ripple Effect from Maningrida performing a song, "Diyama", in which was incorporated a recording with the voice of one of the band member's fathers singing.

18 Personal communication, 2021.

an acoustic-driven lament, in Warlpiri, while the grandmothers fired up a traditional chant around him. It was a one-take only. (Murray 2014, 190)

The "traditional chant" referred to was in fact the Jipiranpa *yawulyu*, led by Murphy's grandmother Fanny Napurrurla Walker, whom Barwick worked with many years before to document this same songline connected to an edible seed ancestor from the Country of Jipiranpa.[19] In this instance, the mixing of old and new styles occurred without a problem for any of the "grandmothers" who had clearly agreed to participate in this recording with their grandson.

As Murray continued to describe of this experience and from his perspective as an influential person in the new music scene of central Australia:

> On the drive back to Alice, I put on that track – "Jipirunpa" – the final song on Brian's 2009 album *Freedom Road,* released by Winanjjikari Music through Barkly Arts. It sounds chaotic, random even, Brian starts on an acoustic guitar, and after a while he starts singing low, a melancholic refrain, and suddenly a bunch of old women erupt with a traditional chant except this chant of theirs has a totally different structure. The piece turns and repeats on itself, compelling you to take in the cyclical melody, it's enchanting, Brian's world-weary vocal rising and falling with the tough grit of the grandmothers until – finally I am forced to concede with Jeff – it makes powerful emotional sense. "I have heard nothing like it." I say. "I love it." (Murray 2014, 192)

These kinds of recordings remain non-existent in Ngaliya Warlpiri Country, though this may be a shift that is further negotiated in the future.

Conclusions

Reflecting on life in Yuendumu in the 1980s, Eric Michaels wrote:

> one must appreciate the mechanism of *jukurrpa* as social reproduction – the management of information transmission as a model across generations – and identify the ways in which novelty must be counter interpolated to the system. But when taking this perspective, simply identifying an expressive act as an artwork can become a problem. The boundaries of performance event and artwork become blurred. Art or video objects become difficult to isolate for analysis because the producers' intent is itself the opposite. Warlpiri artists demonstrate their own invisibility in order to assert the

---

19 See Walker, Barwick et al. 2024; Curran, Carew and Martin 2019.

> work's authority and continuity with tradition. They do not draw attention to themselves or to their creativity. (Michaels 1994, 107)

In the decades since Michaels wrote this, there have been many social shifts in Warlpiri communities that have brought significant pressures and desires to engage with a broader world outside central Australia. This expansion of global connectedness and ease of information sharing has no doubt been influential on the kinds of shifts to traditional protocols that have been discussed in this chapter. As Von Sturmer has set out with respect to the politics of representation: "Every act of representation involves a positioning of the self: each act of representation is an act of self-representation" (Von Sturmer 1989, 127). The above discussion and examples open up many questions about how this is done in a world where a sense of "self" is understood through relationships to others across broad kinship networks, as well as the associated personal connections to *jukurrpa,* Country and songlines.

Many of the media and arts representations that Warlpiri people engage with today require adjustments of the cultural protocols that sustain Warlpiri connections to *jukurrpa* and Country. Significantly, the nature of the fixed representation in multimedia sources requires a more individualised focus with regards to authority than is comfortable for most Warlpiri people, especially in the Ngaliya country in the south. Within the rise of the desert art movement over many decades there has been a shift away from the collective paintings that were popular in the early days (see Yuendumu Doors for example), to those painted by individuals that are nowadays more commercially popular. The rise of categories such as author, producer, musician and artist now have a place within these worlds and have become important ways for Indigenous agency and authority to be better recognised.

Chapter 7

Dispersed sound archives and diaspora communities: reconnecting with old recordings from Hula village, Papua New Guinea

Amanda Harris, Steven Gagau, Deveni Temu, Roge Kila and Gulea Kila

In 1904, a British ethnographic expedition recorded the singing of Vula'a people in Hula village, Central Province, Papua New Guinea. Around 120 years later, contemporary Vula'a people heard this singing for the first time. The work of reconnecting people with old songs was carried out as part of "True Echoes", a project designed to make digitised recordings, long preserved in British collecting institutions, audible to the speaker communities whose songs and languages are recorded. In this chapter, we describe reconnecting the recordings with Vula'a people living in diaspora, away from their home region. Just as the expedition dispersed cultural records across the world, people have also been dispersed through globalised economic and colonial processes. Members of Pacific diaspora communities, living away from their home villages and towns, often keenly engage in efforts to reconnect with traditional culture, to keep alive the cultural practices from which they are distanced. Linking these histories of dispersal, we consider the implications for reconnecting digital heritage recordings with re-located people.

The process of fragmentation of cultural materials in their dispersal to archive and museum collections has been the subject of considerable recent scholarship, with some scholars exploring the potential of digital representations for restoring wholeness to the fragments of culture (Thorpe, Faulkhead and Booker 2020; Campbell, Tipungwuti et al. 2022), and for improving access to archival records (Bell, Christen and Turin 2013; Gibson, Angeles and Liddle 2019; Hoffmann 2021). We consider the complexities of this fragmentation, not just of cultural records, but of cultural practices themselves that have felt the impacts of colonisation and rapid change. Histories of mobility, change and diaspora have long been recognised as an important part of the cultures of Oceania (Diettrich, Moulin and Webb 2011). Returning old sound recordings to a community with long histories of change and migration opens up many questions about processes of cultural heritage repatriation (on this we build on key literature on digital repatriation of and access to sound recordings including Barwick 2004; Bendrups 2015; Gillespie 2017; Treloyn and Dowding 2017; Diettrich 2019; Niles 2018; Harris, Gagau et al. 2019; Koch 2019; Bracknell 2019a). A key question for our chapter is this: what is the relationship between dispersed recordings and speaker communities in diaspora?

The re-imagining of distributed cultural heritage archives has been an important contribution of Linda Barwick's scholarship and we are influenced by her advocacy for "establishing ongoing reciprocal relationships with cultural heritage communities" (Barwick 2004, 253; see also Barwick and Thieberger 2018). Most recently, Barwick's emphasis on "the performative power of the knowledge the archival objects encode" reminds us of the dynamic relational character of old song recordings that can be enlivened through new performances by cultural custodians (Barwick, Green, Vaarzon-Morel and Zissermann 2019, 3; see also Harris, Barwick and Troy 2022a). Our re-engagement with historic recordings produced meaningful reflections on the significance of these old songs, and their relationship to musical practices of the present day.

The "True Echoes" project was designed around participatory research in the villages where the historical recordings were made. Amanda Harris, a musicologist and historian, and Steven Gagau, the local researcher on the project, collaborated on "True Echoes" as PARADISEC colleagues.[1] When pandemic-induced travel restrictions impacted the project's plans, we sought to engage locally with the Australian Papua New Guinea (PNG) diaspora community, while awaiting the reopening of international borders. Indeed, as Van Heekeren wrote of her experience of anthropological fieldwork, "when you return home, relatives of the people you have gone so far to study may now be living just around the corner" (Van Heekeren 2012, x). Steven Gagau does live around the corner from Roge and

---

[1] PARADISEC is the Pacific and Regional Archive for Digital Sources in Endangered Cultures, https://www.sydney.edu.au/music/our-research/paradisec.html.

7 Dispersed sound archives and diaspora communities

Gulea Kila: Vula'a people resident in south-eastern Australia. Steven is also broadly connected with the Sydney PNG diaspora through the Sydney Wantok Association and liaises with Deveni Temu who leads and coordinates the PNG Peroveta Singers of Canberra in community collaboration. These three community members were the key participants in the local research, after they expressed interest in work on their own cultural heritage and past histories of their people and identity, building on their existing interest and record in the area.[2]

Co-authors Deveni Temu, Roge Kila and Gulea Kila had never before had an opportunity to hear the recordings held in the British Library, though they already had exposure to historical accounts of the development of Hula people. Deveni is from an older generation, growing up in the 1950s and 1960s, and Roge and Gulea from the younger generation in the 1970s and 1980s. In recorded discussions with Amanda and Steven in Sydney and Canberra, they have each shared their insights about the transformational period from traditional living to changing lifestyles of modern and westernised living.[3] This diversity of life experiences and knowledge of their own histories and the traditions and cultural ways of Hula people connected the historic recordings with contemporary life and prompted musical responses and re-creation of the old chants and songs.[4]

---

2 Deveni Temu has published several papers on cultural identity and library and information services in PNG, as well as providing expert input into exhibitions at the National Museum of Australia and into the Nigel Oram collection held at the National Library of Australia, see Temu, Ahrens and Faupula 2009; Oram 1942; Temu 1981; 2003. Roge and Gulea Kila participated in discussions with Deborah Van Heekeren on Vula'a history and culture, see Van Heekeren 2012, x.

3 Deveni Temu is not from Hula Village. He comes from Kapari Viriolo villages located east of Hula. His mother is from the Vula'a-speaking village of Viriolo, which is unusual to find amongst the Aroma coastal villages.

4 The group's inputs to co-authorship took a variety of forms. The conceptual framing of this chapter was discussed between members of the group from the time the recordings were first shared in 2020, through the recording of conversations between co-authors in 2020 and 2021, and to the point of developing a written draft of the chapter through 2022 and 2023. Amanda and Steven drafted the first version of the chapter based on two public presentations they had developed together and on the insights that arose from the group's recorded conversations, with Amanda drawing in much of the background literature on cultural heritage and expeditionary histories, and Steven drawing on his expertise in interpreting PNG history and first-person accounts of heritage management. Throughout this process Amanda and Steven's understandings of the history of the Hula recordings was informed and shaped by the perspectives of Deveni, Roge and Gulea and their knowledge of history and contemporary experiences of culture. Deveni, Roge and Gulea also read drafts of the written text, provided corrections and reworkings, and edited their spoken transcripts to shape them into a form suitable for an academic chapter.

Members of Pacific diaspora communities in Sydney live far from home for a range of reasons that have to do with personal choice, economic necessity and educational opportunities. Education in colonial systems has also subsequently enabled people from PNG to access cultural heritage materials held in museums and archives abroad and to reckon with these collections and what they mean to people today. Imperial expeditions and their collection of cultural heritage into institutions are part of the story of colonial histories that have seen both culture and people dispersed away from place. We suggest that engagement with diaspora communities can be crucial to repatriation and reconnection efforts and can complement archival returns to the people still living in the physical location where records were collected. In the next section of this chapter, we trace brief histories of Hula village and Vula'a people, and of the recordings made in 1904 by Charles Seligmann as part of the Daniels Ethnographical Expedition to British New Guinea. After outlining a brief history of place and people, we explore the parallel lives of the physical recordings and those who recorded, and were recorded in, them.

Hula village and Vula'a people

Figure 7.1 A Hula beach with canoe in the distance. From a collection of images taken during the Cooke–Daniels Ethnographical Expedition to British New Guinea 1903–1904. Museum number Oc,B118.45 © The Trustees of the British Museum.

7 Dispersed sound archives and diaspora communities

Hula village, where a selection of the 1904 recordings was made, was home to Vula'a people before Europeans first made contact with them in the 1870s, but had only been established as a Vula'a village around a century before this (Oram 1968, 244; Van Heekeren 2012, 23). Accounts of the origins of Vula'a people identify their previous home region as being in Nakama Kone (Alukuni) in the area of Hood Lagoon, with movement to Gile Gilena (Hood Point) only in the mid- to late-18th century (Van Heekeren 2012, 23–24; Oram 1968, 244). These histories of migration are held in oral histories by Vula'a people today. Roge Kila explains:

> historically, Leva Lui and La'a Lui settled in what is now Hula Village. Upon arrival the Hula people negotiated with the Paugolo and Ririga clans, the original inhabitants, to settle at the current location. The Paugolos and Ririgas allowed the Vula'a to settle there. Initially the houses were built over the sea, on stilts. It was primarily a marine village, so the main survival activities were focused around the ocean. The village folk had to learn their craft around sailing and fishing, like fixing a net, making a fishing harpoon, and eventually operating a motorised dinghy for example. All our lives revolved around fishing and a bit of gardening for vegetables. When I was growing up most of the houses were over the sea but now the village has become land based and there are fewer houses over the sea. (Kila and Kila 2020)

Nigel Oram based his published history on oral accounts of Vula'a people and suggested that the recent establishment of the village was important to understanding processes of Vula'a change and migration (Oram 1968). After the first missionary period 1876–1918, Oram found that ceremonial practices including song and dance were abandoned, and that, between 1945 and 1965, more than half of the Hula population moved to other areas (Oram 1968, 250–251). However, Oram considered people living in and away from the village as forming one society, defined by memories of "full pedigrees from the time of reaching Hood Point" (Oram 1968, 244).

The most recent written accounts of Vula'a people and Hula villages come from Deborah Van Heekeren who measured the veracity of Oram's records against earlier published descriptions by Haddon and Seligmann, finding the records to be mostly accurate. Van Heekeren's accounts and those of Vula'a people she worked with give more nuanced interpretations of historical events and of the relationships between traditional Vula'a culture and recently introduced practices from Polynesian missionaries and British and Australian colonial governance structures. Van Heekeren showed that the introduced notion of "history" is recounted in stories "grounded in a distinctively Melanesian cosmology" (Van Heekeren 2012, 85). Vula'a historicity is embedded in key aspects of Vula'a identity: language and fishing. Fishing is associated with a rich mythology that Van Heekeren has asserted "underscores its cultural value"; Vula'a people's reputation as expert fishers and their orientation towards the sea "continues to resonate in their contemporary sociality" (Van Heekeren 2017, 608).

The resonances of fishing are therefore one of the aspects of culture that Vula'a people take with them through histories of mobility. Van Heekeren has suggested this was intrinsic to Vula'a "experience of place" (both historically and in the present) (2017, 608). Roge expands on the ways that fishing practices connect him to historical practices and ancestors, and are transferrable to his current home in south-eastern Australia:

> [Roge] we call the fish [Gulea] "here we are, here we are, here comes your feed, come and take it" [Roge] I say those phrases because I heard my father say them while fishing. I still say them when I go out there kayaking and fishing, I will call the fish. I'll recall a couple of things that I heard my father say, and he probably heard it from his father as well. "Come take the line, break the line, where are you? Come out and take the line, rip it apart, it's all there, it's yours, I'm presenting it it's yours now take it, it's there [rapu ruki rukia – rip it apart, valea valea – smash it, e'e lovakea – why are you taking so long]". Chanting such phrases is still common in the village. We still say that and when I go fishing with my cousins in the village, we still say those things whenever we cast a line [Gulea] and where there's like a lull period, it's a bit quiet and then and then someone just gets up and suddenly calls out.
>
> [Roge] [in Australia] I go out to Lion Island and they are wondering what's this guy saying, because I'll cast the line and say "e'e rapu ruki rukia" [rip it apart] and "here it comes", because we heard it from my parents my father did that so it must have been something handed down. (Kila and Kila 2020)

Accounts of Vula'a culture have repeatedly emphasised the importance, and elusiveness, of song and singing. C.G. Seligmann, who made the 1904 recordings of Vula'a songs, suggested that "The origin of most of the songs is utterly obscure, and the words for the most part unintelligible. A few songs are however of recent invention" (Seligman 1910, 152). Van Heekeren confirmed that some of the songs recorded by Seligmann had come from elsewhere, and deepened this discussion of the unintelligibility of some song lyrics, citing a *lekwai* song related to her by Walo Kalawa that had no accurate translation, being an archaic song form (2012, 57, 157). Gulea and Roge Kila also noted in auditioning the 1904 recordings that some of the songs sung by Hula people might have been sung in Roro language (Kila and Kila 2020). Deveni Temu suggested that some songs sung by Hula people may have been in the Gulf language of Toaripi, as a result of the timing of the expedition during the Hiri trade, and the sharing of songs between Motu and Hula people.

Figure 7.2 Two Hula men engaged in a ceremonial feeding (spear feast?). From a collection of images taken during the Cooke–Daniels Ethnographical Expedition to British New Guinea 1903–1904. Museum number Oc,B121.111 © The Trustees of the British Museum.

Roge and Gulea Kila confirm the importance of song to Vula'a people:

> [Roge] Singing is a big part of our culture. [Gulea] when we are together we just break into a song. [Roge] We have to sing we can't not sing . . . it is a personal connection to the village. The song allows an emotional and powerful connection to an event in the past, a record of a person's journey, or a historical feat for example. Traditionally when there was a performance, one had to properly prepare for the event. For example, you wouldn't eat for a day, you'd fast and you'd start performing at 3am and then all day and all night. [Gulea] they kind of went into a zone during these traditional dances, it's just like going out like fishing/hunting, they would prepare a certain way, well ahead of the event. [Roge] I know that when I was in high school we did some performances where some of our guys didn't eat for

the day before the performance the next day. So they'd fast and get ready and prepare ourselves and then the next day we performed for a couple of hours (especially in festivals). You feel kind of powerful when you fast for a day and then you're just in a different zone. The performance is probably just ten or twenty percent of it. Eighty percent of the preparation goes into making the costumes, learning the songs, lining up patterns and then getting prepared mentally and all that. (Kila and Kila 2020)

Van Heekeren's attendance at events including funerals at which songs were sung across a number of hours confirmed:

> it is the embodied and performative aspects of singing rather than the meaning of the words which carry the greater significance. To "keep singing" is to participate in a particular mode of being that is fundamental to Vula'a ontology . . . When Vula'a people gather socially, they begin to sing. They sing themselves together, in the sense that the union of their voices announces their collective presence. (2012, 163–164)

Figure 7.3 A group of Hula men and women performing a dance/ceremony. From the Cooke–Daniels Ethnographical Expedition to British New Guinea 1903–1904. Museum number Oc,B120.107 © The Trustees of the British Museum.

Over the last several hundred years, re-locations to different parts of the coast have seen change and migration become characteristic of Vula'a society (Van Heekeren 2012, 24; Oram 1968). The published record of Vula'a cultural practices thus recounts a complex history of cultural change through Vula'a migration over several centuries, and people's more recent embrace of Christianity and engagement with the capitalist economy. Van Heekeren has argued for ways of understanding cultural continuity as "an ongoing process of negotiation and indigenization" (2012, 2). She also contemplated the importance of historical consciousness among Vula'a people:

> Many young Vula'a people do not know the stories that engender the identity of their elders. They do, though, experience a sense of loss in respect of their material culture. As they travel regularly to other parts of the country to participate in sporting events and church-based competitions, they notice that their "traditional" past – song, dance and costume – is not available to them. (2012, 5)

Yet, as van Heekeren has suggested, Vula'a culture is marked not just by change, but by continuities, most especially a continuity of identity that is tied to language, to place, and to the fact that Vula'a people have always fished.

History of the 1904 recordings and their organisation into collections

The recordings made in Hula village in 1904 were captured during the first missionary period, which Nigel Oram dates as 1876–1918. They were recorded as part of the collecting and documentation activities of the Daniels Ethnographical Expedition to British New Guinea by Charles Seligmann, who was building on the interest in British New Guinea developed during his participation in the 1898 Cambridge Anthropological Expedition to Torres Straits (Figure 7.4 shows a recording made with Hula people in 1898). In the middle of this first missionary period, the expeditions visited territory that was under the colonial jurisdiction of Britain, soon to be transferred to Australian administration. Deveni Temu places the 1904 visits within this history of rapid change:

> William Lawes was the first missionary that came via the London Missionary Society, now popularly known as LMS. He was the first white man to ever built a permanent house in whole of Papua New Guinea in 1874. When the trade happened between the Motu and the Hula people in exchange of fish and sago and pots he was there and through that he asked the Hula or Keapara people if he could come and bring the gospel to the village people. So that's 1874. If you take the date of 1904 when Seligmann was there, the

missionary influence was really now gaining power and the change was going to come. That was the beginning of dismantling of the very traditional way of life of the people. The Hula were the first along our coast, excluding the Motu people, that readily accepted this new way of thinking and new way of life, new way of looking at things. (Temu 2022)

Figure 7.4 "Phonograph, Hula": Charles Seligmann or Sidney Ray recording the singing of Vula'a people. From the Cambridge University Anthropological Expedition to the Torres Straits 1898–1899. Image ID N.34987.ACH20 © The Museum of Archaeology and Anthropology, Cambridge.

As they travelled, the expedition members stayed at government outposts and mission stations (Figure 7.5) and relied on local people already working with the colonial administration to corral the participation of villagers in singing for their wax cylinder recorder. Deveni Temu suggests that the tall man wearing European clothing, standing directly behind and watching Seligmann in Figure 7.4, was likely Ahuia Ova. Having worked in domestic service at Government House, Ahuia Ova had a command of English along with Motu, Koita, Hula and other languages (Oram 1979). Ahuia Ova likely introduced Seligmann to villagers, and importantly, explained what type of traditional folk songs and dances they knew

7 Dispersed sound archives and diaspora communities

and in what languages. He would have liaised with villagers, reassuring them and encouraging people not to worry about the recording machine, but to sing as if out on canoes at sea.

1. Port Moresby
2. Gabagaba
3. Tagana
4. Vatorata
5. Saroa
6. Hula
7. Babaka
8. Kamali
9. Kalo

Figure 7.5 Location of stops of the Daniels Ethnographical Expedition to British New Guinea. Map created by Steven Gagau, using the historic map published in Seligman (1910, 40).

As part of her work on the "True Echoes" collections, Vicky Barnecutt traced the path travelled by the wax cylinders Seligmann recorded, which were originally taken back to Cambridge, transferred to the British Institute of Recorded Sound in the 1950s, with this archive being incorporated into the British Library in 1983 (Barnecutt 2021). Other material culture collected on the expedition went elsewhere, including to the British Museum, Pitt Rivers Museum and the London School of Economics and Politics Science (LSE) Library. This dispersal of the collected records of expeditions to institutions able to care for them has not just geographically distanced the records from the places they come from, but has also fragmented the records themselves into separate stores of written records, material culture and ephemeral culture.

Digitisation offers the possibility of making cultural records available beyond the site of the institution that conserves them. A key output of the "True Echoes" project has been a website that makes the cylinder recordings available as well as sharing new materials collected through participatory research by speaker community members during the course of the project.[5] Graeme Were has advocated for the role of digital collections and repatriations in particular, suggesting:

> Digital heritage allows for a new coming together or completeness by foregrounding the dispersal of cultural objects that once existed in one particular time and place, leading to the reinvigoration of dissipated identities and cultural loss through relocation and restitution . . . In reconnecting dispersed treasures housed in separate museums, archives and galleries and on separate computer servers, *the nation or state can be imagined in its entirety* [our emphasis]. (Were 2015, 155)

We contend that it is not possible to arrive at imagining a community "in its entirety" even if we adapt Were's statement to conceive of villages and communities, rather than nations or states. Ethnographic expeditions collected, assembled and interpreted cultural records in ways that were not neutral. Practices of collection were imbued with the interpretative biases of European Enlightenment thinking. They were also informed by now discredited "sciences" (such as phrenology and other comparative physiological pseudosciences) that focused on correlating cranial differences to different stages of human evolution.[6] Expeditionary visits were fleeting and bound by the limits of what "informants" were willing to reveal and by the questions researchers thought to ask. Records collected were just fragments of cultural practice, not cultures in "their entirety".

Expeditions were also not without impact, and it follows that there is no such thing as a wholly unchanged community to which cultural objects can be repatriated. Rather, communities already undergoing processes of change were transformed further through the direct and indirect impacts of collecting expeditions. Even where expedition teams did not physically remove material cultural objects (though most did) and instead took an impression of cultural practice on a wax cylinder, these were acts of engagement and interaction that left tangible traces. As Deveni

---

5 True Echoes: https://www.true-echoes.com/.
6 The emphasis on physical attributes of different groups is strongly evident in both Haddon's (1900) and Seligmann's (1910) records of their various expeditions.

7 Dispersed sound archives and diaspora communities

Temu recalled in his historical account of these recordings (quoted above), the collecting expedition was just one episode in a series of arrivals of foreigners with different interventionist motives. The expeditions were also embedded in colonial frameworks, just as missionary activities interacted with colonial administration, as we now discuss.

The American Major William Cooke Daniels, who funded the 1904 expedition (and after whom it was named) had met Charles Gabriel Seligmann on a fishing trip in Hampshire, in the United Kingdom, after Seligmann had returned from visiting then British New Guinea on the Cambridge Anthropological Expedition to Torres Straits six years earlier. Seeking to capture more records of cultural practices on another trip, Seligmann and Daniels were joined by Walter Mersh Strong and Arthur Henry Dunning. The wax cylinder recordings from the expedition held at the British Library are organised into collections named for the Daniels Expedition, with the contributors "unidentified (singers)", "unidentified (drum)" and "Seligman, Charles Gabriel, 1873–1940 (sound recordist)".[7] This system of organisation, common in archives across the world, places the recording of a song into collections organised by a logic determined by the collectors. These collectors often made no record of the names of singers or speakers recorded and may have misidentified language names and other details. In practice then, "collections" fragment cultural records in the act of gathering and preserving them (Campbell, Tipungwuti et al. 2022). Collecting cultural objects and taking them back to the imperial centre to be dispersed among several different collecting institutions distances them from people and from cultural context, even while making them available to a wider audience.

Though Walter Mersh Strong's name is not visible in the expedition records in the way Daniels and Seligmann are in archives and museums, he left different kinds of traces in the wake of the expedition, and initiated other acts of dispersal. Leaving the expedition in (then) British New Guinea, Strong would become (newly renamed) Papua's first government anthropologist, publishing papers on Papuan language and culture and photographing rock art in the area.[8] He then became part of the Australian administration, founding a program that trained Papuans

---

7   During the course of the "True Echoes" project, these collections were reorganised and renamed (the collection was formerly called the "Seligman New Guinea Cylinders"), but performers have so far been unable to be identified, see, for example, http://explore.bl.uk/BLVU1:LSCOP-ALL:BLLSA7641343.

8   Strong was initially employed as a magistrate, then as a medical doctor, before becoming an anthropologist in 1920. Edmundson 2022 recounted that he was not a keen fieldworker, but published two papers on links between Papuan language and culture and also recorded and photographed some of the earliest rock art in the area.

as medical assistants, sending them to the University of Sydney for training. As the *Australian Dictionary of Biography* recorded:

> In 1933–35 he taught basic science to small groups [of Papuans], then dispatched them to the University of Sydney for several months in a course specially tailored by Dr F. W. Clements. Strong entrusted wide responsibilities to Papuans as extension workers and dispensers, thereby enlarging the reach of the department without bursting its slender budget . . . Strong's ethnographic work is now disregarded . . . He retired in 1938 to a plantation near Rigo which he had acquired from Beatrice Grimshaw . . . Strong died at his home near Port Moresby on 4 October 1946 and was buried in the local cemetery. Much of his estate, sworn for probate at £6669, was bequeathed to the University of Sydney for the education of Papuans and for medical research. (Denoon 1990)

Strong's inclusion in the *Australian Dictionary of Biography* indicates that, though he came from England with the expedition, by 1914 he was embedded in the Australian colonial administration of Papua. We might even say he was deeply involved in the kinds of networks of interconnection through which a line can be traced to the large community of Papua New Guineans who reside in Australia today.[9]

Another member of the colonial administration, Hubert Murray, met with the expedition in 1904 within three weeks of arriving in British New Guinea (soon to become the Australian administered territory of Papua) from Sydney. Following Murray's chance meeting with Seligmann during the expedition's visit, he accompanied him on several investigative outings where Murray began collecting artefacts (Edmundson 2019). Like Seligmann, Murray relied heavily on local interlocutors, including Ahuia Ova (Figure 7.4). Murray went on to become lieutenant-governor of Papua in 1908 as part of the Australian administration, and founded the first Anthropology Museum in 1914. As Anna Edmundson has shown: "there was an important link between anthropology and the Murray administration, as anthropological research became part of an underlying process of indirect rule" (Edmundson 2019, 103). With the museum, Murray had "a concern to collect material culture that was rapidly disappearing under European influence", and in 1911 formalised this in the "Papuan Official Collection", passing an order that officers were not to collect privately but as part of a colony-wide

---

9   Indeed, Strong brokered relationships between Papuan institutions and the University where two of the co-authors work today. On imperial networks between Australia and the Pacific, see also Banivanua Mar 2015.

7 Dispersed sound archives and diaspora communities

collection of material from every regional division of Papua, with the museum constructed in 1914 (Edmundson 2019, 105; see also Lamb and Lee 2023, 6).

These two snapshots from the expedition's wake demonstrate both its embeddedness in larger colonial processes and also its role in the dispersal of both cultural records and people away from their home regions. Today, much of the Papuan Official Collection assembled by Murray resides in the National Museum of Australia, the Daniels expedition's collections are spread across numerous museums and archives across the United Kingdom, and Vula'a people continue to live in large numbers away from their home village, including in Australia and in the United Kingdom. There is no single direct line from the expedition to today that traces the movement of people, but rather the dispersal of records and of people are interlinked processes, each interacting in complex ways with colonisation. In bringing attention to these ripple effects of fleeting expeditionary encounters in PNG, we aim to illustrate the embeddedness of the expedition in a series of colonial actions. Expeditions collected evidence of PNG cultures for preservation, while also being entangled in colonial and mission-led processes of systematic endangerment of cultural practices.[10] Administrators moved people about for education and training in colonial centres (including Australia). The act of arriving on a ship and impressing a copy of a song onto a wax cylinder was thus part of much bigger and more consequential processes.

Songs were not just taken away on wax cylinder, but also taken away through replacement by new religious ideologies, and the musical traditions sanctioned by religious and governing institutions. Michael Webb has shown how Christian hymns came to Melanesia in the 19th century from already established missions in Polynesia. And though many ceremonial song practices now centre on hymns,

> Islanders considered the missionaries' hymns an intrusion into local sound spaces. In Melanesia the physical environment is not a neutral entity but rather an active agent; inhabited by spirits, it is a realm of knowledge and power . . . Islanders carefully evaluated the meanings of hymns and began to learn and circulate them as items of powerful new knowledge. (Webb 2015, 283)

Roge and Gulea Kila assert in Vula'a culture:

> [Roge] mourning songs have been taken over by hymns. I know that when I was growing up, the women would cry and hurl themselves or paint themselves or scratch themselves, put dust on themselves. They don't do

---

10 For another discussion of the adjacent objectives of missions, colonial administration and collecting expeditions, see Lamb and Lee 2023, 5.

that anymore. [Gulea] I think it's Christianity . . . they would . . . scratch themselves and beat themselves you know . . . their face, ash or dust. (Kila and Kila 2020)

Figure 7.6 Portrait of a Hula woman wearing a mourning costume. From the Cooke–Daniels Ethnographical Expedition to British New Guinea 1903–1904. Museum number Oc,B119.53 © The Trustees of the British Museum.

Over the course of the 20th century, Vula'a people became increasingly dislocated from the village, and so in the accounts of Vula'a people today, many report a break in connection to cultural practices and speaking of languages that resulted from being sent to boarding school as the colonial imperative for a single-language education took hold (Megarrity 2005). As Deveni Temu explains:

> by the 50s and by the time I went to boarding school in the late 60s, because we were going to boarding school we were leaving so for the young people that were coming up in the village, that got disrupted. (Temu 2022)

Now for the children of Vula'a diaspora living in Australia, the old recordings seem yet further disconnected:

> [Roge] at first when I when we heard it my kids were silent . . . what is that they said, what are you guys listening to?

7 Dispersed sound archives and diaspora communities

[Gulea] . . . like something out of a horror movie, stop the music, my daughter called out! (Kila and Kila 2020)

The recordings themselves are noisy; the wax cylinders recorded more than 100 years ago have been digitised, and even after audio engineers at PARADISEC had worked on removing background noise from the recordings, the voices of ancestors singing and speaking can be hard to make out.[11] As listeners, we may struggle to hear the sounds not only because of the noise of the old technology, but in other ways. Through the noise, we also hear a century of change, the imposition of different moral and spiritual systems, the sounds of new harmonies that render the old ones foreign. The diaspora community add further layers of sound to this trajectory of change, educated in colonial boarding schools implemented during the Australian colonial administration, they are then well positioned to take up professional roles that take them abroad. Their children grow up in a place where those songs are no longer sung, and in places where they no longer have use for the language, as Deveni Temu emotionally recalled in our conversations (Temu 2022).

What is reconnection in this context?

These histories of change, migration, song and colonisation suggest to us challenges to processes of cultural heritage repatriation that might consider not just the home village as a site for reconnection, but also a wider community of speakers and singers. Anne J. Gilliland has suggested, in a "postnational world":

> it may be more appropriate and useful today for the archival field to acknowledge, respect, advocate for and act upon the realities of always-in-motion diasporas of records in which multiple parties have rights, interests and diverging points of view, than to try to negotiate ownership, protection and physical relocation of records across complex and contested histories and boundaries, power imbalances and stewardship capabilities. Such an acknowledgment moves archival discourse about displaced records away from institution- and nation-state-based ideas about singular provenance, sovereignty, inalienable ownership and physical custody. It focuses instead on records as plural and contingent co-created objects that have certain inalienable and universal characteristics. It also promotes the development of mechanisms for providing pluralised access to them regardless of where they are located and addressing future disputes that may arise over records

---

11 The recordings can be heard through the *True Echoes* website and also in the *Toksave – Culture Talks* podcast available here: https://tinyurl.com/3p4hcapv. On the process of removing background noise, see Kell 2022.

that are generated, transmitted and stored through transnational networking and cloud-based technologies. (Gilliland 2017, 180)

In thinking of repatriation of historical recordings to regions with histories of migration, communities are constituted not by those present in the village at any given time, but a larger group of interconnected diaspora – not only because people themselves identify strongly with place and culture (though this is very important), but also because the actions of expeditions and the movement of people are parts of the same history. It is therefore meaningful to return to the people whose life patterns poetically evoke these histories. In the context of recordings made in Hula village, historical processes can nuance the place of digital repatriation.

Van Heekeren has written that singing puts people into relationship with each other and the world (Van Heekeren 2011). What shape does this world take when we imagine Hula village in 1904 and the Vula'a ancestors singing songs for Seligmann? What relationships were those old people enacting in singing for the expedition? And what relationships are enacted by the recordings coming back and being heard now? After listening to the historical recordings and talking at length with us about them, Roge and Gulea Kila offered to prepare in the costumes they had brought with them and perform for us one of the songs in a genre familiar to them from cultural performances in their childhoods.[12]

Figure 7.7 Hula Lekuleku re-enactment by Roge and Gulea Kila, at Sydney Conservatorium of Music, 17 October 2020. Still from video recorded by Jodie Kell.

---

12 See Kell and Gagau 2023.

7 Dispersed sound archives and diaspora communities

Throughout the course of the "True Echoes" project, participants responded to reconnecting with old recordings by singing songs. Singing has been a response to hearing the old recordings and has complemented the work of translating and understanding the historical songs. This confirms something crucial about Vula'a culture, but also something crucial about diaspora. As Tina K. Ramnarine has suggested:

> questions of identity are inextricable from the past and from [a diaspora community member's] relationship to a former homeland, whether or not that home is several times removed through generations. Where the diaspora has formed as the result of violent encounter in which the past has been ruptured, as has been the case in many colonial projects, a sense of diasporic identity has enabled the diasporic subject to feel connected to a precolonial history. (Ramnarine 2007, 3)

In musical scholarship, diaspora studies have largely focused on communities who take their music with them and disseminate and transform it into new cultural contexts (Troutman 2016; Ramnarine 2019). In these diasporic contexts, musical practice is transformed by its movement into new places, and also held onto by people, as they too move around. But recorded songs can capture cultural practices dispersed to the other side of the world and stored in an archive, while communities transform and shift away from performing it. Responses to these recordings may prompt singing of different kinds of songs, while still linking people to language, place and, in the case of Vula'a community, to fishing. That the return of sung records prompted re-singing in both community members in the village and in the diaspora community[13] suggests a broader conceptualisation of community that can be included in acts of digital repatriation. The act of reconnecting to ancestors through old songs reaffirms continuities, but also the continuities of change.

---

13 See examples on the *True Echoes* site: https://tinyurl.com/w9pejddn; https://tinyurl.com/ymmnjttr.

Part II

Music and Song: Knowing Through Analysis

Chapter 8

Endangered songs in the Kathmandu Valley: contexts, histories and meanings of *dāphā bhajan*

Richard Widdess

Introduction

> It is through song, dance and associated ceremony that Indigenous people sustain their cultures and maintain the law and a sense of self within the world. Performance traditions are the foundation of social and personal wellbeing. The preservation of performance traditions is therefore one of the highest priorities for Indigenous people . . . Without immediate action, many Indigenous music and dance traditions are in danger of extinction with potentially destructive consequences for the fabric of Indigenous society and culture. (Garma Forum on Indigenous Performance Research 2002)

Linda Barwick's work on the vocal musics of Australia and Italy encompasses many different aspects of each tradition, and successfully integrates the detail of musical and linguistic analysis with the wider exploration of meanings, contexts and histories. Among her many concerns are the documentation, archiving and making accessible, in collaboration with their owners, of traditions of song performance and composition, in the face of threats to their existence. In the autumn of 2019, the Music Department of SOAS University of London was fortunate to be able to host Barwick for three months as a Leverhulme Visiting Professor, during which she gave a memorable series of four public lectures entitled "The future of endangered songs". A central theme of her discussion was the nature of song itself, what it means to communities and what it achieves that language alone does not.

The theme of endangered *languages* is very familiar at SOAS. The SOAS website was, until recently, forthright on this issue:[1]

> In our languages lies our accumulated wisdom. Each language is a unique expression of the human experience of the world because it embodies information about the culture of its speakers and the knowledge acquired by previous generations. Thus, linguistic diversity constitutes one of the greatest treasures of humanity, an enormous storehouse of our cumulative knowledge of the universe. As a famous linguist once said, each time a language is lost it is "like dropping a bomb on the Louvre".

The idea that music might be similarly endangered, or rather that its endangerment calls for urgent action, seems to be less of a concern to UK ethnomusicologists than to linguists. But given that the loss of a language is likely to threaten the survival of songs sung in that language, and given that music is itself a form of knowledge even without the presence of language, it follows that the above SOAS statement should apply as much to music as to language (in so far as the two can be separated). It is the duty of ethnomusicologists to explain, to ourselves and to a sometimes sceptical public, what kinds of knowledge, what ways of relating to the world, are embodied in the words and music of songs.

So it was enlightening to hear Barwick spell out, for a mixed audience of ethnomusicologists, linguists and anthropologists, just how important songs are as repositories of knowledge, meaning and human experience. Barwick discussed the processes of creating and transmitting songs in changing environments, and the dynamics of community engagement and documentation. In her first lecture she asked: "What is enabled by singing?" In the Indigenous context in Australia, singing enables the "memorialisation and transmission of knowledge embedded in Country", where Country contains "the essence of the ancestors". Country, ancestors, community and the individual emerged from her account as a complex world that songs remember, nurture and continually re-create. Rather than as discrete, unchanging artefacts, she suggested, "we can think of songs as moments in a never-ending flow of knowledge, forms and practices into new contexts".[2]

I am surely not alone in having reviewed my own work in the light of Barwick's lucid analysis. Much of my recent research has centred on the dāphā tradition of

---

1 In 2019 this passage was included in the Linguistics Department webpage. It has since been replaced with other wording.
2 I have consulted my notes made at the time and a video recording of the lectures.

8 Endangered songs in the Kathmandu Valley

Hindu–Buddhist devotional singing in the Kathmandu Valley, Nepal: a tradition of choral hymn-singing, usually performed by around 10–12 male singers, with accompaniment of drum and cymbals, at temples large and small across the region. Here the "never-ending flow" of song is threatened both by long-term social and economic changes, and by the twin disasters of the 2015 earthquake and the Covid-19 pandemic. The earthquake of 7.8 magnitude that struck on 25 April 2015 caused massive destruction and loss of life across many parts of Nepal, including the Kathmandu Valley. Nationally, nearly 9,000 deaths and more than 20,000 injuries are recorded; 800,000 homes, thousands of educational institutions and health centres, and 750 temples or other heritage sites were damaged or destroyed, and 2.8 million people displaced (Hutt, Liechty and Lotter 2021, 7–8; He et al. 2018; Karki et al. 2022). According to dāphā groups themselves, the earthquake was less damaging than the Covid-19 pandemic of 2020–22, which caused at least 12,000 deaths, severely affected the economy and compounded the problems of recovery from the earthquake (Pandey et al. 2022; Eck 2022; Karki et al. 2022). During this period, the performance and training activities of most dāphā groups were interrupted for months, up to two years or more in some cases. In general, both disasters served to exacerbate long-term, pre-existing problems for dāphā groups, such as difficulties in recruiting and training new singers, lack of financial support, and diminishing commitment to singing in the face of modern social and economic pressures.[3]

What then would be lost if dāphā disappeared? What does dāphā singing enable? What kinds of knowledge do dāphā songs embody in their poetry, language, musical structure and performance? How do dāphā songs remember, nurture and continually re-create country, ancestors, community and the individual? Whence comes the resilience that has enabled the singing of traditional songs to be maintained until now, despite many challenges? In this chapter I will briefly sketch some possible answers to such questions.

I draw here from my book *Dāphā: Sacred singing in a south Asian city* (Widdess 2013). This book describes the tradition of dāphā in the town of Bhaktapur; other towns and villages in the Kathmandu Valley have their own dāphā traditions that may differ in detail from the account given here. *Dāphā* offers the results of frequent fieldwork visits to Bhaktapur, including study of performance (vocal and drum), recordings, interviews with some 18 dāphā groups, and historical and linguistic investigations, from 2003 to 2012; acknowledgments to my many advisers and collaborators will be found in the book (pp. xxiii–xxv). This was the

---

3 Information from an ongoing survey by Nutandhar Sharma and the author.

first book-length study of dāphā in English,[4] but it drew inspiration from several prior works on the music of the Newars, especially those of Gert-Matthias Wegner on the drumming traditions of Bhaktapur (1986; 2009; and now 2023), Paul Greene on Buddhist processional music (2003a; 2003b), and Ingemar Grandin on music and media (1989) and on modality (1997).

A number of recent publications have substantially contributed to understanding issues of endangerment, vitality and sustainability of traditional musics around the world.[5] Here I will occasionally refer to a survey of dāphā groups across the Valley, ongoing at the time of writing, addressing such issues in the wake of the 2015 earthquakes and subsequent Covid-19 pandemic. Pending the results of that investigation, I here focus mainly on the meanings of dāphā for its exponents and communities – what would be lost if dāphā disappeared – rather than on its endangerment and sustainability as such.

I take as a starting point Linda Barwick's formulation of country, ancestors, community and the individual as a framework for examining these meanings, modified as necessary to reflect the particular history and cultural conditions of the Kathmandu Valley (in the following section). I then take a sample dāphā song to show how the meanings of a song do not reside solely in its text, but can be transformed by the change in context of performance from palace to local communities. Some of the social processes by which songs have been transmitted over generations are examined next, especially the teaching process that involves the whole community, and the motivations for, and problems in maintaining such transmission. The next section briefly argues that cultural patterns and perceptions of dāphā, and musical performance more widely, underlie its historical transmission and continued survival, and are embodied in the processes of musical performance. Lest it be thought that society at large is indifferent to the fate of dāphā songs, I then note the efforts of Nepali enthusiasts, working together with a local community, to help revive a dāphā group that has been inactive for a generation, and the political meaning that this endeavour may have for them. In the final section I confront the traditional meanings and values embodied in dāphā songs and singing with the realities of endangerment.

---

4 Books on dāphā in Newar or Nepali languages occasionally appear, but being privately published and circulated, they are hard to access. They include collections of dāphā song-texts (Maharjan 2014; Tāmrakār 2002), and notations of dāphā songs (Mānandhar 2015; K. Śākya and J. Śākya 1988; J. Śākya and D. Śākya 1997; Tāmrakār 2017).
5 E.g. Grant 2014; Schippers and Grant 2016; Titon 2020.

Country, ancestors, community and the individual

The Australian Indigenous concept of Country as a spiritual and material home occupied by ancestors and kin is not precisely applicable to the Kathmandu Valley, but there are significant similarities. The Valley is an area of about 665 square kilometres in the foothills of the Himalayan mountain range. Because of its exceptional agricultural fertility and its position on an ancient trade route between India and Tibet, it has been the most urbanised centre in the region from the mid-first millennium AD onwards. From c. 1200 until 1769, the three city-states of Bhaktapur, Lalitpur and Kathmandu competed for political supremacy and cultural superiority, as is vividly demonstrated in many notable works of architecture – palaces and temples – and myriad artistic artefacts in archives, museums and art galleries around the world – manuscripts, sculptures and paintings. For its inhabitants, the Valley, like each city, temple and individual within it, constitutes a microcosmic reflection of the universe, protected by circles of guardian deities and temples (Gutschow 1982, 15–27; Levy 1992); the "country" is thus a home infused with spiritual significance, a significance often articulated through processional music (Greene 2003a; Wegner 2009). Dāphā songs, through their words, take the singer on imaginative virtual pilgrimage to deities and shrines in distant parts of the Valley, just as community groups often hire a bus to take them there physically on a religious holiday outing (Widdess 2013, 199).

For at least 1,500 years the Kathmandu Valley, known to them as *Nepāl*, has been home to the ethnic group known as the Newars, who practise a combination of Hindu and Buddhist religions.[6] For generations the souls of their *ancestors* have been honoured through the maintenance of clan rituals and other cultural traditions (including dāphā). A lineage of local rulers,[7] the Mallas, ruled the three cities from the 12th to the 18th centuries. In 1768–69, the Newars were defeated by an empire builder from further west, the Gorkhali king Pṛthvī Nārāyan Shāh, who united the three cities, and added a sizeable empire beyond the Valley, centred

---

6 At 1.32 million, Newars constitute about 5 per cent of the total population of Nepal (Government of Nepal 2014). Newars probably account for about half of the population of the Kathmandu Valley. In Bhaktapur, Newars numbered 139,000 out of 304,000 in total; about half the Newar population of Bhaktapur are farmers. Hinduism, in its various forms, and Buddhism are distinguishable at the upper levels of the Newar caste system; at lower levels, such as the farmer community, they are not thought of as different religions, but rather as complementary aspects of a common religious culture. Musicians in particular regularly participate in performances and festivals of both religions: the same dāphā groups sing songs to Śiva and Karuṇāmaya (Avalokiteśvara) with similar devotion.

7 The Mallas were not strictly Newars, their ancestors having arrived from the Mithila region of India in the 13th century.

on Kathmandu. The mountainous terrain and the Gorkha armies protected this much-enlarged Nepal from foreign conquest, but a process of internal colonisation rendered the Newars a suppressed minority. The Shāh dynasty remained on the throne throughout the 19th and 20th centuries. But from 1849 the Rāna clan of oligarchs effectively controlled the country, imposing a policy of national isolation and internal suppression of dissent, until the restoration of the monarchy in 1951. Emerging from a century of poverty and oppression, the Newar farmers, key bearers of musical traditions including dāphā, benefited from land reforms that made them, in the 1960s and 1970s, land owners for the first time; but the same reforms deprived many music groups of land that had been dedicated to support them, by former rulers and pious ancestors (Widdess 2013, 111–113). Following the advent of democratic government in 1991, Nepal faced a succession of major challenges, including a civil war from 1996 to 2006, the deaths of King Birendra and most of his family at the hands of his son in 2001, a suspension of democracy by King Gyanendra in 2005, abolition of the monarchy and transition to a republic in 2008, and most recently, the earthquake of 2015 and the Covid-19 pandemic of 2020–22. Thus after a long period of stasis and hardship under the Rānas, Newars experienced a period of growing prosperity but dramatic change. How far ancestral traditions like dāphā can be maintained in such a volatile world remains to be seen.

The Newar *community* is hierarchically organised in a complex caste system. In Bhaktapur, the majority of dāphā groups belong to the middle-ranking castes of farmers, who traditionally live in compact neighbourhoods in the city; the men go out to work in the fields during daylight hours, so singing dāphā, which is traditionally a male activity, has to take place in the early morning or evening. Singing dāphā is, or was, central to the social and religious life of a farmers' neighbourhood. According to local tradition (Widdess 2013, 105–106), an ancient king decreed that every neighbourhood should provide the four necessities of social life, illustrated in Figure 8.1: a source of water (here, the well), a temple (here, a small shrine of the god Gaṇeśa), a platform providing shelter for trade or social activities (there are two in this picture), and a dāphā group (here sitting to sing on one of the platforms in the early morning). As recently as the 1980s, most farmer neighbourhoods, and some lower caste communities as well, still supported at least one dāphā group, and there was a total of at least 70 such groups around the city.[8] The repertoire of a group often includes songs specifically addressed to

---

8 Information from a survey carried out by G-M. Wegner in 1984. See Widdess and Sharma 2024. For further details drawn from this survey, see below, "Endangerment, survival and revival".

the deity of the local temple, alongside those addressed to other deities, and the local temple festival will be especially celebrated (Widdess 2013, 229–230); there are thus direct links between temple, songs and local community. But today, in Bhaktapur and other cities, residents of caste-based neighbourhoods increasingly use their wealth to move to other areas, potentially weakening their ties to their ancestral neighbourhoods. Local festivals and their attendant music can serve to sustain such ties (Parish 1994, 79).

Figure 8.1 Dāphā in the community: early morning in Lākvalāchẽ neighbourhood, Bhaktapur, 2010. Note the small Gaṇeśa temple (centre, with clock), well (centre right), two covered platforms (left and right), dāphā group (left). Photo: Richard Widdess.

Dāphā performance depends, of course, on *individuals*, who must undergo a special training before being allowed to participate in performance. A significant investment of time and money, by both individuals and the community, is required for transmitting the tradition (see further below, "Social processes"). In some groups, a regular financial payment is required from individuals to subvent the group's expenses, and fines may be imposed for non-participation. But dāphā singing is not about individuals. Voices are expected to blend so that no one voice predominates. Instrumental accompanists and singers of the introductory *rāg* melodies need appropriate knowledge and skills for their special roles, but they are not applauded as soloists. Individuals who are especially knowledgeable are respected as *gurus* (teachers), but performance is a musical expression of community, not individuality. And in stark contrast to the Australian Indigenous and many other music traditions, the composition of new dāphā songs is rare. Songs here are a heritage from the past: according to the author's name that occurs in the last line of many songs, they are mainly attributed to a variety of Malla and Shāh kings, from the early 17th to 19th centuries (see "Social processes").

A dāphā song

Although dāphā singing is now mainly an activity of the farmer communities, it did not originate in that context. Many aspects of the songs, including their melodic and rhythmic structure, and above all their texts, show that they originated in the palaces of the later Malla kings (c. 1600–1769) and their Shāh successors (1769–c. 1850) (Widdess 2013, 31–55). Court musicians, some of them probably from India (Grandin 1997), and court poets writing in the courtly languages Sanskrit, Hindi and Old Newari, were most likely involved in their composition, although they are signed mainly by kings. These languages are incompletely understood by the singers today, and the songs take on meanings and functions more relevant to the farmers.[9]

To take a specific example, the song "Ganamani" is one of the best known and most frequently performed songs in the Bhaktapur dāphā repertoire (Widdess 2013, 263–268). Figure 8.2 represents the main musical materials, text and translation of the song.[10]

---

9 It is not known how far, if at all, dāphā performance practice may have changed during the three centuries of its existence. Many aspects of that practice are shared with other pre-modern genres of South Asian devotional singing, suggesting that they may be original features. Such aspects include the formal structure of the song, with refrain; the antiphonal alternation between two sub-groups of singers; and the multiple repetitions of each line (see "Music and cultural patterns", below).

10 The translation of the text, based on four manuscript songbooks, is by Dr Nutandhar Sharma. The text in the music example is the version sung by the Dattātreya dāphā group. For the reconstructed text see Widdess 2013, 263.

8 Endangered songs in the Kathmandu Valley

Translation by Nutandhar Sharma:

Refrain: O Mother with big eyes, you are the jewel of the retinues, esoteric, unapproachable and deep.

1. The sages and the gods of [the different] directions do not perform devotion and meditation for other [gods beside her]. [If you] meditate on [her], repeat [her] name, do penance, keep attention [and] feeling [on her], [then you will] get wealth, offspring and compassion. O Mother!

2. [I] bow down [to you,] pure queen and mistress of the lord of the world, with graceful face. Cutting innumerable heads of the evil ones, Śivā shines as first among all gods. || 2 ||

3. [You are] seated on all [kinds of animals including] lion, snake, elephant, bull, and holding all [kinds of] weapons. There is no other source of salvation for Śrī Ranajita, O [you who are] pervasive over [all] fourteen [directions]. || 3 ||

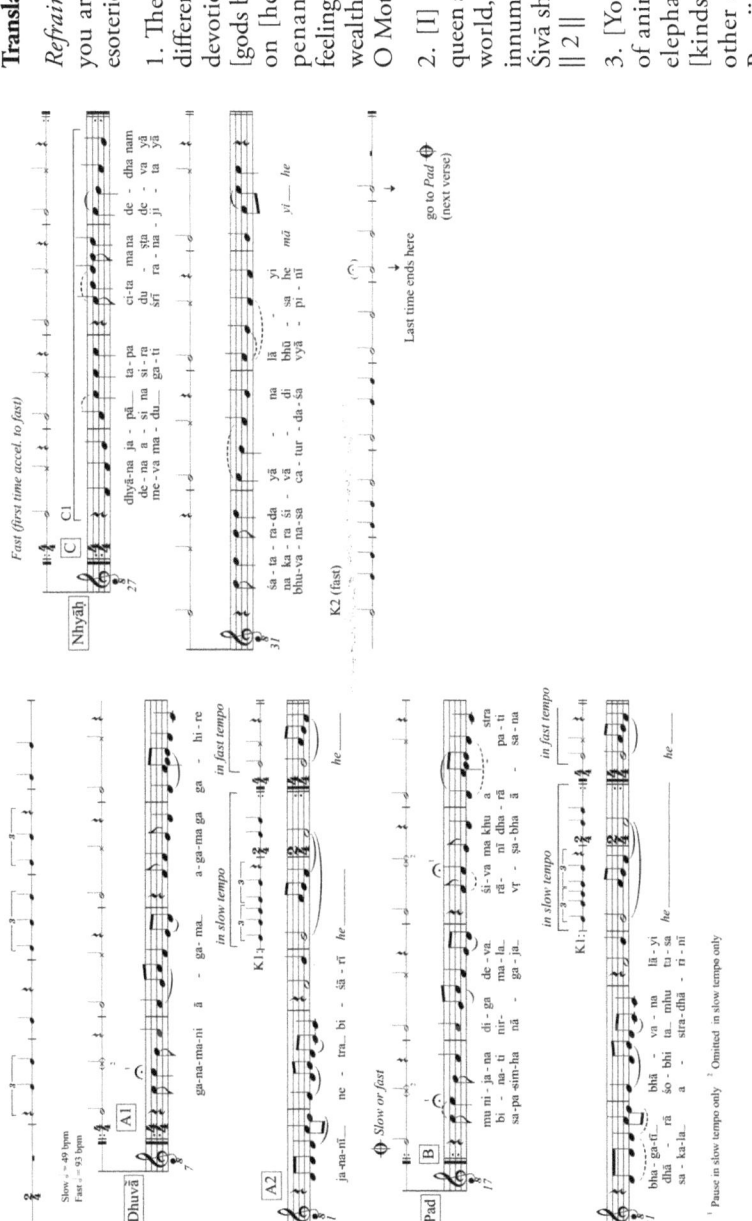

Figure 8.2 The dāphā song "Ganamaṇi". *Rāg*: Āsāvarī. *Tāl*: Cvakh. As sung by the Dattātreya Temple dāphā group, Bhaktapur. Transcription: author. See Widdess 2013, 263–268.

Several features of performance practice distinguish dāphā from other genres of devotional song in the Kathmandu Valley. At the outset, one or two singers sing the *rāg*, a non-metrical introduction, sung to non-lexical vocables, that outlines the melodic material or mode of the song. Following a brief instrumental introduction, the song is then sung by two sub-groups of singers, sitting facing each other (Figure 8.3); they sing alternately, with much repetition of each line of the song, and periodic changes of tempo from slow to fast and vice versa (see "Music and cultural patterns", below). The words of the song are written in a folding book (*thyāsaphu*), one for each sub-group of the singers. Some of the singers play cymbals, of two sizes (*tāḥ* and *jhyālīcā*), marking and decorating the metrical structure, the *tāl* (the words *rāg* and *tāl* come from the Indian classical music tradition). Between the two groups, and directing their performance, sits the drum player, who plays an elaborate, largely pre-composed accompaniment on the barrel-drum *lālākhī*.[11] The style of singing and playing is loud, forceful and, in the fast portion of each verse, energetic.

Figure 8.3 The Dattātreya Temple dāphā group (Dattātreya Navadāphā Khalaḥ), Bhaktapur, 2012. Photo: Richard Widdess.

---

11 For further details of the lālākhī and its repertoire see Wegner 2023.

The language of "Ganamani" is a mixture of Sanskrit, Hindi and Old Newari. As in the songs of Kathleen Fitz Nappanangka analysed by Barwick in her SOAS lectures, the multiplicity of languages contributes to the song's meaning, but here they all evoke the same originary milieu: not the direct ancestors of the farmers, but the vanished world of a courtly, literate, aristocratic and autocratic Newar elite. The last verse of the song tells us that it was composed by Ranjit Malla, the last Newar king of Bhaktapur, who was driven into exile by the invading Gorkhalis in 1769. Ranjit was a prolific poet-composer, and his songs still form the bulk of the dāphā repertoire in Bhaktapur: legend has it that as the cannons of Pṛthvī Nārāyan Shāh were pounding the gates of Bhaktapur, Ranjit Malla was sitting in his palace singing rāgs and dāphā songs. Perhaps "Ganamani" was one of the songs he sang, as it is a hymn of praise to the protecting deity of the royal lineage, the goddess Bhagavatī or Taleju, whose temple is in the palace; Ranjit addresses her as the all-powerful source of his salvation. Figure 8.4a is a representation of Taleju on the "Golden Gate" of her temple in the royal palace, a gate erected by Ranjit Malla in 1753.

None of this historical context is of direct relevance to present-day farmers, who understand the song as dedicated to Gaṇeśa, the elephant-headed son of Śiva (Figure 8.4b). Gaṇeśa is traditionally venerated at the start of any undertaking to ensure its success through his blessings, and he is consequently one of the most popular Hindu deities in Bhaktapur. He is especially popular with farmers, whose lives literally depend on the success of their labour. Almost every farmers' neighbourhood has a small shrine to this deity at its heart (see Figure 8.1), whereas Taleju is only to be found in the royal palace. Dāphā groups sing "Ganamani" at shrines of Gaṇeśa, both in their own neighbourhood and when they visit other neighbourhoods in Bhaktapur; and it is one of the first songs that beginners are taught, to ensure the success of their learning endeavours. This ambiguity or re-assignment of meaning is probably due to the first word of the song, "*Ganamani*", literally "jewel of the multitude". The "multitude" (*gaṇa*) is Śiva's army of lesser deities, demons and ghosts, and Gaṇeśa is traditionally its leader (which is what his name means); so the "jewel of the multitude" could plausibly refer to him. But the rest of the song text, with its repeated cry "O Mother!", is clearly addressed to a goddess, a goddess so powerful that she commands Śiva's legions.[12]

---

12 The goddess is also addressed in the song as Śivā (in Sanskrit, the feminine-gender form of the name Śiva), denoting the female source (śakti) of Śiva's power and energy.

Figure 8.4 (a) The goddess Taleju, as represented on the Golden Gate, Darbar Square, Bhaktapur (1753). Photo: Richard Widdess. **(b)** The elephant-headed god Gaṇeśa. Painted book cover by Madhu Chitrakar, 2010. Photo: Richard Widdess.

In this way, reconstruction and translation of dāphā texts can reveal layers of historical and cultural meaning, ambiguity or multiple interpretation. This is possible because, unlike the songs of a living composer, dāphā songs are historical artefacts, treasured for their antiquity, for which old meanings can be forgotten and new ones created.

Dāphā singers proudly point to the names of royal composers like Ranjit Malla in their songs, just as they take pride in the historical temples and palaces at the centre of the city, built by the same kings (Widdess 2013, 41, 201). Such songs evoke a world of ancestors, even if separated from the farmers both in time and in social rank. But there are few composers of dāphā songs today. What matters now is not the composition of new songs, but what Linda Barwick called the "never-ending flow of knowledge, forms and practices into new contexts".

Social processes

So why has the context of dāphā performance changed from palace to farmers' neighbourhoods, and why is the continuation of performance so important? At the Dattātreya Temple, one of the oldest (possibly 15th century) and most important temples in Bhaktapur, a dāphā group composed of farmers sings every evening, 365 days in the year – except when prevented by national calamity, such as an earthquake or pandemic, or instructed to pause by the central government (formerly, the king) (Widdess 2013, 55). It is likely that the dāphā tradition at this temple goes back at least to the 18th century, and would have been patronised by both the late Malla and the early Shāh kings. In the 19th century the group was composed of high-caste merchants who lived in the square adjacent to the temple. In 1846 King Rājendra Shāh donated land to the group to support its expenses, and appointed a singer to be its leader, stressing that the group should perform daily, without interruption, in the service of God, but also praising the king. Part of the deal, then, was that the group should glorify not only the gods but also the current rulers, presumably through singing songs composed by or about them and containing their names. By the mid-19th century, under the Rāna oligarchy, the composition of such songs had ceased, and an exodus of higher castes from Bhaktapur to the national capital, Kathmandu, had begun. By the early 20th century, farmers were taking the places of the high-caste singers, but continuing their duty to sing daily, which they maintain as far as possible in the present day (Widdess 2013, 47–55).

In this way, the larger temples of Bhaktapur maintain, at some remove, the Malla-period tradition of dāphā singing, which the early Shāh kings of Kathmandu continued to patronise for their own glorification and spiritual benefit. The practice of dāphā spread to the farmer castes partly because they provided services to their high-caste landlords and emulated their culture (Gellner and Pradhan 1995), and partly because religious singing exempted them from a system of forced labour (*jhārā*) (Widdess 2013, 51–55). Now, following social and land reforms in the 1960s, farmers, themselves the landowners, are selling their land for building (to accommodate a rapidly expanding, largely incoming population), and with greater wealth and education are rapidly leaving behind both the profession of farming and the cultural traditions that went with it. Like the higher castes before them, they are increasingly heading for office jobs in Kathmandu, 12 kilometres down the road, instead of to their fields.

Aside from these large-scale temporal and social changes, what does dāphā mean to a neighbourhood community of farmers? Many neighbourhood communities regard it as a matter of their identity and prestige to preserve their own dāphā tradition, and also as a debt, owed to their ancestors, which they will in turn demand of their own children. Dāphā singer Jagannath Lachhimasyu explained to me that his uncle and grandfather specifically charged him to continue the musical tradition by which their name and fame would be remembered (interview 27/08/2010; Widdess 2013, 201). In the words of anthropologist Stephen Parish (1994, 95), "for Newars . . . harm to tradition is tantamount to harm to persons, to the family line – which includes the dead and those yet to be born".

Passing on the tradition is no simple matter. Training in dāphā[13] is an elaborate social process, involving recruitment of a group of students, financial support from their parents and the whole neighbourhood, six to 12 months of daily teaching sessions, and many rituals and feasts: a process so costly, in money, time and energy, that it can only be undertaken at intervals of around 10 years.[14] These days, they happen even more rarely, and the young boys who are taught to sing typically lose interest in dāphā very rapidly, given the competing attractions and demands of cricket, films, mobile phones and school exams (some may come back to dāphā later in life). Yet until recently many neighbourhoods still regarded a training in dāphā or other musical genres as an essential rite of passage for their male children, whereby they gained both the religious and social knowledge that they needed to become fully integrated members of society (Grandin 1989; Bernède 1997).

In 2003 the Yāchẽ neighbourhood of Bhaktapur held a *dāphā pidane pūjā*, an initiation ritual[15] that marks the end of a training program (Figure 8.5). This included the first performance in public of a group of young boys and adolescents who had completed a nine-month training of daily lessons in dāphā singing or playing, during which they learned 55 songs. Twenty-six vocal students, 18 drummers and three natural trumpet (*pvaṅā*) players, ranging in age from 6 to 20 years, were initiated. The day-long religious ritual and musical performance was witnessed by the boys' female relatives; the menfolk were busy in their fields or offices, apart from the priests and the dāphā teachers, the latter identified in Figure 8.5 by their white turbans. Afterwards, the students were presented with traditional gifts to mark their new status as initiates in music – a white turban, a

---

13 For a fuller account of dāphā training see Widdess 2013, 207–17. On Newar musical training more generally, see also Bernède 1997; Grandin 1989, 83–85; Wegner 1986, 12–17.

14 In the ongoing survey of dāphā groups across the Kathmandu Valley, some groups recorded a shorter interval between training programs.

15 This ritual, traditionally performed when learning any musical genre, is an initiation to Nāsaḥdyah, Śiva in his role as deity of music and dance. Once initiated, the student is free to take part in public performance, and may gain the "blessings of Nāsaḥdyaḥ" (see below, "Music and cultural patterns").

Nepali cap, a bowl of sweet yoghourt (a local delicacy) and a few coins followed by a communal feast for 130 people (Widdess 2013, 212–216).

Figure 8.5 Dāphā in the community: concluding initiation ceremony (*pidane pūjā*) of a dāphā training program. Bhaktapur, 2003. Photo: Richard Widdess.

This is the traditional pattern for training and initiation in any Newar musical genre, vocal or instrumental. But it is a matter of debate how much longer the pattern can be maintained in the modern world, given the particular ideology associated with music in Newar culture. Music is considered esoteric and powerful spiritual knowledge: incomplete knowledge is considered dangerous to the mental health of the individual (Widdess 2013, 209). The senior group members who teach dāphā singing and instrumental playing (*guru*s) therefore insist on secrecy during the teaching process, and daily, oral, rote learning for months until sufficient repertoire has been memorised. This process must be framed by elaborate rituals like the *pidane pūjā,* and associated feasts that not only support life but also re-affirm social relations and belonging. Once started, the training program must be completed, however long it takes; *guru*s are reluctant to start training if they are not confident that the pupils will stay the course. And while the *guru*s receive only a symbolic payment for their efforts, the cost of the rituals (including animal sacrifice and feasts) is a significant burden for the community (Widdess 2013, 208). Despite these obstacles, *pidane pūjā*s still happen from to time to time

(Widdess 2013, 137); but many groups interviewed in 2022, from across the Valley, did not know when they would next be able to hold one, and often had not done so for many years. The recent earthquakes and pandemic had forced even the most active groups to interrupt or postpone their teaching schedules.[16] As Grant (2014, 48) has observed, learning and teaching are the "cornerstones of sustainability" for both languages and music genres.

Music and cultural patterns

So what is it about singing dāphā that makes it an appropriate form of enculturation by which the individual is absorbed into the community? Among the defining characteristics of dāphā are the antiphonal alternation between the two sub-groups of singers; multiple repetitions of each line of the song, according to a set pattern; and changes of tempo between slow and fast at prescribed points in the pattern. Figure 8.6 represents the repetition pattern, reading from left to right, for one verse of "Ganamani". The right and left sub-groups of singers sing alternately, punctuated by instrumental interjections, and with several changes of tempo. Thus performance of any song demands not only memorisation of the song, but intense concentration to avoid going wrong in the repetition pattern, and an equal contribution from each participant: there are no soloists, and each sub-group sings the same number of repetitions as the other, in varied order. Thus the student learns to perform a role in a group, and interact meaningfully with others. He learns to be a team player, to contribute without standing out from his peers.[17]

Newars say that a person who cannot coordinate with others, act reliably or behave socially in a gracious or appropriate manner is a person "out of tune" or "out of time". Conversely, one who has learned to sing or play music will also acquire interpersonal skills, charisma and respect in the community; one who has these qualities is "blessed by Nāsaḥdyaḥ", the god of music and dance (Widdess 2013, 120–121, 204). The importance of making an equal contribution to a collaborative social enterprise extends to the social organisation of the dāphā group, where onerous duties such as organising and paying for a feast are allocated to every member in turn, according to a written schedule. This reciprocity also applies to non-musical activities. Thus, if a farmer needs to take the help of a neighbour for a major agricultural task, he will reciprocate by working an equal number of hours in the neighbour's fields at some future date (Widdess 2013, 121–122).

---

16   Information from the ongoing dāphā survey project.
17   When friends and I recently made a short film featuring the Dattātreya group, the group leaders criticised our audio balance because we had allowed some voices to be more prominent than the others. See Sowa, Sowa and Widdess 2021.

8 Endangered songs in the Kathmandu Valley

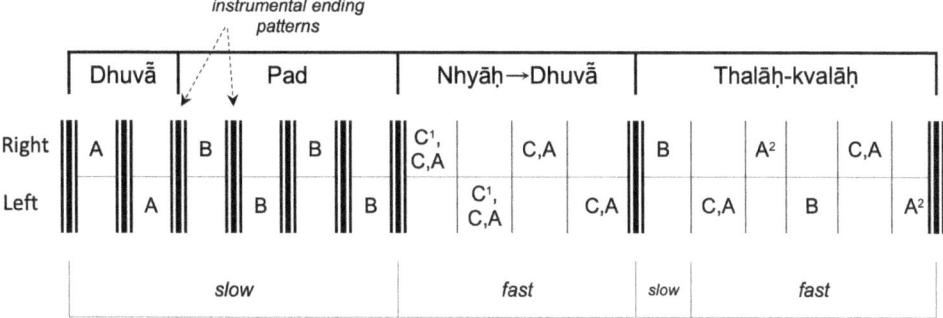

Right, Left = sub-groups of singers
A, B, C = Sections of song: A = Refrain (*Dhuvā̃*), B = Line 1 (*Pad*), C = Line 2 (*Nhyāḥ*)
Thalāḥ-kvalāḥ = permutation of preceding elements

Figure 8.6 Repetition pattern for first verse of "Ganamani" (see Figure 8.2). For vv. 2 and 3, repeat from *Pad*.

As a Bhaktapurian told Steven Parish (1994, 81), if someone is building a house, neighbours will come to help, even if help isn't really needed, because survival in society depends on reciprocity and mutual support. This is *dharma*, moral duty, without which one cannot survive.

These are some of the life lessons and cultural patterns that Newars say are inculcated through music. Others might include respect for the teachers, their knowledge and skills, and for elders generally; education in the religious beliefs and observances of Newar Hinduism and Buddhism; and understanding of the social and religious rituals that consecrate every important act. It is striking that not only the dāphā group as an institution, but also the process of musical performance, with its balanced but alternating roles, seems designed to articulate these wider cultural patterns.

Endangerment, survival and revival

Up to this point, for clarity of presentation, I have uncritically accepted the endangerment narrative in relation to dāphā performance. And indeed there is abundant evidence for a significant decline in the tradition. Dāphā singers themselves recognise this. They freely admit to generational attrition of musical knowledge. Only a small proportion of the hundreds of songs in manuscript songbooks are still sung; in particular, of the many heterometric songs called *gvārā* (in which as many as 11 different *tāls* may be combined: Widdess 2019), only a few are commonly performed. Recruitment of new singers and instrumentalists is increasingly problematic, and of those trained, only a few continue to participate on a regular basis. Government land reforms have deprived many dāphā societies (*guthi*) of the land that previously subvented their expenses. Singers have told me that within 15 or 20 years, dāphā will be "gone" (see Grandin 1989, 83).

And yet the tradition survives with remarkable tenacity. According to a survey of dāphā groups in Bhaktapur carried out by Gert-Matthias Wegner in 1984, and repeated by Carol Tingey in 1992 and by me in 2004,[18] the total number of dāphā group members across 70 groups in 1984 was 3,061. In 1992 this total had declined to 3,021. By 2004 a further decline to 2,646 had occurred. The total number of dāphā performances per year, across all groups, tells a similar story, declining over the same period from 9,116 to 6,684. But this is still an impressive total. Only one group had ceased to function altogether. Is the endangerment narrative a myth?

Survey evidence must be treated with caution. While in some groups, membership is voluntary, in others, it is determined by the number of households in the neighbourhood, with each household obliged by tradition to supply one notional member, even if they do not participate musically. The latter groups thus present an impression of stable membership that may not reflect reality. Similarly each group has a traditional schedule of performances on specific days each year; whether every scheduled performance is actually held is another matter, as it depends on the attendance of a sufficient number of singers, and a competent drum player. The truth about decline lies somewhere between the extremes of pessimistic popular belief and over-optimistic survey statistics.

But while survival depends on sustained membership and continuing performance, revival does not. A group may fall into abeyance for some time, whether months, years or decades, but start up again on the initiative of committed individuals. Some groups are considering enlarging their membership by recruiting female singers, despite traditional restrictions on female behaviour, especially after marriage, which in the past made public music performance quite impossible for Newar women. This barrier to female performance has been relaxing in other genres of Newar music since the 1990s, both in Bhaktapur and elsewhere in the Valley, but only recently in dāphā; there are reports now of a small number of women's groups, including one at the Dattātreya temple in Bhaktapur. There are also a number of female drum players.

Other incipient initiatives include efforts by elite Nepalis to document dāphā traditions and to foster the revival of particular groups, as a reaction to the perceived

---

18 The survey was based on a questionnaire devised by Wegner, as part of a survey of all music genres practised in Bhaktapur. Responses were elicited orally from senior dāphā-group members by a Newar research assistant. The same questions were asked at each re-survey. An online version of the dataset is accessible in Widdess and Sharma 2024.

endangerment of an important component of national cultural heritage.[19] From 2021 to the time of writing, a series of dāphā performances, online discussions, lectures, Facebook postings, YouTube videos and other events has been organised by a Kathmandu-based association called Folk Lok, under the title "Dapha Calling". This initiative originated in response to an appeal for assistance by the Taḥnāni Dāphā group of Kirtipur. Pushpa Palanchoke (2021) has described how this dāphā group rebuilt its performance platform and teaching space, and accepted the help of outsiders to the community, for example in transcribing and recording the repertoire. Particularly striking in this case is the opening of the group's membership for the first time to women, necessitating the first training program to be undertaken by the group for 40 years. The program attracted 30 women trainees and 12 youngsters aged 12–20, including three who are not Newar. The Dattātreya women's group from Bhaktapur performed at the inauguration of the training program (Figure 8.7).

Figure 8.7 The Dattātreya Temple women's dāphā group from Bhaktapur perform for the inauguration of a training program for a new women's dāphā group in Taḥnāni tol, Kirtipur, 2021. Photo: Folk Lok Artist.

---

19 Newar culture is regarded as part of Nepali national heritage when it comes to the prime tourist attractions of architectural monuments such as temples, or visually impressive performances of masked dances. As yet dāphā attracts less national prestige as it does not lend itself readily to de-contextualised, presentational performance.

In her 2021 presentation (to a Boston University conference, "Music, Spirituality and Wellbeing"), Palanchoke argued that the decline of Newar cultural traditions such as dāphā is the result of a process of "Hindu-Brahmanical colonialism" internal to Nepal, following the Gorkhali conquest of the Valley in 1768–69 and the subsequent religious, political and social subjugation of Newar society. This internal colonisation involved gender and caste restrictions, prohibitions on Newar language, and the imposition of Indian classical and Western military music in place of Newar traditional music, forcing Newar traditions to be practised in seclusion if at all. The current revival efforts of groups such as the Taḥnāni Dāphā group, and the Folk Lok organisation, could thus be seen, Palanchoke argues (2021), as a process of internal self-decolonisation. Such revivalist and decolonising initiatives mitigate the prevailing assumption of inevitable decline, and indicate that dāphā remains meaningful to Newar communities as a symbol of their history and identity.

Conclusion

The initiatives of Folk Lok and other individuals and groups are a welcome sign that dāphā songs may have a future as well as a distinguished past. That many groups have so far survived the challenges of the post-1951 era demonstrates the resilience of the genre and the continued support, in some measure, of local communities. But the dangers cannot be ignored. Of the 12 factors affecting the vitality of music genres discussed by Grant (2014, 111–126), the majority elicit concern in relation to dāphā. We have seen that intergenerational transmission (Grant's first factor) is under grave threat; without it, sustainability is impossible. Decline in the number of musicians and others engaged in the genre (factors 2 and 3) follow from faltering transmission. While performance contexts and functions of the genre remain relatively stable (factor 5), reduction in the number of performers imperils the fulfilment of those functions. Without adequate transmission, musical knowledge and skills (factor 8) also decline, leading to change in music practices (factor 4): for example, few singers now know the unmetred, wordless *rāg* melodies with which each song should be prefaced. While the mass media and music industry (factor 6) have so far had little impact on a genre focused on small local communities, government and institutional policies (factor 9) have not compensated, in most cases, for the depletion of financial and other resources (factor 7) following the mid-20th-century land reforms.[20] Grant's 10th factor, the attitudes and perceptions

---

20 The ongoing survey of dāphā groups has identified that some groups in Kathmandu and Lalitpur do receive financial support from the local municipalities. It is not yet clear on what basis this support is provided.

of community members towards the genre, is hard to assess in view of conflicting evidence (which in turn reflects conflicting attitudes), but even a positive consensus is vulnerable to the gradual dispersal of neighbourhood communities. Where such communities persist, positive attitudes towards dāphā may be reinforced by interest and support from relevant outsiders (factor 11), Nepali or foreign, and the sense of local pride that they may arouse. Outside interest is starting to include documentation (factor 12), in the form of recordings, notations and texts of songs, and publications. It is too early to know how effective such initiatives may be.

In conclusion, I argue that dāphā songs, like the Australian Indigenous songs that Linda Barwick has so often written and spoken about, would represent a tragic loss were they to disappear, because of the cultural knowledge and moral principles bound up in them and their associated performance practices. They enable the commemoration of the *country* of Nepal, especially the Kathmandu Valley, in which the gods reside in their innumerable temples; and of the *ancestors*, both the long-dead Newar kings and their vanished courtly world, and the more recent forebears of the singers themselves. Through the complex process of performance, dāphā embodies the principles of reciprocity and mutual dependence that Newars believe are essential for the survival of the individual within society, rather as team sports do in Western societies; and through training and initiation into music, the *individual* learns the social knowledge and skills that enculturate him or her into membership of the adult *community*. Though differently defined and conceived, and formed through very different histories, in both Nepal and Australia, country, ancestors, community and the individual are all evoked or engaged in the complex world that songs remember, nurture and continually re-create through their transmission and performance. And in the course of revivalist initiatives, the singing tradition itself is re-created as part of the "never-ending flow of knowledge, forms and practices into new contexts".

Acknowledgements

I am deeply indebted to all those who have helped me in my research on dāphā over many years: especially my principal research collaborators, Shamsher Bahadur Nhuchen Pradhan (Bhaktapur) and Dr Nutandhar Sharma (Lalitpur), and the many dāphā gurus who have patiently answered our questions. I thank Pushpa Palanchoke for Figure 8.7, and associated information; and the reviewers of this chapter for their helpful comments. I gratefully acknowledge the Leverhulme Foundation's award of a visiting professorship for Linda Barwick in 2019.

Chapter 9

Agents of song: exploring the cultural meanings of Arandic verbs of vocal production

Jennifer Green and Myfany Turpin

Introduction

In traditional Aboriginal songs and in narratives such as sand stories, singers and narrators deftly switch between vocal styles and manipulate their voices to add texture or "flavour" to their performances, drawing on their contextual knowledge of the genres in which these styles typically occur. Our research on these forms of verbal art has shown that the boundaries between talking, singing and humming are not always clear-cut. Several performances that Arandic speakers hesitated to call "singing", one of which is described in detail by Green (2014, 209–219), exemplified this puzzle. In this Anmatyerr sand story, the narrator draws on the ground as she "sings" the entire text, although there are none of the standard features associated with Arandic ceremonial songs, such as repeated lines of rhythmic text and poetic vocabulary. A short extract, which seems to consist entirely of ordinary spoken language set to music, is shown in Figure 9.1.[1] As English speakers, we could find no better word than "sing" as a cover term for the acoustic complexity of this event. This observation led us to begin further investigations into the ways that speakers of Arandic languages carve up the acoustic spectrum of the human

---

1 Archival session name: TYEP-20070916. This line begins at bar 56. See Green 2014, 214–215. The transcription is transposed up a semitone for ease of reading.

voice, and how verbs of vocal production, such as "talk", "sing" and "hum" may refer to sounds produced by various other entities, both animate and inanimate.

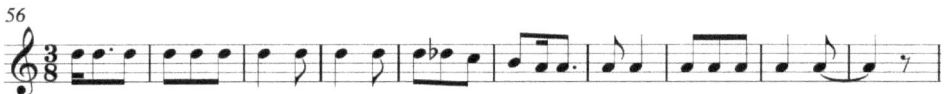

a ke rre na ya ngerr pu rern te tya rtin te tya te ke le nga ki nye ma pa pe nhe

Kwerr	*inang*	*rrpwer-rntw-etyart*	*rntw-etyart*	*kel*	*inang*
girl	3plNOM	pl-dance-PST:HAB	dance-PST:HAB	then	3plNOM

akeweny	*map-apenh-e*
poor.thing	many-SYMP-ART

"The women danced backwards and forwards, the dear things." (Green 2014, 214–215)

Figure 9.1 A segment of an Anmatyerr sand story performed by Janie Mpetyan Briscoe in 2007.

The issue of how verbs of vocal production are applied to Australian Indigenous vocal practices was also encountered by Linda Barwick's supervisor and mentor, musicologist Catherine Ellis, who worked with Antikirinya performers in the north of South Australia in the 1960s. Ellis noted that the correct presentation of "a song" accesses the creative power of the Dreaming and releases the power of the song. For this to happen, the rhythmic, melodic and textual elements of a performance all needed to be "interlocked". "If the structures are not completely interlocked", she wrote, "the performing may, for example, be described as 'sighing' or 'crying' or 'talking' or 'humming', or simply as 'bad'" (Ellis 1984, 152–153). Ellis also found that forms of Antikirinya storytelling, which English speakers might consider to be sung, were not regarded as singing by Antikirinya speakers, but rather as "talking" or "sighing" (Ellis 1985, 61).

The lack of fit between English "sing" and equivalents in other languages has led musicologists working in various other parts of the world to investigate verbs of vocal production (Seeger 1986; Villepastour 2014; Rumsey and Niles 2011). Lundström and Svantesson pointed out that the term "song" is often problematic and may be misleading (Lundström and Svantesson 2022, 2).[2] As has been eloquently argued by Feld in his analysis of sound among the Kaluli of Papua New Guinea, categories of sound are socially constructed and "shared to greater or lesser degrees by natural, animal, and human agents" (Feld 1984, 385–389). What

---

2 Even broader than this is the lack of fit between words for "music" across languages. See Sorce-Keller, this volume.

Feld has identified as "visual-auditory-sensate relationships between people and environment" and "cosmological associations" are fundamental to understanding the complexity of soundscapes and their social relevance (1984, 387). One needs to consider the whole spectrum of a culture's vocal practices, including sounds made by humans as well as by other animate and inanimate beings. As we will demonstrate in this chapter, this is certainly the case in Indigenous Australia, where ownership and agency in what we broadly term forms of "vocal production" can be understood in terms of the complex interrelationships between humans and other species. In an edited volume dedicated to Catherine Ellis, Barwick and Marett stated:

> The very ephemerality of sound draws attention to the evanescence of existence itself. It is this quality of sound that gives singing its potential to empower, to draw us towards our own essence and the essence of the world – the essence known as the Dreaming in Aboriginal culture. (Barwick and Marett 1995, 4–5)

At the lexical level, while there has been much written about the semantics and polysemy of verbs of perception (for example, Evans and Wilkins 2000), less attention has been paid to verbs of vocal production. Two important questions arise: how do the semantics of such verbs limit their lexical possibilities; and how can figurative uses of such verbs draw attention to core elements of their meaning? In central Australian languages, people, birds and animals "talk", as do vehicles and mobile phones. But, despite producing vocalisations with syllabic diversity and temporal regularity akin to music, in the Arandic world birds may talk, cry out, drone or hum – but rarely are they said to "sing". So why don't Arandic birds "sing"? And why does a legless lizard – but not the wind – "whistle"?

In this chapter we explore the meanings of Arandic verbs of vocal production, employing a tool kit of sounds that we played to speakers of Arandic languages to determine whether or not various sounds are systematically mapped onto lexical categories. We focus on three commonly used verbs of vocal production, broadly glossed as: TALK, SING and HUM.[3] The structure of the chapter is as follows. In the next section, we outline our methodology. Then, we discuss the uses and meanings of the three verbs of vocal production. In "Other sounds", we comment on several other verbs that were commonly offered in response to our audio recognition task. In "Signs for sound" we make some brief observations about the verbs TALK, SING, HUM and CRY in the Indigenous sign languages of central Australia.

---

3 We use small caps in the main text to represent English glosses of Arandic verbs of vocal production.

We conclude by summarising our findings, which demonstrate how TALK, SING and HUM describe points on a continuum of the sounds made by humans, animals, and by some inanimates.

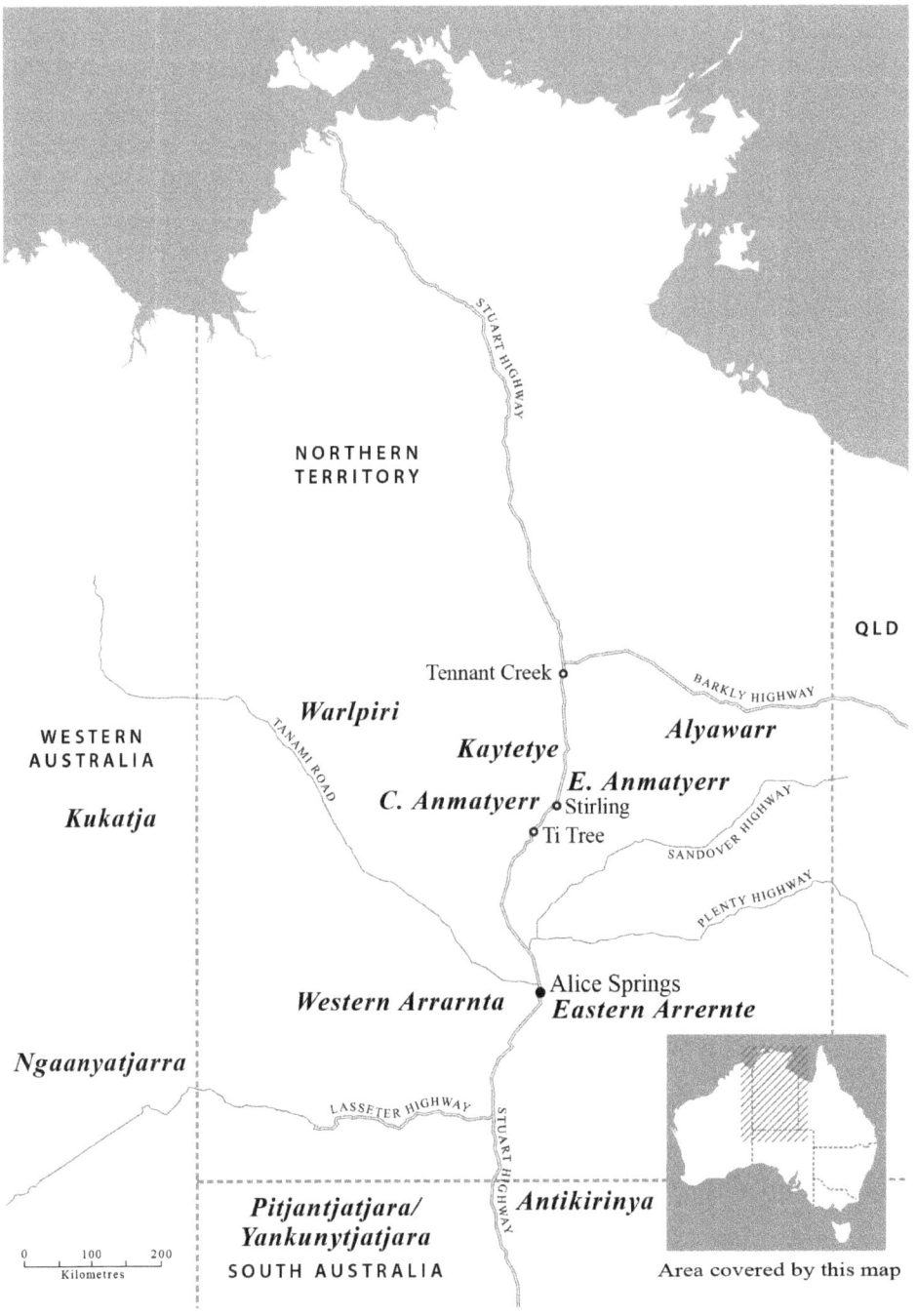

Figure 9.2 The approximate location of languages referred to in this chapter. Map by J. Green.

Methodology

The participants in our exploratory study are speakers of a range of Arandic languages – Eastern and Central Arrernte, Central Anmatyerr and Kaytetye (see Figure 9.2).[4] Many of these men and women are the acknowledged senior experts, and they have worked on collaborative documentation projects that have resulted in dictionaries of their languages, as well as other published resources on song, sign, verbal arts, speech styles and ecological knowledge systems. They live in remote small outstation communities or "homelands" or in regional towns such as Alice Springs.

We amassed a collection of some 70 sounds produced by a range of human, non-human and inanimate entities, but with a focus on bird species. Developed in the spirit of other elicitation tasks designed to explore parameters of the language of sensory domains (cf. Majid 2007), our audio recognition task aimed to help elucidate how Arandic verbs of vocal production carve up the semantic space of sound.[5] Birdcalls were sourced from the Kaytetye bird app and recorded by ornithologist David Stewart.[6] All the sounds were chosen for their relevance to the acoustic ecologies of central Australia, rather than for formal properties such as loudness, pitch or tempo (see, for example, Shayan, Ozturk and Sicoli 2011). We played each item in the sound collection to speakers of Eastern and Central Arrernte, Central Anmatyerr and Kaytetye and audio-recorded their responses. We found that people readily volunteered verbs of acoustic production in their responses to the task. The other sources of our data are written texts that appear in Arandic language and other dictionaries (Green 2003; 2010; Green, Blackman and Moore 2019; Henderson and Dobson 2020; Turpin and Ross 2012) as well as our own recordings and documentations of songs and narrative practices. Table 9.1 lists the Arandic verbs of vocal production considered in the study. While the first three verbs are the main focus of this chapter, the terms in subsequent rows will be referred to briefly. Note that all these verbs are intransitive except for SING. More will be said about transitivity when we discuss this verb.

---

4 The term "Arandic" is applied to the linguistic sub-group of central Australia within the broader Pama-Nyungan language family. Arandic can be divided into two sub-groups, with a number of distinct varieties and up to eleven communilects. See G. Breen 2001, 47.
5 See Appendix B at sydneyuniversitypress.com/keepingtimeappendices.
6 The app is now a website https://thangkerne.kaytetye.com.au/.

Table 9.1 Verbs of vocal production considered in the study.

Arandic form[7]		gloss
angk-	intransitive verb	TALK
aly-, ayl-	transitive verb	SING
arnwer-irr-	intransitive verb	HUM
uny-	intransitive verb	DRONE
ak-, arn-, arrangk-	intransitive verb	CRY
elperlaytn-, arrawenth-irr-	intransitive verb	WHISTLE
aharlaytn-, arlk-	intransitive verb	CALL OUT
aywerr angk-	intransitive verb	MAKE A NOISE

Talk

Specific verbs are used, in many languages, to refer to the sounds that animals make. For example, in English birds are said to "chirp", pigs "oink", and lions "roar". Yet in Australian languages, people and most animals "talk", as do vehicles, mobile phones and machines such as generators. The various meanings of Arandic TALK fall into two broad categories: to produce the sound typical of something; and to communicate a message. Both these meanings of TALK are the basis of the zeugma in the joke of late Kaytetye man Donald Ross, "Bullock bin talk". "Yeah? What'd he say?" (Ross and Whitebeach 2007, 51). In Arandic and other Australian languages, TALK also extends beyond the domain of sound to that of communication more generally, either with or without sound.

Producing a typical sound

Ellis and colleagues argued that "one of the most critical elements in classification of all sound-producing bodies (animate or inanimate) . . . is the actual sound normally produced" (Ellis, Ellis et al. 1978, 68.). We have yet to come across any Australian language where TALK "produce the sound typical of something" can only be said of humans. When emitting their characteristic sound, all humans, animals and inanimate beings are said to TALK (*angk-*), with the seeming exception of dogs, which we consider at the end of this section. The examples below illustrate

---

7 In this chapter we use the Anmatyerr spelling for words that are common to multiple Arandic languages. Terms that are unique to other Arandic languages follow the standard orthographies for those languages, as do language words in the numbered examples.

various uses of the verb TALK. In Example 9.1 and 9.2 the subject is animate (birds and bees), whereas in 9.3 and 9.4 the subjects are inanimate.

Example 9.1

Artety-el	**angk-erl**an-em	alpwertew-alpwert	ahelengkw	weth.
mulga-LOC[8]	**talk**-CNT-PRS	butcherbird	angry	that.one

"The butcherbird **sings out** in the mulga, that 'cheeky' one." (Green, Blackman and Moore 2019, 59) [Aly]

Example 9.2

Ngarntate-pe	**angke**-rrane-rtame	re	**angke**-ngele-angke-ngele,
bee-FOC	**talk**-PRS:CNT	3sgNOM	**talk**-SS-RDP

alperninte-larre-nke	ye	akwe-nyey-alpe-nke	re.
carry-PL-PRS	yes	insert-DO.QUICK&RET-PRS	3sgNOM

"Bees **buzz**, they **buzz** as they carry (pollen) going back and forth filling (the hive)." (Turpin and Ross 2012, 85) [K]

Example 9.3

Kwaty	arrer	**angk**-enh-ety-em,	wak-ek	aylp-eyaw.
rain	close	**talk**-DO&ALONG-HITH-NP	shelter-DAT	go in-IMP

"The **noise of** thunder is coming closer, go inside the shelter." (Green 2010, 103) [Anm]

Example 9.4

Pantey	cassette player	yanh	**angk**-enh.
always	cassette player	that	**talk**-PST:CNT

"That cassette **was playing** 'all day' [incessantly]." (Green, Blackman and Moore 2019, 234) [Aly]

In many languages the verb TALK may combine with a pre-verb or a nominal to mean "emit an X-like sound" (Rumsey 1994, 151). In Arandic languages there are

---

8   See Appendix C at sydneyuniversitypress.com/keepingtimeappendices for the morphological glosses used in this chapter. We use the following abbreviations for Arandic languages: Aly = Alyawarr, Anm = Anmatyerr, Arr = Eastern and Central Arrernte, K = Kaytetye.

dozens of such examples. One such example is *aywerr angk-* "make a noise".[9] This refers to the emission of a sound at a constant rate, such as certain insect noises, the sound of fridges, of vehicles idling (Example 9.5), a whistling kettle or the wind.

Example 9.5

Mweteke	nharte	**aywerre-angke**-rrane.
car	that	**noise-talk**-PRS:CNT

"That car **is running** [i.e., idling]." (Turpin and Ross 2012, 305) [K]

Communicating a message

In the Arandic world, the sounds that birds make are generally not thought to be emulating human speech, and birds don't make sounds that have been taught to them by people. In some rare cases, their calls are regarded as being somewhat akin to human speech and they are thought to be saying something. A "lingua-morphized" version of these birdcalls may come to be lexicalised as the birds' own names (Turpin 2013, 510). For example, in Kaytetye the pallid cuckoo (*Cacomantis pallidus*), whose name is *tyeng-aytey-aytey* ("my younger sibling"), heralds the season when march flies – the cuckoo's younger sibling – emerge (Turpin 2013, 513). Another example is *ipenye-apetyeme*, the Arrernte term for the striated pardalote (*Pardalotus striatus*). This bird's name translates as "a stranger is coming", and the bird signals that someone dangerous is nearby (Henderson and Dobson 2020, 396). Other bird species communicate, in this sense of signalling information. These instances of TALK can be glossed as "call" or "signal", as in Example 9.6 where another small bird is said to be issuing a warning:

Example 9.6

Alethange-we-pe	re	**angke**-nke-rtame	aleterrpeterrpe.
stranger-DAT-FOC	3sgNOM	**talk**-PRS-CNTR	rufous whistler

"The rufous whistler **calls** when there is a stranger around." (Janie Ampetyane 1999) [K]

We encountered only one animal whose sound was not said to be TALK – a dog's bark was instead described with a unique lexeme BARK. This transitive verb can mean "alert people to the presence of something", such as a kurdaitcha (ritual executioner), snake or echidna (the latter a prized food). In Kaytetye, if a dog

---

9 *Aywerr angk-* "make a noise" applies to sounds made by some inanimates and some insects (through stridulation). We include this in our survey of verbs of vocal production as we acknowledge that Arandic languages may not distinguish between sounds made by the vocal cords and those made by other parts of the body.

barks for no apparent reason "it is a way of being told that someone is going to die" (Turpin and Ross 2012, 574). Closer investigation revealed that BARK is not the typical sound made by dogs – more frequently they CRY (see "Cry", below) or *meltye-meltye angk-* (*meltyang angk-, mwelty angk-, urrmelty angk-*), a compound verb based on TALK, which refers to the excited noises dogs make when they are about to go out hunting. Note too that barking is far less common in dingoes, the endemic breed to Australia, than it is in domestic dogs.[10]

In Arandic, as in many Australian languages, the verb TALK has a nominal form meaning "language, word, message": for example, *angka* (compare *wangka* in Western Desert languages). Words that are written on paper are also regarded as exemplars of *angka*, thus TALK as a form of communication need not involve sound. TALK can be used to refer to the practice of using a signed language, as in Example 9.7 below (see also "Signs for sound"):

Example 9.7

Akertere-theye	ayenge	**angke**-rrane,	elty-am-elty-ame	ayenge
sign language-ABL	1sgNOM	**talk**-PRS:CNT	hand-REP-hand-REP	1sgNOM

angke-rrane	ngayele-we	atnwenthe-we	arntwe-we.
talk-PRS:CNT	food-DAT	meat-DAT	water-DAT

"I'm **communicating** in sign language, I use my hands to ask for food, meat and water." (Janie Ampetyane 1999) [K]

TALK also extends to non-sound emitting cognitive action, such as "think to oneself, wonder". This can be seen in the following Warlpiri sentence (the verb TALK is bolded).

Nyanjarni yanulpa katukarirlalku. **Wangka-ja-nyanu** miyalu: "Nyiyarlalu yarlpuruparduju yanu ngurrakarikirraju?"

*He came and looked over and **wondered to himself***: *"Why has my age-mate moved to another camp?"* (Laughren et al. 2023, 425)

Sing

Invariably the first question people asked in response to hearing examples of human singing in our semi-experimental task was, "Who is singing?" This was not surprising – Indigenous songs are "power-laden" (Ellis 1994b) and the identity (or

---

10 Harold Koch notes that the word for dingo in some Australian languages is based on a verb meaning "howl/cry" (personal communication to Myfany Turpin, 4 May 2022).

at least the language group or community) of the singer is of primary significance. With this in mind, we played our examples of singing with caution. It became clear that it was not so easy to abstract away from context to focus on the acoustic signal, a problem that was not so apparent in relation to entities that TALK.

In contrast to the wide range of applications of TALK, discussed above, SING is an activity that is almost exclusively performed by people. In this sense SING accords with ethnomusicological definitions of music as "humanly organised sound" (Blacking 1976; Taylor 2008, 2). As Barwick noted, all music is primarily vocal in Aboriginal Australia and occurs as part of ceremonies (Barwick 2011, 327). SING shares three characteristics that Barwick regarded as widely associated with music, but not speech: it is associated with a specific performance context; it consists of "discrete repeatable pieces"; and it underspecifies referential meaning (Barwick 2012, 171). Across Australia, singing is a way to tap into "the essence known as the Dreaming" (Barwick and Marett 1995, 4–5) in order "to draw on supernatural powers left within the soil in ancient times" (Ellis 1980, 723). The agentive aspect of singing in Australia is well documented. Of the Pitjantjatjara word *inkanyi* "sing" Ellis and colleagues stated: "As well as meaning the act of singing, it also means the act of causing an event through the power of song" (Ellis, Ellis et al. 1978, 79).[11] The Kukatja dictionary (Valiquette 1993, 369) defines the transitive verb *yinkala* as "sing a person (influence a person's state by singing a magical song at him/her)" as well as "impart magical properties to an object".[12] It is perhaps not surprising that SING is often a transitive verb in Australian languages, as it is in Arandic ones.

Below we identify several meanings of Arandic SING. We also show that, for many speakers, SING has now been extended to encompass "new" types of vocal music, such as country music and hymns, often employing *alyelh-*, a de-transitivised form of the verb.

The power of song

In the Arandic world it is typically people who sing. Not only is singing an enjoyable activity, but it is also part of larger events. For example, singing is an essential part of ceremonies, involving both men and women, that are held annually to transform boys into men (Example 9.8).

---

11 Goddard's (1992, 19) glosses for the ambitransitive verb *inkanyi* include "have fun, play"; "laugh, smile"; and "play a musical instrument".

12 A similar polysemy exists in Latin. The term *cano* "sing" was originally associated with augury and magic (Harold Koch, personal communication to Myfany Turpin, 4 May 2022). See also O'Grady 1984, 383, 384.

Example 9.8

Artnwenge	ayenge	ane-yayne,	atyenge	**ayle**-nye.
child	1sgNOM	sit-PST:IMP	1sgACC	**sing**-PST

"When I was a child, I went through ceremony [lit. '(they) **sang** me']."[13] [K]

People also sing to alter the world in a variety of ways – to make someone sick (Example 9.9), to heal someone (9.10), or to manipulate a person's affections (9.11). Frequently the object is foregrounded, and the agent omitted, rendering a passive translation such as that in Example 9.9. In Example 9.9 the word for sorcery is an instrumental noun phrase.

Example 9.9

Ethwe-nge	kwere	**ayle**-nye,	akngw-ayle-nye.
poison-INST	3sgACC	**sing**-PST	mad-CAUS-PST

"He/she **was cursed** through sorcery and went mad [lit. (They) **sang** him/her with sorcery which caused (him/her) to go mad]." (Turpin and Ross 2012, 57) [K]

Example 9.10

Aly-em	awely	arntety	apek	mwerr-irr-etyek.
sing-NP	ceremony	sick	maybe	good-INCH-PURP

Anter	war-el	tha	**aly**-em,	apern-elh-etyek	ra
fat	just-INST	1sgERG	**sing**-NP	rub-REFL-PURP	3sgNOM

mwerr-irr-etye,	irrernt-irr-etyek.
good-INCH-PURP	cool-INCH-PURP

"*Awely* ceremonies are sung to make a sick person get better. I just **sing** them with the fat, so that they can rub themselves with it and get better, cool down." (Green 2010, 64) [Anm]

Example 9.11

Artweye-le	kwere	**ayle**-wethe	relhe	aleyake,	arraylentyine-nke-lke	kwere.
man-ERG	3sgACC	**sing**-PURP	woman	young	transform-PRS-then	3sgACC

"If a man **sings** a young woman, he changes her then." (Turpin and Ross 2012, 189) [K]

---

13 Kaytetye spoken by Peter, recorded by Ken Hale 1959. See annotation 132 on https://angke.kaytetye.com.au/kenhale/kh4561/.

Singing can also imbue certain objects with magical powers. For example, *anter alyem* ("sing fat") transfers the healing power of the song to the fat, which is then used as a rubbing lotion or liniment. The word *awely* "ceremonial genre" can also refer to healing fat itself (Dobson 2007, 19). This "actual/potential polysemy" has been widely documented in Australia (Dixon 1980, 102–103; Evans 1992, 479) and is probably also at the heart of the polysemy in the word *ethwe* "poison" and "sorcery, curse, magic" in Example 9.9.

Song is used to cause an event such as rain. When singing non-human objects to bring about the health of that species, or to bring about rain, the implied meaning is to sing the song or perform the ceremony associated with that object, as in Example 9.12.

Example 9.12

Akwelye	aynanthe	**ayle**-wethe	arntwe	atnthe-wethe.
rain cloud	1plNOM	**sing**-PURP	water	fall-PURP

"We should sing a rain-cloud ceremony to make it rain [lit. sing raincloud]." [K][14]

When both the ceremonial genre or song, and the person or object that is being "sung" are referred to, the former takes the object role and the latter the indirect object role (X sings Y for Z) as in the first clause of Example 9.13.

Example 9.13

Awelye	**ayle**-nke	kwere	mpweyampe-we,	awek-ine-wethe	kwere.
genre	**sing**-PRS	3sgDAT	skinny-DAT	plump-CAUS-PURP	3sgACC

Awek-**ayle**-wethe	kwere.
plump-CAUS-PURP	3sgACC

"*Awelye* is sung for a skinny person, to make them put on weight. To make/sing her plump." (Turpin and Ross 2012, 273) [K]

Example 9.13 also shows that the form of the verb SING and one form of the causative are identical in Kaytetye: *ayle-* (note the additional causative *-ine-* in this example). The example illustrates a possible bridging context, where making someone put on weight (*awek-ayle-*) is achieved through singing. Although it is tempting to see this as a case of polysemy, the Arrernte cognates of these meanings differ (*alye-* "sing" versus *-ile-* "causative"), suggesting a case of homophony.

---

14 Kaytetye Dictionary Database, compiled by Myfany Turpin and held at the University of Sydney.

While singing is primarily a human activity, the capacity to be recognised as "singers" extends beyond humans. In Kaytetye the legless lizard and several species of long-horn beetles and are also said to SING, causing a proliferation of bush potatoes (*Ipomoea costata*) (Turpin, Ross et al. 2013, 22).[15] The longhorn beetle and the legless lizard are both known as *anatye ayle-wene* "bush potatosingers" (Turpin 2013, 509; Turpin and Ross 2012, 110, 111). Longhorn beetles, also called *anatyelepwerreye* in Kaytetye, live on bush potato vines and they produce sound by rubbing parts of their body together (known as stridulation). The association of these species with sound production and with particular powers inherent in song extends across the region. In Anmatyerr and some other Arandic varieties the legless lizard, *iparip*, is said to "whistle" (Green 2010, 336), while in Alyawarr this lizard is called *ngangker-ngangker*, a reduplication of the word *ngangker* "traditional healer, person with magical powers" (Green, Blackman and Moore 2019, 234, 285). The Warlpiri name of the lizard, *yalypinjalypinji*, is a reduplication of an Arandic cognate term *ilpenty*, a genre of "love songs". Two other species of beetles are also said to SING various grass species on which they are found to bring about an abundance of seeds (Turpin 2013, 509). As reported elsewhere in Australia (Turpin 2013) and in other places in the world, the names of species can reflect their cultural significance (Aung Si 2016, 123). The status of these beetles and the legless lizard as singers appears to be an exception, and to our knowledge, for speakers of Arandic languages, no other beings, animate or inanimate, are said to SING.[16] It may be significant that, in the examples discussed above, the lizards and beetles are associated with a plant that is a highly valued food source (bush potato) for people.

Example 9.14 illustrates the whistling and singing of the legless lizard.[17] Here *anatye* "yam" is in the indirect object role ("it sings for yams") and there is no direct object. This semitransitive clause is comparable with the "conative case" (Laughren 1988). The semitransitive clause is rare when the participants of SING are human.

---

15 The ethnospecies referred to are various longhorn beetles of the family *Cerambycidae* (Luo and Huang 2022), Burton's legless lizard (*Lialis burtonis*) and possibly *Delma tincta* and *Delma nasuta*, all of which are endemic to central Australia. The lizard species tend to vocalise when threatened (Weber and Werner 1977).

16 The Pitjantjatjara/Yankunytjatjara Dictionary includes an example of a marsupial mouse which sings (*warani*) "a lonely song" (Goddard 1992, 188).

17 While stridulation is not technically a vocal sound, the movements that make this sound are not visible to the naked eye, so it is not surprising that it is classified as "singing" in the Arandic world.

Example 9.14

Paripe-p-aperte-rtame	**elperlaytnte**-rrane-pe,	anatye-we
lizard.sp-FOC-ONLY-CNTR	**whistle**-PST:CNTFOC	yam-DAT

ayle-rantye	re.
sing-PRS:CNT	3sgNOM

"It's only the legless lizard that whistles and sings up yams." (Hilda Ngamperle 2001) [K]

We argue that these particular species can be agents of SING because the primary meaning of the transitive verb *aly-* "sing" is best understood as an activity that has the capacity to alter or influence another entity by the production of vocal sound.[18]

Performing ceremonial genres

Another meaning of SING foregrounds the ceremonial genre that is being performed, rather than the use of song to influence another entity (compare "put on a corroboree"). In Arandic languages that have a "mediopassive" *-elh-* (Moore 2012), which reduces the valency of a verb, this form of the verb (*ayl-elh-*) tends to be used for this meaning. This is illustrated in Example 9.15. In Example 9.16, the verb is transitive, as Kaytetye does not have a mediopassive.

Example 9.15

Rlengk	**ayl**-elh-enh.arey	arrakerr	awely.
today	**sing**-MED-PL.IMP	2plNOM	ceremony

"You people sing the women's ceremonies today." (Green et al. 2019, 182). [Aly]

Example 9.16

Elpere,	aynanthe	awelye	**ayle**-rwene-wene!
quick	1sgNOM	ceremony	**sing**-QUICK-OBLIG

"Quick, let's sing some *awelye* straight away!" (Turpin and Ross 2012, 578) [K]

Not surprisingly, SING is not the only way to express "perform (a ceremony)". Other verbs include "make", and for public performance genres, such as *ltharte*, the intransitive verbs "dance" and "sit" can be used. In our explorations of sounds many people used SING to describe the performance of non-traditional genres, including hymns, rock music and country music, as well as singing when the genre is unspecified or unknown. Children's songs, which are intoned rhythmically

---

18 We note that the extension of "sing" to certain other animates with powers to influence the world is found in Athabascan vocal genres (Tuttle and Lundström 2022, 135).

on a single pitch, also fall within the scope of the verb SING. These all have accompanying actions and performance contexts (Green and Turpin 2013; Turpin and Ross 2003, 100). Ceremonies and children's songs are multimodal, and the use of SING can encompass the associated actions of painting and dancing.

There is one bird that is said to perform *ltharte* ceremony, the Australian bustard. Kaytetye Elder Tommy Thompson described how male bustards dance (*etnhenke*) and sing (*aylenke*) in this ceremony. Given that participants in our audio recognition task did not use "sing" to describe the bustard's gruff mating call, "sing" is possibly a figurative application in the context of a detailed description of the bustard's *ltharte* performance.

Sounds made by inanimate subjects

Intransitive SING is also used for the musical sounds emitted by musical instruments and other objects such as mobile phones (compare "the violin sang"). Other common ways of expressing these events use Arandic verbs meaning "make, do" (compare "I'm doing guitar") or a borrowed term based on English "play". For the sound of a melodious ring tone on a phone, younger speakers use SING, whereas older speakers prefer TALK. This is particularly so in Kaytetye and may be related to the fact that it does not have a mediopassive.

Evans and Wilkins noted that reflexive and de-transitivised forms of perception verbs are used to derive cognitive and other perceptual senses ("hear" extends to mean "think", "feel") (Evans and Wilkins 2000). The de-transitivised form of Arandic SING similarly derives additional senses in the domain of sound production. The diachronic polysemy of SING to refer to inanimate subjects in its intransitive form (for example, guitars, mobile phones) may have its origins in a widespread synchronic polysemy where subjects of TALK can be either animate or inanimate. Other than musical instruments and mobile phones, intransitive SING is not used to apply to other inanimate objects, such as a kettle or the wind. We encountered very few exceptions to this.

Given the broad range of genres to which SING can be applied, one might think that the sand story performance discussed in the beginning of this chapter (Figure 9.1) would also be regarded as singing. But, as will be seen below, the vocal part of the performance shares a number of features that are also found in "humming".

Hum

The Arandic verb *arnwer-irr-* "hum, intone" is based on the nominal *arnwer* "a humming or buzzing sound" followed by the inchoative *irr-*. People, as well as some insects, are said to hum. When applied to people, HUM refers to the intoning of a melody without opening the mouth, or to singing in a way where it is difficult to make out the words. Humming is also an essential section of many ceremonial performances and other forms of verbal art (Green 2014; Green and Turpin 2013; Turpin and Green 2018). Barwick has described these as "fade effects" (Barwick 1990, 70) and noted that "humming the melodic outline or tapping out the rhythm of the words of the song are both techniques used to aid recall in the course of the performance" (Barwick 1989, 14). Pitjantjatjara performers hum as a method of recalling the poetic text or "looking for a hint of a song" (Ellis 1985, 72; see also Ellis et al. 1978, 74). Ngaanyatjarra linguist Lizzie Marrkilyi Ellis described "humming your way into a song" as part of the process of song making. She recalled how her mother was visited by a *wunymunypa*, "muse", who left her with a humming sound in her ear that led to a song (Kral and Ellis 2020, 203). Ellis and colleagues (1990) concluded, from their study of women's songs recorded at Indulkana in Central Australia, that humming was "an indicator that activities were taking place within the ritual time frame" (Ellis et al. 1990, 105). There are also instances where the distinction between singing and humming is not straightforward, and as Haviland (2007, 171) has noted, "Talk easily fades into singing, and singing into humming". We describe the Arandic uses of HUM below.

Singing without enunciating text

As noted above, one meaning of Arandic HUM is to use the voice musically without articulating syllables. People often do this to pass the time, typically when they are alone and without an audience, as implied in Example 9.17 below:

Example 9.17

Ngarrpe-tyampe	ayenge	"**arnwer-arnwer-arre-rane**	rrkante-le.
alone-too	1sg-NOM	**hum-hum**-INCH-PRS:CNT	fun-INST

"And when I'm on my own I hum along for fun." (Amy Ngamperle 2002) [K]

In the context of learning songs, Glass and Hackett (2003, 245) wrote of the Ngaanyatjarra verb *nguurnmanku* "whimper, groan, coo, say hmmm, hum, wail" that "some people mightn't know one song. Then they listen to the tune and get it right". In some contexts, "just humming" may have negative overtones and reflect loss of knowledge of performance repertoires (Peterson 2008, 114). HUM is also used to describe distant singing where the lyrics are not discernible. A key element of HUM is thus its melodic delivery without producing or perceiving syllables, which are a key feature of oral language.

Performing the introductory section of a ceremonial song

HUM may be used to describe the vocal style employed in the introductory section of a ceremonial song (Green and Turpin 2013; Green 2014; Turpin and Green 2018, 68). The nominal "humming sound" can also occur with the verb SING, as in Example 9.18.

Example 9.18

Arnwere-larlenge-rtame	ampile-yayne-pe	ayle-yayne-ngele.
humming sound-COM-CNTR	recount-PST:IMP-FOC	sing-PST:IMP-S/S

"With a soft drone people would tell stories or sing." (Janie Ampetyane 2007) [K]

One Anmatyerr speaker suggested that it is only women who hum, indicating that this vocal style may be more closely associated with women's performative traditions. In our documentation of men's public singing in the Arandic region, we have not yet encountered any genres with a similar softly intoned introduction (the solo beginnings are often quite loud). There are certainly examples of men humming an introduction to a song elsewhere. Knopoff (1992, 141) noted that the performance of Yolngu clan songs, which are sung by men, also involves an introductory humming section:

> Clan song verses are commonly comprised of three parts – an introduction (*ngurruwanga*, literally "nose-speech" humming), a main body (called *manikay*, literally "song"), and an unaccompanied vocal coda (also called *ngurruwanga*). During the (usually brief) introduction, the lead singer establishes an appropriate clapstick pattern and quietly intones a low tonic. He may sing a few burden syllables, convey information regarding song to the other performers, comment on something unrelated to the music, or begin improvising lines of song text. At the same time, the other singers begin to tap their sticks in accord with the lead singer. (Knopoff 1992, 141)

Singing a non-repeating text

Another application of the verb HUM is in the delivery of improvised or spontaneous texts, which are delivered by one person. Green and Turpin (2018) described one such Anmatyerr performance, aimed at sending children to sleep, that comprises a hummed improvised text with one sung verse that is repeated throughout. The Antikirinya "intoned story" described by Ellis is of the same structure and is said to be "sighed" and then "sung" (Ellis 1985, 60–61). Both were performed by women. We are not aware of similar examples performed by men.

One speaker also described rap music as both "humming" and "telling", while another used the verb HUM to describe hymnal singing. Unlike the intoned stories described above, hymns have pre-existing texts. However, like the intoned stories, they are not bound by the repetition and alliteration patterns of ceremonial songs. The vocal aspects of the sand story performance described in the Introduction to this chapter, which people hesitated to call SING, were sometimes referred to as HUM. This performance was also a story whose text was improvised, with no repeating isorhythmic texts, a fundamental feature of Aboriginal ceremonial genres (Ellis 1968). Perhaps those few speakers who did accept SING as a descriptor of the performance assumed that the text *was* repeated; or they had the meaning "singing for an unspecified reason" in mind.[19]

Insects

Arandic HUM is also used to describe the buzzing sound made by certain insects, such as native bees, wasps and blowflies (Example 9.19). One speaker also described the vocalisations of a horse as both HUM and TALK.

Example 9.19

Urltampe	**arnwere**-irre-me.
native bee	**humming** sound-INCH-PRS

"Native bees make a buzzing sound." (Henderson and Dobson 2020, 232) [Arr]

Some speakers also described certain insect calls as MAKE A NOISE (a hyponym of TALK). We suggest that HUM may refer to sound that varies or fluctuates, whereas MAKE A NOISE refers to a steady sound and so would describe a blowfly moving at constant speed, not one battering against a glass pane, as in our set of sound stimuli.

Other sounds

Our elicitation task also prompted several other verbs that refer to sound emission. Invariably, these proved to be hyponyms or qualifiers of TALK, such as *meltye-meltye angkenke* (dog) "being excited". Two further monomorphemic verbs of vocal production are discussed briefly below.

---

19 As we only played short excerpts rather than whole songs, it would not always have been possible for a listener to ascertain whether the texts were isorhythmic or repeating. Our listeners may have made assumptions about the excerpts of singing they were listening to, based also on contextual knowledge.

Droning, cooing

The verb *uny-* "coo, drone" describes a low-pitched regular sound. A small number of birds are said to make this sound – for example, tawny frogmouths, bronzewings, crested pigeons and emus. The sounds made by barking spiders, goannas and cows can also be described by this verb. Some of these sounds can also be described as TALK, such as the tawny frogmouth:

> *Ingwelarle uringe* **angkerlaneme**. *Apere arntarlkwenge apeke or athengenge. Ingwelarle itne* **angkerlaneme**. *Renhe akenhe* **unyerlanerlenge** *ware awerlanerle. Irrkaye irrkaye wararle kwenele* **angkerlaneme** *ingwemerntele-urreke.*

> The tawny frogmouth **calls out** at night, from the fork of a river red gum, or from an ironwood tree. They **call** at night. You can just hear them **cooing**. They **call** softly all through the night. (Margaret Kemarre (MK) Turner to Jennifer Green, 9 September 2015) [Arr]

The following example of COO refers to the snivelling and mumbling sound of a child, which is likened to pigeon sounds and discouraged:

> *Ime* **unyerlanerle** *arntepele, "Mmmm mmmm mmmm". Alakenhe ime arrpenhe mapele ilerle. "Ampaye! Arntepele-arteke unye* **unyetyalaye**. *Artne apeke arratye artnaye! Arntepe-arteke* **unyerlanetyale"**. *Or people arrpenhe mape alakenhe, "Arnterre angkeyawe! Arntepe-arteke* **unyetyale"**.

> Bronzewing pigeons **coo** like this, "Mmmm mmmm mmmm." Some people tell their children, "Child! Don't **coo** like a pigeon. Cry properly! Don't **coo** like a pigeon." Others say, "Speak up! Don't **coo** like a pigeon!" (Margaret Kemarre (MK) Turner to Jennifer Green, 9 September 2015) [Arr]

Cry

The verbs meaning CRY in Table 9.1 were also used to describe the sounds made by certain animals. Speakers used CRY to describe the noises of cats, curlews, frogmouths, diamond doves, dogs and horses, imputing a position of sadness. Some used CALL OUT, a verb that may suggest sudden distress or the intent to inform others, to describe the noises made by horses, cats, peacocks, pallid cuckoos, butcherbirds, cows and certain frogs. We did not include the sounds that donkeys make in our task. However, Vaarzon-Morel reported that people from Willowra, a remote community in the Northern Territory where there is a sizeable population of donkeys who are regarded by the community as "cohabitants", employ the Warlpiri verbs *yulami* "cry" or *purlami* "call out, sing out" to refer to donkey vocalisations (Vaarzon-Morel 2021, 128; Laughren et al. 2023).

One speaker used the verb CRY to refer to hymnal singing. Although we do not offer a full semantic analysis of this verb in Arandic languages, it is worth mentioning why CRY might be recruited for this purpose. Magowan (2007) noted that, for English speakers, Yolngu mourning sounds like singing. Perhaps the similarity between Arandic hymnal singing and mourning lies in the melismatic setting of the text in both hymnal singing and mourning.[20] This is not a feature of singing in Arandic song genres where each syllable typically only has one rhythmic note attack. Although crying and singing are two different sound structures (Feld 1984, 397), the acoustic similarities between traditional wailing and hymnal singing have led to a convergence of singing and crying in the "new" vocal style of church singing. It remains to be seen just how widespread these patterns of polysemy are in Australian languages. This adds further weight to the primacy of text in Arandic SING – it is not simply about melody. A sense of the re-adjustment brought on by the transition from traditional forms of music to new "hymnal" varieties at Hermannsburg Mission in central Australia towards the end of the 19th century is found in the reminiscences of Pastor Moses Tjalkabota:

> The old men said, "Children, you are now singing wrongly, really wrongly." Then we said, "a, e, i, o, u." "Oh, the children are talking like crows", they said. The children again spoke, and then the old men said, "The children are speaking as though they are crying". (Albrecht 2002, 246)

Signs for sound

It is also instructive to take a cross-modal perspective and look at the ways that verbs of vocal production are instantiated in sign. The speakers of Arandic languages that we consulted are also knowledgeable of the alternate signing practices that are found in their communities where sign is used, predominately by hearing people, to replace speech in particular cultural circumstances (Kendon 2013 [1988]). Sign is used when people are grieving, when hunting or when communicating over a distance, and sign may also be employed as a silent channel of communication during ceremonial performances. Although we did not video-record our discussions about sound, research on sign languages in the region enables us to make some preliminary observations. In these signing systems the verbs TALK/TELL, SING and HUM all have distinct forms. TALK/TELL is formed with a flat hand that is either held in front of the body and "trembled" or moved in an arc-like action away from the mouth. The sign SING is formed with a hand that has only the index finger

---

20 By melismatic we refer to repeating a syllable on a different pitch, as opposed to a sliding to a different pitch without repeating the note attack.

extended, and the motion of the hand is downwards, and sometimes repeated with alternating hands.[21] Kendon noted that the Warlpiri sign SING is also glossed as both *yilpinji* "love songs" and *purlapa* "corroborree" (Kendon 2013 [1988]) suggesting a polysemy between the signed verb SING and signs for some ceremonial genres. It may be that the action of this sign, a repeated downwards movement, is motivated by the particular dancing actions employed in these ceremonies of which song is an integral part. For Anmatyerr signers, the verb HUM is formed with a distinctive "finger snap" that punctuates the motion of the signing hand as it arcs from side to side in front of the signer's body. It appears that the sign HUM is the same as one form of the sign CRY. This may allude to the affective and emotional content of song in general, or perhaps to the rhythmic actions that call forth the traces of a song before the song really begins in full. Another possible motivation is the fact that humming and crying are forms of vocalisation that are textless, a feature that distinguishes both of these from speech and song. The finger snap is typologically rare in signed languages, and in central Australia occurs in some other signs that refer to distance in time and space – such as LONG.TIME, LONG.WAY, which Barwick has suggested may be related to the evocation of ancestral spirits.[22] When it comes to signed utterances about birds, our corpus contains several examples that include the TALK sign, and none that include SING.

Conclusions

In this chapter we have considered the meanings of several Arandic verbs of vocal production, including TALK, SING, HUM, DRONE and CRY. We find that these carve up the semantic space of the acoustic world in ways different from English. Our audio recognition task has proved useful in stimulating many informative discussions about sound, and in finetuning descriptions of the semantic and grammatical complexities of Arandic verbs in this domain. Such focused attention on a particular domain of meaning is a luxury seldom afforded in our task as lexicographers of Australian Indigenous languages. The interdisciplinary approach we have taken has long been on Linda Barwick's "wish list", and it contributes to understandings of how people talk about songs, music and vocal styles in general, and of the ways that various repertoires are interrelated (Barwick 2005c, 59). Further investigations could include a broader range of sound stimuli, and attention to both gender-based and intergenerational differences in the ways that sound is spoken about. Using these methodologies to explore the meanings of

---

21 See Campbell, Carew et al. 2021 [2013].
22 Personal communication, Linda Barwick to Jennifer Green, March 2022.

verbs of vocal production in other languages may reveal different taxonomies of the acoustic world, reflecting local epistemologies and vocal practices.

While talking and singing are universal practices, TALK, SING and HUM describe points on a continuum of human vocal production, including speech, song and other multimodal narrative practices. New musical forms are slotted into this spectrum based on acoustic analogies, features of the text and knowledge about their performance context. The juxtaposition of vocal styles "draws attention to the continuum that exists between the formal and the informal" and "between the Dreaming and the everyday world" (Ellis et al. 1990, 134). Sometimes divergences from ideal forms can cast light on their essential features (Barwick 1995). We have demonstrated how the applications of Arandic TALK are much broader than the English equivalent, encompassing sounds made by humans, animals and some inanimates. We find that the scope of SING is somewhat narrower, and strongly associated with causation and with specific local knowledge about the power of a subject to influence another entity. Perhaps surprisingly Arandic birds are said to talk, warn, weep and coo – but seldom are the sounds they make regarded as song. While some vocal parts of sand stories may be musical, their renditions are not generally regarded as singing because they lack some of the properties associated with more formal performance genres. The few non-human entities that do "sing" are recognised as having particular agency in the complex intertwined relationships between people and other species, and in the songs and ceremonies that people use to sustain and control their biocultural environments. Unravelling some of this complexity contributes to the interdisciplinary study of sound and of musical traditions, a lifelong passion and preoccupation of Linda Barwick.

Acknowledgements

We thank the many speakers of Arandic languages who have worked with us over many years to document their languages and music – in particular, Clarrie Kemarr Long, Eileen Perrwerl Campbell, April Pengart Campbell, Amy Pengarte, Amy Ngamperle, the late Janie Mpetyan Briscoe, the late Alison N. Ross, the late Tommy Thompson, the late Shirley Ampetyane and the late Margaret Kemarre (MK) Turner. Funding for this research was provided by the Australian Research Council (FT140100783, DP1092887, DE160100873, CE140100041). We also thank the editors of this volume, Harold Koch, and two anonymous reviewers of this chapter. An earlier version was presented at the Australian Linguistics Society Conference, December 2015.

Chapter 10

The Hakhun Buffalo Sacrifice (*li jwe*) Song

Reis Flora, Khithong Hakhun, Stephen Morey and Jürgen Schöpf

Introduction

The Hakhun people live in north-east India in both Assam and Arunachal Pradesh states and in Sagaing region, Myanmar. They are one of many hill tribes of South-East Asia, an area known for its linguistic diversity and mobility of population. Within Assam state, they are included with the Tangsa tribe (Barkataki-Ruscheweyh 2017; Morey 2019), while in some other parts of India they are included with Nocte and in Myanmar with Tangshang.

The language spoken by the Hakhun is one of the varieties of Tangsa-Nocte, a diverse group of linguistic varieties spoken on both sides of the India–Myanmar border (Morey 2019), within the Northern Naga group of the Sal or Bodo-Konyak-Jingpo, within the Tibeto-Burman family. Their language has been described by Boro (2017).

In December 2008, Stephen Morey and Jürgen Schöpf were staying at the Hakhun village of Malou Pahar, just above the town of Ledo. Over the previous days we had got to know co-author Khithong Hakhun and the community leader Phulim Hakhun. Phulim directed a performance of a series of dances, summarising those performed across the year, for us to record the following day. There was a rehearsal on the night of 23 December, which we captured on video.

The following morning, we were discussing with Phulim the songs that were present in that performance, with Khithong translating. Rather unexpectedly, we were informed that Phulim would need to leave and prepare for killing a buffalo to eat in the Christmas feast. Phulim and his wife, the late Posim Hakhun, then decided to take the opportunity to demonstrate for us the way in which, in traditional times, the buffalo would be sacrificed, tied to the foot of the steps leading into the house. In everyday Hakhun language, a buffalo sacrifice is called *li jwe* (/li˦ dʒwe˨/), and the festival held at that time is known as *li jwe kuq*. The term *kuq* "festival" is translated a little loosely into English, as it can refer to both a large community event and something celebrated at the family level.

This chapter describes the Buffalo Sacrifice Song and analyses its cultural context, dress, verse structure, poetics, singing, dance steps and accompanying gong playing.

Buffalo Sacrifice (*li jwe*) Song

Data and method

The performance was recorded on 24 December 2008, using two separate video cameras, with Jürgen Schöpf concentrating on filming the buffalo and Stephen Morey on the main singers. The singing was started by Posim, who was then joined by her husband, Phulim, and his younger brother Vaming Hakhun.

The recordings were discussed with Phulim and Khithong, and some of the lyrics transcribed and roughly translated soon after recording. The linguistic analysis presented here is based on a translation by Khithong from the video made by Stephen that was placed on YouTube on 4 March 2021. Khithong Hakhun sent a line-by-line transcription and translation through Facebook Messenger. In the weeks following, both Stephen and Khithong (each remaining in their homes in Melbourne and Malou Pahar respectively throughout) discussed and refined the transcription and translation in multiple Facebook Messenger video chats from March to July 2021.[1]

To bring different levels of analysis together, we employed the software ELAN. This software allows users to time align up to four parallel audiovisual recordings and annotate them on different levels. The output into subtitled video formats is also a highly valued product of our work and is appreciated by the Hakhun community. Our analysis thus combines an emic perspective of this song, informed by ethnographic, linguistic and musicological tools, as well as computer-aided methods.

---

1 See Appendix D at sydneyuniversitypress.com/keepingtimeappendices.

10 The Hakhun Buffalo Sacrifice (*li jwe*) Song

Context

In the Hakhun calendar, the mid-winter month around modern Christmas is called Seyu. At this time, traditionally, a buffalo sacrifice (*li jwe*) was performed accompanied by singing and dancing. A buffalo sacrifice can be performed at the Mwe festival around May, at the time of the construction of a new house or in the month of Seyu. The form and perhaps content of the songs sung during the sacrifice differs according to timing and purpose. The song presented here is that performed at a sacrifice around the 15th day, or full moon day (*lwam nyu*), of the month of Seyu and the song is called both "Seyu Si" and "Ve Si". If performed at the Mwe festival, it is called "Mwe Si".

The song we are presenting here was part of a bigger cultural practice, not all parts of which we have been able to record. We were told that, traditionally, after the buffalo meat is cut into pieces, the head of the buffalo is taken inside the house, and the singer would follow the meat into the middle room of the house or *rum*, and singing would continue, as well as a spoken prayer, *rumbe*. These parts are not included in our documentation.

Traditional practices involved sacrifice to placate spirits. The respective prayers are known as *Rumbe* /rum_Hbe_L/, which literally means "prayer in the middle room". *Rum* in Hakhun language is a most important location inside the house. Guests are not usually invited there and in traditional times this was where prayers were said, near the main post of the house. Phulim did demonstrate the *Rumbe* prayer for us in a video recording made in two parts in 2009. The *Rumbe* prayer is spoken in everyday language, without formal features of a song. The middle room (*rum*) is also the location where the buffalo will continue to be honoured. The song we recorded specifically states that the buffalo horn will be kept in the house, and that the spirit of that sacrificed buffalo will be valued and remain in the middle room (see Table 10.1, C27a). *Arung* is the word for "horn" in everyday language: in song language it is *rungsa*. While we have not yet undertaken a full study of song language in Hakhun, it is clear that some words may vary in form when present in this type of song.

The performance analysed below was not a performance of a buffalo sacrifice proper. The family, as indeed most of the village, has practised Christian beliefs, of the Baptist denomination, since the 1990s. As was explained to us, they had intended to slaughter a buffalo for Christmas and used this opportunity to show us, their foreign guests, how a buffalo sacrifice in the past would have been performed, because we had shown an interest in their traditions.

The performance differed in a number of ways from the historical practice of sacrifice. For one thing, there was only a single gong player, Nyalik Hakhun, daughter-in-law of Posim and Phulim, accompanying the singing and dancing. In a full performance of the ritual there would have been a group playing gongs going in a line before the leading singer. We were told that they understood we wanted to be able to hear the words of the song, so for this recording, the performers decided to reduce the gong playing to a single person. In a rather spontaneous performance of the "Ve Si" ("Seyu Si") song a year later without any sacrifice, the gong playing was more like that in the traditional sacrifice. Normally, gong players lead the group of the performers, followed by the main singer and further responding singers, all of whom also dance.

Dress

In this performance, the dress worn is the traditional dress worn during a sacrifice. Posim wore a strikingly white skirt with a black top and decorations, including bangles and beads. She carried a cup with rice beer and the cockscomb flower (*pweq khi*) (*Celosia* spp.) that grows profusely in the winter season in the Hakhun area. This flower is valued for ritual purposes by many of the Tangsa tribes and others on the India–Myanmar border.

Posim also holds the *nyiapru* leaf (*Phrynium capitatum*) and a decorated rice basket worn like a rucksack (decorated with the same flower and leaf), and at timecodes 6'15"-6'45" (see Table 10.1, C23) the buffalo tail is cut off the dead animal and put into her basket.

Phulim Hakhun wore a striking red shirt, and the traditional Naga "helmet" woven from bamboo strips to which was attached deer skin, hornbill feathers, two wild boar tusks (one on each side), and part of a bearskin with hair. Some elements of the helmet are also mentioned in the song.

Analysis

Our analysis found several different elements in the performance – lyrics, singing, dance steps, body movements, gong playing – relate to what happens to the buffalo. In our analysis we have divided the text into "couplets", pairs of lines that have consistent poetic and musical features across multiple couplets.

Verse form

The main structural element of the song is the couplet. They are abbreviated "C" in our discussion and numbered according to the order in which they were performed. The two lines in a couplet are identified respectively as "a" and "b".

10 The Hakhun Buffalo Sacrifice (*li jwe*) Song

Each couplet has a similar melodic structure, but the melody of the a and b lines is distinct. The division of each couplet into two lines is based on Khithong's initial transcription and "translation" of the song text, which was of this form for C24 (our full linguistic analysis is presented below).

Example 10.1

> *rungsa ban jip theng o*
> horn this your sleeping place
>
> *rung pho ban tung theng o*
> horn this your seating place

Note that Khithong's original transcription separated the word *rungpho* into two separate words, but maintained *rungsa* as a single word. In our analysis below, both are given as single words. Khithong's first translation was more or less a word-by-word translation.

From the perspective of both the music and the text, couplets share a number of features. For example, subsequent discussions with Khithong identified numerous song particles, illustrated here by the syllable "*o*" at the end of each line. Song particles are used to facilitate the fundamental musical structure of the song, and are frequently set to a long note and thus clearly audible in the performance. Although these syllables do not convey lexical meaning, their euphonic sound quality punctuates the end of lines. A song particle usually comprises the single syllable "*a*" or "*o*", and sometimes "*u*" and two syllables such as "*lyo*". The melodic lines support the couplet structure: all a-lines end on pitch 2 and all b-lines end on pitch 1.[2]

Throughout the performance there is a lead singer who also dances, but the singers exchange this lead role, with a short overlap in the case of Couplet 15. Posim sings the first 14 couplets, and the first line of Couplet 15, before Phulim joins her for the vowel at the end of the line, and then for the second line of this couplet. Phulim subsequently sings four couplets, and Vaming follows with three couplets. During the last moments associated with the removal of the buffalo's tail, Posim sings an incomplete couplet, explained more fully below, and then three couplets, and Phulim finishes the song with five couplets, for a total of 31 couplets. Other dancers join in the song at specified moments, particularly for the "rhyming syllable" discussed later in this chapter. This stylistic feature seems to simultaneously illustrate and reinforce group support for the ritual event.

---

2   See Appendix E at sydneyuniversitypress.com/keepingtimeappendices.

Another important structural feature is the *asa he* ("good!") acclamation, which occurs at four different moments. The first instance coincides with the killing of the buffalo where it is shouted four times (at Couplet 12, Table 10.1). But in the following instances, *asa he* is shouted only twice each time. These occur at the end of Phulim's first section as leader, after C19, then at the end of Vaming's lead, after C22, when singing and dancing stop for the removal of the buffalo's tail, and at the end of the song, after C31. In all four instances, Vaming initiates the acclamation.

During the final moments of Phulim removing the buffalo's tail (at 6'34"), Posim sings the first line of C23. She then waits approximately 10 seconds to continue singing. During this time, Phulim finishes cutting off the buffalo's tail and places it in the basket Posim wears on her back. These two events evidently distract Posim from singing. She nonetheless continues her basic dance-step beat for five beats, then continues by singing a new a-line, beginning on the left foot this time, and renders a complete couplet (C24).

O structure – relation of dance steps, metre, rhythm and pitch

What we have termed "dance-step beats" of equal duration are basic components useful for establishing the metrical outline of the entire performance. These "dance-step beats" reflect both the underlying basic beat of the song and the basic pulse of the dance. A couplet consists of a unit of either eight beats or seven beats. Whereas a-lines are consistently four beats in length, b-lines are either four beats or three beats. The tempo of the dance-step beats increases somewhat, from 36 per minute at the beginning to 42 per minute at the end.

Singing occurs during the first three beats in each line of a couplet. The syllable sung on a beat is generally given strong emphasis, except at the end of a couplet. The fourth beat in a couplet is characterised by a rest in the text and the melody. Nonetheless, this beat is consistently articulated by a dance-step beat. As Posim begins the performance on her left foot, the four beats during C1a are danced L R L R. She also dances C1b with the steps L R L R, and a similar rest in the text and melody occurs on beat 8.

Whereas the a-lines always consist of 4 beats, with the single exception of 26a (3 beats), half the b-lines have 4 beats and the other half have 3 beats. The latter unit occurs in C13–17, 20–22, 24, 26–31: basically in the second half of the performance. Five exceptions to the standard length for a line can be attributed to a mistake or unsettling events occurring during the performance. These exceptions arise during C4b and C12a (6 beats), C6b and C23b (5 beats), and C26a (3 beats).

The standard length of a couplet (lines a and b combined) is thus seven beats (50 per cent) or eight beats (45 per cent). The length of each note is not indicated

10 The Hakhun Buffalo Sacrifice (*li jwe*) Song

precisely in Flora's transcription. Although the fundamental dance-step beats are isochronous, the rhythmic components of the song associated with a specific dance-step beat are enigmatic and await further study. Speech rhythm may be the explanation in some instances. To indicate brevity in this context, the short notes, similar to an anacrusis before the "beat", as distinct from the long notes, are represented by smaller numbers, which have stems with flags attached, and also sometimes show other symbols associated with Western notation, such as more-or-less horizontal beams.

Pitch

The text is sung using three basic pitches, identified in the notation by the numerals 1, 2 and 3. They are a whole tone apart sequentially, and 1 represents the lowest pitch. The lower two pitches are basically stable. They occur as longer tones of duration and as ornamental pitches. Pitch 3 is clearly different. Except when performed in a short ornamental capacity, pitch 3 is characteristically the starting point for an immediate descending glissando during a long note. This particular feature is an important and distinguishing attribute of the scale. A fourth pitch, at the interval of a minor third above pitch 3, is not prominent and occurs only eight times in an ornamental capacity.

Initially, a similarity with the anhemitonic pentatonic scale as found in the Western heptatonic major scale may come to mind, but in this instance such a similarity is not appropriate. The absence of a pitch at the interval of a major sixth above the lowest pitch, pitch 1, or at a minor third below it, together with the descending glissando after pitch 3 that is used to begin a long note, sets the scale associated with this song distinctly and uniquely apart from the pentatonic. The pitch material in this song may be usefully schematised, in number notation, as follows:

Example 10.2

$$1\text{--}2\text{--}3\backslash\ ^{1\text{-}2\text{-}3\text{-}4}.$$

The larger numbers indicate a pitch available for a long note. The superscript numbers indicate a pitch that may be used ornamentally, which only has a very short duration. A dash indicates the interval of a whole tone, and, in the case of pitches 1 and 2, a long note on the same pitch. The backslash symbol "\" above (which is shown as a descending curve in the transcription) is found only after pitch 3 and represents the characteristic downward glissando after pitch 3 which starts a long note.

In addition to the three pitches used for long notes, the schema in Example 10.2 shows that four pitches can be used for ornaments, indicated there by superscript numbers. The longer dash in the line after superscript 3 indicates the interval of a minor third. The level of pitch 1 is just below 270 Hz or cps, the latter pitch being equivalent to "middle C" in the Western system. All three participants sing at the same level and in the same range.

Music analysis

Table 10.1 displays the form of the total performance, as determined by its various structural aspects. Read from left to right the table shows the song unfolding over time, while the columns represent different simultaneous elements in the performance: singer, couplet, beats, gong and so on. Thus, the first row, marked "L", records the performance of each lead singer: Po = Posim, Ph = Phulim, Va = Vaming. The second row, "C", illustrates the sequence of couplets, which are identified by an Arabic numeral. The third row, "B", gives the number of beats in each couplet, first the a-line and then the b-line.

The fourth row, "G", identifies the couplets when Nyalik plays a gong. Row five, "E", records events related to the buffalo; namely, when the buffalo is successfully held down and tied (X), the couplet during which it is killed with a spear by Phulim (K), and the couplet when its tail is cut off (T), also by Phulim. The sixth row, "A", shows the moments when the acclamation *asa he* is shouted. Finally, the vertical line after C22 represents a hiatus in song and dance for approximately 40 seconds before the tail of the buffalo is cut off during C23a. In summary, the structure of the *li jwe* song and ritual under discussion may be grasped by reading the vertical columns in the table from top to bottom, and from left to right in sequence.

The affirmative shout *asa he* disrupts the metric organisation. The duration of the first acclamation of four shouts is 6 beats. This acclamation causes Posim's performance during C12a to be inaudible, and also causes her to add two dance-step beats at the end of this line. The second acclamation of two *asa he* shouts, occurs after C19 and lasts for three dance-step beats. Interestingly, from the beginning of the third acclamation, just after C22, when *asa he* is shouted twice again, she completes three dance-step beats, which is followed by a silent dance-step beat, before she stops her dance movement.[3] Initially, the fourth dance step seems to illustrate a mistake: that is, an added beat after the *asa he* acclamation, which is shouted twice, has ended.

Recently it came to light that *asa he* acclamations traditionally occurred as a unit of three, not as a pair or four times. In a video chat with Stephen (17 November 2021), Khithong noted:

---

3   See Appendix E at sydneyuniversitypress.com/keepingtimeappendices.

10 The Hakhun Buffalo Sacrifice (*li jwe*) Song

Table 10.1 Overview of the *li jwe* event.

L	Po										Ph								Va				Po			Ph					
C	1	2	3	4	5	6	7	8	9	10	11	12	13	14	15	16	17	18	19	20	21	22	23	24	25	26	27	28	29	30	31
B	44	44	46	44	45	44	44	44	44	44	64	53	43	43	43	43	44	44	43	43	43	43	45	43	44	33	43	43	43	43	43
G						G	G	G	G	G	G	G	G	G	G	G	G	G	G	G	G	G		G	G	G	G	G	G	G	G
E								X				K											T								
A										A			A					A				A									A

Key:

L Lead singer

C Couplet identifier

B Beats per line (a-line followed by b-line)

G Gong

E Events relating to buffalo: X – held down and tied; K – killed; T – tail cut off

A Acclamation *asa he* shouted

> This is actually important. It should be three. The forefathers said three times is equality – [*asa he*] coming from father, mother and child . . . which make up an exact and complete family. Thus, the forefathers told us that three was the correct number for this.

The symbolism associated with a unit of three shouts consequently strongly implies that a buffalo sacrifice is good for every member of a Hakhun family. Keeping this information in mind, Posim's four dance steps after C22 may well illustrate a somewhat faded memory for the earlier and more traditional Hakhun acclamation of three *asa he* shouts. During a *li jwe* song performance, that unit would require more than three dance-step beats.

It should be noted that although the *asa he* represents the whole family, it was traditionally only shouted by males. As Khithong said: "traditionally *asa he* shouting is done by men only during the time of *rumbe* and buffalo sacrifice. But these modern days, ladies [may] also join, like singing songs in church."

Posim's talking to observers, in three sentences at the end of C4b, does not notably compromise the overall couplet continuity, nor does her extra left-foot beat at the end of C6b, which can be attributed to the gong playing starting at that moment. But both instances, which happen early in the performance, disturb the apparent melo-metric (combination and relation of melody and metre) song structure that we hear and see emerging.

Posim seems to prefer the longer 8-beat couplet, and the men seem to prefer the shorter 7-beat couplet. Posim and Phulim sing together during C27, but they sing two different texts. Afterwards, for couplets 28–31, Posim joins Phulim at the end of each line. Overall, the ambiguity of the b-lines having 4 or 3 beats may highlight an instability perhaps due to the fading of this tradition, and the lack of practice before the performance of the song.

Language and poetics

The words of this *li jwe* ((Buffalo Sacrifice Song)) are mostly the same words as would be found in the spoken language, though there are some forms that were identified by Khithong Hakhun as "song language". Consider the "a" line of Couplet 1. This and following examples are presented in four lines:

  (i) the Hakhun text as agreed by Khithong,
  (ii) a phonemic rendition of Hakhun using some phonetic marks,
  (iii) a gloss, or word by word translation, and
  (iv) a free translation of the whole sentence.

10 The Hakhun Buffalo Sacrifice (*li jwe*) Song

Example 10.3

Cheq	nye	a	tanlim	kuq-ri.
cʰeʔ	ɲeᴸ	aᴴ	tanᴹlimᴴ	kuʔ-riᴹ
born	new	SO.PRT	increase	give-PROX.1PL

"The new-born are increasing for us."

Khithong indicated that in spoken language this would be realised as "*Cheq nye talim kuq ri*", with two differences between spoken and written text: first that the song particle *a* would not be present in spoken language; and secondly that the causative prefix *ta*- /tə-/ in spoken language is realised as *tan* in song language.

An understanding of the poetics of these songs relies on the observation that there are perhaps four types of words in these songs:

   v. content/lexical words carrying most of the meaning
  vi. grammatical words like imperative markers and agreement markers, such as *ri* and *ki* in Couplet 25
 vii. expressives that are often reduplicated (like tütü)
viii. song particles like *a*, *o*, &c, glossed as SO.PRT.

The "song particles", as we have termed them, might be called vocables in other types of analysis. They do not have ordinary semantic meaning and would not be listed in a dictionary, but they are an essential part of this particular song style. They can split compound words, as we see below in Example 10.5. Song particles are also found in the Pangwa Tangsa Wihu song (Morey and Schöpf 2019).

An important feature of this song style is that a single solo singer generally sings the text, but other singers join in on what we will term the "rhyming syllable", a song particle or vocable. In Example 10.4 we see C24 and C25, where in the a-lines, this was the particle *o* sung on a high pitch and marked with a high tone. In the b-lines it was particle *a*, sung after the word *tung* in 24b and after *van* in 25b. This "rhyming syllable" in the b-lines is lower in pitch and marked with a low tone and occurs after four syllables that are not song particles, usually content words, though they may be grammatical words like *ri* in 25b. On the melodic level, this constitutes what we can call a kind of pendulum structure, or pitch alternation of the phrase final vowels, or notes. The tones marked in the second line of the transcription are citation tones, except in the case of the "song particles" where we see high tones in a-lines, and low tones in b-lines. Consider couplets 24 and 25:

Example 10.4

C24 a. Rungsa　　ban　　jip　　theng　　**o.**
　　　ruŋᴸsaᴸ　　banᴹ　　ʒip　　tʰeŋᴸ　　**oᴴ**
　　　horn　　you　　sleep　　place　　**SO.PRT**

　　　"This horn is your sleeping place."

　　b. Rungpho　　ban　　tung　　**a**　　theng　　o.
　　　ruŋᴸpʰoᴸ　　banᴹ　　tuŋᴸ　　**aᴸ**　　tʰeŋᴸ　　oᴸ
　　　horn　　you　　　　**SO.PRT**　　place　　SO.PRT

　　　"This horn is your sitting place."

C25 a. Bwe　　jip　　a　　ri　　van　　ki　　**o.**
　　　bweᴴ　　ʒip　　aᴴ　　riᴹ　　vanᴴ　　kiᴹ　　**oᴴ**
　　　tired　　sleep　　SO.PRT　　PROX.IPL　　come　　IPL　　**SO.PRT**

　　　"Come here to us to rest from your weariness."

　　b. Bwe　　tung　　a　　ri　　van　　**a**　　ki　　o.
　　　bweᴴ　　tuŋᴹ　　aᴸ　　riᴹ　　vanᴴ　　**aᴸ**　　kiᴹ　　oᴸ
　　　tired　　sit　　SO.PRT　　PROX.IPL　　come　　**SO.PRT**　　IPL　　SO.PRT

　　　"Come here to sit and rest."

An example of a reduplicated word like *tütü* "having" is found in the text from the dance performance recorded on 24 December 2008 (later on the day that the Buffalo Sacrifice Song was recorded). In this couplet, presented as Example 10.5, we see the reduplicated word split by the rhyming syllable.

Example 10.5

　　a. Sero　　a　　dungrip　　nü　　**o.**
　　　sun　　SO.PRT　　rise　　DEM　　**SO.PRT**

　　　"Every (day) the sun will rise."

　　b. Rumrwen　　a　　me　　tü　　**a**　　(tü　　o).
　　　every time　　SO.PRT　　peace　　having　　**SO.PRT**　　(having　　SO.PRT)

　　　"And all the time we are having peace."

The phrase *tütü* is a single word but because the first syllable is the fourth non-song particle in the second line of the couplet, the rhyming syllable *a* is inserted in the middle of *tütü*. In this recording, there were no other singers joining in at this point in the song, but if they had been, they would have joined in the bolded syllables.

Many of the couplets show the feature of parallelism: that is, the same topic is expressed two times with similar words, a feature that has been found in many (oral) literatures of the world.[4]

Singing

The performance roles are distinct. In this performance, the lead singer was joined by the other two dancers on the final song particle or word of a couplet line ("rhyming syllable"), while the audience generally did not take part in the performance, except that several male members present joined in the "*asa he*" shout (see above for a discussion of the *asa he* "acclamation"). The gong player, Nyalik, did not sing in this instance; in other instances captured on video, the several gong players also do not sing.

The evidence currently available for identifying a consistent underlying melodic structure or form for the Hakhun *li jwe* genre is not very strong, because of the small number of couplets in the song under discussion, and we have not yet been able to compare this performance with others. With this caveat in mind, we believe that four components suggesting basic melodic features can be extracted from the performance of the song documented in the video.

1. The a-lines end on the mid- or high language tone and the middle music pitch.
2. The b-lines end on the low language tone and the low music pitch.
3. The overall phrase contour for a couplet, consequently, is descending.
4. An ascending interval often occurs between a single "ornamental" note and a following long note, and also often occurs in a pair of short "ornamental" notes.

These four points clearly reinforce other analytical data, which establish that certain elements in the descending shape of each couplet provide a notably more complicated overall sound image for a couplet in this *li jwe* song than a simple step-wise descent often associated with a descending melody. An analysis of four renditions of the first line in this song will illustrate this observation.

Posim renders the important phrase "*cheq nye tanlim*", glossed as "born new increase", in four distinct instances: lines 1a, 3b, 10b and 15a. Posim sings this text at the very beginning of the ritual, which may be significant, and each rendering exhibits a notable and impressive variation.

---

4   See Jakobson 1966. Turpin 2017b is an example discussing parallelism in songs in Australian Aboriginal languages.

In line 1a, Posim begins the song strongly with her first dance-step beat on "*cheq*", which is accented, and then "*nye*" is articulated immediately and implicitly emphasised by a long note, using the song particle "*a*" on pitch 2. Next, Posim gives primary emphasis to "*tanlim*" through two musical devices: first, by using the high pitch level 3 for "*lim*", which characteristically descends immediately, and second, by singing the euphonic sound "*m*" during the "long note" on dance-step beat 2.

In line 3b, by comparison, Posim stresses "*nye*" and "*tanlim*" in a different, symmetric manner. Each word is highlighted with an ascending and descending melodic interval, respectively, during a long note. This pattern is separated, within the total context of this *li jwe* song performance, by a dramatic two-part upper ornament on "*tanlim*" itself. This second version, with its clear shape of an arch, very effectively enhances the impact of the text. In both versions, the verb at the end of the phrase is "*kuq-ri*", "give to us".

In line 10b, Posim renders the word "*nye*" with a new and third melodic flourish. This time, she uses the weight of a dance-step beat for "*nye*", instead of placing it on the first word "*cheq*", as in the two earlier instances. The word "*tanlim*" in 10b is rendered as a short "ornament" on only one pitch, pitch 2, before the song particle *a* that follows "*tanlim*" is sung on pitch 1, for a long note. The rendering of "*tanlim*" here, in a relatively unadorned simplicity, is all the more notable with respect to how "*tanlim*" is sung by Posim in its two earlier occurrences. The meaning of "*tanlim*" ("increase") is thus highlighted here by Posim singing a third melodic configuration for this word.

In line 15a, "*nye*" occurs again on a dance-step beat, for a second time in succession, and is also given a fourth variation of melodic flourish. Posim renders "*tanlim*" here identically to her singing of this word in line 1a. In the last two instances of this phrase, the auxiliary verb at the end is *la*, "LET".

To summarise, although Posim sings the evocative words "*cheq nye tanlim*" four times, twice in an a-line and twice in a b-line, all four renditions are clearly different. In this ritual context, the interplay and rendition of the same words with respect to three different parameters – a dance-step beat, long notes, and the ornamental flourish preceding a long note – demonstrates the musical skills of the singer, Posim. Additionally, a circumscribed scale of three basic pitches and the use of a higher fourth pitch once ornamentally, together with the limits imposed by the length of a line and an overall descending shape in general, add notable value to the accomplished variations for the text "*cheq nye tanlim*" performed by Posim in this song.

10 The Hakhun Buffalo Sacrifice (*li jwe*) Song

We interpret this as an individual variation, and, speculating further, as an indication that there is no fixed melo-rhythmic structure behind this song. Rather, the evidence in this performance suggests that the structure of a *li jwe* song is variable to a certain extent, and subject to what may be described aptly as "hinge points" – such as the pitches available for a long note, which are sung usually with a song particle, and the number of beats or dance steps in the line of a couplet – around which the song is re-created for each and every performance afresh.[5] Seen as this, the song can be perfectly the same in an emic view, while clearly showing variations when individual performances are recorded and studied in detail.

The closest indication we find for a relatively specific yet tentative melo-metric template may be derived from the last five couplets led by Phulim in this recording, C27 through C31. In each of the 10 lines, a descending glissando from pitch 3 is performed during the first long note, respectively during dance-step beat 1 and dance-step beat 5. In the a-lines, pitch 2 is employed for the two remaining long notes, which are sung on beats 2 and 3 respectively. The song during dance-step beat 4 is always silent: no text, no musical tone. This silence reinforces the end of the a-line and also separates it from the b-line. But when Nyalik is playing a gong, the silence of the song at the end of an a-line is filled in somewhat.

In the b-line, the long note on beat 6 is pitch 1. The b-lines always end on a lower pitch than the a-lines and generally a glottal stop characteristically ends the couplet, on beat 7, also on pitch 1. Thus, the lower pitch and the final glottal stop together clearly differentiate b-lines from a-lines. This glottal stop is not notated in the linguistic transcription because we view it as a feature of the singing, not of the language. Note that there are language words with final glottal stops, such as "*duq*" ("hand") and "*kuq*" ("give") in C26b, written with *-q* in the orthography.

In this model, it is tempting to include an ornamental note on pitch 1 before each long note in the a-line. In a similar manner, it is tempting in the b-line to include an ornamental note on pitch 2 before the long note for beat 5, and also for beat 6. The ornamental pitch before the ending glottal stop on pitch 1, whenever an ornament is used at this point, is also on pitch 1.

Generally, Phulim and Vaming follow this model more or less consistently. Posim, by comparison, is more flexible in her rendition of such a template. The descending glissando from pitch 3 for a long note is sung by Posim on the second dance-step beat in two couplets, C1a and C15a, which comprise the same text. Additionally, she does not sing pitch 3 for either an ornamental note or to initiate a descending long note in four lines: 9a, 10a, 11a and 26a. Here the only components of the

---

5   See also Turpin 2007 relating the concept of "hinge points" or "hinge syllables".

scale employed are pitch 2 for long notes and as an ornamental note, and pitch 1 as an ornamental note. The text is different in each line.

Others joining in on the last syllable of a line is a common feature of many Hakhun songs. A more detailed discussion of this would require more Hakhun songs to be published and analysed.

We would like to highlight two observations regarding timbre. The third syllable of several a-lines is a song particle, and displays a short rapid repetition of its respective vowel, especially when sung by Phulim (for example, C17–18). In a musical analysis, it could be heard as the rendition of creaky voice, a vowel quality found in many languages of this region. Secondly, the vowels of b-line endings tend to increase in modulation (tremolo), a fact we already have established regionally as well.[6]

Dance

In other performances of Hakhun songs, the dance was performed in single file, led by gong players and immediately followed by the lead singer, in turn followed by more singers and dancers, all in line and together in step. In this performance, because there were not multiple gong players, this style of performance was not followed, although Khithong Hakhun did tell us that a full performance of the Buffalo Sacrifice Song would be done in this way. It remains unclear whether there is a rule starting a dance with either the left or the right foot, although this performance commences with the left foot. This dancing in sync requires practice and we were told that there had not been enough practice before the performance that we recorded. The dance is organised in a cycle of four parts on a single dance-step beat. These four parts can be described as follows:

   (i) the basic dance-step beat when the knee bends, then
   (ii) the knee rebounds
   (iii) the knee bends again, and
   (iv) the knee rebounds again.

Thus, in total, two knee bends occur for each dance-step beat. This is particularly clearly visible for Phulim in C16–19 and C27–31. Combining the left and right foot steps, the dance that occurs on every two beats, a left foot step followed by a right foot step, can be described thus:

---

6 See Morey and Schöpf 2019.

1. The leading foot (left in this instance) is placed on the ground, carrying the full body weight. Simultaneously both arms, holding the dance items, make a downward movement.
2. The (left) knee rebounds, carrying the full body weight while the right foot is either on the ground without weight or even a few centimetres above the ground. A second knee bend and rebound then occurs. Both arms may slightly follow the rebound to some extent.
3. The right foot is placed on the ground to the right side of the left foot, carrying the full body weight. Both arms may follow with the downward movement as in step 1.
4. The right knee rebounds, carrying the full body weight while the left foot is either on the ground without weight or even a few centimetres above the ground. Both arms may slightly follow the rebound to some extent.

What we have called "knee rebounds" are an already documented feature of other dances in the region,[7] where it is referred to as flexing the knees. Generally, Posim raised both arms at the beginning of a phrase, be it either a or b, and lowered them on or near beat 3 of that phrase, sometimes with a bit of emphasis on the lowering motion. Posim's dance-step beats were generally much more emphatic than either of the men. After a dance-step beat by Posim, her other foot was clearly off the ground in preparation for the next beat. This was not so clear with the men. Every placement of the foot can involve an inward or outward turn, alternating towards the left or right of the dancer. There are inconsistencies in the dancing that may be explained by the fact that neither performance was preceded by rehearsals.

Gong playing

The buffalo sacrifice was traditionally done with playing gongs, although as already noted in this performance gong playing was reduced so that the text of the song would be clearer on the recording. *Yam tum* is the Hakhun name for a low tone gong. Khithong pointed out that "there should be more gongs, at least 6, better still 10–15 females would play the gong". An onomatopoetic citation of the gong playing was given to us as "*ting ting tung tung ting ting tung tung*". In fact, gong 1 is the lower pitch, and the lower gong is the leader, so the musical organisation of the pattern would be better expressed as *tung tung ting ting tung tung ting ting*.

In a full traditional performance, gong playing would commence before the singing. Two gongs we had the chance to record in 2009 were in an interval of 535 cents, basically a "wide" fourth apart. The beating pattern was a four-beat cycle:

---

7   See e.g. Vatsyayan 1987, 127.

1. beat on the boss of the gong, letting the beater rebound so that the gong sounds freely
2. beat on the boss of the gong, letting the beater rebound so that the gong sounds freely
3. touch the boss of the gong with the beater to stop the sound
4. silence

In the 2009 performance, with two gong players, the patterns were shifted against each other by two beats: see the following transcription (O = ringing beat, X = stopped beat (damping beat), − = silence):

Gong 2 (2009):   −−OO−−OO−−OO−−OO−−OO−−OO−−OO

Gong 1 (2008 & 2009):   OOX−OOX−OOX−OOX−OOX−OOX−OOX−

Thus, the resulting pattern is efficiently described by the onomatopoetic citation above. Throughout this research, we entertained the hypothesis of a (somewhat "elastic") coordination between the couplet structure and dance on one hand, and the gong playing (4 gong patterns per line of song = 8 per couplet?) on the other, but there is no clear evidence in this performance to support or reject this. The other performance of 2009 that we recorded has not resolved this issue either. Khithong Hakhun made the point that these performances were not thoroughly rehearsed, and it may be that the lack of coordination between the couplet structure and the gong playing was due to that.

Sustainability

We assume Phulim initiated the singing of the Buffalo Sacrifice Song because he had worked sufficiently with us to know it would meet our interests. Whether it was of interest to him to revitalise the song is more elusive. We think when he performs rituals of pre-Christian beliefs, it is for him documentation not revitalisation. We are not sure he could easily separate the singing from the ritual. Khithong has stated that there is interest among younger people to keep the traditions, but we are unaware of the detail of any efforts to sustain aspects of performance since the ritual has been abolished. At the very least, the recording and documentation provides a possible reference for the community if such an effort were to be started in the future, and this is now the only way to hear the late Posim.

The recording was to some extent controlled by Phulim and Posim, when we consider that the gong was placed away from the cameras, and there was only one, unlike the "Impromptu dance" of the year later. We are entirely reliant on Khithong's translation and on his information about the context and cultural background of the song; it may be that if we were able to sit with Phulim and other elders to discuss these things with him we would get possibly richer answers.

Conclusion

Wolfgang Marschall (2008, 221) observed that "only in the rarest instances are musical instruments used to accompany singing . . . Instrumental music and dance go together, dance and singing go together, but there have been few links between instrumental music and singing". This song presents a different picture: the performance of a song (originally part of a ritual event) that includes simultaneous gong playing and solo and group singing together with dancing. Concurrent gong playing, singing and dancing in this tradition is particularly notable. The Hakhun Buffalo Sacrifice Song genre, of remarkable complexity in its own right, adds significant new data to the variety of cultural traditions documented heretofore among the peoples of north-east India, including Nagaland, and the western hill regions of Myanmar. To the best of our knowledge, discussion of a Buffalo Sacrifice Song, now apparently an extinct genre, has not appeared previously in the wide-ranging literature of the region.

We want to place this paper as an example of a renewed interest in the careful description of Naga songs, from the point of view of both text and music. Kaiser (2008) is a study of the complexity of song traditions and the difficulty of translating the song texts and their importance as a repository of cultural history. Kaiser's paper, however, only deals with the texts and not the music. Another valuable resource is the CD and accompanying booklet, which offers a highly informative survey of music from fifteen separate Naga communities (van Ham and Stirn 2004). With reference to our study, however, no Buffalo Sacrifice Song, which would be useful for comparative observations, is included among its 34 tracks.

In recent times in India, Posim, now deceased, Phulim and Vaming have been important carriers of Hakhun music culture generally. Additionally, their proactive efforts have enabled what is an important Hakhun cultural event, considered in this paper, to be documented for the record in meaningful detail.

Chapter 11

Music analysed: 20th-century ethnomusicology vis-à-vis Western music theory

Marcello Sorce Keller

This chapter is an attempt to survey how ethnomusicologists have, during the 20th century, approached the study of non-Western and traditional repertoires; the conceptual tools they chose for the task, their effectiveness and limitations. This attempt does not claim to comprehensively treat such a daunting topic. It is, less ambitiously, the result of what this writer more vividly recalls about his personal itinerary across both ethno- and historical musicology.

Sharing this itinerary may be like going down memory lane for old-timers like myself, while it might bring to the attention of younger scholars, as well as to practitioners of other disciplines, intersecting music studies (social sciences in particular), a segment of literature which – in my perception – no longer receives the consideration it deserves. A look at it in the light of contemporary perspectives may well reveal how some of what was done in the past may justify updating and then might become productive in contemporary research.

Why muse on analysis today

I began to study ethnomusicology in the early 1970s with Bruno Nettl, when John Blacking, Alan P. Merriam and Mantle Hood were also in their prime.[1] If we

---

1 Bruno Nettl was the one more frequently involved with transcription and analysis: Nettl 1958a; 1958b; 1964; 1987.

examine today their contributions, which so much characterised the field during the second half of the 20th century, one easily realises how much it has changed since then. The Fab Four of 20th century ethnomusicology paid much attention to the cultural dimension of music making and were, at the same time, curious about what makes sonic events tick. Moreover, their outlook was either explicitly or implicitly comparative.

Today comparative work is infrequent.[2] The practice of transcription, once part of the habitual training for students of ethnomusicology, followed by some sort of analysis, is also rather infrequent today (Hopkins 1966; Ellingson 1992). Clearly, since those days, much has happened: audiovisual ethnomusicology has become an area of primary engagement and a host of fascinating themes, not addressed by earlier scholarship, now occupy centre stage – among others, cultural engagement, ownership, agency, minorities, identity, gender, post-colonialism, intangible cultural heritage, power, conflict, ecosystems, preservation, maintenance, sustainability. It all goes to show how lively the field of ethnomusicology really is, and how powerfully intertwined sonic activities are with just about everything in human life . . . the good, the bad and the ugly: conflict, war, discrimination, and so on.[3] Apparently, enthusiasm for the newly opened areas of investigation has made some of the older ones lose some of their attractiveness.

It is somewhat of a paradox that transcription and analysis should recede into the background precisely at a time when computer science provides us with new and powerful analytical tools. To be sure, a minority group within the field is taking advantage of recent technology, but it is not representative of mainstream interests, those appearing in the foreground at conferences and in major publications.[4] No doubt interest in transcription and analysis has to contend with the perception

---

2 Merriam himself already noticed such a decline of interest in comparative work in his influential *The Anthropology of Music*: Merriam 1964. It may have been caused, at least in part, by the fact that cultural relativism, as professed by Franz Boas, Margaret Mead and Ruth Benedict, was at times interpreted as saying that cultures are so intrinsically different as to make comparison scarcely meaningful. To be sure, resistance to comparison, and transcription and analysis, has been attributed as well to their association with socio-cultural evolutionism and other various factors: Bohlman and Pegg 2001.
3 I use the term "sonic" in referring to sound proper as well as to "noise"; it has become common in analytical discourse since at least the 1970s: Cogan and Escot 1976.
4 See, for instance, the *Journal of Analytical Approaches to World Music*: AAWMjournal.com.

of the drawbacks they entail. One among others is how they are unsuitable to investigating how body movements relate to sonic actions.[5]

Hence my wish to look back and recall how theoretical and analytical discourse were pursued during the 20th century; not just in ethnomusicology but also in that branch of music studies concerned with the Western literate tradition, which, in the Anglo-American space, goes under the name of "music theory". There we have two areas of scholarship occasionally interacting with one another, while more often going their separate ways.

When traditions become theoretical

Patterns of social behaviour, even if beneficial for survival, do not necessarily become objects of theoretical discourse.[6] Most "social actions", in Talcott Parsons's terminology, establish themselves out of experience, habit or accepted wisdom (wise or not that it may be) (Parsons 1951). That applies as well to what in the West we call "music". In this particular context, theory and compositional practice developed in dialogue with one another, but that was not the case everywhere.[7] Of course, it needs to be pointed out how absence of theoretical frameworks does not mean absence of quality standards. It simply means they are not explicit and spelled out in an organised manner.[8]

It is quite a question to ask: under what circumstances may sonic practices become the object of theoretical elaboration? Whether or not cultures possess a concept embracing a wide range of practices, one comparable with a Western European

---

5 Anthony Seeger puts it this way: "Musical transcription, for a long time the starting point of analysis and later revealed to be very problematic, has been shown to be a useful tool for raising questions, but not for providing answers, about musical traditions. When combined with other techniques, transcription can contribute to analysis but should not be confused with it": A. Seeger 1987, 139.
6 Classical Greece produced literature, arts and philosophy galore, but no science of economics: no systematic study of how wealth can be produced, consumed and distributed – all activities which did not become the object of theoretical discussion.
7 In the 14th century, treatises by Philippe de Vitry (*Ars Nova*, 1320), Jan de Muris (*Ars Novae Musicae*, 1319) are already composition-oriented.
8 It is at any rate debatable to what extent Western theories have to do with the assessment of quality, perhaps with the exception of Schenker, whose aim was to explain why a masterpiece is a masterpiece: Schenker 1994–97. It is clear that – for instance – the Blackfoot Indians, whose song making does not rest on theoretical assumptions and explanations, intuitively judge quality of performance: Nettl 1989. Similarly, in Western "classical music", although it so much revolves around performance practice, there are no generally shared and accepted criteria to evaluate its quality.

concept of "music" seems to play a role. It does not often happen. Actually, an overview of sonic practices across the world reveals how the term "music" is not universal; no equivalent for it exists in most languages (Slobin 2011, 3). However "musical" some alien sonic practices may appear to Western ears, they are likely to be categorised by insiders in conceptual boxes they feel unrelated to one another; not, therefore, as genres of the same matter.[9]

In other words, what makes the concept of "music" so imposing in Western culture is, more than anything else, its hyper-inclusive nature. It brings under the same roof a range of practices that (in terms of production techniques, form and function) actually have little in common; in other words, it is a fuzzy concept (Sorce Keller 2010). Hence the perception of its pervasiveness, of something encountered almost everywhere and at any time. Should the concept be made more restrictive, its outreach would appear less imposing and attract less attention.[10]

Wherever, on the contrary, sonic practices (sound-centred, sound-complemented, sound-enhanced, and so on) are not felt amenable to be put into one single conceptual basket, their heterogeneity to a degree hinders the formation of a monumental avatar demanding theoretical engagement. It so appears that cultures possessing a meta-language for their sonic practices are those that refer to them with umbrella terms/concepts capable of covering a cluster of them. Good examples are Classical Greece, India and China. For example: the Greek term "mousiké" (μουσική) covered all that is encouraged by the Muses; "music" as we intend it today, plus poetry, dance, gymnastics, and at times even enchantments and medicine. The Hindu word saṃgīta (संगीत) refers to practices associated to the performing arts. The Chinese word Yīnyuè (音乐) carries various meanings, all referring to activities including sound (whether sound-centred, complemented, enhanced . . .).

But we should not overlook how theory is often found in conjunction with professionalism and notation.[11] Comparative musicology, at the turn of the 20th century, considered explicit theory, professionalism and notation as defining

---

9   Jean-Jacques Nattiez questioned whether it makes sense to speak of "music" in relation to cultures that do not use this concept: Nattiez 1990, 41. I share such misgivings. This is one reason that, where umbrella terms such as "music" are not present, I suggest speaking of "sonic actions", "behaviour" or "practices": Sorce Keller 2010.

10 In the West, a funeral lament, a rock concert and an oratorio are all categorised as "music". Should function become the primary consideration, they would appear to be different things. Even denizens of the so-called "classical music" tradition still call "music" (albeit of second-rate standing) all that lies beyond their practice.

11 A triplet of characteristics, truly an "ideal type", since each one of them may be present in a variety of forms and degrees.

11 Music analysed: 20th-century ethnomusicology vis-à-vis Western music theory

"high cultures"; an ethnocentric view, since, in the West, theory, notation and professionalism are central to the high-brow tradition.[12] Putting such "high cultures" on a higher pedestal than the so-called (at the time) "primitive" ones appears today untenable.[13] In fact, theory, notation and professionalism only express specific dimensions of sophistication valued in the West. Others exist that easily escape the attention of the Western mind.[14]

Analysis in search of a theory

If we think of "analysis" as the act of taking stock of and identifying what is most significant in the course of sonic utterances, then "theory" is the set of norms and constraints, expressing what one can actually do, likely to be accepted and perhaps valued within any given tradition.

Historically, analysis and theory served in Western culture two main purposes: transmission of the compositional craft (something ethnomusicology only to a limited extent investigated across traditions); and understanding what choices music makers arrive at, and under what constraints.[15] Ideally analysis has a focus: one can more aptly take apart an object of interest when knowing what to look for, and choose the appropriate tools for the job. One could think of such tools

---

12 The accepted view is that ethnomusicology, as defined in the 1950s, builds upon the previous experiences of the *vergleichende Musikwissenschaft* (comparative musicology), with the addition of those made in the field of cultural anthropology.

13 The concept of "high culture" was established during the second half of the 19th century, in the wake of evolutionism. Back then, it seemed reasonable to assume that cultures develop by stages, from simple to complex forms. The highest degree of complexity was – needless to say – seen in Western culture. Non-Western tonal systems appeared from that standpoint less developed and complex: Yasser 1932.

14 Judith Becker put it this way: "Complexity is not intrinsic to the music itself; it is the relation between the sophistication of the intent of the player, the musical performance, and the sophistication of the reception by a listener. Accidental variation, even though infinite, does not count. Skill does. Calculated, deliberate alteration of pitch, duration, rhythm, overtone structure (tone quality) attack, or release according to prescribed constraints creates a kind of complexity in a single line which is as demanding of the artist as any single passage in a Beethoven Symphony. A Japanese Shakuachi player or a solo singer of a Mongolian 'long song' are particularly striking examples of this kind of complexity" – 1986, 347.

15 Ethnomusicology has one more: to comprehend what function performances, genres, or entire traditions play in their habitat.

as being like fishing nets, the meshes of which are large or small, depending on the kind of fish one wishes to catch.[16]

Analysis, therefore, is to a considerable extent subjective. Even electronically generated sound spectra are at best only as objective as a picture-photograph (Jairazbhoy 1977b). Naturally, a subjective view need not be arbitrary. One's assumptions and goals can be clarified at the outset and so, in the end, results of the investigation tell us as much about the scholars as about the object of interest.

Another way of making sense of analytical endeavours is to observe to what extent they come from someone operating from within or from without the culture (which is, of course, a matter of degree). When facing alien traditions, without explicit theory, when scholars cannot gain sufficient knowledge from practitioners of the tradition, the pure outsider's approach is the sole possibility.[17] Observing function and modes of production is then a good way to start. By taking a performance apart at a later moment, there is a reasonable chance the individuality of single constituent elements might reveal itself: how they hang together and how they help the overall entity tick. That is how early comparative musicologists, armchair scholars, used to proceed, because they could not practise fieldwork, and anyhow their interests were so universal as to make impractical the very idea of it. In this situation, anybody who could provide recordings (travellers, colonial officers, all untrained in ethnography) was quite welcome. Naturally, such people could only provide minimal contextual information about where, when and how recordings were made. But today it is possible to work, at least to a degree, from within, when one has gained basic familiarity with the tradition (previous contacts and fieldwork), and whenever repertoires rely upon accessible insider theories. The possibility always remains that one may wish to go beyond and develop (outsider) theories promising further insights; like when Jonathan Stock suggested that

---

16 By way of example: if we dig into a Bruckner symphony, it does help to have in mind the classical sonata form model. Then it is not hard to realise how, instead of using it in its simple form, containing a first and a second theme, the composer comes up with extended thematic "clusters" for both the first and the second theme. The concept of sonata form is a net hardly capable of catching something in other contexts.

17 Here the problem comes up of how useful it may be to analyse cultures with tools that are alien to them. The question is encountered in Western musicology as well. It is in fact legitimate to ask whether older music benefits when analysed by the theoretical categories of its own time: Schubert 1994. In dealing with world music it is obvious to assume that insiders have a practical understanding of it (knowing through performance and/or habitual experience of it). In our age of cultural cross-fertilisation, insiders perhaps wishing to see how outsiders may relate to their own practices and then looking at how ethnomusicology approaches them is one good way to do it.

Schenkerian analysis could to some extent be used in ethnomusicological research (Stock 1993, 215–240).

Conservatorium students, who almost solely deal with the "common practice period" in European art music (1600–1900) routinely apply Hugo Riemann's theory of "harmonic functions" (Riemann 1893) – approach from within – that is, Western music analysed with tools belonging to the culture itself. In the different context of the Hindustani or Carnatic tradition, outsiders can profit from accessing the Râga and Tala systems as they are extensively discussed by an age-old insider literature and, in that sense, learn how to approach it from within. In the case of European medieval or Renaissance music we would be truly working from within if relying on coeval theory, which is seldom done. When instead modern concepts are applied, that is also an outsider's approach since, arguably, contemporary scholars are alien to the culture of the Middle Ages and the Renaissance, perhaps as much as they would be to the cultures of Java or Papua New Guinea (Everist 1992).

In the absence of notation developed by the culture itself, one can consider what insider informants can tell about what (from their standpoint) matters most in the sonic utterances they produce and utilise. How usable their information is depends on many factors.[18] Ethnomusicologists in any case strive to acquire as much familiarity as possible with their object of research through fieldwork (a sine qua non after World War II), and/or participant observation.[19] But in the end they will almost inevitably end up applying at least some conceptual tools alien to the culture they study. That is understandable, since the knowledge gained is not meant for the benefit of insiders, who are usually satisfied with their own way of understanding what they do, but rather to wider audiences, and for the benefit of intercultural understanding.

That is not to say that when insider theory and notation are available (articulating in a meta-language what sonic repertoires are about), one can proceed unhindered by obstacles. For one, culture-bound theories express the particular point of view of their makers, which may not necessarily lend itself to cross-cultural communication. Moreover, no theory or notation system can ever fully describe the tradition it relates to, just like no grammar can fully describe all the characteristics of a language. There seems to be an economy principle guiding cultures to systematise only what appears of primary interest. For instance, rhythm and metre in the Arab-Islamic tradition received – on a theoretical level – less attention than melody.

---

18 The difficulty of comprehension between scholar and informant has been often experienced since the early days of fieldwork practice: McAllester 1954.
19 Advantageous as fieldwork and participant observation obviously are, they are only viable in quite circumscribed situations.

In the West, only during the 19th century did orchestration became the object of treatises; and only in the second half of the 20th century did tone colour, texture and temporality became objects of serious inquiry.[20] The question is therefore how to look for a theory in the absence of it; and how to use existing ones in order to, ideally, offer something worth learning to both the insider and the outsider. Ultimately, this is a problem of cultural translation (Bohlman 2011).

At the turn of the 20th century, comparative musicology used to catalogue all pitches present in a performance, repertoire, genre or even an entire culture.[21] The study of scales, modes, metre and rhythms, with the intent of figuring out how a set (or subset) of pitches relates to one another occupied an entire generation of scholars.[22] As a result some general understanding of tonal systems was indeed gained, albeit with an ethnocentric tinge: concepts of scale, mode, tonal systems, metre and texture are central to Western musical thinking – and less so elsewhere. It anyhow emerged that interval relationships often work similarly in different cultures[23] and that in the domain of European folksong "gapped scales" are widely used (pentatonic with no semitones, also called "anhemitonic")[24] – a sort of "universal" as they are to be also encountered in many areas of the world.[25] Following on such acquisitions, melodic types and tune families could be identified within specific repertoires (Heinitz 1921; Bayard 1950; Bronson 1959–72; 1969; Suppan 1976–83; Bartók 1981).

---

20 Stockhausen's article on the perception of time in music remains to this day historically relevant (Stockhausen 1957).

21 *Gebrauchsleiter* was a term introduced by Hornbostel to indicate the tones actually used in a particular piece, and *Materialleiter*, in a contrastive fashion, to indicate the reservoir of tones and intervals out of which the music maker may choose the most appropriate for a single performance: Hornbostel 1912.

22 Bartók 1981; Danielou 1968; Heinitz 1931; Hornbostel 1912; Lach 1925; Schneider 1964.

23 Almost everywhere the octave, the fifth and the fourth are treated as focal, stable intervals.

24 Interestingly, the two "gaps" characterising the pentatonic scale may at times be occupied by "filler notes", which suggests a tendency for the pentatonic to become heptatonic.

25 Five-tone, anhemitonic scales are encountered in places as far apart as China, Hungary and the United Kingdom: Szabolcsi 1943; Wiora 1957. The concept of "universal" has been and continues to be problematic and controversial: Nettl 2005, 42–49.

Transcription as analytical procedure

"Transcription", and more generally "notation", is the process of mirroring sonic events by graphic symbols.[26] That entails a somewhat arbitrary translation from a "time" to a "spatial" dimension. In Western culture, where composition was for centuries conscious manipulation of form through notation, a mental representation of sound in spatial terms is immediate and unchallenged.[27]

In what we call "classical" or "art music", notation is no less than the embodiment of the work of art itself, a normative guide to proper performance.[28] Scholars, obviously, utilise it for other purposes. The notation they need is "descriptive" rather than "prescriptive", and a means for forcing upon the transcriber the most perceptive listening possible (jazz musicians habitually transcribe, to make sure no detail escapes their attention) (C. Seeger 1958).

Once a transcription is made, especially when trying to mirror something quite unfamiliar, one needs to formulate hypotheses, even if they may be proven false later, about what may be the significant elements in it (in other words, the "phonetic" versus "phonemic" dilemma). That is why insider notations are valuable: they offer a culture-specific view of the events they describe. Out of the overwhelming complexity of sonic events (that electronically generated spectra make visible) insider notations choose the essential (in their cultural setting), among what can actually be graphically represented, although not necessarily crucial. The tricky part is that notation leaves out what is both important and graphically expressible, but so established in oral tradition that there is no need to write it down – performers know what to do anyway. To put it differently, it cannot be ruled that all the essentials will be graphically represented. The major challenge is then to find out to what extent literate traditions rely on an oral tradition (in a

---

[26] "Transcription" is a sub-category of notation, since it logically requires the pre-existence of notation. Transcriptions and non-transcriptive notations (that is, prescriptive, solely intended to guide performance) among the prescriptive tablatures are a special case. Tablatures flourished in Europe through the 16th and 17th centuries and throughout Asia. They are instrument-specific. Without the instrument in your hands, they do not yield much information at all about how graphic symbols may translate into sound. In other words, by looking at a tablature a mental image of the piece cannot be gained.

[27] Not so in other contexts where sound may be considered as wet or dry, masculine or feminine, perfumed or smelly, and so on.

[28] UNESCO in 2001 included the autograph of Beethoven's 9th Symphony into the International Catalog Memory of the World.

jazz chart, for instance, it is practical to write straight quarter-notes; that performer will give them variable duration and accents according to the style of the piece).[29]

In absence of clues about the logic underlying sonic events, scholars need to look in all directions; open-minded investigations often lead to valuable discoveries. Jean-Jacques Nattiez was quite right in comparing musicological research with the activity of a sleuth (Nattiez 2007, 30–58). For instance, time and again investigators came to realise that melody, polyphony and rhythm – such primary constituents of Western music – in other contexts may be less relevant or even be absent, while function, tone colour and texture may be primary carriers of meaning. The very concept of a "note", for instance (that is, precise pitch, a discrete entity, neatly separated from the others), needs to be cautiously applied to traditions where glides between pitches are frequent and significant (like in India and the Middle East). In considering all such variables, it appears evident how transcription indeed is a first level of analytical inquiry.

Transcription has a history that considerably precedes ethnomusicology. During the 19th and early 20th century, musicians and folklorists often transcribed traditional or (as they were indicated at the time) "exotic" melodies.[30] They could not even rely on the phonograph – a novelty that, when finally available in the early 20th century, was bulky, heavy and expensive. Those early transcriptions appear today inadequate. But they are still historically significant, by showing us what their authors could discern in foreign-sounding repertoires and, in reverse, what may have escaped their attention (Barwick 1988). In dealing with oral traditions, East

---

29   The study of the interface between the written and the oral was initiated at the beginning of the 20th century by followers of the *Rezeptionstheorie*: Dessauer 1928; Meier 1906. But in those days exchanges between the oral and the written circuits were considered forms of corruption, not creative interventions as they are seen today: Barwick 1990; 1999; Sorce Keller 1990. Goody 1987 is a general discussion of how the oral and the written interact.

30   The European folk melodies as well as the extra-European melodies transcribed in Table N of Jean-Jacques Rousseau's *Dictionnaire de Musique* were widely known for quite some time and frequently quoted by composers (for example C.M. von Weber, Hindemith), who had no other source to find something exotic: Rousseau 1998 [1767].

11 Music analysed: 20th-century ethnomusicology vis-à-vis Western music theory

and West, transcribing techniques were for years the object of discussion.[31] The Western staff, often inadequate, was often times complemented by "diacritics".[32]

Occasionally even new notation systems, tailored for specific repertoires were devised.[33] Electronic instrumentation, of which the Seeger melograph was an early example, came into use in the 1960s (C. Seeger 1958, 184–195; Moore 1972). Advantageous indeed is how they give us images of sound, more analogical to human perception than other forms of representation. Even untrained people can easily find correlations between what they hear and what they see.[34] Today, even public domain sound-editing software (like, for instance, Audacity) yields intuitive images of tone colour. At any rate, spectra do not distinguish between "piece" and "performance", not necessarily relevant in many locales.[35]

Ethnomusicology, officially born with the American Society for Ethnomusicology in 1955, was from its inception much influenced by Anglo-American cultural anthropology. It comes from the clear persuasion that however much can be learned by studying sonic events in themselves, it is crucial to consider how they do not occur in a vacuum: place, time and function do shape how they are made and perceived. It may seem obvious to say so today, but the reality is that much of Western music history and analysis has been dealing with reputed immortal masterpieces, without considering how their transposition in time and place alters their import. It is, in fact, easy to observe how sound makers by necessity need to relate, for instance, to the background noise surrounding them. They also operate differently, depending on whether what they do is meant to be a centrepiece event or, rather, something marginal and complementary. Context always is crucial. A few instances may suffice to clarify the point: operatic singing developed out of the necessity of being heard in large theatres at times when no amplification existed; crooning in American popular song came about when the microphone allowed a soft singing voice to stand out even when accompanied by a large

---

31 In November 1963, during the Eighth Annual Meeting of the Society for Ethnomusicology at Wesleyan University, one session was devoted to a "Colloquium on Transcription and Analysis". Participants were, among others, Robert Garfias, Mieczyslaw Kolinski, George List, Willard Rhodes and Charles Seeger: England 1964.
32 They are graphic signs modifying the meaning of other pre-existing standardised signs. Diacritics are used in order to adapt Western notation to non-Western repertoires or oral traditions more generally. Their use was introduced by two of the founders of comparative musicology in Germany: Abraham and Hornbostel 1909.
33 IMC-UNESCO 1952; Korde 1985; Schuiling 2019.
34 Cogan 1984.
35 "Shazam", the application so many young people have on their smartphones, does in fact recognise performance, but not different renditions of the same song.

orchestra. In extreme cases, a different framing of a performance may engender misunderstanding of the meaning it originally intended to carry – which is not necessarily something to regret. In fact, new aesthetic experiences may develop, tailored to the new time–space situation. It happened, for instance, when the hippie generation made sense, in its very own way, of Ravi Shankar when he performed at Woodstock in 1969 (Sorce Keller 2001; 2021). What is intriguing about such forms of re-contextualisation and cultural translation is how they activate "creative listening": that is, the ability to attach new meaning, new import, to sonic utterances that originally they were not meant to have. Our grandfathers could only appreciate Verdi or Wagner, but not both of them. Today it is our creative listening ability that makes it possible for us to make sense of both those great composers – by experiencing them, no doubt, in a way much unlike how they were experienced at the turn of the 20th century.

Ethnomusicologists are, no doubt, more alert than other scholars to relationships between performance and its context, and it is easy to see why. Historians of Western music deal with compositions put on paper by authors who almost never knew where, when and under what circumstances performance would take place – often not even for the premiere. Hence, interest in the original text (the score) largely outweighs any interest in how pieces interact with different locales, at different times, although we do know that, when authors knew the destination of their compositions, they made use of that knowledge.[36] Ethnomusicologists, on the contrary, do not study scores but rather witness live events, events that almost never are realisations of a normative text. The transition to ethnomusicology as we know it today, after World War II, is in fact through the awareness of how important it is to be an eye-witness: hence the practice of fieldwork, first developed in anthropology and sociology, become a sine qua non for serious research, at least on small target areas. Putting it more generally, personal experience of sonic events leads one to appreciate how much what historians of Western music call "extra musical" contributes to the meaning of what is considered to be strictly "musical".[37]

---

36 That happened more frequently in the domain of opera. Italian opera composers would habitually adapt their works for Parisian performances, taking into consideration the expectation of the French public (as did Giuseppe Verdi with *Don Carlos*). Another example is harmonic rhythm in Bach: less dynamic in cantatas and oratorios (meant for the church, where a high reverberation is expected) than in his harpsichord pieces (meant for home performance).

37 One example: Gilbert Rouget convincingly maintains how the "power of music" in triggering a "trance" state of consciousness may unfold quite differently, depending on time and place; the relations between sonic events and trance mainly depends on the system of meaning shared in any particular cultural context: Rouget 1980.

11 Music analysed: 20th-century ethnomusicology vis-à-vis Western music theory

It is fascinating how witnessing sonic activities may at times reveal that sonic activities, although most often functional to the environment for which they were planned (or in which they were transported and, so to say, translated), can also be dysfunctional. This one aspect has been most apparent in the domain of protest songs, and in that branch of contemporary ethnomusicology studying conflict and war. Only seldom was this aspect highlighted in apparently anodyne repertoires that, although on the surface not appearing antagonistic to the established social order, yet may serve ideological purposes of some kind or another (Sorce Keller 2012, 113–140).

Finally, while giving much attention to the functional, or dysfunctional, role of performances or repertoires, the risk is that of insufficiently observing sound itself, which the present writer feels has occurred in much scholarship produced in this new century. Just like historical musicology often turns out to be "literature about music", ethnomusicology runs an equal risk of becoming the study of the social relationships surrounding sonic activities. Both are forms of circumnavigating the sonic continent, without actually ever putting boots on the ground.[38] How our "musical others" may feel about such forms of "circumnavigation" is, of course, an interesting question waiting for an answer.

Analysis: pros and cons

Probably because analysis is so problematic, it always had friends as well as foes, and not solely among ethnomusicologists.

Even practising musicians nourish misgivings about it. For one thing, they seldom wish to analytically examine what they do. They possess a "practical consciousness" of the craft, rather than a "discursive consciousness" of it, and the former is often felt to be quite satisfying. Scholarship, of course, is concerned with the latter.[39] It also needs to be noted how many residual Romantic attitudes are still alive in Western culture among the general public. They support the fallacy that methodically investigating a work of art, dissecting it as it were on the anatomical table, is tantamount to humbling or even offending its poetic content.

---

38 A concern also expressed by Joseph Kerman: "My own hesitation before contextual studies ... is founded on the impression that they really are usually tilted much too far towards the consideration of contexts. They usually deal too little with the music as music": Kerman 1985, 180.

39 "To deserve the name, I contend, knowledge must be communicable and in that sense public and also useful, I mean, capable of being transmitted into successful action", Gordon Childe 1956, 4.

Adepts of Western art music also at times lament that predominance of analysis might distract from giving due importance to historical inquiry, and criticism: that is, examining the meaning music conveys, the pleasure it triggers and the value it holds for society. Such a concern was once voiced by Joseph Kerman in an article titled "How We Got into Analysis, and How to Get Out" (Kerman 1980). But he himself conceded that analysis "does at least concentrate one's attention on individual works of art rather than on historical generalization or bibliographical minutiae" (Kerman 1985, 115).

Ethnomusicology, it must be conceded, never developed "criticism", if by that the effort to gauge aesthetic quality is intended (surely the least quantifiable element of any activity), nor has it been keen in verifying authorship (which most everywhere is no useful concept to go by). Even less has it been striving to produce critical editions, although in the past the idea of finding and documenting "pure", "uncontaminated" traditions was quite present in the field, no doubt part of ethnocentric attitudes, and so difficult to phase out.[40]

Theories for the entire world

Both Bruno Nettl and Stephen Blum extensively discussed the role and forms of analysis in ethnomusicology (Nettl 1964, 98–203; 2005, 92–112; Blum 1992, 165–218). They particularly highlighted the role of "schools": the German school of comparative musicology (led by E.M. von Hornbostel), the German-American (initiated by Franz Boas), the Anglo-American (started by Cecil Sharp), the Hungarian (founded by Béla Bartók and Zoltán Kodály) and so on.[41]

Interestingly (with the exception of the early Hornbostel school, eager to scan the entire planet), many approaches mostly focused on local situations. So too, more systematically than others, did Béla Bartók with his analytical and classification work tailored to Hungarian folksong (Bartók 1981; Sorce Keller 1984). But a few scholars did cultivate the ambition of developing approaches suitable for cross-cultural application. Among them, Mieczyslaw Kolinski (1901–1981), who also strove to avoid as much as possible the ethnocentric bias of traditional analysis cultivated in Western music (Falck and Rice 1982). Alan Lomax (1915–2002) also stands out in this respect. However controversial his general conclusions were,

---

40 All sonic activities and products are actually the result of hybridisation processes of some sort, genres and authors alike.
41 An idea of how much analytical approaches differ can also be gained by the collection of articles edited by Kay Kaufmann Shelemay in the series The Garland Library of Readings in Ethnomusicology, in particular vol. V, *Cross-Cultural Musical Analysis*: Shelemay 1990.

11 Music analysed: 20th-century ethnomusicology vis-à-vis Western music theory

his effort to look for correlations between the specific manner in which social groups take up roles in the performance, their modes of voice production, tonal blend, pitch quality and texture was quite original (Lomax 1968). Texture, the way melodic and rhythmic elements, plus polyphony, register shifts, volume, silence and so on merge in performance thus determining its aural impact began to be explored by students of Western music only a few years later (LaRue 1970; Cogan and Escot 1976; Cogan 1987). Undeniably, texture quality (what rock musicians call "sound") is the most immediately striking aspect of musical style anywhere: what listeners instantly perceive as something that either draws them closer or, on the contrary, repels them. Let us consider, for example, how immediate the response can be to the texture of a gamelan (it is thick, leaving hardly room for moments of silence), or to the Japanese gagaku (where silence characterises the genre as much as sonic events).

There have been other attempts at developing methods of cross-cultural analysis, some of them inspired by linguistics.[42] A later one was the ambitious attempt by Jay Rahn to apply to a broader range of musics across the world the theories that Benjamin Boretz had developed for the Western repertoire (Rahn 1983; Boretz 1969).

None of the above, or the other approaches not mentioned here, found much following, which is tantamount to saying that ethnomusicologist do not share paradigms as Western music scholars do (Rameau, Riemann, Schenker and so on). Why that is the case can be explained, at least in part, by the fact that confronting profoundly diverse sonic realities makes it hard to develop approaches equally effective for many of them. All theories aspiring to do so remain in the history of the field as inspiring models of intellectual engagement, waiting to be updated and to nourish future endeavours.

Conclusion

Most ethnomusicologists through the 20th century and up until today have been all-rounder scholars: fieldworkers, audio and film operators, analysts and even archivists. Barwick is exemplary in having touched nearly all areas of interest to the field (Barwick 1988; 1989; 2003; 2005b; 2009; 2011a; 2011b). This needed versatility is, arguably, one of the most attractive and fascinating aspects of ethnomusicologists' form of intellectual endeavour. Equally fascinating is how in ethnomusicology, day after day, new areas are opened to investigation, not previously

---

[42] The influence of linguistics in ethnomusicology began to be felt in late 1950s: Becker and Becker 1979; Blacking 1971; Kolinsky 1982; Nettl 1958a; Powers 1980.

discerned. They are all intellectually engaging and, in my view, even potentially useful beyond ethnomusicology. It seems to me, in fact, that if politicians were aware of how music works (in situations where cultural engagement, ownership, minorities, identity, gender, post-colonialism, intangible cultural heritage, power, conflict, sonic ecosystems, preservation, maintenance and sustainability are at play), their agenda would reflect a better understanding of society (Pettan and Titon 2015). That is because ethnomusicology has made it more evident, beyond any possible doubt, that how humans engage with sound always matters, anywhere and everywhere. Yet, in the absence of shared approaches, it is difficult to put together a wide-angle view – a model – of the sonic shell covering our planet and of its dynamics – which would seem to be the ultimate goal. More specifically, the fundamental unanswered question, at present, remains the following: why do some specific sounds function the way they do, and not others? Or could other sonic concoctions serve the same purpose equally well? John Blacking implicitly expressed that question when he wrote:

> We need a unitary method of musical analysis which can not only be applied to *all* music, but can explain both the form, the social and emotional content, and the effects of music as systems of relationships between an infinite number of variables. (Blacking 1971, 93)

I certainly do not know whether we will eventually ever get there. It just seems to me unthinkable that any progress in that direction may come without a strong analytical engagement in ethnomusicology.

Chapter 12

Singing Moonfish, hearing Country

Genevieve Campbell with Yikliya Eustace Tipiloura

Describing to me how songs are composed for ceremony, senior Tiwi song custodian Yikliya Eustace Tipiloura[1] said, "ngintiri wartuwanimunguma" – we heard the bush.

wartuwani "bushland"
mungu "brain, mind"
-ma "become"

He explained that to hear something is for one's mind to absorb it; he hears the place and he knows it. *Mungumuwu* means "to know or be aware of something"; "to sit or place one's mind there". Tiwi Elders often refer to the people about whom they are singing through allusion to associated places, totemic animals or plants, kinship relationships and ancestral stories. Full understanding of any song text relies on the hearer's ability to decode the buried message by applying their own accumulated knowledge to the poetic inventions they are listening to. The singer (who would traditionally also be the composer) presumes that the listener can connect the dots. Situational context is core to most songs, with composers mining the stories, names and symbolic connections of the people for whom they are singing. Their listeners, in turn, accumulate cultural knowledge through regular participation in gatherings where songs tell of the Palingarri (deep past) ancestral stories, of totemic beings and of the interwoven structures of kinship

---

1 Eustace Tipiloura's unique Tiwi name is Yikliya. He was also widely known by his Christian name Eustace. To avoid confusion with other singers sharing the Tipiloura name in the archive and in respect for Yikliya and the addition of his cultural knowledge to the literature, I will refer to Yikliya throughout this chapter.

systems. Kinship connections, shared oral history and an unbroken presence in a relatively small place create a degree of communal knowledge – of plants and animals, natural features and sacred sites.

As the basis on which many Tiwi song texts are built, the allusions to Country, ancestor and kinship are not just an affirmation of belonging, but an act of knowing, of speaking a code that is only understood by those who have the cultural authority and ownership to know it. Allusion, in its creation of a layer of opacity to the outsider, serves to safeguard cultural information and necessitate interpersonal inculcation – with the holders of the knowledge relied upon and in turn revered for their artistic ability to continue to create it. Educated Tiwi listeners (as with any musical genre) will have emotional and intellectual responses to what they are hearing, partly based on what they expect to be hearing of that music. Each of the classical Tiwi melodies, intrinsically attached to a ritual function and performance context, elicits a response – whether one of ritual protocol, sorrow or joy. Across all these melodies are the variations, ornamentations and artistic embellishments (whether extemporised or composed) that allow listeners to hear individuals with their own vocal and poetic styles. Tiwi listeners also hear similarities along family lines of vocal techniques and timbres, and the passing on of subject matter, ancestral names and places.

The comparative value given to oral and written systems of recording, "proving" and disseminating knowledge is the subject of numerous academic discussions about cross-cultural comparison of epistemology and indigenous knowledge systems in the anthropological space (Bolisani and Bratianu 2018; Chiu et al. 2010; Odora-Hoppers 2002) and the incorporation of First Nations peoples' knowledge systems in ecological and environmental research (Ericksen, Woodley et al. 2005; Birch 2016; Goulding, Steels and McGarty 2015; Laughren, Curran et al. 2016). The emerging recognition of First Nations cultures' deeply valued and performed acknowledgement of human/non-human co-inhabitation of the world is valuable, but still has a comparatively small research voice. My work with Tiwi song custodians has always had a primarily performance- and practice-led focus, so we find ourselves part of emerging discussions on the contrasting understandings of what knowledge is. Whereas observational research, especially with the collection of recorded materials, tends to remove facts from their context and place, to then be (re)-written down (usually by outsiders), away from the source, Indigenous knowledge is grounded in the ongoing and interactive connection between the knowledge holder and the content, subject and physical context.

I was very fortunate to spend some (but not enough) time with Yikliya Eustace Tipiloura, a senior culture man respected in particular as a leader in song composition and the performance of ceremonial song following the "old" or "hard" ways.² In several sessions over the course of about five years we listened through a series of Tiwi Purruruti (Moonfish) songs, making some transcriptions and translations. The songs had been recorded in a Yiloti (Final) mortuary ceremony held in 1966, which he remembered. In 1966 he was among the young men who did not yet lead the singing, but he listened to the old men and picked up words and said, "really I'm still learning from them now off this cassette tape recording". We had plans to spend many more hours working on the recordings of the Moonfish songs. He reported back to me a number of times that those recordings had inspired his new compositions, both for our performances together and for ceremonies he led for his community. He told me that he had used "some of those really hard words, you know? Those special old words with really good meaning". Aside from their poetic value, the Moonfish songs gave Yikliya and his family important affirmation of lineages of custodianship of a particular area of his ancestral Country. These had always been known and valued, but here in these songs was "proof" (if that was needed). It was "unwritten, unsaid, just known" (Ayre and Mackenzie 2013) and now we knew that it was being sung.

Yikliya was a catalyst for my application, in 2018, for a University of Sydney postdoctoral fellowship and with him as my central consultant I proposed building the project around Moonfish in a discussion of mortuary songs and their role as conduit between the living and the dead. On his lead, we planned this also to be the framework on which to build a descriptive "method" for composing ceremonial songs, as he and other senior knowledge holders saw the decline in capacity in this area having a growing negative impact on their community. Yikliya died³ a few weeks before the application deadline. I succumbed to a deep sense of failure that I'd not been able to win funding, to get my foot in the door to facilitate research and work with him on his songs. I'd presumed that, at his age of just 70, he would remain healthy and alive for some time yet. I'd taken his presence for granted. I wallowed in self-pity and a cynical sense of the irony of the situation – my proposed project title was "The impact of death on Tiwi song practice in the

---

2   The "old" or "hard" way is used by many Tiwi people to describe the classical song forms, language and poetic devices of the classical song practice, the composition of which is now out of reach of all but a small handful of senior singers.

3   In Tiwi culture, the name, image, voice of and places and songs closely associated with a deceased person are "closed" (not to be spoken, seen, heard) for a period of mourning. This period can vary depending on family wishes, but it is usually until the Yiloti (Final) mortuary ceremony has been held, about one year after their death. After this, the spirit of the deceased has been released and restrictions are lifted. Mr Tipiloura's name and words are included here with the knowledge and permission of his family.

context of artistic creativity, cultural maintenance and community well-being". I remember very clearly Barwick telling me to leave the application as it was and simply to add a caveat at the end, to the effect that, if there was any need for evidence of the impact of Elders passing away before they have the chance to teach their songs, this was it.[4]

The songs aren't closed as such, but since Yikliya has passed there has been reticence to continue work on the Moonfish recordings among the senior singers remaining, as they were considered his to study and his to sing from. He was the person who had custodianship and took responsibility for learning these words and their poetry. My transcriptions therefore remain incomplete, and it is only the information he shared that I include here. I present only the segments of song that Yikliya wanted to put into writing. The whole remains intact as a resource of Tiwi oral knowledge, and as recent discussion in the literature acknowledges (Curran, Barwick et al. 2019), that is often its most valuable and meaningful form.

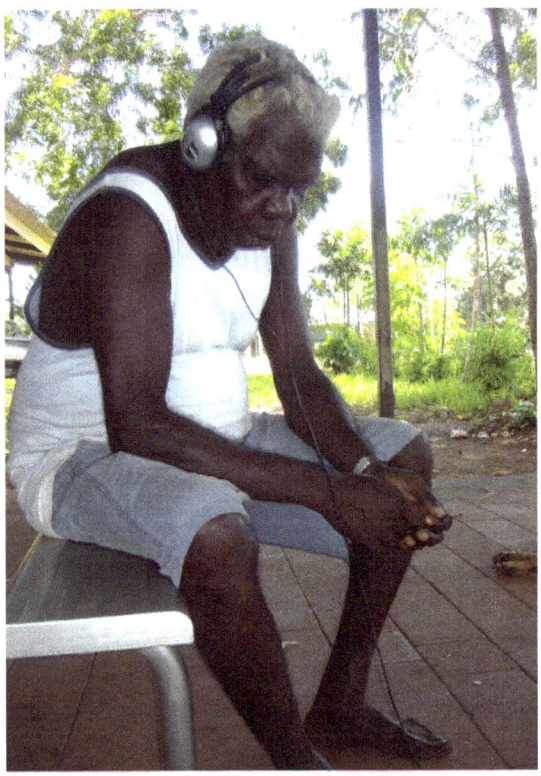

Figure 12.1 Yikliya Eustace Tipiloura listens to the Moonfish recordings, Wurrumiyanga, 2010. Photo: Genevieve Campbell.

---

4   Perhaps the untimely loss of my proposed research colleague hit home with the panel, because my application was successful. While the Moonfish songs did not feature in my re-adjusted Fellowship project, I did work with Tiwi Elders in assessing the inter-relatedness of song skills necessary for eschatological processes and individual and community wellbeing.

We listen to 1966. We can hear that a large crowd has gathered for Ceremony. Some are there to perform as ritual workers, having been paid (in cash, smokes, or beer later on). All are there to participate in some way. All will watch, clap in time with the dancers and follow the procedure, some from an outer circle distance and most coming into the circle to dance when it is their turn alongside others in their kinship group, relating to the deceased. Perhaps sitting on the ground off to one side is non-Tiwi researcher and art collector Sandra Holmes, who is there with permission and the knowledge of family to make an audiocassette recording of the event. Some people, such as the main singers and close family, would know they were being recorded, and perhaps were paid by Holmes.[5] Others might not be aware she was recording at all. There is no real way of knowing how this might have affected the singers/dancers/mourners or if it determined any choices of words or procedure. What we can tell is that this was a large gathering and an important event.

Sandra Holmes catalogued this recording of Yoi[6] as "for a man" (whom she presumably didn't name out of respect). Through a series of over a dozen songs, Holmes noted "this is the same song" and "another song about Moonfish".[7] While they are all about Moonfish, they are not the same song, but each has distinctly different words, imagery and intent. On a backdrop theme of Moonfish, the songs elegantly shift and change to support and to mirror the ceremony as it moves through its various stages and participants. Moonfish is a totem significant to people of the Wulurangku Country group, custodians of the central and northern land of Melville Island and of the reefs, estuaries and creeks in which the fish are found. So in song, Moonfish is an acknowledgement of Country, but also an anthropomorphising of the country itself. The country is alive and active in the movement of the Moonfish, the lifeblood of the place is in the nourishment it gives and in the seasonal refreshing of the life in the creeks. The Moonfish in these following songs are the vitality of this special place, sacred to certain families.

The Yiloti ceremony was held across the third, fourth, fifth and sixth of June 1966, near Milikapiti, for Mampurringamirri Pilakui (also known as Charlie

---

5   Mary Elizabeth Moreen, now a senior culture woman at Milikapiti, recalled her parents (Allie and Polly Miller) being paid by Holmes for their time as interviewees and singers.
6   The "Yoi" in this context refers to the danced and sung event – a large gathering of mourners within a series of mortuary-associated rituals held after a person's death, often spanning around one year. It is after the Yiloti (Final) ceremony in that series that restrictions on the name, image and recorded voice (if relevant) of the deceased are lifted.
7   The material discussed here relates to AIATSIS catalogue: S03_000184A and S03_000184B, recordings made by Holmes on 04–06 June 1966.

Fourcroy).[8] We can hear that it is a large crowd, and Yikliya confirmed that around 100 people would have been coming and going across the four days. There might have been a few non-Tiwi attendees who knew Charlie Fourcroy but in the main this was a ceremony for Tiwi people. On the first evening, the Yilaniya (smoking) ceremony was held with Pupartingirriti (Long Len), Tankila Punguatji and Walter Punguatji leading the singing, with the larger group joining in as they picked up or "caught" the words, as Yikliya described it. The songs performed across about three hours on the first evening all refered to Moonfish (the ancestral totem of the dead man – his "Dreaming"),[9] and although none overtly mentioned death, a spiritual journey, the dead man himself, or his Country, the songs related to all of these. Together the songs traced the swum paths of the fish and created a series of images and allusions to the ritual journey the deceased was taking as he moved to the next state of his existence, leaving his family and friends behind. On the audio, we hear Eleanor Mungatopi whispering asides to Holmes, acting as interpreter and guide, and giving information, comments and descriptions of what is going on and what is being sung. As she was the primary Tiwi source at the time and the person making the translations, it is important to include her words here. When Yikliya listened to the recording, he listened to Eleanor Mungatopi as well as to the participants of the ceremony. This provided an interesting time overlap, as he listened to an event that he had been present at, knowing more now than he did back then of what he was hearing. Some of the sung phrases were difficult for Yikliya to decipher because of the noise of the large gathering at the ceremony, the sometimes-inconsistent quality of the audio, and some gaps in his own understanding of the poetry created by the senior singers who in 1966 had a living memory connection to the generation of composers and singers before them.

It makes sense that for people surrounded by water there would be numerous and descriptive words for it – for the sea, the rain, the creeks and waterholes, the waves, and the tide. The action of water in all its forms has a demonstrable impact on people's daily lives and so in songs there are richly poetic depictions of interaction and engagement with it, of the anthropomorphism and personalising of it, and the metaphorical symbolising of people, places and relationships in it. This series of Moonfish images shows us how certain associated words, when woven through songs, also create an aural sense of place.

---

8   I can mention his name now that his ceremony is over. The name Charlie Fourcroy was coined by the Mission because he lived at Jikilaruwu, near the colonial place Cape Fourcroy, on the south-western coast of Bathurst Island.

9   "Dreaming" is used by Tiwi people when speaking in English to refer generally to one's Country-associated ancestral totem identity.

The primarily monotonic and isorhythmic melodic form sung here is consistent with the Jipuwakirimi.[10] After pitch fluctuations at the start of a line (at the performative discretion of the lead singer) the pitch settles to a repeating string of syllables across regular beats that enables group participation and dancing. This continuing pitch, interspersed with interjections from individuals and the group, creates an almost unbroken flow of notes gently undulating around a "tonic" by about three tones. When considered separately the short songs strung together across the hours-long performance are aural flashes, images of water, creeks and fish. When listened to as a whole they become the journey of the deceased and an overarching narrative of the ceremony itself. Just as the melody undulates and the singing ebbs and flows as soloists begin and are joined by the group who enter to dance and then retreat from the circle, the volume of voices ebbs and flows and the songs become almost an onomatopoeic description of tidal wash.

The first song sets the scene. These words were all that Yikliya could decipher, but from them he offered the extrapolation in italics below.

-mawula (twist/turn) mirripaka (sea) mirripakama (rough sea, waves)
The waves are flipping the moonfish around in the water.

This, he said, is like the deceased is "walking . . . strong and alive and energy, you know? There in his country". The moonfish are found in the creek to the southeast of Milikapiti, so these first few songs place them there and so, by extension, place the lineage of the deceased there in their country.

Kutampila wingayampitirrirra mangurrulumpwarni
The sea tide is coming in.

This segment of text includes the sung form of *mangulumpwarni*, itself a now archaic word meaning "tide". In this segment, the first sung phrase, it might seem to be a simple narrative device – setting the scene by telling us that the tide is coming in. Listening further though, we hear that it connects physically (as it does etymologically) the various states of water in this place, forming an aural and poetic thread through all the songs in this ceremony. As we listen through each reiteration of this first song and then repeating iterations of the songs that follow, we hear more words for the water in this place, all adding to the accumulated aural and poetic image of the physical place where the moonfish are found. As we will see, this also creates a multilayered, multisensory and multi-temporal image of the aural, physical, spiritual and ritual place.

---

10 Jipuwakirimi is the central song type of the group-participation song and dance events that constitute mortuary ceremonies. For further description see G. Campbell 2023.

With the passage of time not all of the words in the recording are clearly transcribable, due to the audio quality of the recording, changes in language, and the artistic licence taken by singer composers. Nor then are they exactly translatable. However, many of the words that describe the tides, water, creeks and mangroves are etymologically connected. Approaching these with a Tiwi dictionary in hand gives us a clue as to how to translate them, but we have to remember that, when they were sung, these words were altered, through addition, deletion and/or repetition of syllables, word breaks were shifted and vowel sounds were modified. The singers worked with their contemporary spoken language and shaped it according to the rules of Tiwi song metre and the freedoms of extemporisation.[11] All of these changes were the artistic and creative licence of the composer-singers, and so it is not for me (or indeed current Tiwi listeners) to decide which words exactly the singers were presenting. Here are words that Yikliya heard many times among the recording.

Mirrakawuyanga – an area west of Milikapiti, and one of the nine ancestral Murrakupuni (Country) areas with which Tiwi people identify as traditional owners, through patrilines.[12]

Marripwanga (and a sung variation) marripuwanga – the mangroves found right at the water's edge on the coastline around there.

Mirrituwunga, mirrimparinga, pamparinga – the mangroves that line creeks further inland, away from the sand.

Also woven into the songs' phrases are *-mangimi* (to flow, as water does), *manungumunga* (the brackish water where fresh meets salty) *mawukuwamunga* and *mangulumpi* (salt water). The similarity in sounds between these words, especially when embedded into the sung metre, were described by Yikliya as "the sound of the water there and how it sounds when we sing water". The words themselves create a lexical image of the physical place as people hear the nouns and adjectives that describe the area. As well, as the words are sung, with their syllables that sound similar repeating and flowing along with the rhythmic metre, an aural image appears in the listeners' minds of the sound of the creeks, the water and, so, the Country where the Moonfish (the ancestors) are. All of those words that *mean* and are *understood to be* those creeks also then come to *sound like* those creeks, as listeners associate them with songs about them.

---

11 For more on the linguistic and musical techniques of classical Tiwi song composition, see G. Campbell 2023.

12 The map (Figure 12.2) shows the Murrakupuni (Country) areas and the three main towns. The places in which the moonfish swim in the songs referred to here are the creeks, coastal shallows and reefs in the place called Mirrakuwuyanga.

12 Singing Moonfish, hearing Country

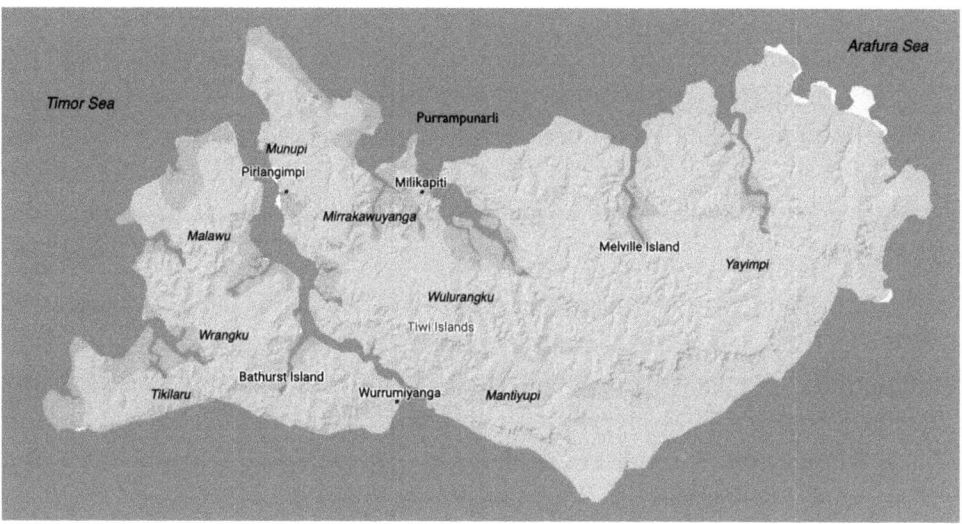

Figure 12.2 The Tiwi Islands, showing the area these songs originate from and belong to. Map data © 2024 Google

The songs continued. Yikliya said he heard words that described "Two creeks running different ways". This sets the location of the song quite precisely, with the land around there being made up of tidal inlets and freshwater creeks curving around and past each other. We hear *makatinga* – the fresh water in the creek. *Makatingari* (Yikliya pointed out) is the ritual washing time at the end of the mortuary ceremonies. So, he hears both the place and the ritual action, as the moonfish in the water enact the ritual washing that Moonfish people will now do themselves. The cleansing of sorrow and lightening of mood as the mourning restrictions (physical and emotional) are lifted with the washing away of the painted ochre face and body designs that are representations of the deceased and (literally) of the earth they were made from. One song names Purrupiyama (on the north coast of Melville Island), and Murrupiyanga (the reef along the eastern coast of Melville), the two farthest points of the paths and places named in the songs – the paths the deceased took while he was alive.

Kutatampila winga ampitirri kiyarramangiliyatapuni
The fish are in the strong current now, a sea swell coming in

Murrupyianga angitiliyamirri watingitirriki tili manginguwaga . . . mirraputi ngama
The moonfish are swimming there at Murrupiyanga [in that spot with the brackish water]

Murrupiyanga tilayamirra awatiyuwuntirra manunguwurra
His spirit [the deceased] is holding the tide there at that place, his place

Holding time still: on that state of the tide before it turns, just at the liminal stage when it is neither coming in nor going out. This imagery, sung at this point in the ceremony is the symbolic in-between that the participants are in at Ceremony. The person has "passed away" but he hasn't gone yet. Not departed. He stays where he belongs, in his country, along the Murrupiyanga, the reef, the totemic place for these Wuranjawi and Wuriyupila people of the associated mudskipper and fire clans.

"He can't really go until we've finished that final ceremony so we've got to sing all through all those songs and dance each person while he waits. Hangs around . . . waits until he is sure he has to go," said Yikliya, a little too loudly, with headphones on as he followed the journey, clapping one hand against his knee in time with singers half a century ago, hum-shadowing their melodies, sometimes singing fragments of words as he picked up a phrase on repeat.

Tiwi deceased are never considered "gone" to another place altogether, but to have passed from one existence to the next, in this same place. Midway through a Final Ceremony such as this then, the singers and ceremony participants are in a sense holding the deceased in the state of not-still-here but not-yet-there. The deceased is on the not-yet turned tide, like the moonfish, the inhabitants of that place in both existences. At this point we can see too how the deceased is becoming his ancestral self, his totemic identity, and is waiting on the tide with the (other) moonfish.

Kutatampirrarra kuntingimangimarrungurruwa
Swimming under the rock on the other side, over there

Tiliyamirra wartiyunguntirrakuntingi manunguwurra
Going quickly, being swept along, with the tide

At one point in the recording, we hear Eleanor Mungatopi say: "He went to that place by himself and he saw a lot of fish and he came back and to tell all his relations to go to that place and make their camp there". Yikliya heard the singer naming the walking track and the paths to get to the place where the creeks are. This two-way arrangement of creeks is very good for fishing, making it an important place for the custodians and traditional owners and a place that has been lived and walked on for generations.

A family member from the Bathurst Island side adds his song straight on from the last.

Wanga nuwa mirranawi Tipurrikuwamirri
That person [your son, his name] Tipurrikuwamirri Old man making a net out of vines.

Yikliya also heard *mangurrumwunga* in one iteration and guessed that this was describing the cross-hatched painted ochre body designs the men would have been wearing. On the tape we'd heard Eleanor Mungatopi explain that this song is about an old man making a fishing net out of vines. Perhaps she, as a young woman, heard the more literal meaning or perhaps she simply chose to give only the literal meaning to the visitor while knowing full well the double significance. When Elders listened in 2020, they heard the push and pull of the water, dragging the moonfish between the sea and the land, and younger speakers tell me that *mangumwunga* (a newer way of saying the older word, with the *rru* elided) now means "tug-of-war". Perhaps these visual correlations go further to the push and pull of a thrown net as it is cast out and retrieved. Either way, all understandings combine to add to the image of the two-way state of the moonfish, of the water, the place and the liminal state of the deceased as the songs that will release him from this to the next existence are still being sung.

Timarralatingimirri Daisy (the sister of Langiyamanu Doris, who was Charlie Fourcroy's widow) sings as an amparruwu.[13] She sings in the voice of the dead man, as he is leaving, crossing the water and warning people not to follow him.

Kurukanga wakawayi [this is a non-translatable vocalisation often used in widow songs]
Awungarra Parrilantu nuwingumati lakuwularighi
Ngintumukujurranuwala. . . kujurranu kujurranumajirrakurti miyirraniyi . . .
Awungarra juwunikurawu aranawu ngiya yawuni yariki kulumurrunga

I'm going to leave, going to paddle that canoe
Going across to the other side [Parrilantu]
You'd better be careful while you are going there
I will watch out, I'm fine, I'm a crocodile too.

She repeats "arranawu" (be careful) in a part-sung, part-wailed entreaty to everyone to be wary of the Mapurtiti (the spirits of the dead)[14] who are lurking around, and of the spirit of the dead man who might take someone with him as he is about to depart to the next existence. He is safe to cross the water because he's a crocodile man, through his Dreaming.[15] The others don't have the same protection from their Dreaming ancestors or from the Mapurtiti so need to be careful.

---

13 The widow's song is sung by the amparruwu (the widow) or their classificatory kinship equivalent.
14 The Mapurtiti are the spirit beings of the next existence. They live in the same country, frequent the same places and interact and behave as they did when they were alive.
15 Dreaming is the commonly used English term for a Tiwi person's Yoi, transferred through song and dance and connected to their ancestral Country through their father's bloodline.

The Moonfish songs continue, with different singers adding their line, which is repeated a number of times while people dance. Yikliya suggested this translation: "*The moonfish get stranded by the tide and get stuck on the sand and die*".

The symbolism of this line is extraordinarily powerful. The death of the moonfish, succumbing to the pull and betrayal of the tide, to fate. The metaphorical reference to death, to mortality and to the overwhelming power of nature is clear. Those to whom I played this song in the archive recording gave "translations" such as this:

We all have to die one day.
Those moonfish are like the man who died.
There is no turning back sometimes.

Another song came towards the end of this same ceremony. It suggested that the deceased, who has now become Mapurtiti, was now standing at the edge of the water. His shadow scared the moonfish away. Here the moonfish become the living clanspeople. They don't follow the Mapurtiti but are "scared" away back to the living. Yikliya suggested similarities with "Grim Reaper" symbolism, although here the reaper was casting his shadow on the animal representations of the living people. The people in this song *are* moonfish and, as there is no "us and them" for Tiwi people when they consider their Country and the ancestors within it, the song implies that "we are those moonfish and we are warned by the Mapurtiti".

The next songs returned to the journey of the moonfish, adding more stanzas to this almost four-hour-long sung poem.

Alakirri awaji-ngunjirra-kunti-ngimpi mayawurrinki pirripawuma awartiyungwuti
The moonfish is going inside the rock on the bottom of the sea, swimming underwater.

Milikamawartinguti-rrutungimayawurrinki
That big rock in the sea.

The moonfish returned to where it was safe, the undersea rock caverns and hollows that protect them when they swim in deeper water. We then heard two more songs that re-established the moonfish safe home in its Country. Singing this (and hearing it) at that point in ceremony creates a sense of ease, that all is now well, for the fish and for the kin who call them their Country.

Mantirrimpuka awartiyungwuti wurrakungtini mayawurrinti
Mantirrimpuka awartiyungwuti nguntupayi

The moonfish is eating seaweed
Seaweed, the fish is swimming through it

Another song in this series was added, then another and another. Each song was repeated continuously for anywhere from a minute to five or so. As the main singer presented his seaweed phrases, individuals among the assembled group picked up the words after a few iterations and joined him. Then, as a group singing in unison, they continued as individuals came forward to dance. We could hear people talking over the singing, encouraging dancers to come forward and we also heard the lead singer take a "solo" for some iterations, and seamlessly switching from one lead singer to another, and back again. Perhaps he indicated this with a gesture, but also (our only indication on the recording) he did so by adjusting his volume to become the "lead" again. Yikliya told me that if someone thinks up another song, he would let people know and they would round off the previous one before he then jumped in with his new words.

Even through the audio alone we could hear the collective, collegial and mutually supportive nature of this performance event.

Mantarripuka wangitipiliyawantimirri mantarripuka wartinguntirrakuntingimi mayawurrinti

This was the same song as the previous one about the fish going inside the rock and finding seaweed, but a young boy's name, Tipiliyawantimirri, takes the place of the fish. Perhaps he was present and was being encouraged to participate. "Maybe he is singing that young fella's name into his song to tell him to join in. He doesn't want to stop the singing you know? Keeps going and calls that young boy", observed Yikliya.

The next song changed the mood and brought us back to the ritual purpose: mourning. Yikliya listened: "Men are trying to catch the moonfish but their hands get cut by the spines". The injury the men suffer as they try to catch the moonfish symbolises the pain of bereavement and is personified through a doubled imagery – the mourners feel the pain of the ancestors. Ten minutes further along the singing, now about an hour into the recording, Yikliya said: "Three brothers the same skin as Mickey Geranium . . . tell about where you can go fishing and where you cannot". This is a marking of custodianship of Country, he told me, as the places that are associated with the deceased (his Country) are sung into the circle to make it clear to everyone that they are now sacred places to be avoided and "left alone for a while": that is, the area is now closed to respect the mourning period. This was the penultimate Moonfish song. It signalled the new status quo of the living now that the deceased was moving on. We heard the long cries and wails called out by all the participants, in answer to Mickey Geranium calling out to Country to signify the end of the Moonfish section of the ceremony.

I wrote down all Yikliya's passing thoughts, pausing the recording while we painstakingly noted down snippets of old words that he tried to sing slowly, a difficult task because once the words lost their sung rhythm and tempo and became spoken, Yikliya automatically reverted to spoken forms. It is only in the flow of song that he could accurately represent them. As for so many other of my attempts at translation, these moonfish songs include multiple possible understandings and inferences.[16] Listening today to song words from 1966 that were formed in the old language held by then senior singers, or were newly invented poetry for the occasion for which they were composed, we can only approach them from our point of (multisensory) view. Just as Tiwi listeners hear the "sound of the trees" in the words of songs about the dense bush across a full day of repeated strings of songs with one central subject, the resulting repetition of words, synonyms or similar-sounding words creates a type of poetic soundscape. In this instance it is the words that echo around the "sound" of the estuarine waters in the sung words, including numerous, varying iterations of *manguwu* (quoted above), that create a sort of lexical onomatopoeia or a musical and poetic imagery. We also hear accumulating metaphoric imagery. *Mipirranjinga* (murky, dark ocean water) and *mipirranjini* (murky, cloudy freshwater, as in a waterhole) appear in a few of the phrases. We hear *warti* in these songs a lot. It means "underwater" and also "mist or dense, low cloud". *Wartingimi* is "to swim under, through the water (not on top of it)" and *wartinga* is "to move through the dense bush". At one point in our listening, Yikliya told me that one line of song explained that the singer "can't see the Moonfish because they're underwater ... just like he can't see those living family properly, but he can't find where he should go yet, since he passed away". Here again is imagery of the murkiness, mistiness, cloudiness of the in-between for the deceased and his kin. The obscuring of sight is an image we hear in many Tiwi songs composed for mortuary ceremonies, especially at the Yilaniya (the smoking ritual) during which the possessions of and places frequented by the deceased are cleansed with the white smoke of a green-leaf fire. As well as for cleansing, the smoke serves to alter and disguise the place of the living. Family walk through the smoke to disguise themselves from the spirit of the deceased and to encourage them to leave. In the dark murky water, the Moonfish ancestors were shrouded in their watery equivalent of the smoke of the Yilaniya that shrouded their Tiwi clanspeople.

---

16 This is also an important consideration more broadly. See Barwick, Marett et al. 2007 and Walsh 2010.

Audio Example 12.1 Yikliya Eustace Tipiloura singing Moonfish (Recorded by G. Campbell, 2015).

Yikliya recorded his own Moonfish song in 2015 – a conscious collation of the imagery and words he had "picked up" from the recordings. As we've continued to listen to Moonfish since he passed away, the words and the voices have become more shrouded in the opacity of allusion and inference as the extra layer of his custodianship has now settled on them and so informs new Tiwi listeners' understandings. Especially in the context of funeral rituals, perhaps every culture in the world has musical traditions that create an aural atmosphere, aural cues that envelop mourners in a recognised aural space that can provide comfort, allow for the expression of grief or provide a framework or structure through which the participants progress. In the context of returned recordings of mortuary rituals, Tiwi listeners go through many of the emotional responses they remember from their own experiences. It is here that implied and inferred meaning in melodies is particularly strong because not only are people hearing the songs themselves, but they are hearing the sadness of those attending the ceremony. The presence of the Moonfish songs in the recorded archive makes them items of historical and sociocultural value because they can tell us who had died, when they died and who was there to mourn them. Current custodians of Tiwi song culture are glad to have Yikliya's voice added to the archive, as these songs that are no longer sung (and may never be again) continue to be sung by him and his ancestors through their recorded voices and through their ancestral resonances, in the bush, to be heard by those who can hear them. This description of our experience with Moonfish is just one of the many connections Tiwi listeners are discovering with their ancestral lands among the recorded archive of Tiwi song. For people whose whole cosmological explanation for the world comes from the earth, from nature, and continues to maintain intrinsic connection between current living people and their ancestors, in the place they've always been, it makes sense that the sounds of that place are the origins of words, stories, songs and dance.

Chapter 13

Musical analysis, music sustainability and thrivance: returning to "What can one 'know' about any sort of music by means of musical analysis?"

Sally Treloyn and Tiriki Onus

Introduction

In the 1990 paper "Central Australian women's music: knowing through analysis versus knowing through performance" (hereafter "Knowing through analysis"), Linda Barwick asked "What can one 'know' about any sort of music by means of musical analysis?" (Barwick 1990, 76). In part, the paper responded to a central problematic of ethnomusicology, regarding the role of musical analysis as a method to understand and present understandings of aspects of musical systems. This was a matter that Barwick also addressed in "Creative (ir)regularities" (Barwick 1989), which took as a prompt an implication in Peter Sutton's "Mystery and change" (Sutton 1987) that "close descriptions and essentially musicological analyses of Aboriginal songs" sit in opposition to a "deeper and more balanced approach" focused on "the relationships between music and the wider context of Aboriginal culture" (Barwick 1989, 12; Sutton 1987, 77). Throughout her career, Barwick has answered this challenge, presenting many analyses of Indigenous musical systems from various regions, including central Australia, the Daly, West Arnhem Land, the Kimberley and southern Australia. These have produced knowledge about many aspects of creative practice that encompass a "wider context". These aspects range from studies of individuality, gender and creative agency (Barwick 1995), to mechanisms of knowledge transmission (Ellis and Barwick 1987; Barwick 1989; 1990); cognition (Barwick 2012); continuity, change and innovation (Barwick 2011; 2017), and beyond. Importantly, Barwick has also engaged with a second, but related, core problematic of analysis – relating to questions of authority (who has it in research and who should have it?) and benefit (who benefits from analyses and ethnomusicology more broadly?).

Barwick's work as a scholar, collaborator, teacher and mentor has contributed an immense body of work towards the challenge of better understanding First Nations creative practice in the academy and society at large, and the ethical challenges attendant with this. Barwick's work has informed the work of contemporaries across generations and has directly contributed to the practice of ethnomusicology, linguistics and beyond, as this volume attests. This said, it remains a fact that the analytic methods of these disciplines remain fraught and entangled in ongoing experiences of settler colonialism, contributing to ambivalent regard for analyses.

This chapter revisits Barwick's question "What can one 'know' about any sort of music by means of musical analysis [today]?" (Barwick 1990, 76), considering this question in two contemporary contexts: musical analysis and music sustainability. We (the authors) do this in relation to our distinctive identities and positionality: one, Onus, a First Nations Yorta Yorta and Dja Dja Wurrung creative, singer, scholar, and academic and community leader; the other, Treloyn, a non-Indigenous ethnomusicologist. We approach the chapter as colleagues, working together at the time of writing at the Wilin Centre for Indigenous Arts and Cultural Development in the Faculty of Fine Arts and Music at the University of Melbourne, where our collaboration includes co-teaching subjects in Indigenous music and listening, research, and service. We also write from a position of affection and respect for the impetus of this volume, Linda Barwick, as friends, colleagues and, in the case of Treloyn, also a student and mentee since 1997.

In the first part of this chapter, we discuss musical analysis of First Nations musical practice. In the second we consider music sustainability research, which has gained prominence in recent decades. Building on the response of Onus and other critical scholarship to ethnomusicological representations of Indigenous music, through these sections we attend to the tendencies of analysis towards objectification and voyeurism, and of the rhetoric of sustainability towards extinction narratives. In the third and final section, we return to Barwick's question "What can one 'know' about any sort of music by means of musical analysis" today, where the verb "can" is considered in relation to what can be understood, as well as in relation to risk of harm. Recognising the vital role that attention to sustainability plays across domains, we introduce a productive counter-narrative to sustainability, drawing upon the term "thrivance" (after Jolivétte 2021). We use thrivance to describe a way of regarding First Nations creative practice that is strengths-based, that prioritises First Nations authority, and that is attentive to continuity and how musical practices are valued in their communities of practice. Considering examples from Barwick's work, we conclude that thrivance offers potential for a safer form of musical analysis.

Relations of musical analysis

To prompt our writing of this chapter, we (Onus and Treloyn) first reflected on our experiences of reading and witnessing ethnomusicological accounts of Indigenous music. Onus reflected on frequent experiences of discomfort and feeling unsafe when listening as an audience member to presentations on First Nations people's practices by non-Indigenous people. Such presentations rest upon the notion that outsiders have a voyeuristic right to observe. Onus's reflection adds currency and insight to observations and views expressed elsewhere, that transcription and analysis operate in the shadows of colonialism as "tool[s] of colonial acquisitiveness, a means of appropriating and exhibiting sensory experiences" (Ellingson 1992, 110; see also Myers 2019). Onus's reflections also highlight a critical question of authority – particularly, who has it, who claims it and who should have it – in the representation of First Nations music. Thirty years ago, Catherine Ellis similarly reflected: "Why is it important to know certain things? To whom is it important? What damage may be done . . ." (Ellis 1994a, 3). More recently, Michael Walsh warned: "While it [analysis] may be fascinating to the analyst of song language it can be difficult to decide who should have access to it" (Walsh 2007, 140).

While scholars such as Barwick have established a critical frame with which to approach analysis of Indigenous music, and while analysis presents opportunities for supporting the agendas of Indigenous musicians and musical communities (see below), it remains a fact that analysis, and representation in ethnomusicology more broadly, is fraught, a situation that extends also to linguistics (see Gaby and Woods 2020; Bennett 2019) and elsewhere. Given this, it is understandable that ethnomusicologists and others may feel disinclined to keep analysis in their methodological toolbox (see, for example, Magowan 2007). Others, such as Barwick, have striven to harness and advance the potential of analysis to understand the perspectives and artistry of Indigenous singers, song practices, and the contexts in which they operate, and to support and strengthen Indigenous rights. Barwick, as with Ellis before her and many colleagues and students, has critically engaged with questions of authority, by ensuring that analytical directions are informed by the perspectives of singers (Knopoff 2003, 48). Further, Barwick has deployed analysis and analyses to support the authority, agency and self-determination of singers and their communities. Examples include contribution to land rights (e.g., Justice Gray and Office of the Aboriginal Land Commissioner 2000), and making research data accessible to source communities as a matter of social equity (e.g., Marett and Barwick 2003; PARADISEC).

Additionally Barwick's writing on the status of analysis has contributed to a critical understanding of listening across musical-cultural worlds, and of cross-cultural representation more generally. Both "Knowing through analysis" and "Creative (ir)regularities" interrogate the philosophical core of analysis, providing a rationale for analysis not as a pursuit of capturing a truth about the musical system being considered, but rather more as a mode of coming-into-relation-with around a shared though differently experienced manifestation of music (see also Cross in this volume):

> [A]nalysis is a process of understanding rather than a methodology for producing "truth". What I know about this music is not a measurable quantity, but a constantly changing way of relating to the music. Each time I listen to or analyse a performance, I experience the music differently. Although I presume that the ways in which I experience it are very different from the ways in which performers do, it is nevertheless the case that the manifested form of the music, which they perform and I analyse, is a shared component of our experience. Through "performing" my analysis of this sound pattern, I am asking and sometimes answering questions that are relevant to my understanding of the world; just as I understand that sound pattern to be one manifestation of performers' understanding of the world. (Barwick 1990, 60)

Barwick, following on from the theorisation of the analysis presented in "Knowing through analysis" and "Creative (ir)regularities", has shown many cases of how analysis may be undertaken as a process to understand one's pre-existing ways of listening in relation to others' ways of performing, and as a process to dynamically transform the former through engagement with the performance of another. While such a methodology is predicated on the availability of the music of First Peoples to non-Indigenous peoples (noting that this was prior to the emergence of leading Indigenous ethnomusicologists in Australia) and thus references coloniality and risks the voyeurism described by Onus above, it also speaks to and arguably honours the agency of Indigenous musicians who chose to work or sing with known outsiders. It is an approach that attempts to take "personal responsibility" within ethnomusicology (Knopoff 2003, 46–47). Reflecting this also, Clint Bracknell has observed that contemporary ethnomusicology in Australia is, by and large, focused on long-term relational accountabilities (Bracknell 2015b).

While there is further work to be done, critical engagement with the core problematics of ethnomusicology, such as that undertaken by Barwick, establishes a framework for analysis grounded in questions of authority and accountability. In the following section of this chapter, we consider another, equally fraught, preoccupation of ethnomusicology in Australia, music sustainability.

Relations of music sustainability

Returning to the prompt for this chapter, a conversation between the authors about the experience of witnessing ethnomusicological accounts of music owned and held by First Peoples, Onus further reflected that such scholarship often perpetuates extinction narratives. When scholars rationalise that transcription, analysis and other forms of representation are done in aid of addressing music endangerment, I (Onus) am reminded of the same attitudes that herded my great-great-grandparents into photographic studios "lest they become extinct". In this, there was an assumption that all is lost, that there was no future, including that future that I and my children inhabit. This defeatist extinction narrative was taught to me in schools in the 1980s and is repeated in many forums today. Therefore, it is troubling when an uncritical undertone of this is present in academic research. In these contexts, I am mindful of the normalisation of a deficit lens on First Peoples' lives. While it is difficult because it acknowledges the harm, it is important to both acknowledge and refuse this normalisation as a Yorta Yorta and Dja Dja Wurrung person who aspires to a different experience for my children and community.

From plural methodological and theoretical origins (see Wild 2006; Toner 2007), ethnomusicology in Australia has long been interested in music sustainability, a topic that has come more into focus over the past two decades or so. This is reflected in and is in part due to the foundational Garma Statement in Indigenous Music and Dance that explicitly ties documentation by ethnomusicologists to the challenge of preventing the "extinction" and "loss" of music and dance practices (Garma Forum on Indigenous Performance Research 2002). It calls upon ethnomusicologists to do this work along with the project of recording and repatriation, under the direction of Indigenous authorities and knowledge holders (Marett et al. 2006). This attention to sustainability is also in line with global movements in ethnomusicological research in Asia (e.g., Grant 2014; Howard 2016; Harris 2017; Widdess in this volume), North America (e.g., Titon 2009; 2016), and elsewhere.

Largely influenced by the work of Jeff Todd Titon (2009; 2016), and Huib Schippers and Catherine Grant (Schippers and Grant 2016), today music sustainability is treated as an ecosystem problem that enfolds the social, political and economic contexts in which music practices occur and music practitioners operate. This approach is attentive to diversity, change and growth and their limits, interconnectedness and stewardship. A great deal of research is both community-led and focused on supporting and throwing light on local expertise to recover and re-nourish musical practices (e.g., Treloyn, Martin and Charles 2019; Bracknell 2020a; Troy and Barwick 2020).

But non-Indigenous approaches to endangerment and more recently sustainability have – not unlike transcription and analysis – been the subject of scrutiny and critical ambivalence and require sensitivity in their treatment in particular contexts. Firstly, collection itself – a hallmark of ethnomusicology and linguistics – for the purposes of storage and preservation, and often analysis, shares uncomfortable histories with stealing, traditions of cultural appropriation, and colonisation (Treloyn and Charles 2021). In the comparative musicology school, recording technologies – harnessed in the name of preservation – were co-opted to support ideologies of social evolutionism, monogenesis and diffusion, via comparison of musical systems. The emphasis on recording and archiving as a method for preservation has also been associated with deficit views of Indigenous cultures as extinguishable and dying (Grant 2015a), as noted in Onus's reflection on extinction narratives in Indigenous music scholarship.

Secondly, there has been increased focus on the rhetorics of music sustainability. Catherine Grant suggested ethnomusicologists consider taking up more active language in discussion of music endangerment such as that which is used in linguistics, including "language death" and "genocide", partly as an act of acknowledging that forces of domination are responsible for these forms of change: "They do not die, they're killed", wrote Grant (2015, unpaginated). However such language, speaking again to Onus's reflections, also risks subjecting First Nations experience to extinction narratives, and privileges the mythology of the power of colonisation over Indigenous practices. In the Canadian context, Beverley Diamond has considered how Indigenous lives and experiences may be further subjected to the Western and colonial gaze via narratives of victimhood (Diamond 2015, 268–270; Treloyn 2022, 15).

In a comprehensive review of the topic from a North American perspective, Titon unpacks the basis of music sustainability in cultural conservation and preservation, including the limitations and problematics of these terms. Titon noted that the ecological trope (after Spitzer) is potentially entangled with cultural evolutionism in the positionality of researchers (also after Spitzer) (Titon 2016; Spitzer et al. 2007). In the Australian context, where the treatment of Indigenous peoples has been compared to the treatment of non-human resources, flora and fauna, this critique of the term and rationale of sustainability has significant relevance for ethnomusicological projects of sustainability.

Titon proposed that the term "music resilience" may be more appropriate to the work of ethnomusicologists in relation to music sustainability, where resilience references "a system's capacity to recover and maintain its integrity, identity, and continuity when subjected to forces of disturbance and change" (Titon 2016, 158). Whereas sustainability suggests goals and ends, rather than means, Titon explained, resilience "offers a strategy" (Titon 2016, 158). Resilience, as framed by Titon, presents an opportunity for ethnomusicologists to embrace strengths-based language and methodologies in relation to musical communities, where new, local approaches to revival show "not archival preservation, but sustainability within living cultural groups" (Titon 2016, 172). In the context of ethnomusicology that approaches First Nations practices in Australia, this concept of "music resilience" provides a promising option. It acknowledges the harm done to knowledge systems and practices by the dominant peoples and structures of colonisation, while rejecting the discourse of deficit, and foregrounding a strengths-based regard for systems of sustainability carried in knowledge systems themselves.

More recently, beyond ethnomusicology, there has been a rejection of the cultural resilience frame. In the context of Indigenous inclusion in tertiary education institutions, Onus notes that speaking of resilience places the burden of colonialism on Indigenous peoples; that, rather, we should ask what we are asking Indigenous peoples to be resilient to, and how can we dismantle and change that. Perspectives such as this underpin a reframing of discourse about Indigenous lifeways, away from extinction narratives, towards thrivance, a term that encapsulates a strengths-based and self-determined view of contemporary Indigenous practices. Opelousa and Atakapa-Ishak sociologist Andrew J. Jolivétte wrote:

> To be resilient is to constantly respond or be on the defensive to things that happen to you as a result of colonization, whereas thrivance is the active acknowledgement and activation of Indigenous knowledge, joy, and relationships to live lives devoted to centering, honoring, and educating current and future generations . . . without always centering them within the context of . . . colonialism and genocide. (Jolivétte 2021, 477)

The question then arises: might an approach to Indigenous music grounded in principles and language of thrivance lessen the risk of harm associated with analysis and ethnomusicology more generally?

Music analysis and thrivance

A full consideration of the potential for thrivance for musical analysis is largely beyond the scope of this chapter. But, in this final section of the chapter, returning to Barwick's question, we wonder: "What can one 'know' about any sort of music by means of musical analysis?", where the verb "can" is measured both by what can be learned about music and social context through analysis, but also in terms of what can be done with analysis (noting its potential benefits) without harm. We begin with a brief consideration of intersections between examples of musical analysis and the concept of thrivance. Noting the impetus for this volume, we find these in Barwick's oeuvre.

Titon's frame of musical resilience as "a system's capacity to recover and maintain its integrity, identity, and continuity when subjected to forces of disturbance and change" (Titon 2016, 158) clearly resonates with much analysis of Indigenous song, particularly that which has been practised in times of environmental change. Barwick's analysis of Djanba in Wadeye (previously Port Keats Mission) in the 1950s and 60s, for example, shows the ways that Murrinh-patha (Yek Diminin clan) composers Robert Dungoi Kolumboort, Harry Luke Palada Kolumboort and Lawrence Kolumboort drew upon varied musical styles to create the new genre Djanba, to address social inclusion in the new, complex mission. As Barwick explained, the musical style developed for Djanba exhibits a "constructive fostering of variegation" that was also echoed in dance style, body paint and lyrics, and that supported their "struggles to embrace cultural difference" (Barwick 2011, 349).

Moving beyond resilience, Barwick (2011) showed that – while the invention of Djanba was in response to massive social change brought by colonisation – it was achieved by the continuation of innovative and creative compositional strategies that are part of a long history of musical culture in the region. As such, the example may be an orientation towards musical thrivance, attentive to activation of knowledge transmission and relationships, rather than framing musical practice in terms of disruption and recovery.

Such an approach to musical systems and musicians is also evident in Barwick's earlier analyses, such as those presented in "Knowing through analysis" and "Creative ir(regularities)" that are attentive to the functions of musical complexity. Much ethnomusicological analysis of central Australian music pursues patterns that characterise the organisation of melodic, verbal and rhythmic elements. Barwick (1989) suggested that the practice of varying the principles that organise performance, resulting in complexity, exemplifies a common aesthetic that is central to First Nations societies that the article considers, and serves to preserve musical systems. One effect of variability is that apparent "irregularities" perceived on one level point towards and maintain regularities on other levels of the text/rhythmic hierarchy, and facilitate the maintenance of the musical form by conserving "the most important elements of each system" (Barwick 1989, 27; see also Barwick 1990, 70; Ellis 1997, 60). Here Barwick followed on from Sutton's suggestion that "contradictions" and "irregularities" "may themselves be systematic and integral to a society's means of self-maintenance . . . and [it] is the dialectical interplay of both regularities and irregularities which constitutes the system" (Barwick 1989, 27, after Sutton 1987, 88). Viewed as thrivance, the complexity revealed by this approach to analysis celebrates the ways in which musical artists and systems activate and centre relationships in musical transmission. Attention is paid to the locally held values for musical reproduction, and the relational complexity of musical systems and traditions.

Arguably, both deficit and extinction narratives that are common in scholarship on Indigenous practice, to which Onus and others have pointed, are in fact diminished by this approach. Much can be learned in this regard from the work of Barwick, and Ellis, John von Sturmer, and others in the 1980s in this regard. Barwick has pointed out that the complexity of Indigenous musical practice may even "resist . . . the universalising aims of analysis" (Barwick 1989, 14). In the same volume that Sutton published "Mystery and change", von Sturmer in "Aboriginal Singing and Notions of Power" made an appeal for the vital importance of analysis in relation to the power of Indigenous singers and song:

> Is it the song which allows the controller/owner and/or performer to produce the effects, or is it the power which is seen to be vested in the controller and/or performer which allows the song to produce its effects? In short, to put the matter crudely, is it the singer or the song? (von Sturmer 1987, 7)

To not focus on performance, von Sturmer suggested, would be to risk "re-assert[ing] the artifactualising of Aboriginal social and cultural life" (von Sturmer 1987, 16).

Returning to tangible benefits that can result from analytical methods, beyond producing a better understanding of musical systems and their contexts, several scholars (e.g., Bracknell 2015b; 2020a; Curran 2020a; Curran and Yeoh 2021; Barwick and Turpin 2016) have also conducted musical and textual analysis in service of community-led sustainability initiatives, particularly oriented towards music sustainability (or thrivance). Most recently, Barwick's use of analysis has, in collaboration with linguistic analysis with Jakelin Troy, for example, provided valuable information to revive Ngarigu performance practice that was otherwise cloaked in a settler colonial parlour music arrangement (Troy and Barwick 2020).

Undeniably, questions of authority, as flagged by Onus and others (see "Relations of music sustainability" above), will remain current in debates about and approaches to analysis, including in explicitly collaborative approaches (Treloyn and Charles 2021). Reflecting this, as Bracknell has observed, ethnomusicology in Australia as a discipline, including that which uses musical analysis, is community-led to a degree that is not seen elsewhere in the world (Bracknell et al. 2019).

Conclusion

Musical analysis has at once been a hallmark of and a contested method in ethnomusicology in Australia. Examples show that musical analysis can contribute to better understanding Indigenous musical creative practices and broader social contexts, to community-led initiatives for sustainability, and to domains of education, land rights and beyond. But the fact remains that musical analysis is vexed, and is valued in multiple and sometimes competing ways. Experiences of harm can be rendered when analyses are read, witnessed or taught entangled in larger histories of objectification and voyeurism, and a persistent narrative of extinction, that are associated with larger histories and structures of colonialism. We have a wider "wicked problem" that resists resolution (see Grant 2015b) and that leads us back to Barwick's question "What can one 'know' about any sort of music by means of musical analysis?" In this chapter, we return to this question, attentive to both knowledge production, as well as to an ethical prerogative of care for those who are subjected to, engaged with and witness to musical analysis. As touched upon in the final section of the chapter, the notion of thrivance – a strengths-based and self-determined view of contemporary Indigenous practices that centres on relationships and people – may offer some guidance for music analysis. Through a brief look at samples from Barwick's analyses, concepts of innovation, complexity and collaboration are shown to be aligned with a thrivance approach. We conclude that thrivance offers ethnomusicologists a way to use and present musical analysis that has less potential for harm, and that is grounded in Indigenous authority and artistic strength. If we value responsibility, relationships and care in our disciplines, we must consider not just who listens to the music and languages we analyse and how, but also who listens to and reads our analyses and how. Such considerations continue to be crucial to understanding what we can "know" about music from analysis, or any method.

Part III

Dialogic Futures

Chapter 14

Karaoke corroboree: subtitled music videos and language revitalisation

Clint Bracknell

Introduction

This chapter will discuss the use of subtitled online music video content to support the recirculation of endangered languages and song traditions in the urban and rural Noongar region in the south-west of Western Australia, including the capital city of Perth. Democratisation of video production technology has increased from the 1970s onwards, with developments in portable, easy-to-use and comparatively cheap camcorders preceding the international proliferation of smartphones, consumer-grade video editing software and online video sharing platforms (Henley 2020, 197). While new communications technologies contribute to globalisation and the risk of "cultural grey-out" (Lomax 1968, 4), Indigenous people frequently mobilise a variety of media "as new vehicles for internal and external communication, for self-determination, and for resistance to outside cultural domination" (Ginsburg 1991; 1992; Neuenfeldt 2007). The UNESCO Expert Group on Endangered Languages identified "response to new domains and media" among its nine factors contributing to language vitality (Brenzinger et al. 2003). As just one example of the proliferation of Indigenous languages in new domains, Sami languages of northern Europe:

> are used in various domains that range from everyday interaction to political life (e.g. the Sami Parliament), education (e.g. Sami speaking classrooms),

> the media (e.g. television, radio) and diverse areas of popular culture (e.g. Sami-language karaoke, rock, rap and tango). (Pietikäinen et al. 2008, 83)

Accordingly, each new online platform provides additional channels for engaging in efforts to sustain and revitalise Indigenous languages, with social media long being recognised as:

> an active space for gathering and sharing language through Facebook pages and groups, Twitter feeds and hashtags, Instagram accounts and videos posted to TikTok and YouTube to promote language use in the home, share lessons, and nurture humour and joy in the process of learning. (Rosenblum 2021)

Although the challenges inherent to language revitalisation remain, the International Decade of Indigenous Languages (2022–2032) began amid increasing engagement with Aboriginal and Torres Strait Islander languages across media in Australia.

As a pronounced example of the renewed energy around Indigenous languages, the number of people identifying as speakers of the Noongar language in the Australian Census more than tripled, up from 475 people in 2016 to 1,536 people in 2021 (Austlang 2022). Although census data does not account for fluency or frequency of language use, it clearly demonstrates increasing identification with the language among the 30,000 Noongar people in Western Australia, most of whom primarily speak varieties of Aboriginal English and Australian Standard English. Despite challenges to its vitality, Noongar people continue to value Noongar language and have actively pursued a language revitalisation agenda since the 1980s. The Noongar region was the first area in Western Australia claimed by the British in 1829 and the past two centuries have seen most Noongar families subjected to frontier violence followed by rigorous government policies of segregation, cultural assimilation, and the suppression of Noongar language and expressive culture (Bracknell 2020b).

Corroboree to karaoke

Frequent outdoor "corroboree" performance incorporating song, dance and visual design long supported the vitality of Noongar social and ecological systems, language, and song traditions (Bracknell 2017a). Corroboree music is principally vocal and based in language. This term is the anglicised version of a word meaning "dance" in an Aboriginal language from Western Sydney, New South Wales (Stubington 2007, 228) and is frequently used in Australian Standard English to describe Aboriginal performances. In Aboriginal English, "corroboree" is frequently used to describe unrestricted or "everyday" music rather than the more serious "ceremony" or "business", which can be restricted on account of kinship, seniority or gender. For most Aboriginal people engaged in itinerant pastoral work across Western Australia throughout the early colonial period and into the 20th century, corroboree performances were the nightly entertainment.

Corroboree performances crossed Aboriginal linguistic and cultural boundaries, bringing people together in shared participatory understanding (Turpin and Meakins 2019; Turpin, Yeoh and Bracknell 2020). Linguist Luise Hercus interviewed Mirning singer Charlie Traveller at Umeewarra in South Australia in 1965. Traveller worked as a shepherd in the early 1900s at Nanambinia in the Esperance region (Dimer 1989, 29). On the audio recording of the 1965 interview held today in the Australian Institute of Aboriginal and Torres Strait Islander Studies audiovisual archive, he sings in Noongar and Mirning – rare 20th-century examples of song recorded in either language.[1] Traveller also describes how corroboree repertoire was shared across Western Australia and into the Northern Territory:

> Lot of corroborees I seen all over the place. Western Australia and the Kimberley, North Perth. All different tribes coming in there. All the drovers, cattle drovers, musterers, they having a big camp every night singing . . . I taught them my songs . . . They all like. Alice Springs mob like this song what I got. (Traveller in Hercus 1965–70)

Traveller's account illustrates the dynamic vitality of corroboree throughout the early 20th century.

But, from 1905 until 1971, successive Western Australian government Acts based on a policy of Aboriginal cultural assimilation placed implicit restrictions on Aboriginal languages and cultural expressions (Haebich 2000). Specifically, these included the *Aborigines Act 1905*, *Native Administration Act 1936* and *Native (Citizenship Rights) Act 1944*. As knowledge of the lyrical and musical conventions of Aboriginal song genres is often among the first casualties of language loss, the encroaching dominance of English threatened the creation and sharing of Noongar songs (Walsh 2007). Despite these constraints, senior people remembered corroborees being performed during this period in private gatherings away from towns (Wallam et al. 2004).

---

1 Other Noongar songs were recorded in the 20th century by Wilf Douglas (1965–1967), Norman Tindale (1966; 1968), C.G. von Brandenstein (1967–1970; 1971–1976), Sandra Wooltorton (1986), and Tim McCabe (1994–1997).

The late Albert Knapp, a senior Noongar language speaker, described a performance his mother witnessed in the first half of the 20th century in the south coast region of Western Australia:

> My old mum was telling me they used to go corroboree down just the other side of Ravensthorpe . . . they kept up their dancing and singing and that, I don't know how long it used to go for. It ended up mum killed herself laughing, as he [old Mr Dabb] ended up coming down and playing the piano accordion for 'em. (Bracknell 2015a, 76)

Noongar performance practices from the early colonial period through the immediate postwar era are marked by resilience and the incorporation of new harmonic instruments like guitar and piano accordion. Still, from the early 20th century through to the late 1960s, there is a relative dearth of references to corroboree being shared publicly, let alone with recordists. This absence from the public record directly coincides with the existence of stringent assimilationist legislation. Interestingly, as non-Aboriginal support for Aboriginal civil rights increased in the 1960s and influenced changes in government policy (McGregor 2009), various researchers would record performances of Noongar songs "remembered" by usually the last people to witness their fully-fledged performance (Bracknell 2015a).

As Noongar language was suppressed, so too was corroboree. Noongar adapted and found new ways to gather, perform and support each other. From 1946 to 1960 the Aboriginal-operated Coolbaroo League ran a popular music dance club in Perth and surrounding regions for Aboriginal people and their non-Aboriginal advocates (Haebich 2008). By the late 1970s, new opportunities in tourism and the arts led to the emergence of new opportunities for Noongar dance, now accompanied by the didjeridu of northern Australia. The instrument was seemingly "co-opted to fill the silence of songs no longer sung" (Bracknell 2024), at a time when certain senior Noongar nevertheless still held old song repertoire.

In more recent times, Jim Morrison and Anna Haebich have described how the social functions of corroboree performance are echoed in contemporary Noongar participation in karaoke. Karaoke is popular across many Indigenous communities in Australia, as also evidenced by the "Laura Idol" karaoke competition at Laura Festival in far north Queensland (Thompson and Connolly 2006, 347). Developed to augment the jukebox and facilitate amateur singing in public, the technology and performance conventions of karaoke originated in Kobe, Japan, in the 1970s (Kelley 2016; Lum 1996). It spread globally as a popular form of entertainment, with geographically and linguistically diverse groups adopting karaoke into their cultural practices and ascribing culturally specific meanings and functions (Matsui

14 Karaoke corroboree: subtitled music videos and language revitalisation

2001; Xun and Tarocco 2007). In the context of "Noongaroke" funeral fundraising events in Perth, Western Australia, during the 1990s and 2000s, karaoke "fitted neatly into family gatherings to mourn loved ones by providing an attractive way to sing and dance and to restore wellbeing in the manner of earlier corroboree events" (Haebich and Morrison 2014, 2). Rather than merely reflecting the effects of globalisation and the pervasive influence of homogenous popular culture, these karaoke gatherings foreground:

> [the] unmistakable sounds of Noongar talk – the words, tones of voice and the accents – as families reminisced about the good and sad times and the texture of the singers' voices and their choices of nostalgic rock and country songs – "Johnny B. Goode", "Brown-eyed Girl", "Neon Moon", "Satin Sheets", "Seven Spanish Angels". (Haebich and Morrison 2014, 4)

Just as the most requested tracks on the popular Noongar Radio request program "Inside Out" are country music songs from the USA (Bracknell and Kickett 2017), the Noongaroke repertoire primarily included English-language rock and country. These musical choices are not the result of cultural assimilation, as country music is far from being the most popular genre in broader Australia. Aboriginal people have long identified with country music after initially hearing it in touring shows of the 1930s (Smith and Brett 1998). Its popularity may be due to Aboriginal people feeling "closer to cowboys than they do to city people" (Kartomi 1988, 21), the portability of its most ubiquitous instrument – the guitar – and the genre's emphasis on lyrical themes associated with family, land and loss (Furlan 2005).

While English-language country music karaoke remains popular among Noongar, the past decade has also seen Noongar-language singing re-emerge across a range of domains including popular music, public dance performance, Welcome to Country speeches and prestigious arts collaborations. Over the past decade, Gina Williams has released four albums of contemporary music sung in Noongar and premiered an opera with the West Australian Opera company. Senior Noongar singer Barry McGuire recently collaborated with the West Australian Ballet company and electronic dance music artists for Britain's iconic Glastonbury Festival. An album of electronic music–infused new Noongar songs in the old style by Maatakitj premiered for Perth Festival's 2022 Noongar Wonderland dance event, was nominated for "album of the year" in the Western Australian Music Awards and led to a 2023 collaboration with the USA's Kronos Quartet. Given that music and performance are linked to effective Indigenous language revitalisation in New Zealand and Hawaii (May 2013), increasing the presence of Noongar song in not just live performance events but audiovisual media too could further encourage language revitalisation in the south-west of Western Australia.

Indigenous media and language revitalisation

Video content created by regional and remote Indigenous media organisations including the Central Australian Aboriginal Media Association (CAAMA) and Warlpiri Media Association can be seen to have bolstered many of the Indigenous languages still considered "strong" and spoken across all generations today. In 1988, CAAMA co-founder Freda Glynn explained:

> TV will be going into those communities 24 hours a day in a foreign language – English. It only takes a few months and the kids start changing . . . We're trying to teach kids you can be Aboriginal and keep your language and still mix in the wider community and have English as well. (in Ginsburg 1995a, 275)

In less remote regions of Australia where Indigenous languages are more rarely spoken across all generations, video content has been produced to address similar concerns. Since April 2011, the television series *Waabiny Time* has aired on National Indigenous Television (NITV). It introduces the Noongar language of the south-west of Western Australia to young children. Songs are a key component of *Waabiny Time*, although it is unfortunate that some of the singers on the show less familiar with the sounds of Noongar language occasionally mispronounce key words. This emphasises the need for content creators to have adequate access to language capacity-building opportunities before getting involved in creating language revitalisation resources.

As engagement with television has waned amid increased access to the internet, the Indigenous media sector has expanded to include online content creation and community IT projects. Slogget and Parker discussed how:

> [t]he attraction of new media for young people makes the digital world not only a potent tool in content capture and delivery, but also an effective tool in cross-generational engagement that empowers elders who want important knowledge to be available to youth, and empowers young people as agents in the preservation of this knowledge. (Slogget and Parker 2013, 228)

The "digital world" can involve cutting-edge production technology and more utilitarian solutions. First created in 2011 in order to engage Aboriginal youth preoccupied with television, Wunungu Awara: Animating Indigenous Knowledges (formerly known as the Monash Countrylines Archive) demonstrates the application of new media technologies such as rich 3D animation to create content for tablets and smartphones based on the regional stories, songs and languages of Indigenous community groups (Monash University 2022). At the more pragmatic side of the scale, a digital music database was established at the Wadeye Library and Knowledge Centre in the Northern Territory in 2003 and continues to be central to sourcing, recording, archiving and digitally sharing songs to use at local funerals. In both cases, Indigenous peoples are actively engaging in digital media to share language and song (Barwick 2017).

A not-so-empty orchestra?

Communities all over the world have mobilised karaoke technology and conventions to nourish languages other than English. Despite the primarily oral nature of many endangered languages, literacy is often identified as an essential component of language revitalisation. Samoan political leader Tui Atua Tupua Tamasese Taisi Efi (2005) stated:

> The written medium, today, is critical to the preservation of Indigenous languages. The traditional methods for learning the indigenous languages of oral cultures like ours are increasingly being replaced by new technologies for learning. The most significant, however, is still the written word. (Efi 2005, 66)

In Kuppam, India, the creation of a digital jukebox of popular folksongs using Same Language Subtitling was motivated by "the potential to address wide empowerment dynamics through social and cultural regeneration and affirmation as well as literacy gains through the 'first world' tools of karaoke" (Arora 2006, 128).

Karaoke can also be a means for diasporic populations to maintain identity and engage with a heritage language. Describing Filipino-Americans who speak English as a first language singing Tagalog karaoke songs, Pascasio asserted:

> To claim that karaoke is a form of pure mimicry and therefore culturally empty is an argument subject to different interpretive and epistemological frames . . . For Filipino Americans, the act of mimicking is not necessarily bereft of cultural or political meaning. On the contrary, it locates karaoke as a technology of decolonization and creative experimentation. (Pascasio 2021, 110)

Karaoke has also created great interest among Khmer heritage speakers in the United States in learning to read in Khmer (Wright 2007). Karaoke provides music, text and video, while encouraging public singing, priming it as an effective means for practising language and literacy skills while solidifying personal and collective identity.

At the 2016 United Nations International Expert Group Meeting on Indigenous Languages, Tatiana Degai discussed online videos of old folksongs in her endangered Itelmen language from the remote Kamchatka Peninsula of eastern Russia. Subtitled in the original Itelmen as well as the dominant Russian language, the videos inspired locals to sing along at public celebrations, giving rise to what has been dubbed "Itelmen Karaoke". As Degai and colleagues discussed, "Itelmen Karaoke" was more than just the opportunity to learn songs:

> Many of the singers, whose songs are presented . . . are gone, especially singers of traditional songs called khodilas. Nevertheless, through this tool, their descendants gain access to this ancient tradition and an opportunity to learn a form of singing known by their fathers, grandfathers, and great-grandmothers. While these songs were retained mostly in the archives of linguists, they now have become accessible to the wider community not only to hear, but also to learn. (Degai et al. 2023, 12–13)

In its mobilisation of karaoke in support of an endangered language, "Itelman karaoke" is an exemplar of how archival audio can be effectively recirculated in its home community.

Nevertheless, use of the term "karaoke" to describe the phenomenon of singing along to subtitled music videos is potentially misleading. Karaoke – a clipped compound of the Japanese *kara* "empty" and ōkesutora "orchestra" – videos typically include scrolling graphic lyrics, nostalgia-evoking stock footage, instrumental backing music and an absence of recorded lead vocals to leave room for novice vocal performances. The Itelmen videos effectively subvert this key karaoke convention. Rather than excluding lead vocals, they feature group vocal performances. Singing along with other voices with the support of synchronised video and text seems more likely to facilitate singing in a little-known endangered language like Itelmen, or Noongar, than singing into a void all by yourself.

Singing without shame

Overcoming the "shame factor" associated with language revitalisation has been a key challenge in the context of Indigenous languages in Australia. Despite domestic and international interest in Indigenous languages and music among non-Indigenous people increasing in recent decades, Aboriginal linguist Jeanie Bell (2013) described a wide range of attitudes Indigenous people may hold towards the revitalisation and public exposure of their languages and cultures. Due to trauma associated with forced cultural assimilation, some older Aboriginal people may "voice their opinion that traditional language and culture should remain in the past", and others may be reluctant to participate in language activities "due to shyness or the belief that they do not have enough language knowledge"

(Bell 2013, 402). Ethnomusicologist Margaret Gummow described Bundjalung people in New South Wales being overwhelmed when listening to archival audio recordings of old songs, and hesitant to sing in public, explaining that:

> [T]oday, many Aboriginal people are possessive of their culture and rarely perform songs on request. The songs and language that are still remembered are precious possessions from the past that owners hang on to. This is understandable when we consider the history of European contact. (Gummow 1994, 48)

It is also understandable that many Indigenous people are reluctant to have themselves, their languages and cultures put "on display" for the entertainment of newly interested non-Indigenous audiences, especially when many of these opportunities can cause intra-group tension connected to the politics of Indigenous cultural identity.

These complex issues notwithstanding, karaoke seems to function socially as an antidote to shyness and insularity. Asian restaurants in the United States started incorporating karaoke in the 1990s, which functioned to engineer camaraderie among Asian diasporas (Pascasio 2021). Among Asian minority groups in the United States, Canada and United Kingdom, a sense of community and solidarity was found to be more important in karaoke than the aptitude of singers (Chun 2004; Ong 2009). In Australia and the United States, karaoke presents one of the only socially acceptable forums for amateur singing in public spaces apart from sports arenas where Australian fans shout post-victory football team songs and most Americans still sing their anthem (Brown 2015). Settler-colonial Australia has imposed a restrictive emotional regime on Noongar people, smothering expressive culture (Bracknell 2020b). Our communicative culture was once routinely musical, but these imported hang-ups around singing leave karaoke as one of the only safe spaces for a Noongar to sing, albeit in English.

Archival Noongar song videos

To capitalise in the popularity of karaoke among Noongar, several subtitled Noongar-language music videos have been produced over the past decade. This "karaoke" technique has proven popular and effective in recirculating songs from archival collections among small community groups. As is often the case with Aboriginal music, considerations associated with how song items should be shared and performed can complicate the re-popularisation of songs that have long fallen out of popular use. As a result of the increased cultural value recently attached to endangered languages and song traditions, individuals, groups or organisations may feel the need to impose new restrictions on songs that were widely known and shared in the past. Nevertheless, many projects based on archival Aboriginal song recordings being returned to their home communities illustrate the potential of archival audio to enhance music and language revitalisation. They also emphasise the need for dedicated time and appropriate spaces to practise and perform old songs (Wafer and Turpin 2017).

Between 2017 and 2019, I led an Australian Research Council–funded project "Mobilising song archives to nourish an endangered Aboriginal language", which involved repatriating recordings of Noongar songs held in archival collections to their south coast Noongar community of origin. Although the descendants of the singers recorded in archival collections and the broader community of stakeholders were interested in the songs, there were few regular opportunities to practise singing. As an initial response to community requests for a way to practise and share the songs, I developed short videos for six archival songs, each with a static background – usually a picture of a senior Noongar person standing in a landscape related to the song content – but with the synchronised subtitled song lyrics in a large font. These videos were designed to be viewed on a smartphone. Although most Noongar own a smartphone, internet access is not a given. Additionally, the descendants of archival singers and other stakeholders mandated that the songs be shared gradually, so simply putting the subtitled videos online for anyone to potentially access would not have been appropriate. Bluetooth peer-to-peer sharing of these videos seemed the most effective and suitable solution. Digital peer-to-peer sharing of the videos allowed for descendant and community control over dissemination. The close physical proximity required for Bluetooth file-sharing also facilitated a kind of social interaction not dissimilar to how songs were shared orally in the past.

The descendants and stakeholders were the first to receive the videos and subsequently showed and shared them with other Noongar people as they saw fit. When the technology worked, it was effective and empowering. Unfortunately, Apple's "airdrop" proprietary technology will not allow peer-to-peer file-sharing with non-Apple smartphones via Bluetooth. This technical hitch derailed the use of Bluetooth file-sharing as a neat solution for archival Noongar song recirculation. Nevertheless, building on the relative popularity of the subtitled song videos and a desire for visual representation of the tune of each song led to the development of nine new subtitled videos featuring new audio recordings of archival songs accompanied by animated graphic scores developed with composer Jean Michelle Maujean. On the direction of the descendants and stakeholders, these videos were uploaded to a password-protected section of the Wirlomin Noongar Language and Stories organisation website to be shared into the future as that organisation sees fit.

Koorlangka karaoke

While online technologies allow for various levels of password protection to restrict access to certain content, Ayonghe and Ategha assert:

> This is the age of mass communication, of news reaching people in a matter of hours, of multimedia experiences and a world where audiences demand the right to share the latest text, be it a film, documentary, song, or book simultaneously across cultures. (2018, 45)

Increasingly, Noongar people and the broader community interested in learning Noongar language are searching for relevant and engaging online content. On commencing a subsequent Australian Research Council–funded project "Restoring On-Country Performance", senior Noongar advisers Dr Roma Yibiyung Winmar, Annie Dabb and Barry McGuire suggested that, to better serve the language revitalisation aspirations of the broader Noongar community, I (as lead chief investigator) should prioritise the development of language and song resources that could be freely shared, without limitations to access.

To this end, in 2020 I established the website mayakeniny.com and began production of a series of children's song videos with karaoke-style subtitled Noongar lyrics, titled *Koorlangka Karaoke* (Budrikis and Bracknell 2022). The songs had been translated by Dr Roma Yibiyung Winmar and incorporated into her Noongar language teaching program at Moorditj Community College for many years. A total of 10 videos were filmed during Perth's first lockdown period at the beginning of the Covid-19 pandemic. Over two afternoons in Dr Winmar's own back and front yards, linguist Dr Amy Budrikis filmed her singing each song as I provided off-camera guitar accompaniment. The videos were edited and subtitled, and artist and film-maker Cassandra Edwards added hand-drawn digital animations. Dr Winmar suggested that young viewers would be more engaged in the videos if they had a strong beat, so I overdubbed guitar, bass, backing vocals and electronic drums.

These videos were produced quickly and, for maximum public engagement, posted on social media platforms including Facebook, through links to the "Mayakeniny" YouTube channel. *Dambart Yerderap* (*Three Little Ducks*) was the first video shared via the Kurongkurl Katitjin (School of Indigenous Studies at Edith Cowan University) Facebook page. Within two weeks, it received 9,000 views, 157 "like" and "love" reactions, 121 "shares" and 41 positive comments such as "I love this so much," "That is wonderful," "Moorditj!" The video was shared widely within and outside of the Noongar community by organisations including community radio stations and childcare centres. It generated calls for more resources like this to be used in schools. Some people left comments to let us know they had shared the videos with their children and grandchildren.

The popularity of these videos is not only due to the demand for online Noongar language resources, but also thanks to the respect Dr Winmar has earned over many years as an active member of the Noongar community, teaching Noongar language to generations upon generations of students. Noongar community responses to Koorlangka Karaoke demonstrates the potential reach and impact of subtitled music videos in an endangered language, particularly when shared on social media. While the Koorlangka Karaoke videos were used in classrooms and more informally by parents and grandparents to teach children, they did not encourage the same kind of community participation as Degai's "Itelmen Karaoke", or even the English-language "Noongaroke". Social media platforms like Facebook encourage interaction within the online space in terms of "liking" and commenting on content, but they do not necessarily encourage user participation in face-to-face activities and embodied practices like performance.

Noongar Wonderland TikTok videos

TikTok is an online application for smartphones that enables the creation of user-generated content in which users lip-synch or dance to music hosted by the TikTok platform, often with animated synchronised song lyric text. As is the case with many online video platforms, this user content can be shared, liked and commented on by other users. One intriguing aspect of TikTok is the way its users frequently instigate "challenges", whereby other users are expected to emulate or respond to the content in an original video (Montag et al. 2021). Among other activity, this phenomenon frequently results in users practising dance moves, often in pairs or groups, and learning the lyrics to songs so they can create their own video responses to challenges.

On the advice of senior Noongar as part of the "Restoring On-Country Performance" project, I had developed new Noongar songs based on the musical and lyrical conventions of old Noongar songs, embellished with dance music beats.[2] Noongar performer and Master's Degree candidate Trevor Ryan choreographed new dances for these songs and directed a group of Noongar dancers to present them at the outdoor event "Noongar Wonderland" held as part of Perth Festival 2022 (Ryan 2022). Each song and dance evoked the ecological place of sharks, dolphins, stingrays, bobtail lizards, dragonflies and groundwater in the Noongar region. We encouraged Noongar people and the broader public to participate

---

2 This music was released as *Noongar Wonderland* by Maatakitj featuring Paul Mac in 2022.

in the performances, and via various surveys administered by Perth Festival and Noongar Master's Degree candidate Kyle J. Morrison, most performers and audience members indicated that this participation in Noongar song and dance increased feelings of connectedness to the local environment (Morrison 2022; Bracknell et al. 2021).

As the audience for Noongar Wonderland was limited to 1,500 people over three nights, Trevor and I wondered if sharing the repertoire via TikTok could be effective not just in increasing feelings of environmental connection, but as a language-learning activity. One Saturday in October 2022, Trevor Ryan gathered with linguist Amy Budrikis, Noongar director Kylie Bracknell, and three young Noongar dancers to film the first viral Noongar-language TikTok dance challenge videos. These were subsequently subtitled with the Noongar song lyrics and will be live on the TikTok platform at the time this chapter is published. We hope that with the support of subtitled text and the action-based online community, these videos may prove useful as another domain for Noongar language and song revitalisation.

Conclusion

The use of online subtitled video content is just one of many possible ways to support Noongar language and song revitalisation. In lieu of regular opportunities for everyday interaction in Noongar language and the limited number of Noongar language teachers supported in the school system, online digital media offers relatively straightforward and barrier-free ways to increase the presence of Noongar language in daily life. The legacy of corroboree performance – connecting people across linguistic and cultural boundaries – provides a potentially useful framework for considering the goals and strategies of language revitalisation in online spaces. While some serious knowledge and information can only be held by the right individuals, young people eager to connect more deeply with their Indigenous language and Country need "open" repertoire that they can learn, share and experiment with.

Although there was no choice offered as settler-colonial policies attempted to strip away Noongar song and language, culture is always changing. Noongar, like most Indigenous people worldwide, choose to mobilise new instruments and technologies as we see fit. Karaoke combines text, music, video, camaraderie and a licence to sing. It can be a perfect vehicle for encouraging engagement with endangered languages, particularly when – as in the case of "Itelman Karaoke", Koorlangka Karaoke and Noongar Wonderland – the empty space in the music left for a solo amateur singer is filled in with a crowd of Indigenous voices to sing along with. As pandemics and suburban sprawl continue to conspire to isolate us from each other, online trends like TikTok "challenge videos" could be leveraged to enhance the vitality of minority languages, especially when that format carries many of the useful qualities of karaoke. As is the case with anything online though, its success may depend largely on how many people "like" it.

Chapter 15

Tjendji (Fire) and *Tjerri* (Sea Breeze): what Indigenous wisdom has to tell us about the climate emergency and the biodiversity crisis

Payi Linda Ford and Allan Marett

Introduction

In his 2009 book, *Dying words: endangered languages and what they have to tell us*, Nicholas Evans (citing Bernard 1992) warns us that "any reduction of language diversity diminishes the adaptational strength of our species because it lowers the pool of knowledge from which we can draw" (Evans 2009, 19). In the following year, Marett observed in response that if this is true for language, it is even more so for traditions of music and dance, particularly in Aboriginal Australia, where songs are the most valued and revered repositories – the foundational documents if you like – of Indigenous knowledge, wisdom and history (Marett 2010).

These ancient repertories of Aboriginal song have since European settlement been decimated – worse than decimated – brought almost to the point of extinction. Despite the heroic efforts of Indigenous Australians, the great majority of the cultural traditions of ceremonial song and dance were lost as a result of the unlawful and brutal occupation of Indigenous lands by the British colonial forces and their settler-descendants. It goes without saying that when we lose these traditions of ancient song, we also lose the wisdom and knowledge embedded within them. Miraculously, a significant number of song traditions survive today and these offer unique sources of knowledge and wisdom, which we might draw upon in our quest to overcome the many difficulties facing the world and its many beings at this time.

A key premise of our chapter is that the current ongoing destruction of the environment is enabled not just by greed, but by worldviews that rest upon certain assumptions about the relationship between what is conceived of as "sentient", "animate" and "alive" and what is conceived of as "non-sentient", "inanimate" or "dead". Living beings are regarded as sentient and all other phenomena as non-sentient and inanimate – basically as dead matter. It is this deep rift between living beings – and in particular human beings – and their physical environment that often underpins the treatment of the environment in disrespectful and destructive ways.

There is an extensive literature that attests to the fact that Australian Aboriginal societies regard Country – and its many phenomena: clouds, rocks, trees, wind – as sentient and in a dynamic relationship of mutual reciprocity with the human world. Marett, for example, in his book on the *wangga* of the Daly region, observed that "the land, as in many other Aboriginal cosmologies, is thus conceived of as alive and sentient – not only the source of all life, but also responsive to human events" (Marett 2005, 29).[1]

Worldviews that regard the relationship between the animate and inanimate in this way provide important models that we can draw upon in our search for new ways to confront climate change and other environmental catastrophes. We can look for guidance to societies that recognise and enact within their cultural practices a deep sense of reciprocity between humans and the physical world, and to this end, our paper will consider three instances drawn from Australian Aboriginal culture that reveal how reciprocity and more sustainable worldviews tend to draw the lines between the animate and inanimate world differently.

First, Payi Linda Ford discusses her painting, "Wadi kan ngun pip wa!" ("Seasonal Fire"), which focuses on her *ngirrwat, Tjendji* (Fire), and the practice of giving fire to Country. She tells us:

> *Ngirrwat* is the word in my language for what is often translated as "Dreaming," or "Ancestral Being" and *ngirrwat* are intimately connected to the sentient landscape. The *Tjendji* (Fire) *ngirrwat* tells me when, where and burn the country. It is part of who I am.

---

[1] See also, for example, Myers 1986; Poirier 1996; Povinelli 1993; Rose 1996.

Secondly we focus on a *lirrga*[2] song about the same *ngirrwat*, "Fire", and specifically upon a performance of a song about this *ngirrwat* that Payi's uncle, Captain Woditj, gave at the final mortuary rites for her mother in 2009. Performances such as this enact deep mutual obligations between people and people, and between people and country, but as Payi will tell us, in recent times climate change has led to fire management becoming more dangerous and unpredictable.

Our third case study is a performance by Maurice Ngulkurr of a *wangga*[3] song about a *ngirrwat*, Sea Breeze *(Tjerri)* that is closely related to the Fire *(Tjendji) ngirrwat*. We focus particularly on the way in which the sentience of a natural phenomenon such as wind is reflected in the text of this song. We show how patterns of reciprocal obligations are expressed in the song, and how these underpin the critical role that songs such as these play in the ecology of Payi's Country, Kurrindju, in the Daly region of north Australia.

"Wadi kan ngun pip wa!" ("Seasonal Fire" (2005)): a painting by Payi Linda Ford

I, Payi Linda Ford, a Rak Mak Mak Marranunggu woman from Kurrindju, in the Finniss River region, south-west of Darwin, Northern Territory, Australia, will now discuss my *ngirrwat* Dreaming, *Tjendji* (Fire) in order to locate myself within Country and in relation to the *wali* and *wangga* ceremonies, to which I belong.

"Woewoe Kurrindju yimin mi-thita pitpit wa, waki ninni!" These words, in my Mak Mak Marranunggu language, mean "Oh my country Kurrindju, I am giving you fire to make you warm and clean". I received this form of words, together with the authorisation to give fire to Country, from my mother and her father, and I call out these words whenever I give fire to my country. Giving fire to Country is a reciprocal process. In return for my giving fire to her Country to clear it for hunting and to encourage new growth, my Country gives me food and many other benefits.

---

2   *Lirrga* is a genre of public, didjeridu-accompanied song sung by the Marringarr people of the Daly region. *Lirrga* are received by living songmen from their deceased relatives, and are one of several genres sung at mortuary and circumcision ceremonies.

3   *Wangga* is another genre of public, didjeridu-accompanied song. Language groups that own *wangga* include the Marranunggu. Like *lirrga*, *wangga* are received by living songmen from their deceased relatives, and are one of several genres sung at mortuary and circumcision ceremonies. For more detail see Marett 2005; Marett, Barwick and Ford 2013.

Figure 15.1 "Wadi kan ngun pip wa!" ("Seasonal Fire" (2005)). A painting by Payi Linda Ford. Photo: Mark Ford.

My acrylic painting called "Wadi kan ngun pip wa!" or "Seasonal Fire" was painted on Belgian linen in 2005 as part of the Aboriginal process for my doctoral thesis "Narratives and Landscapes: their capacity to serve Indigenous knowledge interests".

This painting illustrates the annual fire pattern throughout the year.

- Warm ochre-coloured dots embody the characteristics of the fire's moodiness embellished in the course of its movement across the savannas down onto Patj Patj, Munjirr-Munjirr, Miyerr-Miyerr, Melambelangu, Munjimima floodplain-country, where it meets the salt water of Fog Bay.
- The central white ochre dots denote the fireplaces of my Rak Mak Mak Marranunggu people.
- The light-yellow ochre dots indicate early seasonal burning along the ridge country.
- The large dark shades of red and orange ochre dots signify cooler fires.
- The large green dots indicate the wet and damp areas underfoot where the vegetation is ready to burn.
- The darker shades of red ochre dots depict hot, slow fires.
- The smaller red ochre dots are fast, spirited fires.
- The medium red ochre dots depict the heat intensity of the late fires over the lower floodplain country.

So, to summarise, this painting of seasonal fires in the Rak Mak Mak Marranunggu Country, Kurrindju, illustrates how the fires are set alight at different places at different times of a calendar year.

"Tjendji" ("Fire"): a *lirrga* song, sung by Captain Woditj

The *lirrga* song, "Tjendji" ("Fire"), is sung in Marringarr, a language that is closely related to my languages Mak Mak Marranunggu and Marrithiyel. All three languages belong to the Marri language family, which forms part of a wider complex of Daly languages and their associated clans groups known as Marrawalgut. People who belong to the Marrawalgut ceremonial complex share songs like "Tjendji" and "Tjerri". Since time immemorial, *wangga* and *lirrga* songs such as these have been created and performed by songmen to reflect the moods of the Country. As a member of the Marrawalgut group, I am able to draw upon these songs to link us to Country.

"Tjendji" ("Fire") is often sung at *kapuk* ceremonies for Marrawalgut members. *Kapuk* ceremonies are the last of a series of mortuary rites that are performed to allow the spirit of a deceased person to leave the society of the Living and join with the Ancestors, and Fire plays a central role in this ceremony.

This song, "Tjendji", has a particular significance for me that links me to my Country. It was sung by my uncle Captain Woditj (see Figure 15.2) and other songmen for my *ala* – my mother – Ngulilkang Nancy Daiyi's final mortuary rites in August 2009 on the Finniss River coastal floodplains, at Kalngarriny and Meneling near Litchfield National Park. Allan Marett and Linda Barwick also both attended these ceremonies, and sang with the *wangga* and *djanba* groups respectively (Ford, Barwick and Marett, A. 2014). My spiritual relationship with the song, through my Marrithiyel connections to her *ngirrwat*, *Tjendji*, is very powerful.

The text of the song, which is in Marrangarr, describes Fire burning at Nerendji on the Moyle River floodplain, near the Little Moyle River.

Fire at Nerendji burnt down on them /

It's burning along over there now on the little Moyle.

The Fire *ngirrwat* is shared by the Marrangarr and Marranunggu language groups, as well as other language groups within the Marrawalgut complex.

Figure 15.2 Captain Woditj singing the "Tjendji" (Fire) *lirrga*. Photo: Mark Ford.

> *Tjendji Nerendji ya nganan=wurri vinyi+wir+kut = a*
> Fire at Nerendji burnt down on them (x2)
>
> *Kurna=vingi kidi+pir kani muyil yipesri*
> It's burning along all over there now on the little Moyle

Figure 15.3 "Tjendji" ("Fire"), composed by Dennis Nardjic: translation by Clement Tchinburrurr and Lysbeth Ford.

 **Audio Example 15.1** "Tjendji" ("Fire"). Sung by Captain Woditj.

15 *Tjendji* (Fire) and *Tjerri* (Sea Breeze)

In the epilogue to his book, *Songs, dreamings and ghosts*, Allan, flying back to Darwin from Wadeye, also reflects on the fires he sees burning on the Moyle floodplain, which bring to mind another *lirrga* song, one composed by Captain Woditj's Marrangarr countryman, Clement Tchinbururr.

> Soon, as the towering cumulus surrounding us promise, the wet season will be upon us, flooding the land . . . For now, though, the country below is still dry, still showing signs of having been burnt. For millennia people have looked after country in this way.

> *Fire!*
> *The people of the Muyil set fire to Yenmura-Ngurdandar.*
> *Cold dry season country!*
> *Burning away from me at Wangnenggi,*
> *The whole Muyil floodplain will be on fire by now.*
> *It's burning there, even where I can't see it,*
> *There at the little Moyle River, far away from me.*

> Burning country is another of the ways that people make their presence known to the sentient landscape. It is part of what humans are obliged to do – to look after country, so that it in turn will nourish them (Marett 2005, 233).

As in Captain Woditj's much shorter song text, Clement's *lirrga* song names specific places on the Moyle (*muyil*) floodplain as it tracks the route of the fire: *Yenmura, Ngurdandar, Wangnenggi*. It also mentions the fact that these fires are set in the cold season, *ringi*.

The Sea Breeze *ngirrwat* and the Fire *ngirrwat* are strongly connected.

The Sea Breeze gives life to Fire so that it can burn the country. When Sea Breeze blows from the west, the gentle winds pick up and whistle to the fire to race across the grass that has fully dried out, even though underneath the grass, there is still moisture in the ground. The fire burns across the top of the grass and the water that is lying beneath it. This happens just after the early burns are started in May–June each year.

Later, in September–October, however, the late dry season weather and the wind combine to burn grass and other fuel that was not burned earlier in the year. As a result of climate change such fires are now not so easily managed. Vegetation has increased in density, and so have the fuel loads. Moreover, nowadays wind directions can change instantly and unpredictably causing much hotter and more dangerous fires. The late dry season has become a dangerous time for us.

"Tjerri" ("Sea Breeze"), a *wangga* song sung by Maurice Ngulkurr

Our third example is a specific song about Sea Breeze (*Tjerri*), which was given in dream to the Marriammu songman Charlie Niwili Brinken, by his deceased ancestors, known as Mayawa. Charlie Brinken in turn passed the song to Maurice Ngulkurr (whom we see in Figure 15.4), who sang it for Allan and helped him translate its text. *Wangga* songs, which are given to the Living by the Dead, are owned and performed by most language groups in the Daly region, including the Rak Mak Mak Marranunggu clan.

Figure 15.4 Maurice Ngulkurr points in the direction of the *Tjerri* (Sea Breeze) Dreaming site. Photo: Allan Marett.

> *karra mana tjerri kagan-dja kinyi-ni kavulh*
> Brother Sea Breeze! He is manifesting himself right here and now, as he has always done
>
> *karra mana tjerri kinyi-ni kavulh kagan-dja*
> Brother Sea Breeze! He is manifesting himself, as he has always done, right here and now
>
> *purangang kin-pa-diyerr kavulh kagan-dja kisji*
> The sea is always breaking at the creek, right here, like this

Figure 15.5 "Tjerri" ("Sea Breeze") composed by Charlie Brinken. Sung by Maurice Ngulkurr.

15 *Tjendji* (Fire) and *Tjerri* (Sea Breeze)

Audio Example 15.2 "Tjerri" ("Sea Breeze"). Sung by Maurice Ngulkurr.

Figure 15.5 shows the text of "Tjerri". Close attention reveals a worldview where phenomena – including things that in certain mainstream worldviews would be seen as inanimate – are regarded as alive and self-generating in the present moment according to deep ancestral precedent.

Let us consider the first line. Here the first word, *mana* (brother) is used to address the Sea Breeze Dreaming. This implies an inherent intimacy. "Sea Breeze" is family. This is followed by the phrase "he is manifesting himself right here and now, as he has always done". In Marriammu this is: *kagandja kinyi-ni kavulh*. As is common in Aboriginal languages, the verb is agglutinative: that is, it consists of a verb stem to which elements are added before and after to inflect for person, mood, tense and so on. The verb stem of *kinyi-ni* is *–nyi-* which means "to make or do". Put *ki* in front – *ki-nyi* – and it means "he/she/it makes or does", but since we know that the subject is male – brother Sea Breeze – we have used the masculine pronoun "he" throughout the translation. The suffix *–ni* makes the verb *kinyi-ni* reflexive: "he makes himself". Linguist friends tell us that these sorts of self-reflexive verb constructions occur most frequently within the poetics of song. And in such contexts they can be regarded as unique and special poetic expressions of a deep truth: the self-reflexive – indeed self-actualising – nature of ancestral beings – *ngirrwat* – such as the Sea Breeze. Self-generation is an intrinsic quality of Dreamings, which require no agency beyond themselves for their existence.

While "Tjerri" is unique to its environment and culture, the worldview that underpins it is not unlike that expressed in songs from other parts of Aboriginal Australia. The self-generating nature of Dreams was, for example, referred to by T.G.H. Strehlow, who maintained that the core meaning of *altjira* (the Arrernte term cognate with *ngirrwat*) was as follows: "that which derives from . . . the eternal, uncreated, springing out of itself", or that which has "sprung out of its own eternity" (Strehlow 1971, 614; see also Swain 1993, 21). And the way the Murrinhpatha at Wadeye spoke to Stanner about the Rainbow Serpent Dreaming (*Kunmangurr*) also resonates. Kunmanggurr was said to be a *kardu bangambitj*, a "self-finding" person (that is, "self-creating and self-subsistent") (Stanner 1989, 249).

The *eternal aspect* of the Sea Breeze is expressed by the co-verb *ka-vulh,* which follows *kinyi-ni* and means literally "he lies" or "he has always lain there", while the *here-and-now-ness* of the Sea Breeze Dreaming is indicated by the word *kagan-dja*, which precedes *kinyi-ni* and means, literally, "right here and now".

So to summarise: *Karra mana Tjerri* Brother Seabreeze *kagan-dja* right here and now *kinyi-ni* he is manifesting himself *kavulh* as he has always done. Or to put it another way, Dreamings such as Sea Breeze (*Tjerri*) stand in their own unique place – that is, they are self-generated – while simultaneously maintaining deep connections with other beings throughout space and time. In our view, texts such as this embody an ancient wisdom that is indigenous to this land – a view of the world that has, for millennia, sustained and nurtured the relationship between humans and the environment in this country that we now call Australia.

While the worldview articulated here is substantially at odds with what we have loosely called "a mainstream western view of the world", it is not alone. There are other wisdom traditions that resonate closely with that of Indigenous Australia. As a long-time Zen practitioner and teacher, Allan is most familiar with examples of this that occur within the Zen tradition. The 12th-century Japanese Zen Buddhist poet-philosopher, Dōgen Zenji, for example, speaks of "self-actualising dharmas [phenomena]" that both leap into being as the present, and are simultaneously eternal. We will argue the value of engaging with such ancient wisdom traditions, and in particular the wisdom tradition indigenous to this land.

The songs "Tjendji" and "Tjerri" offer us critical lessons about climate change and adaptability to the environment in which we live and function. It is through knowing, being and activating *Tjendji* that the Rak Mak Mak Marranunggu people co-exist with the environment and manage their biodiversity in a way that offers sustainable outcomes. As Payi tells us:

> through my *Tjendji ngirrwat,* I have cultural roles and responsibilities to fulfil as determined through my lineal linkages to the Country to which I belong, that is, the country of my Rak Marrithiyel Makali-Grandmother Milyanga and Rak Mak Mak Marranunggu Tjabutj-Grandfather Djekaboi. This *Tjendji* and *Tjerri* knowledge is passed onto my children and so on into the future.

Yu! ngangi wedjim waki tjan Tjendji Tjerri marri!
Yes, our joint (Allan and Payi's) Fire and Sea Breeze story is finished now.

Acknowledgements

This paper was originally part of a panel entitled "Listening to the Ancestors", presented at the 2021 Australian Academy of the Humanities Annual Symposium, which had as its theme "Culture, Nature, Climate: Humanities and the Environmental Crisis". Papers in this panel focused on the Aboriginal ceremonial arts – song, dance and visual design – and how the knowledge embedded in these forms might inform our response to the multiple environmental challenges that we face today.

Chapter 16

Music as formative social action

Ian Cross

Problematising "music"

Since the work of the Strehlows last century (see Hill 2002), music, largely in the form of song, has been increasingly recognised as integral to the proper functioning of the Indigenous cultures of Australia and has become a key feature of the workings of restorative justice in that country. As Alick Tipoti (quoted in Koch 2013, 38) put it: "the songs and the dance and the storytelling . . . are like our documents to prove that it [the land and waters] belongs to us". They reflect the ways in which "Creative Ancestors moved across an undifferentiated topography during the original 'Dreaming,' shaping a featureless world" (Hill 1995, 308). "Songs" here seem to have functions that are effectively assertions of legal rights, making claims that have deontic force in that they affirm, and even compel, obligations among people and between groups.

From a Western-centric perspective, this seems odd; how can songs – music – be used for such purposes? In contemporary global Western culture music is, at its most exalted, an aesthetic object (Ingarden 1961), while in common currency it constitutes a commodity with entertainment value and little else (see, e.g., Adorno 1945; Holbrook 2000). Indeed, in very recent digital incarnations music seems to exist primarily as a means of capturing attention, extracting user information and hence monetising engagement with streaming platforms (Drott 2018). How can such an apparently trivial pursuit possibly have the authority to function as a means of establishing ownership – as a means of asserting, and even instating, basic human rights?

Over the last several decades, research on Indigenous Australian musical practices has shown that they foreground features that may be present in Western musics but that have tended to be disregarded in most accounts of manifestations of those musics. While Indigenous Australian song can appear to be entertainment, Barwick and Turpin (2016, 114) noted that it has distinct social functions in that it can "defuse conflict and build social cohesion", serving (Barwick and Turpin 2016, 126) as part of "a way of displaying and managing group identity within a complex social landscape involving diverse complementary groups and many gradations of social difference". Indeed, Indigenous song is understood by its performers and owners as a "mode of intervening in the world", acting to maintain the order of things (Curran, Barwick et al. 2016, 367). While some germs of music's social potential – such as its roles in the realisation and presentation of identity, or in seeding the emergence of subcultural formations – are reflected in contemporary Western musicological theory and discourse, Indigenous song in Australia seems vastly to exceed the scope and powers of music as understood in Western contexts.

In order to reconcile – and to understand the significance of – the apparent peculiarity and the compelling lucidity of Indigenous Australian perspectives on music, it is useful to start by re-evaluating conventional Western definitions of music. The *Oxford English Dictionary* (2021) defines music as "The art or science of combining vocal or instrumental sounds to produce beauty of form, harmony, melody, rhythm, expressive content, etc." While this may have sufficed in late 19th-century Europe, it has been overtaken by developments in popular music over the last hundred years – it can scarcely be applied informatively to much grunge, thrash metal or hip-hop, for example. The definition supplied by the musicologist Irving Godt (2005, 84) appears to offer a slightly broader and more carefully delimited version:

> Music is humanly organised sound, organised with intent into a recognisable aesthetic entity as a musical communication directed from a maker to a known or unforeseen listener, publicly through the medium of a performer, or privately by a performer as listener.

Both the dictionary and the academic definitions given here effectively assert that aesthetic attributes are criteria in judging whether or not something constitutes music. But, as the ethnomusicologist Bruno Nettl noted, "there are societies and musics where these criteria make no sense at all" (Nettl 2005, 18).

Cross-culturally, "music" seems to be extremely variable in form and in function. Indeed, development of a general definition that can be applied to the heterogeneous phenomena identifiable as "music" across cultures seems to be either quite intractable or simply superfluous (see also Barwick 2012). For example, Rice

(2013, 1) suggested that ethnomusicology explores not music but what it is to be "musical", defining this as "the capacity of humans to create, perform, organize cognitively, react physically and emotionally to, and interpret the meanings of humanly organized sound". While much more inclusive than Godt's account, Rice's account is equally applicable to language and to music while excluding the dimension of movement that would be considered integral to "music" in many cultures (see, e.g., Nketia 1982). For some ethnomusicologists and music sociologists, defining music is viewed as neither feasible nor necessary. Born and Barry (2018, 458) claimed "both music and social movements . . . are best figured not as organic totalities but as constellations of heterogeneous mediations". In the end, the heuristic proposed by the ethnomusicologist Klaus Wachsmann (1971, 384) might be as close as we can get to a generalisable definition:

> I could say to myself that those phenomena outside my own immediate culture to which I now attach the label "music" because I recognise and acknowledge them to be music, are merely so labelled because, rightly or wrongly, they seem to me to resemble the phenomena which I am in the habit of calling music in my home ground.

What, precisely, are those phenomena that are recognised as music on "my home ground" in the present day, from a conventional, Western, musicological perspective? By and large, they remain Western art music of the last 300 years or so, but admitting into the fold an increasing range of popular musics. These ideas of music tend to have something in common. They frame music as primarily an aural phenomena (Cross 2012), treating music as confined to what Turino (2008) terms the *presentational* field in which a clear distinction is drawn between music producers and music listeners. Music tends to be conceptualised from the perspective of the listener; music is predominantly something to which you listen, not something you do. A framing of music as presentational is not confined to recent Western contexts; many musics beyond the bounds of WEIRD cultures (Western, Educated, Industrialized, Rich, Democratic[1]) can also be interpreted as presentational. Music in the presentational field appears to be particularly susceptible to processes of commodification (Appadurai 1994), in which exchange value comes to be the primary sense in terms of which something is valued. These processes, bound to the 18th-century emergence of ideas of intellectual property (Hunter 1986) and 19th-century technological developments in capturing music

---

1 See Henrich, Heine and Norenzayan 2010.

as sound,[2] have led to the appropriation of many non-WEIRD musics into the presentational field under the banner of "world music".[3]

But, as Turino (2008) noted, there are other fields of music. Perhaps the most prominent is the "participatory" field, in which there is no sharp delineation between performer and audience, with roles capable of being reversed or merged: the audience may simply be, or have the potential to become, the performers. Participatory music, often in the form of song, is prevalent in many traditional, non-WEIRD, cultures, but is also pervasive in a wide range of WEIRD contexts (such as the chants of football fans[4]). While participatory music can seem trivial and casual, it is almost never mere entertainment. A typical consequence of engaging in making music together is that participants come to experience a heightened sense of bonding or mutual affiliation (again, well evidenced in respect of football chants[5]), a phenomenon central to what Victor Turner described as *communitas* (Turner 1969). Turino (2008, 59) developed a coherent account of the attributes that participatory music is likely to display that may underpin its efficacy in creating bonds between those making music together: it is likely to comprise short open, redundantly repeated forms with "feathered" beginnings and endings, to downplay individual virtuosity, to be highly repetitive and to exhibit a constancy of rhythm or groove. It invites participation.

The constancy of rhythm typical of participatory music lends itself to dance; most world cultures that foreground participatory practices in their music make little if any distinction between music and dance.[6] Indeed, music and dance can be thought of as culturally mediated and multimodal realisations of the same set of underlying capacities, as the findings of Sievers, Polansky et al. (2013) suggest. In the Australian context, Barwick (2012) adopted my own suggestion that since "the concept of music is amalgamated with that of dance in many – perhaps the majority of – cultures" it would be "parsimonious to treat music and dance as intrinsically related or simply as different manifestations of the same phenomenon" (Cross 2007, 654) in her observation that "in Pitjantjatjara, one of the Western Desert languages of Australia, the word *inma* encompasses not only music, but ceremony, accompanying dance, body painting, and ritual paraphernalia" (Barwick 2000; Ellis 1985, 70–71). Barwick (2002, 68) had previously implied that, for at least some Indigenous Australian cultures, music and dance may not only be

---

2   See, e.g., Chanan 1995.
3   See, e.g., Feld 2000; Stokes 2004.
4   See, e.g., T. Clark 2006; Kytö 2011.
5   See Knijnik 2018; Lee 2018.
6   See, e.g., Gourlay 1984; Nketia 1982.

virtually inseparable but that they also fulfil significant social functions when she noted that "Public *dance-song* genres [my emphasis] play a central role in establishing relationships of mutual support and obligation between the various language groups in Wadeye".

A substantial and still increasing amount of empirical research over the last 15 years or so has provided confirmation of Barwick's claim in demonstrating that both moving together and making music together can lead to positive effects on personal memory and on pro-social behaviour ("behaviours that are intended to benefit others": see Jensen 2016). Dancing together has been shown to lead to enhanced person perception and memory (Woolhouse et al. 2016), as well as a sense of enhanced interpersonal closeness (Tarr, Launay and Dunbar 2016). Working with children aged between 8 and 13, Rabinowitch and colleagues (2013) found that a program of musical group interaction comprising interactive musical games enhanced the development of the children's capacity for empathy, while experiments with adults by Pearce and colleagues (2016) showed that group singing can increase a sense of mutual affiliation between participants. Vuoskoski and colleagues (2016) found that even just solitary listening to music could lead to an enhanced sense of cross-cultural affiliation; it seems that music, even in presentational forms, can elicit the sense of *communitas* that characterises participation in active and interactive music making.

It should be stressed that any instance of presentational music is likely to entail participatory features. Presentational frames can assign quite specific activities not only to performers but also to audiences, which must be accomplished appropriately for a performance to unfold successfully – in Western classical (Bishop and Goebl 2018), Western popular (Swarbrick, Bosnyak et al. 2019) and non-Western contexts.[7] Moreover, audiences may exhibit significant levels of coupling in their physiological responses to musical performances[8] as well as in their neural activity, both among themselves and with performers (Hou, Song et al. 2020). Similarly, any instance of participatory music can be appropriated, at least in part, into the presentational domain.[9] The labels "presentational" and "participatory" constitute useful categories in terms of which to explore the form and function of music across different cultural contexts, though any given instance of music is likely to exhibit greater or lesser proportions of features of each field.

---

7   See Swarbrick, Bosnyak et al. 2019; and see, e.g., Ram 2011, on the role of rasikas – connoisseurs – in Indian art music performance.
8   See, e.g., Czepiel, Fink et al. 2021; Tschacher, Greenwood et al. 2021.
9   For a paradigmatic case see Feld 1996.

Music as cultural heritage

Indigenous Australian music is no exception, exhibiting both presentational and participatory features. It is just as susceptible to being appropriated into commercial presentational forms as any other form of music; happily, those processes have at times been fruitfully managed by Indigenous performers in their appropriation of musical forms and norms of the hegemonic WEIRD culture for Indigenous ends.[10] But even in traditional Indigenous cultural contexts music exhibits both presentational and participatory features. The songs – and as Barwick noted, "the traditional musical genres of Aboriginal Australia consist entirely of vocal music" (Barwick 2012, 171) – are for the participants as well as for the community members who have legitimate access to them, both present and past. Those songs embody the histories of the ways in which singers, audience and land interact, and have interacted, as understood in terms of Dreamings (Hill 1995). Events articulated in song constitute the ways in which the rights, rites and responsibilities of Dreamings become distributed among those who experience themselves or their ancestors as agents in those events.

Here we might find a preliminary answer to the question of how it is that music can support the claim that the land can belong to its Indigenous inhabitants even when exiled or dispossessed. A song belongs to those who know its significance through creating it or participating in it, most likely being functional in the formation and transmission of collective memory (Hirst, Yamashiro and Coman 2018) through processes of mnemonic convergence (there is good evidence that music helps consolidate words, and probably higher-level linguistic structures, in memory[11]). Song in Indigenous Australian culture reflects its participants' relationships to the land, linking places, events and people, and in every performance the song binds the singers and dancers together, reinforcing their identity *as* a group (Marett 2005; Barwick 2002). As Barwick and Turpin (2016, 127) pointed out, "ceremonies are not simply entertainment, but expressions of Aboriginal law". They noted that:

> Shared conventions in music, poetics, dance, body decoration, and song subjects allow each repertory to highlight the Dreaming stories and places that are specific to that clan's identity. This traditional use has extended in the last 40 years to legal contexts where performance of *yawulyu/awelye* has been accepted as demonstrating native title to land. (Barwick and Turpin 2016, 130)

---

10 See, e.g., Corn 2010; Dunbar-Hall and Gibson 2000.
11 See Tamminen, Rastle et al. 2017.

These conventions embody a set of common understandings expressed in specific performance practices that relate to specific clan identity and can thus specify legal title. Hence the song is a recollection and assertion of the group's place in the world as well as a means of sustaining the group's identity and of mediating its relationships to other groups, a form of intangible cultural heritage that acquires power through its performance.

It might be asked why land rights should not simply be asserted through language. After all, language enables explicit assertions about states of affairs such as the existence of a particular group of people and their rights to a particular territory. But explicit and unambiguous assertions may pose more problems than they resolve; in order for such an assertion to "work", it requires all interested parties to accept the claim made, otherwise conflict is highly likely to ensue. The use of song allows conflict to be deflected or postponed. As Turpin and Stebbins noted of Indigenous Australian song:

> A song text itself is often what Sperber and Wilson (1986) call "weakly communicative". This means that the hearer is required to make many inferences to receive a message, and as a result many interpretations of the message are possible. (Turpin and Stebbins 2010, 2)

This ambiguity appears to be a feature of music in general, a feature that I have described elsewhere as "floating intentionality" (Cross 1999, 2005) and one which has powerful efficacy in the management of social relationships (particularly at times of social uncertainty, such as births, marriages, deaths – changes of social status and interpersonal significance). In song, language can become untethered from its everyday and socially shared meanings; meanings may be private and unshared, though the embedding of those meanings in music and song can afford the unspoken *sense* to all concerned in making and experiencing the music together that they are experiencing the "same" significances (Cross 2015).

Marett (2005) provided an instance of such a phenomenon in his account of the "tripartite ceremonial system" in Wadeye in the Northern Territory, where conflicting claims to access had emerged between members of the three different language groups. The tripartite ceremonial system was produced by Elders of the groups involved and required members of one particular language group to perform their own particular song genre within the significant ceremonial occasions (such as *burnim rags*) of the other language groups, each of whom possessed their own proper song genres. As Marett (2005, 23) noted, this system "continues to function to the present day and is pointed to as a source of ongoing stability within the community". As he pointed out (2005, 35), "song texts often contain elements of ambiguity that permit a variety of different exegeses", and it appears likely that it is this ambiguity that allows the tripartite ceremony to maintain a degree of social harmony across the three groups. Nevertheless, though ostensibly ambiguous, song language may bear quite specific meanings, though in Indigenous Australian song the meanings of the words may be evident only to those who have come to have access to the "inner truths and outside appearances in all aspects of being" that "make Dreamings and people co-presences in one world" (Sansom 2001, 3).

While language in the special context of song can exhibit floating intentionality, so may language in everyday interaction. When speech is employed in the "phatic" register (Malinowski 1923), utterances can also become detached from their usual meanings, serving to minimise potential for conflict and to promote sociability (Senft 2009; 2018). Phatic communicative interactions in speech share functions with joint music making; they help to manage situations of social uncertainty by reducing social tension (Senft 2018), and they can express and enhance a sense of social group identity (Wiessner 2014) or "conviviality" (Rampton 2015). Phatic speech interaction thus seems to share properties with those attributed above to participatory music making; the results of a series of studies we have conducted in Cambridge and in Santiago show that not only do phatic speech and interactive music making share affiliative functions, they can also share aspects of form. These results have led me to conclude that music, and speech in the phatic mode, constitute manifestations of a super-ordinate human capacity for affiliative communicative interaction that has profound and positive significance for the management of social life. It can be suggested that this capacity for affiliative communicative interaction is foregrounded in song in the articulation of Indigenous Australian traditions in the present day, and is likely to have been instrumental in the persistence of Indigenous Australian lifeways across historical and prehistorical time.

Music as affiliative interaction

In a series of experiments we explored interaction in spontaneous speech and in music, recording pairs of same-sex friends (all native English speakers) for about an hour each, talking, doing simple non-musical tasks, and making music together. We found that intonation peaks in speech ("accents", generally articulated as f0 peaks in pitch contour) when pairs were making music together tended to be aligned with the pulse or beat that was evident when participants were successful in making music together (Hawkins, Cross and Ogden 2013). We then explored turn transitions in their speech (when one speaker cedes the floor to another) in the conversational interactions, finding instances where a periodic pulse seemed to pass from one speaker to the other, coordinating the timing of their contributions.

Analysis showed that when participants were interacting in the phatic register, at turn transitions the last few speech accents of one speaker's utterance could produce a regular beat that predicted the timing of the first speech accent of their respondent (Hawkins 2014; Ogden and Hawkins 2015). Moreover, in such cases the pitch of the second speaker's utterance was also likely to form a musical pitch interval with that of the first speaker's turn (Robledo, Hawkins et al. 2016). Hence attitudinally aligned turn transitions appear to exhibit coordination in rhythm and in pitch across turns, a type of coordination usually considered to be associated with music rather than conversational interaction.[12]

Our "Joining-In" findings led to an experimental collaboration with a group of Chilean researchers in which we explored the effects of spontaneous musical interaction on subsequent conversations, using both phonetic conversation analysis and motion capture (Robledo, Hawkins et al. 2021). We asked pairs of same-sex strangers to have a brief conversation and then *either* to make – improvise – music together (MI group) *or* to build a tower with wooden blocks together (HB group) and then to have another brief conversation. In the second conversations in the MI group, we found an increased proportion of turn transitions organised around a shared beat as well as a highly significant increase in movement coordination (body sway) compared to the first conversation session. In comparison, the HB group (who had built towers together) showed a decrease in frequency of rhythmic turn transitions and no effect on movement coordination. In sum, after musical interaction, pairs of same-sex strangers showed a substantially increased temporal coordination in both their (unconscious) movements[13] and in their conversations compared to a similar group who had simply played a non-competitive (but reportedly enjoyable) manipulative game. The pairs of strangers in the MI group who had made music together had come to behave more affiliatively: in effect, more like friends than strangers.

I would suggest that this property of musical interaction – its capacity to enhance a sense of mutual affiliation even between strangers – is central to the efficacy of song in Indigenous Australian traditions. As Barwick (2012), and Barwick and Turpin (2016) noted, songs help to maintain a sense of group identity, strengthening bonds between those who persistently make music together. Songs also structure and maintain knowledge, articulating and conserving the "inner truths and outside appearances in all aspects of being" (Sansom 2001, 3) that underpin attachment to territory, serving to document and assert land rights. But song understood both as a manifestation *and as a source* of affiliation in communicative interaction also

---

12 But see also van Puyvelde, Loots et al. 2015.
13 See Latif, Barbosa et al. 2014.

allows for a crucial flexibility in determining *who* may belong to a group and *how* a group relates to a territory.

The survival of hunter-gatherer lifeways: music as formative social action

Unlike in many WEIRD societies, occupancy and use of territory in contexts such as those of Indigenous Australia, in which land and place are central to identity and lifeways, are both fixed and variable. As Berson (2014) noted (after Stanner) Indigenous Australian territoriality can be conceptualised in terms of "estates" and "ranges". Estates (or "Countries") represent the territory owned or held by a community that may constitute a patriclan or be bound by a shared Dreaming; ranges are the areas over which a group hunts or forages, and, depending on ecological circumstances, may overlap with ranges of other groups with whom food may be shared (Berson 2014, 393) "not for the aesthetic pleasures of ritualized exchange but rather because reciprocity was critical to survival". Hence the role of song and ceremony in determining legal rights has been taken to be relevant to estates rather than to ranges.[14] It has been suggested that these legal rights depend on continuity of lineage and tradition, a position supported by some anthropological sources from the 1930s that infer a pre-contact stability of lifeways.[15] It is certainly the case that songs can establish a degree of continuity of lineage and tradition in at least some cases; the foundational land rights cases (*Mabo v. Queensland* 1992) hinged in part on the fact that recordings of songs made in the 1950s and 1960s were strikingly similar to recordings made more than a half-century earlier by the University of Cambridge Torres Strait expedition of 1898 (Koch 2008, 160).

But long-term continuity is not easily accessible to hunter-gatherer groups in fragile and dynamic environments. While the invasion of 1788 and its borderline genocidal consequences (Tatz 1999) constituted a watershed in destroying or disrupting much of Indigenous Australian culture, dramatic changes to populations can be traced back to pre-contact times. Clark (2006) described documented early 19th-century cases of exile or abandonment of sites leading to their assimilation into the estates of other groups, as well as instances of extinction of clan groups through processes of fragmentation and fissioning, leading to the absorption of their territories into those of neighbouring or related groups. Other instances of population changes with much greater time depth in Indigenous Australian societies have been inferred using linguistic phylogenetics, as in the work of

---

14 See Koch 2013.
15 See Berson 2014, 410–411.

Memmott and colleagues (2016) on related language groups around the Gulf of Carpentaria over (at least) the last millennium. A recent paper by Bird and colleagues (2019) may help in understanding and interpreting issues of stability and change in such contexts. It provides a helpful theoretical and empirical treatment of the compositions, continuities and social embeddings of contemporary hunter-gatherer groups, based in part on a case study around the foraging groups and social organisation of the Martu in Australia's Western Desert.

Bird and colleagues (2019) started by noting that most contemporary hunter-gatherers live in surprisingly fluid groups, where links between non-relatives predominate and where groups are themselves linked in large-scale social networks. This effectively argues against a primacy for biological kinship in the formation and identity of hunter-gatherer groups, suggesting instead that the determinants of group (culture) membership will depend on lifeways and the contexts within which these are situated, and that groups are drawn from "networks of social organisation maintained in relational, rather than material, wealth accumulation" (Bird et al. 2019, 96). This "relational wealth" takes the form of mutual ties and obligations, and the personal and ritual frameworks within which these are understood and maintained; relational wealth provides "a delayed return of social capital" (Bird et al. 2019, 98) and constitutes a prime motivator of group membership as well as a source of cultural attachment.

In their case study of a contemporary Australian hunter-gatherer society, the Martu, Bird and colleagues (2019, 101) noted: "Martu local organization is made up of hearth groups, residential groups, foraging groups, estate groups and *tjapal* – large aggregations of people from many different estates and language groups". These groups are not hierarchically structured; instead, hearth, residential and foraging groups are variable in their size and composition, with hearth groups frequently including members of more than one language group, while foraging group composition is "dominated by affinal relationships and distant genealogical kinship" (Bird et al. 2019, 105). The large-scale aggregations, *tjapal*, are "gatherings of people from across complex networks of dispersed estates and language groups" (Bird et al. 2019, 101). Hence the structure of Martu society exhibits a degree of social redundancy in forming cultural relations through the cross-cutting of hearth, foraging, residential and estate groups, which, it could be argued, makes for considerable social resilience in the case of challenging environmental conditions. Though Bird and colleagues (2019) – somewhat surprisingly – make only one passing reference to song, I would argue that in the context of Indigenous Australian practices, music (in the form of the Dreamings, song and ceremony that constitute a substantial aspect of relational wealth) serves to effect affiliative alignments and may constitute a primary framework for the processes through which cultural and group attachments are formed. These processes are in the moment and face to face; they cannot be reified and detached from their contexts and maintain any real efficacy, though like a seed, a recording of a song may lie dormant as a germ of a tradition that may flower when planted in an appropriate context. In effect, from an Indigenous Australian perspective, processes of Dreaming and song might be constitutive of cultural identity to a greater extent even than biological kinship.

In the view of Bird and colleagues (2019), hunter-gatherer societies are construed as constituted through trans-generational networks bound together by relational wealth; relational wealth, according to Borgerhoff Mulder and colleagues (2009), is that form of wealth which manifests as "social ties in food-sharing networks and other forms of assistance and that is of high importance for hunter-gatherers". In the Australian case that Bird and colleagues (2019) explored, that relational wealth consists of common Dreamings that provide shared ways of narrating and understanding the environment, its history and its inhabitants. These common Dreamings are manifested, sustained and taught through face-to-face, collaborative, processes of music and public and private ritual. In the Martu example we can understand a society and its traditions as being sustained through processes of communicative interaction that are manifested as song and that create flexible affiliative bonds that can help manage changes of state in the social networks that comprise the society so as to enable it to adapt to changes (such as environmental threat) that could threaten its survival. Song helps both to maintain groups and to manage changes in group structure and membership while retaining continuity of tradition in the form of Dreaming, providing a flexible and adaptable means of fitting group to land – and vice versa.

Conclusions

In conclusion, for Indigenous Australian cultures, songs have tended to be conceived of as intangible cultural heritage, a means of structuring and conserving knowledge. Hence, as Alick Tipoti put it (Koch 2013, 38), "songs and the dance and the storytelling . . . are like our documents, in effect, title deeds". But songs are more than that. The experiments by ourselves and others referred to in this chapter suggest that making music together is an excellent way of establishing attachments that, while transient, may still be powerful enough to dispel immediate tensions; musical participation may also (particularly when repeated) be sufficient to establish durable group membership. Hence we can think of music as a means of enhancing affiliative attitudes, of inducting individuals into a group and potentially effecting changes in group membership. Music is a good way to not only structure cultural knowledge, conserve collective memory and bond groups together, but also to *form* groups and manage changes in their composition, thus providing a flexibility that is likely to have been required for hunter-gatherer survival and thrivance (see Treloyn and Onus, this volume) in the complex and challenging Australian environment.

Of course, in the present day yet more layers of complexity are added to the complex processes involved in maintaining and adapting Indigenous culture when traditional Indigenous and contemporary Western understandings of property, possession, music and rights are severely at odds. As Hill (1995, 309) put it, Indigenous Australians "view rights to land as originating with the design of the world rather than with alienable legal title . . . land is seen as part of their 'extended selves', something to be preserved and maintained". But in the last few decades it does seem that effective and sensitive mechanisms for managing the conflicts likely to arise between these quite different ontologies and epistemologies are being developed at multiple institutional levels in Australian society. Gray cited section 3(1) of the *Aboriginal Land Rights (Northern Territory) Act 1976* (Cth):

> *traditional Aboriginal owners*, in relation to land, means a local descent group of Aboriginals who: (a) have common spiritual affiliations to a site on the land, being affiliations that place the group under a primary spiritual responsibility for that site and for the land; and (b) are entitled by Aboriginal tradition to forage as of right over that land. (Gray 2020, 330)

This helpfully provides a quite flexible definition, allowing for changes in the composition of "traditional Aboriginal owners". But I suggest that this and other legal formulations are likely to require continual monitoring and adjustment to take account of what we are now learning about how music, as a form of affiliative communicative interaction, can manage social relations so as to restructure groups and deontic attitudes across multiple levels, remaking not only Indigenous but national and global understandings of our social worlds.

Chapter 17

Daluk Bininj, Ngarri-djarrk-ni/lovers, let's sit down together: popular love songs of western Arnhem Land

Jodie Kell and Tara Rostron

Introduction

Love and relationships are central to social structures and love songs have been a key force in music making throughout history. This is still true today, with love songs dominating music charts and evident in many localised popular music styles (Scheff 2011, 14; Arrow 2017, 285).[1] Yet the musical expression of romantic love, referred to in this chapter as "love songs", tends not to be a subject of serious study. Music historian Ted Gioia (2015, x) has said, even though the most common topic of music making throughout history has been love, there is little consistent analysis of love songs as they are perceived as a "soft topic". We argue that the reasons for this neglect have to do with gender bias, considering women play a prominent role in the creation and performance of popular love songs, as illustrated by Gioia (2015). When music is perceived as an important arena for the mediation of values and ideas (Ottosson 2016, xii), we propose that love songs should be seen as political as they possess the power to influence social change.

Focusing on contemporary music in West Arnhem Land, we explore a comparatively recent movement of women musicians in the region who are utilising the intercultural space of popular music to compose, record and perform. As members

---

1 For statistics on Australian music charts, see ARIA n.d.

of the Ripple Effect Band, we use an autoethnographic approach to examine two love songs from the band's repertoire as case studies.[2] We argue that the process of creating these love songs has contributed to the development of women's musical practices in the region and in so doing has provided a voice for women to express their perspectives on cultural knowledge and social issues.

Ripple Effect Band is the first professional all-women's rock band from Maningrida in West Arnhem Land, and is exceptional in the Australian music scene as one of the few women's bands emerging from a remote community. The band formed in 2017 and independently released *Wárrwarra* in 2018, an EP of four songs in four different Indigenous languages (Ripple Effect Band 2018). Following this release, Ripple Effect Band performed in many local Arnhem Land festivals, at venues across the NT, and toured nationally. The band's latest single "Waláya", released in February 2023, is featured on major streaming platforms and the Ripple Effect Band YouTube channel, putting the song and the band firmly in the public sphere (Thomas 2023). Noongar music maker and language revivalist Clint Bracknell (2023, 32) described the band as "unique in Australia" due to an approach to multilingualism that sees band members regularly swapping instruments and taking turns to sing lead with all members providing back-up vocals no matter what language is being sung. As women coming from different backgrounds, having Indigenous and non-Indigenous members as well as a range of language groups, Ripple Effect Band has a fresh new sound characterised by strong ensemble singing, collaborative song writing and women controlling the production process.

The two love songs that are the focus of this chapter are commonly part of the band's live performances: "Love Song", composed in 2003 by Maningrida High School students (Hayes-Bohme, Cooper et al. 2003), and "Loving and Caring", composed in 2021 by the authors (Ripple Effect Band 2023). "Love Song" was originally recorded in R&B style with electronic sequenced beats, but Ripple Effect Band performs it with rock band instrumentation. In this chapter we explore why this song has continued to be popular with women in Maningrida and ask how it has contributed to women's musical practices in the region. "Loving and Caring" was released in July 2023 and the band has regularly performed it live since 2021 (Rostron and Kell 2023). The song was composed over several months and, as co-producers, we chose it as one of the two singles leading up to the 2024 album,

---

2   This is an autoethnographic account in which the authors Kell and Rostron are the composers and music producers of the song "Loving and Caring" discussed in this chapter, as well as members of the Ripple Effect Band. In order to avoid ambiguity, we distinguish between ourselves as authors/song composers and producers by using the first-person pronouns we/our/us and as part of the Ripple Effect Band as a whole, including the other members, by using the third person pronouns they/their/them.

17 Daluk Bininj, Ngarri-djarrk-ni/lovers, let's sit down together

Mayawa (see Figure 17.1). While it is too early to analyse the song's reception, we use personal accounts of composition, production and formative time spent on the road to examine the intent of the band's music making and ask what it means when love songs are composed with the purpose of negotiating social relationships.

Figure 17.1. Album cover for *Mayawa*, featuring "Loving and Caring", the subject of this chapter. Ripple Effect Band, 2024.

This chapter is co-authored by two band members, Jodie Kell and Tara Rostron. Our positioning as female-identifying musicians, one Kune *daluk* "Woman, Indigenous Woman" (K)[3] and one *balanda* "non-Indigenous" woman,[4] brings a particular perspective to a discussion of love songs. As well as an insider viewpoint, our different backgrounds as co-producers inform our musical and textual analysis and shed a light on intercultural processes. Co-founders of the international research platform Social Impact of Music Making (SIMM) Project, Brydie-Leigh Bartleet and Lukas Pairon (2021, 271) commented that, in the

---

3   This study uses a range of languages from the Maningrida region, using the specific language relevant to the context. Words in language will be noted in italics, followed by the English translation and the language group in brackets. The languages used are Kune (K), Burarra (B) and Ndjébbana (Ndj).
4   *Balanda* is a derivative of the Macassan term for Dutch people which is commonly used across Arnhem Land to refer to non-Indigenous white people.

burgeoning field of socially engaged practice, practitioners offer unique perspectives on creative processes and the outcome of these processes. We use a practice-centred collaborative approach that is the result of a long-term relationship between the authors and other musicians involved in the project. We collated material documented through recorded interviews, media interviews, film footage and song recordings and explored the relevance to the themes of this chapter, as well as other literature, through recorded telephone interviews in 2022 and 2023. Kell did the bulk of the writing for the article so, to distinguish this from Rostron's contributions, Rostron is quoted directly in separate indented text, transcribed from interviews conducted in 2022 and 2023.

It is pertinent to note here that we are addressing the gender imbalance in the practice and the documentation of Australian popular music. The 2017 *Skipping a Beat* report showed that "male advantage is a pervasive feature of the Australian music industry" (Cooper-Coles and Hanna-Osborne 2017, 2), pointing out that women are under-represented as composers, producers and musicians despite making up half of those who study music. Historian Michelle Arrow commented that it is important to note that "a sharply demarcated gender division has structured the expression of love in popular music" (Cooper-Coles and Hanna-Osborne 2017, 286) and went on to say that most performers and songwriters in the Australian music industry have been male, as well as the music historians and mythologisers. When music is a major driver of Australia's creative economy as well as being part of the daily lives of Australians at work and in leisure, we question what it means for women to be excluded from this social forum and how this affects the power structures of society. In her analysis of the music making of Aboriginal men in central Australia, Åse Ottosson (2016) described contemporary Aboriginal music as an important space for the construction of male identity and a male-dominated forum where social issues can be discussed and explored without conflict. Through the intercultural space of contemporary music making, the women of Ripple Effect Band are claiming a space for their voices to be heard in this forum too, putting their stories and perspectives into the frame.

> When I play music, I want to encourage and inspire other people, especially young people. I hope to be a role model for women to stand up, speak out and be confident in who they are. (Rostron 2022)

Australian popular music: reflecting or constructing notions of love

In this section we explore the reasons why love songs have been overlooked as a serious topic of study and argue that, because love songs concern the very nature of our intimate relationships, they have the potential to upset the power balance of social structures. In this way love songs can be seen as political, not only reflecting but also constructing notions of relationships that contribute to social change. Gioia (2015, 8) commented: "the history of the love song is also the history of the repression of the love song." He explained that, because innovation in love songs tends to come from marginalised people, "outsiders", including women (whom Gioia says have played a large role in the creation and performance of love songs), their contribution has been diminished or even eradicated. The radical and disruptive nature of love songs being at the heart of intimate relations has meant that "the established powers resist innovations in love music" that challenge authoritarian rule and patriarchal institutions (Gioia 2015, xi).

Love itself is a force musicians can use as a way of working with others. Creative practices are informed by the different backgrounds of artists, but bound by relationships that allow for trust and deep communication. Brydie-Leigh Bartleet (2016) described love as a social practice that can inform and underpin intercultural arts collaborations, such as the creation of contemporary popular music. Focusing on love, we are challenged to consider ways of engaging that seek relationships that reach across otherness while accepting difference. bell hooks (2000, 76) commented: "[the] important politicisation of love is often absent from today's writing". She saw love not as a feeling but as an active force that "leads us into greater communion with the world" and has the capacity not only to improve the life satisfaction of individuals but to contribute to ending domination and oppression (hooks 2000, 76).

For Ripple Effect Band members, making popular music is an active way of indicating social connection and negotiating agency. Marcus Breen (1987, 4) described popular music as expressing the ways in which people live their lives. By creating an image of their lives, it has the potential to empower them into action. Socio-musicologist Simon Frith (2007) suggested that the power in popular music lies in its ability to evoke emotions that influence the experiences of the listeners. Rather than examining how a song reflects society, he asks how it constructs meaning and provides opportunities for us to experience ourselves in a different way (Frith 2007). In Australian popular music, cultural historian Hsu-Ming Teo (2017a, 31) says said that examining the expression of love in popular culture draws attention to how productive "playing around with discourses of romantic love has been for creating culture and nation, and vice versa". As the first women in Maningrida to be composing and performing love songs, Ripple Effect Band offers alternative perspectives on social relationships to those previously expressed by male musicians. As they have developed as music producers, band members intentionally use this perspective to suggest more loving ways to relate to one another.

Historians of popular music in Australia have tended to focus on genres of music, such as punk, rock, Indigenous rock or hip-hop with little reference to love songs (e.g. Homan and Mitchell 2008; Hayward 1992; Breen 1987). James Cockington's book *Long way to the top* explored the depiction of an "ordinary" love story in the wedding on the television series *Neighbours* and Kylie Minogue's subsequent rise to fame as a pop artist, but this account focuses on popular culture rather than specifically analysing popular music. Analysis of Australian Indigenous contemporary music commonly highlights socio-political themes such as place, identity, language and racism but writing about love songs is absent.[5] Peter Dunbar-Hall and Chris Gibson (2004) discussed the influence of transnational Black culture on the R&B music of the Indigenous duo Shakaya, but they overlooked the political stance of their hit song "Stop Callin' Me" (Nicastro, Stacey and Wenitong 2002), a protest song about sexual harassment (Dunbar-Hall and Gibson 2004). Using the medium of pop music as a safe space for a critique of social relationships, Simone Stacey and Naomi Wenitong call out a man for stalking, a form of predatory sexual harassment.[6] By failing to mention their most popular song, Dunbar-Hall and Gibson have rendered the duo's socio-political stance invisible.

Released in 2002, the song was successful, peaking at number 5 and then spending 17 weeks in the top 50 ARIA singles charts, reaching platinum status and scoring the duo a support for Destiny's Child tour of Australia. We suggest the popularity of the song can be attributed to resonance with the shared experiences of women. It is empowering to hear the sassy confident defiance and, as Black Indigenous women, Shakaya was a major influence on the members of the Ripple Effect Band. The neglect of this song's importance in Australian music history is surprising because, while not strictly a love song, it is remarkable in its expression of Indigenous women's perspectives about social relationships.

Hsu-Ming Teo's edited book (2017, 4–5) considered how Australians have portrayed love in popular culture and how this relates to love as it is practised in society.

---

5 See, e.g., Bracknell 2019b; 2023; M. Breen 1987; Castles 2016; Dunbar-Hall and Gibson 2004; Ottosson 2016.
6 Nicastro, Reno, Simone Stacey and Naomi Wenitong, "Stop Callin' Me", Shakaya, 2002.

17 Daluk Bininj, Ngarri-djarrk-ni/lovers, let's sit down together

It includes a chapter on love songs in rock and pop music by historian Michelle Arrow. Arrow traced the history of popular love songs in Australia, describing the "raucous, masculine carnality" of rock music as "celebrating a musical hybrid of sexual aggression and sentimental mateship" (2017, 302). She commented that Nick Cave's celebrated love songs, "Into my Arms" and "Ship Song", are distinctive in their romantic lyrics as Oz Rock tends to focus on non-romantic types of love: "Love gone wrong, homosocial love, love of nation, sentiment, and increasingly love steeped in irony" (2017, 310).

The pop tradition, on the other hand, has pitched itself to a female and non-binary audience and is more concerned with a romantic view of love. Arrow (2017, 300) stated: "typically, Australian music was at its most successful internationally when it articulated universal themes of love and romance, rather than the distinctively grizzled takes on love that were central to the pub rock tradition." Even the growing focus on individualism and a more casual approach to sexual relationships in pop music is expressed as a form of self-empowerment. This is apparent in Irena Rex's analysis of Kylie Minogue's film clip for the song "I've Got to Be Certain", in which Minogue presents a strong assertive image, expressing her confidence to state her views on social issues. As well as being commercially viable, pop music is more welcoming to women who could carve out a career within the restrictions on acceptable performance modes (Arrow 2017, 287).

Controlling the processes of music production can provide a space for asserting power and agency for women. In discussion with Indigenous musicians Shellie Morris, Toni Janke, Lexine Solomon and Kerrianne Cox, Katelyn Barney (2007) examined the motives for these women to produce their own recordings. The women stated that they were making music for future generations and to document and raise awareness of social issues affecting Indigenous Australians. Engagement with music production enables women to take control of the agenda of music making. This has empowered members of the Ripple Effect Band to use what Gioia (2015, xii) called "the defiant force of the love song" to construct identity and question social structures as Indigenous women. In this chapter, we ask how the expression of love through song is contributing to notions of identity and social connection in West Arnhem Land.

The Top End sound: popular music in Maningrida

Maningrida is in West Arnhem Land, about 500 kilometres east of Darwin in the Northern Territory of Australia. One of the largest remote towns in the Northern Territory, it has a population of 2,500, as well as more than 30 outstations or homelands. The traditional owners are the Dhukurrudji clan of the Kuníbidji people who speak Ndjébbana language. Since it was established as a government trading post in the 1940s, Maningrida has diversified to include people from across Arnhem Land. Linguist Jill Vaughan (2018) described it as one of the most multilingual regions in the world, with 14 languages spoken daily in the community.

Maningrida's remote locality has contributed to the development of a unique and vibrant music scene, incorporating a mix of music genres such as ancestral song cycles, gospel songs, electronically produced hip-hop music and reggae rock bands. Ancestral music and dance ceremonies, known as *bunggul,* continue to play a vital role in marking social occasions. In the introduction to the exhibition Jarracharra "the dry season" (B), Burarra curator Jessica Phillips (2020, 47) stated how music in Maningrida has been and continues to be a way of bringing people together and maintaining and strengthening languages and cultural traditions.

Maningrida's music traditions have been documented since early recordings made in the 1950s, but analysis of the breadth of traditional music styles is beyond the scope of this chapter. We focus on the development of contemporary popular music practices in the region, which can incorporate ancestral music forms, and we will discuss this as a characteristic of the regional style. The introduction of radio to Arnhem Land in the 1950s initiated a major change to musical practices in the region with the start of guitar-based ensembles. Fifty years later, the construction of mobile phone towers in the early 2000s enabled access to the internet through individually owned smartphones. This technology brought into the bush global influences and transnational networks, which have been adopted and adapted in a distinctive cultural mix. The influence of music genres popular with Black American artists such as reggae, R&B and hip-hop was reinforced by exposure to Indigenous artists from within Australia who were using popular music forms as a platform for addressing socio-political issues. Artists such as Archie Roach and Shakaya were achieving mainstream success and the Centre for Aboriginal Studies in Music in Adelaide nurtured Indigenous bands such as No Fixed Address, who recorded the first Indigenous reggae song, the political anthem "We Have Survived" in 1981. In 1992, Warumpi Band released "Jailanguru Pakarnu/Kintorelakutu" and its success gained "legitimacy for recording songs in Aboriginal languages" (Homan and Mitchell 2008, 257).

Locally, Yothu Yindi, from East Arnhem Land, formed as a "bold new intercultural exchange" between Yolngu and *balanda* musicians (Corn 2023, 45), releasing their ground-breaking album *Homeland Movement* in 1989. Their music is representative of Indigenous bands from the region north of Katherine in the Northern Territory, commonly referred to as the Top End. Peter Dunbar-Hall and Chris Gibson (2004) analysed the compilation album, *Meinmuk Mujik: Music from the Top End* to investigate elements of the distinctive local music style, which they call "The Top End Sound" (Dunbar-Hall and Gibson 2004). The 1997 album has 24 tracks from 14 bands and solo performers in nine languages and "it typifies the contemporary Aboriginal music soundscape in a number of ways" (2004, 192). Even though the music scene has changed since that time, their description of the characteristics of the Top End Sound remains relevant to our discussion of popular music in Maningrida today.

Encompassing a range of genres including older and more recent music styles

Music performance events in West Arnhem Land commonly include a range of genres. For example, funeral ceremonies can involve ancestral music and dance styles from East Arnhem (*manikay*) and West Arnhem (*kun-borrk*), dedicated gospel songs recorded on iPads and mobile phones and hybridised forms of dance using coloured cloth and synchronised moves as signifiers of identity and connection. Community music festivals are a modern form of music and dance gatherings, which commonly include *bunggul* at sunset followed by rock, reggae and hip-hop bands into the night. Ethnomusicologist Reuben Brown (2016, 292–294) argued that the music performed by contemporary music bands at Gunbalanya's Stone Country Festival had a lot in common with the traditional performances that preceded them. Indeed, many of the performers move between the two forms, taking ancestral song traditions and "re-framing them" in new ways for popular music performance. Brown described Kuninjku singer Crusoe Kurddal performing the Mimih song set both on the dance ground and on stage with Maningrida's Sunrize Band. Sunrize Band also recorded two versions of "Wak Wak" (Black Crow) on their 1993 album *Lungrrurrma*, with the upbeat blues version followed by the *manakay* (see Dunbar-Hall and Gibson 2004).

This style of re-imagining of ancestral songs into popular music forms was pioneered by Eastern Arnhem Yolngu musicians starting with Soft Sands in the 1960s. Aaron Corn's explorations of guitar-based bands across Arnhem Land demonstrates how musicians adopted new styles, forms and instrumentation but, through their re-contextualised local uses, accommodated Indigenous concepts, values and beliefs

(Corn 1999, 3–4). Yothu Yindi's lead singer Mandawuy Yunupingu's approach to composing music drew inspiration from *ga̱nma*, a place where "fresh and salt bodies of water converge, each retaining their own distinct properties, yet producing something new and fruitful through their interaction" (Corn 2022, 43). This concept encapsulates the way Yothu Yindi mixed *manikay* into rock or reggae songs, alternating Yolngu and *balanda* references (Stubington and Dunbar-Hall 1994, 243–259), which is a distinctive feature of the Top End Sound.

Multilingualism

Linguist Isabel O'Keeffe examined how "the manyardi/kun-borrk song traditions manifest the linguistic diversity, multilingualism and underpinning language ideologies of the Western Arnhem Land region", arguing that they act as "emblematic keys to identity" (2016, 342–343). Likewise, the rock bands of the region sing in a range of languages, which results in festivals and concerts involving multilingualism. Clint Bracknell saw the "rock band format" as a framework for intercultural performance "with the common musical language of the rock band potentially facilitating the foregrounding of Indigenous languages and worldviews" (2023, 23).

Reference to Dreamtime imagery

Arnhem Land musicians such as Yothu Yindi express land-based belief systems, incorporating aspects of *manikay* into rock music production and adding cultural background information to "give others an understanding of Aboriginal life and an idea of where we're coming from" (Dunbar-Hall 2004, 198). In Maningrida, Letterstick Band named its album *Diyama* after a *kun-borrk* and the band included a traditional version as well as a version where the *kun-borrk* is sung over a rock beat with modern instrumentation on the album (Letterstick Band 2004a). Aaron Corn (2002, 77–79) said, of Letterstick Band, that the band's song writing was influenced by the aesthetics, elements and themes of *manikay* and *borrk* genres, "balancing the continuity of local music traditions against creative engagement with new musical media and technology".

"Diyama" was originally sung by band members David and Colin Maxwell's father Mulumbuk, who was recorded by anthropologist Les Hiatt in 1960. It is an expression of the song of ancestral mermaid spirits who inhabit the waters of the An-barra homeland of Gupanga. Kell and Jinmarabynana (2022, 180) explained how the musical innovations of three generations of An-barra musicians "have transformed the expression of ancestral spirits using new musical forms and utilising music technology". As well as Letterstick Band's version, Ripple Effect Band's song "Diyama" was composed by Mulumbuk's granddaughter Stephanie James and Kell. The song moves between a ballad telling the story of the mermaids and David Maxwell singing the *kun-borrk* over rock band instrumentation. The history of this song demonstrates how musical innovation in the Top End, arising from engagement with new forms of technology and introduced forms of music, "enables song custodians to respond to changing contexts" (Kell and Jinmarabynana 2022, 180). For women, using contemporary popular music making is a way to safely bypass gender restrictions to compose and perform songs that express their connection with Dreaming stories and sites.

The prominent use of *yidaki/mako* "didjeridu" and *bilma/manberlginj* "clapsticks"

The absence of this distinctive characteristic in women's rock bands from the Top End points to a history of gendered music practices of the region. In West Arnhem Land *bunggul*, women do not join in the singing or play instruments. It is against cultural protocols for women to play *mako* "didjeridu" (K) or *manberlginj* "clapsticks" (K). Women participate as dancers, and those with cultural responsibilities may direct aspects of ceremonial performance and contribute to discussions about the meanings of the songs, but they are not allowed to perform as musicians or singers (Brown 2016, 67–68; Clunies-Ross 1989, 110; Hiatt and Hiatt 1966, 4; Kell, DjÍbbama et al. 2020, 162; O'Keeffe 2016, 12–13).

These gender restrictions have influenced the popular music scene in Arnhem Land. In 1999, Aaron Corn noted that rock bands in Arnhem Land were made up almost entirely of men, reflecting the traditionally divergent roles of men and women in secular life (1999, 9–10). Music historian Liz Reed (2002, 26) similarly argued that inequality in the intersection of race and gender caused Indigenous women to be absent from the Australian music industry. When Ripple Effect Band started in 2017, it was often the only female band at community festivals and the band still finds very few women playing in community rock bands as it tours around. We do acknowledge the importance of the women from Wildflower, the first professional West Arnhem Land band to feature women as musicians and composers. Coming from Manmoyi, Wildflower released its debut album *Manginburru Bininj* in 2009. Brown (2016, 67–68) claimed that Wildflower is unique because "[the band expresses] how *daluk* [K: women] can partake in the *bininj*-orientated domain of public song". The band members do this by drawing upon matrilineally inherited knowledge passed on from their aunt, Jill Nganjmirra, rather than patrilineally inherited *kun-borrk*.

Members of Wildflower and Ripple Effect Band are among the few women to play instruments, compose music and sing in public in West Arnhem Land but they are part of a growing movement of Indigenous women musicians both locally and across Australia. Artists such as Ruby Hunter, Jodie Cockatoo-Creed, Tiddas, Shakaya, Jessica Mauboy and the Stiff Gins paved the way; today there is greater support and exposure, and pop singers Thelma Plum and Emily Wurramura and hip-hop artist Baakaa are achieving national success. Composers Deborah Cheetham, Nardi Simpson and community music producer Shellie Morris have received academic accolades and the popularity of Electric Fields and Mo'Ju point to a greater acceptance of gender diversity. All of these artists are constructing new forms of Indigeneity, reacting to modernity and highlighting perspectives as female and non-binary artists, with their music political by its very nature as it is challenging social structures and stereotypes.

Love songs in West Arnhem Land

There is a genre of *kun-borrk* specifically concerned with love known as the *jurtbirrk* love songs of West Arnhem Land. Ronald and Catherine Berndt did extensive fieldwork in Arnhem Land in the 1950s and wrote about social life, including the aesthetic of music performance (Berndt and Berndt 1951). In 1979, Ronald Berndt published a book specifically about the love songs of Arnhem Land, including a song cycle from Goulburn Island in western Arnhem Land (Berndt 1976). Research on this genre of love songs was continued with the recordings of the *jurtbirrk* songs of the Iwaidja language group, which were released on a CD in 2005 (Barwick et al. 2005). Linda Barwick, Bruce Birch and Nicholas Evans (2007, 6) explained that these songs, often referred to as "love songs" in English, are a genre of didjeridu-accompanied songs that are individually composed and owned and usually deal with romantic or emotional topics. Through analysis, we will explore how the performance and recordings of *jurtbirrk* influenced elements of love songs composed by young women in Maningrida.

We also draw upon the composition styles of popular local bands, Letterstick Band and Wildfire Munworrk Band in particular, as they are family to Ripple Effect Band members. Love songs are not prominent in these bands' repertoires, but Ripple Effect Band have played covers of "Gama Jin-ngardipa (Broken Love)" by Letterstick Band (Letterstick Band 2004b) and "Kune Love Song" by Victor Rostron, which has recently been refashioned into Wildfire Manwurrk's single "Mararradj" (Rostron 2021). These songs express a nostalgic broken-hearted sense of love that contains a similar sense of lost love as in "Love Song", but we argue that, as women, Ripple Effect Band is bringing new perspectives and we examine how the process of creating these love songs has contributed to the development of women's musical practices in the region and what this means for women's agency.

A new form of expression for young women in Maningrida

"Love Song" is the first love song written by women in western Arnhem Land. Wildflower released its first album in 2009 after "Love Song" was composed and the album did not include any love songs. In terms of older music forms, Linda Barwick and colleagues commented that there are "no known instances of a woman composing or performing a *jurtbirrk* song, although women very much enjoy listening to, and talking about, the songs and the events portrayed in them, and also compose dances for and dance to *jurtbirrk*" (Barwick, Birch and Evans 2007, 11). Rostron and I have experienced this countless times, sitting down with groups of women listening to recordings of "love songs" that become a stimulus for laughter, discussion and "women's talk", but despite this interest, the composition and performance of love songs remained gender restricted.

In 2003, a group of high school students – Thomasina Hayes-Bohme, Charlynna Roy, Rowena Cooper and Jodie Cooper – formed a band, MGB, with encouragement from Kell who was their teacher at the time. They attended a hip-hop workshop at the school and they began song writing and recording audio tracks over sampled beats. The group brainstormed ideas, with much laughter, deciding to write about their own experience of relationships. The result is a song about a girl in Maningrida whose boyfriend is in Darwin and the sparse lyrics express a feeling of loneliness and concern as she waits for his return.

Since then, "Love Song" has become an enduring local pop song and it is regularly performed with rock band instrumentation. In the 2000s, Maningrida school bands such as MGB, Ocean Band and the Front Street Girls performed this song in Maningrida as well as on tour at Garma Festival and in Darwin. Ripple Effect Band regularly include the song in its set, often as the opening number, and in 2021 the newly formed high school girls band played "Love Song" at the Maningrida Lúrra Festival, nearly 20 years after it was first composed. It is commonly heard at informal music sessions involving women in Maningrida, accompanied by acoustic guitar, or played in community music rooms. We suggest that the transmission of this song, with younger girls learning from their older peers, and its shared sentiment as a song composed by local women have made women feel comfortable and confident to play it. In this way it has contributed to the developing women's musical scene in West Arnhem.

> We're still playing "Love Song". Why are we still playing it? Because we want to show current students in Maningrida that's the first song we learned to play. We want to pass it on, like we helped the young girls perform in Maningrida festival in 2021.
>
> Do you know why they feel comfortable playing "Love Song" from school? Because of us, because we are still playing that "Love Song" wherever we perform on stage. Those young women in Maningrida school, they feel comfortable because of us and because we passed them that song. (Rostron 2022)

Analysis of the song shows an innovative blend of old and new musical forms drawing influence from *jurtbirrk* love songs of the region as well as globally popular R&B and hip-hop styles of the 2000s. The lyrics contain a feeling of unresolved emotions that resonate with listeners and its enduring popularity must also be due to the song filling a gap by presenting the perspective of young Indigenous women's view of social relationships.

The style of the original recording of "Love Song" is R&B, a style emerging from Black American music culture. It combines rhythm and blues associated with Detroit's Motown label with elements of pop, soul, funk, hip-hop and electronic music. Rostron recalls that when she was at high school around the time "Love Song" was composed by MGB, young people accessed music through CDs; the *So Fresh* compilation CDs sold at the local shop were a major source of music listening. The *So Fresh* compilations from 2002 to 2003 include several love songs, many of which are in pop, hip-hop and R&B styles. The male artists celebrate romantic love (Usher: "U Got It Bad") or sexy love (Nelly: "Hot in Here"). Female artists have a tough, sexy sound (Pink: "Get the Party Started") but also include songs about relationships (Alicia Keys: "Girlfriend"; Shakaya: "Cinderella" and "Stop Callin' Me"; Destiny's Child: "Emotion"). The global nature of the *So Fresh* compilations is part of what Dunbar-Hall and Gibson (2004, 120) referred to as "transnational spaces within which cultural exchanges and borrowings occur". The influence of these confident Black women singing about their views on relationships was impetus for women in Maningrida to start using song writing to publicly express their perspectives on romantic love.

The instrumentation of "Love Song" consists of software-created beats with keyboard, electric and bass guitars. The song opens with Rowena Cooper speaking, a common trope in R&B and hip-hop songs,[7] but in vocal style and lyrical structure, "Love Song" differs. Rather than the melismatic vocal style of R&B, or the fast rhythmic patterns of rap, "Love Song" vocals are unhurried repetitive melodic lines. In the same way that Linda Barwick and colleagues compared the style of *jurtbirrk* to being "along the lines of blues songs that emerged from African-American culture in the 20th century", we contend that "Love Song" has strong similarities to the structure and content of *jurtbirrk*, which are composed about aspects of everyday life and consist of "brief, evocative statements in accessible language, usually consisting of two lines of text, which are repeated in predictable combinations" (Barwick, Birch and Williams 2005, 9–10). Unlike most contemporary popular songs, "Love Song" does not have a repeated chorus. Instead, like *jurrtbirrk,* the verses consist of a series of short repeated poetic statements such as the second verse, translated here from Burarra.

An-nurra a-bona Darwin
My boyfriend has gone to Darwin

Gala marngi gin-barra ani-jakabarra
I do not know when he will return
(repeat)

The economy of expression follows the allusive nature of traditional music of the region. Linguist Murray Garde (2005) found that in *manyardi/kun-borrk* song texts, the literal meanings of the songs are generally clear, but contextual meanings are often vague, perhaps intentionally, so that the meaning can only be inferred by those who are familiar with the particular event, incident or emotion described or may only be fully known by the original composer. In this stanza, on the surface it is a simple statement but the sense of uncertainty about return dates resonates with anyone who has lived in Maningrida or other remote communities in Arnhem Land. The familiarity here comes from the fact that many women in Maningrida, or any remote community, can relate to the feeling of worry and distress when their lover or partner is away from them in bigger cities, as they wait back in community for their safe return. The song becomes a vehicle to speak to women about their experiences of love, at times drawing the allegory to themselves.

The lasting popularity of "Love Song" among women in Maningrida is partly due to its place in the history of the women's music in Maningrida and the transmission of the song has contributed to the development of women's music

---

7   For example, "Ignition Remix" (R. Kelly), "Nu Flow" (Big Brovaz), "Cleanin' out My Closet" (Eminen), "Cinderella" (Shakaya), "Two Wrongs" (Wyclef Jean and Claudette Ortiz).

practices in the region. It mixes the lyrical minimalism of traditional *jurtbirrk* love songs with more recent styles and instrumentation and it also displays elements of the Black American music style R&B, as the influence of transnational Black culture introduced new forms of expression for young women in Maningrida. The intercultural space of contemporary popular music, with the hybrid mix of influences, allowed women for the first time to compose and sing about romantic love from their perspective. This was an important development in the history of music making in the region and its place in the mediation of social structures.

"Loving and caring": the power of music to influence social change

Figure 17.2. Authors Jodie Kell and Tara Rostron, who composed "Loving and Caring", performing as a duo in Newcastle, NSW, in 2022. Photo: Paul Dear.

Eighteen years after MGB wrote "Love Song", the authors of this chapter, Rostron and Kell, composed "Loving and Caring" (see Figure 17.2). We spent a lot of time together both in Darwin and on the road in 2021, performing, running workshops and producing the album, and we often talked about including a love song. The composition process was very different from the impromptu workshopping of the earlier love song; it was more intentional and took place over a longer time frame of months rather than the week it took to write, rehearse and record "Love Song" in 2003. Examining the process leading to the composition and subsequent audio recording of the song sheds a light on the power of music to encourage social change, the value of cross-cultural collaboration and the dynamics of gender in music production.

Having time together to converse deeply about our personal beliefs and aspirations, as well as listening to other artists for inspiration shaped the song. Yorta Yorta Dja Dja Wurrung composer Lou Bennett identified the management of time and space as one of the key challenges in Indigenous and non-Indigenous collaborations: "I believe that a story/song has its own agency and having agency means having the right to time, space, and stillness" (2023, 14–16). David Byrne, from Talking Heads, said that "collaborating is a vital part of music's essence and an aid to creativity", which includes interpretation, realisation, and the sharing of musical references (2012, 138–151). Clint Bracknell discussed the place of cross-cultural collaborations to "challenge and re-frame notions of Indigeneity" (2019, 115–116). In composing "Loving and Caring", these discussions about the motivation behind the song were formative and our different perspectives gave us the freedom to step back and see a bigger picture of what we wanted to say about relationships.

As the first women musicians in Maningrida, Ripple Effect Band members must consider perceptions of their music and lyrics carefully. This was particularly pertinent when writing about love. Music performance is a public presentation and love is a private emotion. In Arnhem Land communities there are cultural protocols concerning a woman's brothers and uncles that prevent her talking publicly about personal matters. We pondered how we could express concepts of love without causing trouble between band members and their partners or families. Jealousy is a major issue in Maningrida, as it is in many remote communities (Senior, Helmer and Chenhall 2017, 206–207).

> If I sing as a young woman, if I sing love songs in public on the stage, my boyfriend could get jealous or other women can get jealous. For example, if a woman has a boyfriend with her and I'm a single woman, I'm singing on the stage and she gets jealous, she tends to turn around and argue with her boyfriend. That's part of jealousy. It's a big problem, jealousy. Mainly lovers and young people. That's how suicide is happening a lot around community here, because of that jealousy. (Rostron 2022)

When Rostron and I were composing a love song, we found that we could manipulate musical elements to work safely within these protocols. We came up with the idea to use metaphor and allusion to avoid generating feelings of jealousy.

In the second verse of the song, we connected the cycles of a relationship to the replenishing cycles of the seasons in Maningrida. Rostron explains:

> *Yekke* is the dry season like this time now. When we burn grass and the trees. Everything's burned and that's how everyone feels, bad and depressed. Everybody's starting to fight even lovers feel no good, it's because the trees are burning. *Kudjewk* is the wet season. That's in November and December when it starts raining. When it starts raining, all the trees and grass start growing. The rain and thunder rolls. That's how we feel, like it's our heart beating. When the thunder rolls, it hits the ground, like it hits your feeling and that's where you're starting to love someone. The trees and leaves are growing and everything, is starting to show love. But especially lovers. That's the main thing. (Rostron 2022)

We wanted to create a positive image of relationships, moving on from the emotions of "Love Song" where the woman is powerless, waiting in community and feeling lonely and worried. Rostron explains how she wanted to compose a love song that presented positive relationships, suggesting how people can relate to each other.

> I want to make people to stay more positive than before. Not like "Love Song", you know, sitting around and wondering, too much thinking and worrying, they need to push themselves forward and think straight. Instead of just going around and around in cycles and keeping it inside. That's not good. Sometimes you need to let it out. I think this is a new, good message for everyone. (Rostron 2022)

In his analysis of US Top 40 hits over two decades, American sociologist Thomas Scheff (2011, 21–23) questioned why so many popular love songs legitimise and help to generate unhealthy responses to our emotions and dysfunctional types of relationships and what the implications for interpersonal and societal relationships were when people connected to these songs. He called for love songs that celebrate positive love relationships and promote a degree of connectedness and balance through communication and mutual understanding. We propose that "Loving and Caring" is such a song.

> "Loving and Caring", it's like family, friends and lovers, how to look after each other and communicate with each other and how to love and care. (Rostron 2022)

We were aware of the toll of domestic violence on this community. We have both experienced physical violence and the threat of violence, as well as supporting family members, friends, and their children through stressful situations. We wanted to use music as a way of sending a message of hope, and some practical advice

17 Daluk Bininj, Ngarri-djarrk-ni/lovers, let's sit down together

about how to approach relationships. In this way, we were approaching the song as a means of enacting social change, hoping to break the cycle of jealousy, arguing and domestic violence.

> Songs can give people ideas and sometimes make them change a little bit such as inspiring them to stop thinking about the past. Like a new voice that when they hear it, they will say, "Oh, okay. I know this gives me an idea about how I can look after my family or friends or someone that I love and that I want to be with". (Rostron 2022)

One of the main messages of "Loving and Caring" is the importance of communication in relationships. Throughout the song, the singer directly addresses her partner, such as in the first verse.

Njale yinjilng warreminj kangurdulme
Hey, why are you so upset?

Kan-marnime ba ngabengkan
Tell me so I know.

Njale mankarre yikarrme kure kukange
What message are you holding onto in your heart?

At the end of each chorus, the lyrics call out,

Ngayih marne djare nguddah
I really love you

Yimri konda nuk ngarri-djarrkni, ngarri-djarrkni
Come over here and we'll sit down together

The song expresses a sense of confidence. The singer is in control, negotiating the terms of the relationship. Music historian Liz Reed has said this is a theme that runs through Indigenous women's music in Australia. We have already discussed the lyrics of Shakaya, and Reed (2002, 33–37) has described how other female artists such as Tiddas, Ruby Hunter and Leah Purcell were starting to articulate their autonomy as independent women in the 1990s. In her song, "True Lovers", Hunter also addresses her partner directly, asking if he feels about her the same way she feels about him (Hunter 2000).

Ruby Hunter believed in the power of music to heal and release and in her lyrics she proposes that, while relationships can be difficult, it is possible to work things out with reason (Reed 2002, 36). This sentiment is also apparent in "Loving and Caring", where the singer asks her partner to come and talk things over. In this way, as Tess Reed commented, rock music can provide a medium for "mediating gendered customary behaviour", with song lyrics being a safe and neutral space to raise issues and teach appropriate behaviour (Reed 2002, 28).

"Loving and Caring" displays elements of the rock genre, such as the guitar-driven instrumentation and the verse–chorus–bridge structure, but the recording also contains other stylistic influences. Driving from Maningrida to Alice Springs down the Stuart Highway, we listened to music that was to inspire our song writing: R&B hits from the 2000s such as songs by Mariah Carey and Shakaya, and more recent Indigenous artists such as Thelma Plum, Baker Boy and Barkaa. We were also influenced by a series of Indigenous community hip-hop videos produced in Maningrida by the Greater Youth Service, Malabam Health Board and NAAJA collaborating with Indigenous Hip Hop Projects to explore themes such as respectful relationships and domestic violence (Indigenous Hip Hop Projects. 2015). The songs are very popular and can be found on YouTube, including "Make it Through" and "Ripple Effect Maningrida", which was the inspiration behind the name of the band. Rostron was around when these videos were produced, and she participated in some of them.

The impact of these artists and projects is apparent in the transnational elements of both Black American R&B sounds and Australian Indigenous hip-hop, which includes the incorporation of electronic beats mixed with the live drums, the use of synthesisers and sampled sounds, dense lyrical content, the use of spoken words and the inclusion of rapping. Motivated by Baker Boy, from Milingimbi, North-east Arnhem Land, who raps in Yolngu Matha and English, Rostron raps in her language of Kune and English. She drew inspiration from other Indigenous women rappers, such as Naomi Wenitong from Shakaya and Barkaa, a Malyangapa, Barkindji woman from western New South Wales, whose debut release in 2020, "For My Tittas", reached national success with lyrics that call for Black women to feel proud and strong. Listening to Indigenous women rappers gave Rostron the confidence, as an Indigenous woman, to try this more rhythmic form of vocals to send out a message to her community about social relationships.

The song was recorded over a period of months in a range of locations and a distinctive feature of this process was the control over all aspects of production by us as female producers. We wrote the harmonic structure of the song using acoustic guitar and then worked on ideas using Logic software on Kell's computer: programming beats, recording in guitar and bass and using this recording to add sections to the song. We recorded the bass guitar and rhythm guitar tracks at PAW studios in Yuendumu, the drums and main vocals at Dr.G. studios at Skinnyfish Music in Darwin and the rap on Kell's laptop at the Music NT rehearsal rooms in Darwin. We spent time together in Kell's Ackeron Street Studio in Newcastle, adding more guitar, keys and extra vocals, and pulled it together with a pre-mix that we sent to Sydney-based audio engineer Antonia Gauci for the final mixing process, which was done with our input. Having this lengthy production schedule gave us creative licence to shape the style and feel of the song, and to navigate intercultural collaboration involving women in a male-dominated space, with Indigenous and non-Indigenous artists and audio engineers working in remote, regional and city-based locations.

Producer and academic Paula Wolfe argued that the creative practice of self-production, where artists produce their own music for commercial release, has challenged the gender bias of the music recording industry. Rather than relying on studios, the "burgeoning access to digital recording technology" has changed the positioning of female producers and allowed them greater control (Wolfe, 2020, 93). Linda Barwick, in her discussion of contemporary funeral songs in Wadeye, commented that music technologies have allowed a democratisation of the means of making music, leading to "a fundamental shift in musical practices around funerals in Wadeye", including a greater prominence of women in composing and leading songs (2017, 166–167).

> When we are writing and producing music, I feel closer to the music. I can feel something is holding me and telling me I am doing fine. It is positive. It gives me a power. A power to make this love song and give advice to people about relationships, about change. (Rostron 2022)

If we consider how music is a forum for social mediation, then taking control over the stages of music production becomes a powerful act. As composers, producers and members of Ripple Effect Band, we have felt in control of "Loving and Caring" and we composed it with the intent of influencing how lovers relate to each other. The resulting song, "Loving and Caring", exhibits elements of transnational musical cultures that have been localised through the use of Kune language and by addressing the fabric of society, romantic love, it is a political statement, about the rights of women to express their perspectives on love, and about a vision for the mediation of social constructs.

Conclusion

Through the medium of song, the young women of MGB began a tradition of women-focused songs that can provide their perspective on love and social relationships. Composed in a modern setting of a school classroom where the women were separated from the socially dictated silencing of women's voices, "Love Song" challenged the gendered restrictions surrounding song. Its lasting popularity comes from the way the song resonates with women's experiences of love, and a sense of ownership and pride as the first song composed by women in Maningrida. This popularity and reiterations of the song performed by women musicians in western Arnhem Land points to its impact on the musical practices of women and subsequent expression of new forms of agency.

In composing "Loving and Caring", Rostron and I have demonstrated that as musicians we have grown and matured and taken control over the process of music production. This gave us the opportunity to compose with intent, and we have written a love song that aspires to enact social change. By presenting an image of relationships that promotes good communication as key to getting along, we hope to influence couples, lovers and all people in relationships to find a way to love each other with care and respect. In this way, Ripple Effect Band is using music making to mediate Maningrida women's social positioning and to act as role models for other women to feel confidence to ask for new ways of loving, and new values in relationships.

Through analysis of the history and context in which two love songs were written and performed by Ripple Effect Band, and the song writers' intentions, we have demonstrated how popular love songs are inherently political as they address and aim to mediate socio-cultural relationships and perceptions of the role of women in these relationships. The neglect of studies of love songs has occurred partly through gender bias in both the music industry and the documentation of the history of popular music that have been dominated by men. Through a practice-based approach within an intercultural collaboration, we are contributing to new perspectives on popular music and negotiating greater agency for women.

Chapter 18

Arrungpayarrun ta alan "We'll follow their path"

Reuben Brown, Isabel O'Keeffe, Ruth Singer, Jenny Manmurulu, Renfred Manmurulu and Rupert Manmurulu

Introduction

Following in the path, track or footsteps of one's Elders and ancestors is a common idiomatic expression used by Bininj and Arrarrkpi singers of the *manyardi/kun-borrk* song tradition of western Arnhem Land. In Mawng, one says *arrungpayarrun ta alan* "we'll follow their path". This can describe practices involving intergenerational transmission of song, dance and song knowledge; consideration of performance aesthetics including rhythmic mode and song order; processes of receiving new songs in dreams or composing new songs; and principles that underpin these practices (Brown 2016; Brown, Manmurulu et al. 2018; O'Keeffe 2017). In a similar way, Franca Tamisari (1998, 262) wrote that Yolngu of east Arnhem Land conceive of maintaining the "the Law of, or right way of, performing songs and dances" as following in the footsteps of ancestors. Tamisari noted:

> Following in the footsteps of the ancestors is not limited to deepening a well worn track which endures over time, but in assuming everchanging spatiotemporal dimensions, it establishes a creatively productive dialogue between people, ancestors and land. (1998, 262)

These dialogues are also evident in the ways people follow the path of Elders and ancestors in the *manyardi* song traditions, and through the "intergenerational nature of research collaborations" (Brown and Treloyn 2017, 58) in our field of applied research on Indigenous song and dance practices.

In this chapter we analyse some key principles of *manyardi* expressed in Mawng, reflecting on a 15-year collaboration between a team of linguists and musicologists, including Linda Barwick, and *manyardi* ceremony leaders, including the Manmurulu family, knowledge holders of the Inyjalarrku (mermaid) song-set from Goulburn Island. These principles include ideas about fostering intergenerational *manyardi* performance and research relationships "like family", as Jenny Manmurulu expresses it; *manyardi* bringing back memories; performances of *manyardi* maintaining dialogues between past and present performers; and working together to enliven *manyardi*. We pay tribute to scholar, mentor and friend, Linda Barwick, and to collaborator and senior ceremony leader for Inyjalarrku – the late Nawamut David Manmurulu – by tracing something of the *alan* "path" they have laid for future generations. This *alan* relates respectively to carrying out intercultural, interdisciplinary, collaborative and participatory research on Indigenous Australian song (Barney 2014; Ford, Barwick and Marett 2014), and to passing on *manyardi* song and dance practices. The chapter includes reflections from the Manmurulu family on their collaboration with Linda Barwick – beginning with their first meeting at Warruwi in 2006 to the present – following the *alan* "path" in *manyardi* performance and research collaborations.

Following the *alan* "path" in *manyardi* performance and research

Manyardi (known as *kun-borrk* in Bininj Kunwok) are didjeridu- and clapstick-accompanied songs from the western Arnhem Land region of the Northern Territory. They are performed for both formal occasions that involve dance, including funeral ceremonies, *Mamurrng* (diplomacy) ceremonies, *Inyimanj ja najaman* (girls' puberty) ceremonies, local festivals and celebrations, and also informal occasions that may not involve dance (including trips to significant sites, or song documentation and elicitation sessions with researchers from outside the community). Songs are organised into named repertories or "song-sets" with each song-set affiliated with a particular linguistic variety of the region and, by extension, to the land and people affiliated with that linguistic variety. Songs may be composed or received in dreams and are in everyday language (often referred to as "love songs") or in untranslatable spirit language (often referred to as "spirit" or "Dreaming songs"), such as the Inyjalarrku "mermaid" Dreaming songs (Apted 2008; 2010; Barwick, Birch and Evans 2007; Brown 2016; Brown, Manmurulu et al. 2017; Garde 2005; O'Keeffe 2007; 2010; 2017). Table 18.1 lists the diverse song-sets recorded or discussed by the Western Arnhem Land Song Project, and their affiliations.

Table 18.1 *Manyardi/kun-borrk* song-sets recorded and/or discussed during the Western Arnhem Land Song Project.[1]

Song-set code	Song-set name in language[2]	English name	Language of song texts	Language affiliation of song-set
IT	Itpiyitpi	Grasshopper	Bininj Kunwok (Kunwinjku), Mawng, Kun-barlang	Mawng
KL	Kun-barlang	Kun-barlang Love Songs		Kun-barlang
KN	Kun-nalk	Crying	Bininj Kunwok (Kunwinjku)	Bininj Kunwok (Kunwinjku)
LU	Rlumpuk	Pigeon	?Mawng[3]	Mawng
NA	Nakurrututu	Mudfish	Mawng	Mawng
MY	Mimih/Yawkyawk	Mimih (pandanus) spirits/Mermaid	Bininj Kunwok (Kuninjku)	Bininj Kunwok (Kuninjku)
KK	Kaddikkaddik	Oyster Catcher	Kun-barlang, Spirit language	Kun-barlang
MK	Marrwakara and Mularrik	Goanna and Frog	Spirit language, Mawng	Mawng
DY	Diyama	Stripey Cockle	Spirit language[4]	Burarra
IL	Inyjalarrku	Mermaid		Mawng
JK	Jalarrkuku	Floating Island		Manangkardi
KA	Kalajbari	Frigate Bird		Iwaidja
MN	Manbam	Bowerbird		Marrku
MP	Mirrijpu	Seagull/Silver Gull		Manangkardi

---

1 See Barwick, Birch et al. 2011–2015.
2 Most of the song-set names are in the same language as the language affiliation of the song-set, but some names are untranslatable.
3 *Rlumpuk* songs are no longer performed and there are no recordings of any of them of which we are aware; the song-texts were love songs in Mawng.
4 *Milyarryarr* also include some everyday Marrku words (an Iwaidjan language that is no longer spoken): Brown and Evans 2017.

Song-set code	Song-set name in language	English name	Language of song texts	Language affiliation of song-set
MR	Milyarryarr	Black Heron	Spirit language (cont.)	Garig/Ilgar, Marrku, Manangkardi, Mawng
NG	Ngarnaru	(untranslatable)		Manangkardi
NJ	Nginji/Ngili	(untranslatable)/ Mosquito		Mawng
KB	Karrbarda	Long Yam		Bininj Kunwok (Kunwinjku)
KU	Kurri	Blue-tongue Lizard		Bininj Kunwok (Kunwinjku)
ML	Marlwa	Pandanus spirit		Bininj Kunwok (?Kunwinjku)
YA	Yanajanak	(untranslatable)		Amurdak

Manyardi song-sets are seen as owned primarily by an individual songman and are typically passed on from fathers to sons, but also from and to other male relatives. Performing one's inherited songs is conceptualised as following in the footsteps or path of one's Elders, as Rupert Manmurulu explains about his performance of Inyjalarrku songs: "I'm following the footsteps from my *ngabbard* ['father'] and my *mawa* ['father's father'] right. And if I speak in Mawng I say: *Ngunjarrung ta alan* \'I'm following their path'."[5]

It is not just the song-set's repertoire of songs that is passed on, but also the associated dances, dance styles, composition and performance practices (Brown 2016; O'Keeffe 2017). For the Manmurulu family, this also includes the practice of travelling for performances across Arnhem Land and beyond, engaging with those outside of the *manyardi* traditions, including *Balanda* (non-Indigenous) people. As Jenny Manmurulu explains, David Manmurulu's father George Winunguj and his father's older brother Lazarus Lamilami used to perform together. This included a *Rom* (diplomacy) ceremony performed for the *Balanda* photographer Axel Poignant in 1952.[6]

---

5 Rupert Manmurulu, RB2–20210215-RB_01.wav, 00:23:14–00:23:30. Recordings referred to in this chapter are archived in PARADISEC under collector ID RB2, https://catalog.paradisec.org.au/collections/RB2.

6 See more details in Brown, Manmurulu et al. 2018; Harris 2020; Poignant and Poignant 1996.

> Like this Inyjalarrku it's been passed on from Old George [Winunguj] and Lazarus [Lamilami], and then they passed it onto their sons and the sons are passing it on to their sons . . . The two brothers [Winunguj and Lamilami] used to go together and the big brother [Lamilami] used to sing while the little brother George [Winunguj], he has performed [dance] through the *Yumparrparr* [giant] . . . Roslyn [Poignant] has written in that Nagalarramba Encounter [*Encounter at Nagalarramba* (Poignant and Poignant 1996)] and it shows how they both worked together, went together and worked together.[7]

Reflecting on the continued intergenerational transmission of Inyajarrku, Jenny Manmurulu also comments on her late husband David Manmurulu's commitment to passing the Inyjalarrku songs on to their sons, Reuben Manmurulu, Rupert Manmurulu and Renfred Manmurulu, even though the sons also spent time away from the community at boarding school (see Figure 18.1):

> And like from David [Manmurulu], when my boys came home, or like going to boarding school, coming home on holidays for holidays, and then he told them, he's been telling them to join in or follow Nawamut [David Manmurulu's skin name], to sing so when he pass away or get too old and then they can, you can carry on. And if, when you have your own children, then you'll tell them to sing and pass it on.[8]

> And now my boys . . . they're passing it on to their boys. And for me, [I'm] passing my dancing techniques too, [to] my granddaughters and other girls too.[9]

This intergenerational transmission has included David Manmurulu passing on the performing of the *Yumparrparr* "giant" dance (which was inherited from his father Winungudj and accompanies certain Inyjalarrku songs) to Rupert Manmurulu. The three generations of *Yumparrparr* "giant" dancers are shown in Figure 18.2.

Jenny Manmurulu also details the way that David Manmurulu taught her the Inyjalarrku dance styles when she married him, so that she could then teach them to other women:

> It took me a while to start dancing myself, but Nawamut [David Manmurulu] he's been teaching me the different style of dancing of the Inyjalarrku . . . *Imajpungkinang ilangaling. Innyarlukpangung kapin warramumpik. Ngeyantung la ngyerukuning alaj innyarlukpangung* [He used to get up and

---

7 Jenny Manmurulu, RB2–20210215-RB_01.wav, 00:19:55–00:21:22.
8 Jenny Manmurulu, RB2–20210215-RB_01.wav, 00:45:32–00:47:00.
9 Jenny Manmurulu, RB2–20210215-RB_01.wav, 00:32:27–00:33:11.

dance like the women. I would see him and I would show (the women) how he was dancing]. So when he used to get up and dance, or even in the house by ourselves, start singing, get up and perform like a lady dance . . . And then I used to follow, dance with him . . . he used to tell me . . . this is the style of dance for this song, *ta nukapa ta ayuk nuyu, nuka ja manyardi* [the style (of dancing) that belongs to this (particular) song].[10]

Women typically dance for a range of song-sets, which may include those of their father, mother's father and brothers, and husband, and different songs may be learned from different kin and Elders across a lifetime, as Manmurulu reflects on her learning of different *manyardi* dances:

I used to watch my mum and her sisters, including my grandmother . . . I used to dance with them when I was just growing up, but when I grew older, like I forgot all about it . . . I knew the song very well, but I forgot the dancing style or dancing technique. And two old ladies showed me how to dance, old Rosemary [Urabadi] and Nita [Garidjalalug]. Like we told them that you have to teach us and then we'll carry on teaching the other girls and they'll pass it on to the next generation. Anybody who knows, get up [and dance] and we'll follow. It doesn't matter if you make mistakes, that's part of our learning.[11]

For all children in western Arnhem Land, dancing *manyardi* is encouraged as their *alan* "path" laid down by previous generations and to be passed onto future generations, as Manmurulu explains:

We tell the younger ones that you have to get up and dance because most of your family been dancing and that's your *alan* ["path"] *Kurrungpayarrun. Kutpunpanuki warak pata wera* ["You follow this way. You'll show the others how."]. Like you start dancing now and then pass it on to your next generation.[12]

---

10 Jenny Manmurulu, RB2–20210215-RB_01.wav, 00:33:22–00:34:41.
11 Jenny Manmurulu, ICLDC presentation, 00:08:37–00:09:27.
12 Jenny Manmurulu, RB2–20210215-RB_01.wav, 00:47:53–00:48:19.

18 Arrungpayarrun ta alan "We'll follow their path"

Figure 18.1 Four generations of *Inyjalarrku manyardi* performers. Top: George Winungudj playing didjeridu for his sons, including David Manmurulu (far left in the yellow top), circa 1970s. Photographer unknown, from Manmurulu family private collection. Bottom: David Manmurulu (centre in red top) with his sons and grandsons, 2010. Photo Beth Luck, used with permission.

Figure 18.2 Three generations of *Yumparrparr* "giant" dancers. Top: George Winungudj, 1952. Photo: Axel Poignant (published in *Poignant and Poignant* 1996, 141), used with permission. Centre: David Manmurulu, 2012. Still from Gus Berger, used with permission. Bottom: Rupert Manmurulu, 2013. Still from Grubin Films, used with permission.

The first time that members of the Manmurulu family (David, Jenny, Reuben and Rupert) gave a public presentation on Inyjalarrku and *manyardi* in which they shared their philosophy of *arrungpayarrun ta alan* was at the 2007 Indigenous Music and Dance Symposium, with co-presenters Linda Barwick and Isabel O'Keeffe. Rupert Manmurulu finished the presentation with a statement about some young men not following their Elders but going a "separate road". He emphasised the way that he and his brothers were continuing to perform Inyjalarrku and passing it on to their children. Fifteen years later, with the passing of his father, David Manmurulu, in 2021, and with his own sons and nephews following his path by singing and playing arawirr (didjeridu), Rupert Manmurulu's statement has added poignancy:

> I just want to say one more thing. Apart from my dad there's a lot of families back there they've got their own songs and they've got sons, nephews and whatever else, you know and their sons and nephews they don't look forward you know towards what their father been doing and their grandparents, they just want to go separate road, you know. But for us, you know, [we're] proud of my dad, you know. He's been there, done it, so you know, if one day, his days might go on [i.e., he might pass away], me and my brother [Reuben Manmurulu] here, we'll still be singing and all that, continuing on.[13]

Barwick facilitated dialogues between members of the Manmurulu family, researchers (herself, O'Keeffe and others in the audience), and other ceremony holders and practitioners from around the country, as well as providing the opportunity for David Manmurulu to lead a *manyardi* performance at the end of the presentation, allowing the songs to be "brought alive". This dialogic approach to research, including the dialogic approach to presenting at conferences, has been a path that *Balanda* collaborators (Reuben Brown, Isabel O'Keeffe, Ruth Singer and others) have since followed in our ongoing collaborations. We echo the idea of Payi Linda Ford, Marett and Barwick, who wrote of their research collaborations: "the integration of our interests within a shared culturally meaningful framework has offered us new ways to engage with each other, and in turn created new research pathways of knowing, being and doing" (Ford, Barwick and Marett 2014, 62).

Barwick's approach has been underpinned by her long interest in the "process of performance" and on the effect of performers' experiences – her own and that of other women, as well as others – on the analysis of song traditions (e.g., Barwick 1992) and her commitment to engaging with Indigenous song traditions as "a vital part of contemporary life" that are "active and potent responses to the exigencies

---

13 Rupert Manmurulu, 20070818MA-ILXX 00:48:18.682–00:49:39.408.

of everyday life" (Marett and Barwick 2007) and contemporary "sites of creativity" (Barwick 2000b). This commitment has also driven her ongoing and collaborative advocacy for Indigenous musics, music makers and scholars within the academy. As Bracknell and Barwick (2021, 78, citing Arau and Clemens 2013) wrote:

> Resisting settler colonial attempts to suppress and eradicate them, Indigenous musics will always carry immense power to connect and effect change in this place. Given the history of denigration, ignorance and appropriation towards Indigenous musics, advocacy for Indigenous self-determination must be the central mandate of Australian music institutions. Enabling tertiary music institutions as brave spaces from which Indigenous music-makers and Indigenous scholars can speak truth and be heard will benefit the practice, teaching and research of all involved.

Our team of musicologists, linguists and Arrarrkpi singers and dancers engaged in research on *manyardi* has benefited from opportunities to learn from the collaborative work of Linda Barwick, and David and Jenny Manmurulu as well as other Indigenous music makers and scholars in Australian music institutions. We conceive of our continuing collaborative research on *manyardi* (for example, Brown, Manmurulu et al. 2017; 2018; O'Keeffe, Barwick et al. 2018) as following the *alan* "path" of Barwick's interdisciplinary and intercultural projects documenting *manyardi* (Barwick, Birch and Evans 2007, 7; Barwick et al. 2011–2015). In their analysis of Iwaidja *jurtbirrk* songs, Barwick, Birch and Evans similarly saw their work as "taking place within a long and ongoing Australian tradition of cross-disciplinary engagement". They argued for the great benefit of this interdisciplinary approach to research on Indigenous Australian song and to focusing on song and song poetry:

> Song, as a medium, gives us a special opportunity to reveal some of this fine cultural knowledge, which is in the minds of language speakers – both as songmen, and as "ordinary" speakers – but which may only appear in the rare moments so delicately portrayed in this song genre. The multiple focus brought by interdisciplinary work can increase our sensitivity to the richness and logic of what is there. (Barwick, Birch and Evans 2007, 29)

More broadly, across a vast number of research projects, publications, conferences and symposia, and in her role as supervisor and mentor, Linda Barwick has led her field by creating and sustaining dialogues – between Indigenous and non-Indigenous, between generations of scholars and practitioners, between scholars of different disciplines. In the following sections we consider how these collaborations and dialogues connect with principles within the *manyardi* song traditions.

"Like family"

As we have seen in the previous section, the *manyardi* song tradition is highly relational, with song-sets and their associated dances and compositional and performance practices being passed on throughout generations of extended families and kin networks. Similarly, Jenny Manmurulu conceptualises the research collaborations between her family and researchers, including Linda Barwick, as being "like family" with reciprocal relationships – the Manmurulu family inviting researchers to hear Inyjalarrku, and researchers inviting the Manmurulu family to share at research forums, including the first presentation they gave with Linda Barwick at the Indigenous Music Symposium in Darwin in 2007 (where they stayed at the Northern Australian Research Unit). As Jenny Manmurulu explains in her reflections on first meeting Linda Barwick at Martpalk (Warruwi Community):

> That's when we first met her [Linda Barwick], that's when Isabel [O'Keeffe] was based at Martpalk. That's where she [Isabel] heard the Inyjalarrku song and then she told Linda about that song and when she [Linda] heard it, she said "Oh! We better go and see them!" We were like family. We were all looking after each other – Linda [Barwick], Allan [Marett][14] and Isabel [O'Keeffe]. Like, *nungmalal mira ta ngarrarrangung ngarrunpatpang ta ngarrimung* ["it's good how we were like family to each other"], it's been really good how we used to get together like one big family. After coming out to watch us dance the Inyjalarrku – hear the song and dance – and then they invited us to come to NARU [Northern Australian Research Unit].[15]

Jenny Manmurulu has expressed similar sentiments when discussing other collaborations with Brown, O'Keeffe and Singer: "We're working as one big family now" (Brown, Manmurulu et al. 2018). These collaborations have included invitations from the Manmurulu family for researchers to perform *manyardi* alongside them in both ceremonial and academic conference settings (see, for example, Figure 18.3 showing Barwick and Marett with Jenny and David Manmurulu at the Annual Indigenous Music and Dance Symposium in Darwin in 2011; and Figure 18.4 showing Barwick dancing with Jenny Manmurulu). Reflecting on the performance of *manyardi* at the International Council for Traditional Music World Conference in Bangkok (Thailand) in 2019, Rupert Manmurulu considers the invitation that he and Renfred Manmurulu gave to Indigenous performers from the Kimberley (Pete O'Conor, Lloyd Nulgit and John Divili), as well as non-Indigenous researchers (including Reuben Brown,

---

14 Barwick and Marett are personal and professional partners.
15 Jenny Manmurulu, 20210204 Tribute to Linda presentation, 00:00:00–00:01:50.

Isabel O'Keeffe, Sally Treloyn and Aaron Corn), to "help out" with the *manyardi* performance as "extended families":

> They were helping us out sharing the *manyardi*, it wasn't only the two of us [me and Renfred Manmurulu], you know, we had extended families: Reuben [Brown], Isabel [O'Keeffe] and the Kimberley boys [Pete O'Conor, Lloyd Nulgit and John Divili] and Sally [Treloyn] and Aaron [Corn].[16]

These research collaborations exemplify what Brown and Treloyn (2017, 58) described as the "relational process of research embodied through performance", which draws on Cree scholar Shawn Wilson's discussion of an Indigenous research paradigm that is "relational and maintains relational accountability" (Wilson 2008, 70). Similarly, Ford, Barwick and Marett (2014, 51) have pointed out these kinds of relationships and invitations depend on "reciprocal respect and trust that can only be earned through longstanding and ongoing commitment and engagement".

The relational research collaborations between the Manmurulu family and researchers including Linda Barwick and Allan Marett were particularly strengthened through the 2012 *Mamurrng* (Diplomacy) ceremony at Warruwi for Reuben Brown commissioned with funding from an Australian Research Council Discovery grant led by Barwick, Marett and historian Martin Thomas.[17] The Mamurrng was initiated by the ceremonial giving of a lock of Brown's hair to David Manmurulu at the Annual Symposium for Indigenous Music and Dance in 2011. As part of the reciprocal nature of such ceremonies, at the end of *manyardi* performances, Marett performed two *wangga* (songs from the Daly Region of the Northern Territory), which he had been given permission to perform by songmen Kenny Burrenjuck and Frank Dumoo,[18] accompanied by David Manmurulu and other Warruwi musicians on the didjeridu and with Linda Barwick leading the women in performing the associated dances. In reflecting on this in 2021, Jenny Manmurulu commented on people's surprise at Warruwi, and her response to them that emphasised Barwick and Marett's longstanding relationships, engagement and work with ceremony holders and performers at Port Keats (Wadeye).[19]

> You know how we presented that *mamurrng* to you [Reuben Brown], and *Arrarrkpi* [Indigenous people] from Martpalk, they got really surprised how

---

16 Rupert Manmurulu, RUIAC presentation 2 December 2020, 00:30:31–00:32:13.
17 See R. Brown 2017 for a detailed description and analysis of this ceremony.
18 See Marett, Barwick and Ford 2013, 13.
19 See also Barwick 2002; 2005b; 2011; Barwick, Marett, Walsh et al. 2005; 2010; Barwick, Marett, Blythe and Walsh 2007; Ford, Barwick and Marett 2014; Marett 2000; 2005; Marett, Barwick and Ford 2013.

they see Allan [Marett] singing that song [*wangga*] and David [Manmurulu] blowing the didjeridu [for him], and Linda [Barwick] was dancing [*wangga*], you know. And the people at Warruwi, you know, they were asking, "where did they learn?" And I told them that they've been working at Port Keats area, and they've learned all the songs and knowledge, you know, and the dancing styles.[20]

Invitations for the Manmurulu family to present and perform at academic conferences are also considered by Jenny Manmurulu to be an important part of the respectful reciprocal relationships that were established by Barwick and Marett. Jenny Manmurulu reflects on subsequent collaborations and presentations with Brown, O'Keeffe and Singer as taking over from their lead, but notes that Barwick and Marett continue to be "in our head" or in our thoughts as we co-present and perform together:

It was a really good experience working with Linda [Barwick] and Allan [Marett] – how we first met them, and they invited us to come for this symposium [for Indigenous Music and Dance], probably three or four times here in Darwin and then twice in Canberra [and in Melbourne]. And even though that like you [Reuben Brown] and Isabel [O'Keefe and Ruth Singer], taking over [from them] like working closely with me and David and the boys [Rupert and Renfred Manmurulu], but we still had Linda [Barwick] and Allan [Marett] in our head, you know, [thinking] "they should've been here!"[21]

Jenny Manmurulu's comments, particularly that we "still had Linda and Allan in our head", also highlight the "intergenerational nature of research collaborations" (Brown and Treloyn 2017, 58) and the dialogic nature of the *manyardi* song traditions that are expressed in the Mawng expressions, considered in the following sections about how songs make people remember and how people bring songs alive.

---

20 Jenny Manmurulu, Tribute to Linda Barwick 20210204, 00:00:56–00:02:09.
21 Jenny Manmurulu, Tribute to Linda Barwick 20210204, 00:00:56–00:02:09.

Figure 18.3 Allan Marett, Linda Barwick, Jenny Manmurulu and David Manmurulu at the Annual Indigenous Music and Dance Symposium in Darwin, 2011. Photo: Reuben Brown, used with permission.

Figure 18.4 Jenny Manmurulu and Linda Barwick perform *manyardi* at the Musicology Society of Australia Conference in Perth, 2018. Photo: Musicological Society of Australia collection, used with permission.

Kangmarrangulin "song brings back memories"

K-ang-marranguli-n
PR-3LL-song.move.audience-NP

"It (the song) breaks our hearts/brings back memories"

Kangmarrangulin is an idiomatic Mawng expression that encapsulates the idea that performing and/or hearing *manyardi* brings back memories and allows ongoing dialogues with the past as people remember loved ones and ancestors, such as those who performed *manyardi* before. The expression *kangmarrangulin* can also be used to talk about how visiting places or the changing seasons (for example, the wet season wind blowing) bring back memories. Related to how it makes people remember is its other meaning about how hearing *manyardi* can be deeply moving emotionally, translated as "it breaks our heart" (O'Keeffe, Singer and Coleman 2020). Jenny Manmurulu explains:

> *Wey kangmarrangulin nuwu!* ["Hey, your song makes us remember/breaks our heart!"] It's more about a person who starts singing and then the people say "oh, it reminds us back when he start singing, now he's continuing singing". It brings me memory that when I went away and now I came back home and I'm starting to listen [to] the same song, it breaks my heart. When I start dancing on different songs in Inyjalarrku and it brings memory back to me, I think about my sister-in-law, old Agnes Mirrawayin, because she teach me a lot and when my memory comes back, I just closed my eyes and see her vision in my dream, and I do the dancing. That's why people say, "oh, you got really lovely technique" you know, because she just come back to my memory and then I start following her way, how she's been dancing. So that's what *kangmarrangulin* means.[22]

Jenny Manmurulu also compares remembering and memorising songs and dance movements to archiving, and comments on the ways that archival records are incomplete but can help to trigger memories of songs and dances that have been passed on.

> We [*Arrarrkpi* "Indigenous people"] don't have the archive or anything... but it's there already... it's what we've memorised, most of our stuff that we've been taught from our Elders. Like *manyardi*, it's been recorded there, but no documents on ladies dancing... But this Inyjalarrku song, the old

---

22 Jenny Manmurulu, ICLDC presentation, 00:14:32–15:30.

songs that they've been recording . . . the dancing style is still there . . . and we can still memorise [the dance] if it's been passed on.²³

The incompleteness of archival recordings that Jenny Manmurulu comments on is also an issue that Barwick has engaged with deeply in her scholarship, including discussions about the "aural snapshots" or "partial records" of the archival song recordings of the 1948 American–Australian Scientific Expedition to Arnhem Land (Barwick and Marett 2011), the potential "conundrums and unexpected consequences" of archival returns (Barwick, Green, Vaarzon-Morel and Zissermann 2019), and commitments to working with contemporary musicians/custodians on "contemporary efforts to re-evaluate, and where appropriate, revitalise significant cultural records" (Troy and Barwick 2021). This scholarship has considered the dialogues between archival sources and contemporary musicians/custodians and many of these musicians/custodians, including Bracknell, Dowding (Treloyn and Dowding 2017) and Martin (Treloyn, Martin and Charles 2016), have shown how singers in archival recordings speak to fellow countrymen listening in the present. As Bracknell (2019a, 8) wrote, reflecting on community efforts to consolidate and recirculate the Noongar song repertoire:

> The archive is valuable, but contains so many questions that require authentic, informed and sometimes creative decision-making on the part of descendants of singers and their nominated community experts . . . a possible revival of Noongar song repertoire is simply not possible with the archive alone and requires deep intellectual and creative investment on the part of relevant Noongar people. Such processes of dialogue with archival sources has become characteristic of contemporary ethnomusicology.

Barwick's methodologies aimed at creating access to cultural materials for custodians (e.g., Barwick, Marett, Walsh et al. 2005; Barwick and Thieberger 2018; Barwick et al. 2021; Barwick, Green, Vaarzon-Morel and Zissermann 2019, etc.) have been instrumental in facilitating these processes of dialogue. They also reflect the idea that Aboriginal song traditions are "active and potent" as Marett and Barwick (2007, 4) wrote:

> Aboriginal song traditions today are a vital part of contemporary life, that these are not living museum pieces as some of our politicians would have us believe, but rather active and potent responses to the exigencies of everyday life – indeed they are one of the primary mechanisms by which Aboriginal people respond to and adapt to change.

---

23 Jenny Manmurulu, RB2–20210215-RB_01.wav, 00:36:40–00:39:20.

The next section considers a Mawng idiom that encapsulates ideas of the "active and potent" role of song traditions in dialogic engagements in the present.

Karryaryakpakpa ja manyardi "We bring the song to life"

Karry-aryakpa-kpa ja manyardi
1pl.in/3MA-make.wet/enliven-KRDP-NP MA song
"We make the song happy, bring it to life (by engaging/dancing)"

The Mawng ideomatic expression *karryaryakpakpa ja manyardi* "we bring the song to life" is commonly used by *manyardi* performers to describe the way that *manyardi* singers, instrumentalists, dancers and other participants need to work together to enliven a song performance or "bring it to life", in the same way that water refreshes the thirsty and parched or brings a plant to life. Performing *manyardi* enacts a dialogue between those involved, with the singers and instrumentalists bringing the dancers to life and dancers and those in the audience enlivening the singers through their participation: dancing, clapping and calling out. If there is no dialogue through participation, singers can "feel bad" and the "song will go bad".[24] Rupert and Jenny Manmurulu explain this dynamic:

> Rupert Manmurulu: Sometime when we're singing and nobody don't clap for us or singing out *arrapujpa* ["(good) songman!"], all that, sometimes the singers get bored, and we go off track a bit. If somebody sing out for us or start clapping when we're singing, you know, or dancing that's like –
>
> Jenny Manmurulu: enlivening the singers . . . And like when they start singing, you know . . . they [the young boys] just get up and start dancing, like we don't tell them all "get up and dance!", they just hear the clapsticks and they just get up and start dancing.[25]
>
> Rupert Manmurulu: I always, you know, keep elbowing my two brothers to say like sing, you know, to get the true *manyardi* [song] from inside in us, let it out where you make people start singing out for it, clapping, you know, and then they'll start, we'll start feeling good about ourselves [as singers], you know. And then that's when the boys start, get up and they dance, you know. And then from one person you get up and dance, and then you got two and then three and then many more.[26]

---

24 David Manmurulu, quoted in Brown, Manmurulu et al. 2017.
25 RB2–20210215-RB_01.wav, 00:42:16–00:43:10.
26 Rupert Manmurulu, ICLDC presentation, 00:17:47–00:18:53.

The Manmurulu family consider this same principle at work as they share presentations about and performances of *manyardi* in new contexts outside Arnhem Land, such as at festivals (for example, in Mowanjum, Western Australia), academic contexts (for example, the Annual Symposia for Indigenous Music and Dance, and the International Council for Traditional Music World Conferences) or even online (for example, live videos of *manyardi* performances streamed by families on Facebook), connecting with family members living away from their traditional Country, including young people at boarding schools or homestays. As well as invitations to perform and work together "like family", these invitations are also made to help "bring songs to life". Reflecting on the performance of *manyardi* at the International Council for Traditional Music World Conference in Bangkok (Thailand) in 2019 (see Figure 18.5), Renfred and Rupert Manmurulu commented on the way that having Indigenous performers from the Kimberley in Western Australia (Pete O'Conor, Lloyd Nulgit and John Divili) and non-Indigenous researchers (including Reuben Brown, Isabel O'Keeffe and Sally Treloyn) joining them, along with members of the conference audience whom they asked to volunteer to dance, could also be described as *karryaryakpakpa ja manyardi* "we bring the song to life", which made them as singers feel "over the moon":

> Renfred Manmurulu: In this [Bangkok, Thailand] performance, you can see like Reuben [Brown] yourself, you started off dancing with Kimberley boys [Pete O'Conor, Lloyd Nulgit]. And then when we called out for a couple more to come down, join in . . .
>
> Rupert Manmurulu: And we were very proud of Isabel [O'Keeffe] and Sally [Treloyn] joining in . . . you need two clapstick man and one didjeridu player so we actually asked Johnny [Divili] if he can help along [with clapsticks]
>
> Renfred Manmurulu: Which he did . . . then the start [of the] dancing with Isabel, that soaked up the atmosphere, where everyone all start joining in, they wanted to be part of it, dancing and stuff like that. And the most important thing is that word *karryaryakpakpa ja manyardi*.[27]
>
> Rupert Manmurulu: For Thailand, you know, we had Pete [O'Conor] and Lloydy [Nulgit] and Reuben [Brown] dancing. And then we started to, you know, ask the audience, like for volunteers to come and dance. And then a few of the blokes came rushing in, came down and started dancing. It made us, I don't know, we was just over the moon, me and Renfred![28]

---

27 Renfred and Rupert Manmurulu, 20201202 RUIAC presentation, 00:28:3100:32:06.
28 Rupert Manmurulu, ICLDC presentation, 00:19:11–00:19:28.

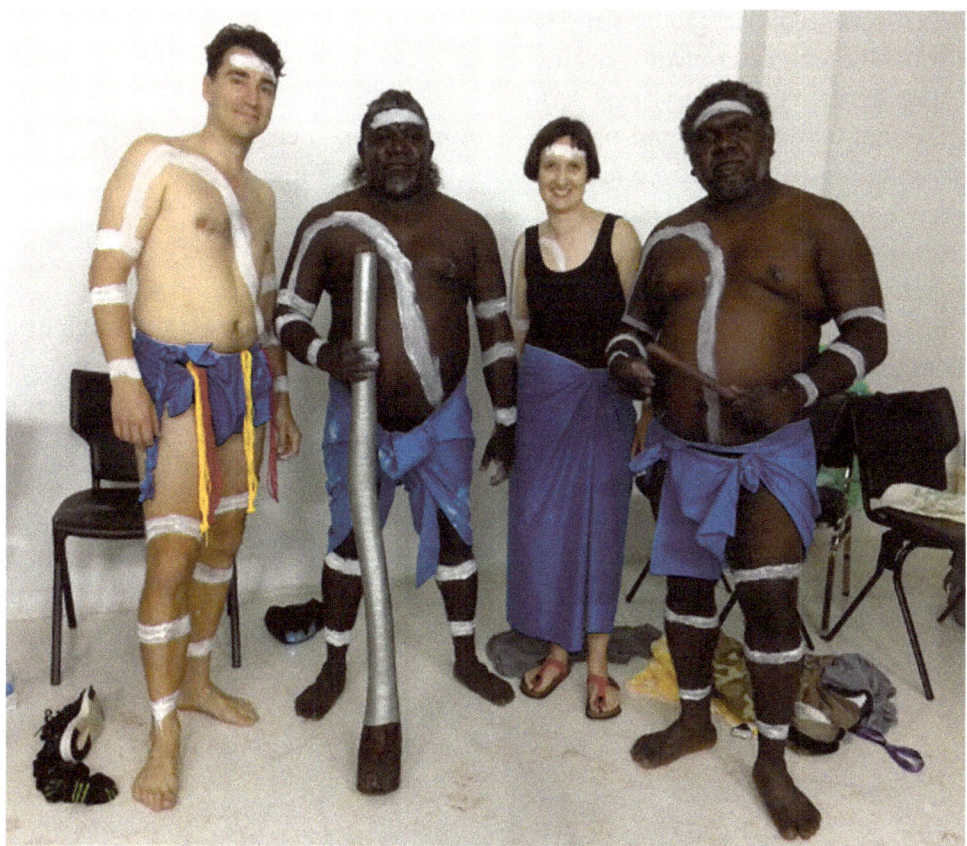

Figure 18.5 Reuben Brown, Rupert Manmurulu, Isabel O'Keeffe and Renfred Manmurulu prepare to perform *manyardi* for the International Council for Traditional Music World Conference in Bangkok, Thailand, 2019. Photo from Isabel O'Keeffe's private collection, used with permission.

Conclusion: sustaining *manyardi* through continued dialogue

In this chapter we have considered some of the ways that *manyardi* performers follow the *alan* "path" of their Elders and ancestors and lay a path for the next generation, as well as the ways that researchers like Linda Barwick have laid a path for our collaborative research to follow. Barwick's collaborative approach, working "like family" with the Manmurulu family, other *manyardi* ceremony holders and performers, as well as ceremony holders and performers of other Indigenous song traditions, has frequently involved engagement in performance. Her approach has opened dialogues between researchers and practitioners from different cultural backgrounds and helped to set a precedent for dialogues through performance in diverse contexts, including at the Annual Indigenous Music and Dance Symposium. By fostering performance and research relationships, sustaining dialogues between past and present *manyardi* performers and researchers, and working together to enliven *manyardi*, we can make important contributions to the vitality of *manyardi* traditions and to collaborative research on Indigenous Australian song. We echo Jenny Manmurulu's words that it has been "a really good experience working with Linda [Barwick] and Allan [Marett]" and we still "have them in our head" as we continue along the *alan* "path" that they and ceremony holders, like the late David Manmurulu and his family, lay out before us for our ongoing, creative dialogues.

Acknowledgements

The authors thank Linda Barwick for her mentorship, friendship and scholarship; the late David Manmurulu, who contributed his knowledge in the form of conversations and interviews, which are drawn upon for this chapter; and also Fregmonto Stokes for research assistance transcribing interviews and conversations cited in this chapter.

Chapter 19

Singing from the mountains: when things really go right in Indigenous research – a story of creative collaboration and Ngarigu cultural renewal

Jakelin Troy

Introduction

> I've heard that song before, when Eucumbene was being flooded by Snowy Hydro, the women all came together and sang it . . . you have got the rhythm, but you should sing it faster.[1]

> Our hope is that our work might inspire new performances and new creations by Ngarigu people on Country, and thus contribute to the great ongoing dialogue between people and Country. (Troy and Barwick 2020, 103)

During the worldwide catastrophe of the Covid-19 pandemic lockdowns, 2020 to 2022, universities went online, travel ceased, and fieldwork and sitting down with Indigenous communities to undertake collaborations became impossible. But, during this time, I had the chance to think quietly and deeply about my Country. I walked most days on Mount Rogers, behind my house in Ngunawal Country,

---

1 Uncle John Casey, Ngarigo Elder, speaking at an online gathering about renewal of Ngarigu song performance, September 2021.

Canberra, and looked across to my Ngarigu Country, the Snowy Mountains of southern New South Wales. Each day I would paint a small sketch of the landscape, often an image of those distant mountains. This peripatetic practice gave me time to gaze from afar and, from that perspective, observe closely my Country and contemplate how to write more personally about my connection to Country (Troy 2020). I also thought about walking on Mount Rogers with Linda Barwick, my friend and research collaborator, and how on that walk we shared how we each loved the mountains and had such similar desire to care for that Country. At this time, we also began to collaborate on recovering a song from my Country, for my people to perform, "The Song of the Women of the Menero" documented by naturalist John Lhotsky in 1834 (Lhotsky 1834). We published our thinking, proposing: "By claiming Lhotsky's 1834 sheet music publication as a record of Ngarigu creative practice, stemming from the heart of Ngarigu Country, our primary aim is to care for Ngarigu performative culture, honour Ngarigu Country and nurture contemporary Ngarigu creativity (Troy and Barwick 2020, 103).

Here I explore our collaboration on this song and how it has had profound resonance with my Ngarigu community and has helped us to be again "singing from the mountains". I ground my story in the narrative of how Barwick and I brought back into contemporary life this song of my people that was buried in the archive, and which is now affectionately known by my community as "The Snow Song".

In writing about the Ngarigu song project I wish to share my experience of when things really go right in Indigenous research. For me they have really gone right because I, a Ngarigu researcher, have had the chance to have a deadly collaboration with Linda Barwick, a non-Indigenous researcher. Deadly is the best way to describe this collaboration because in Aboriginal English it means "great, marvellous, wonderful". "Deadly" came into our lexicon from Indigenous Irish people transported to Australia in huge numbers by the British from the start of their invasion of Aboriginal Countries in 1788 (Troy 1991). The Irish and their immigrant history of Australia is also part of Barwick's and my personal stories. Both of us descend from people who were forced by governments to come to Australia or came chasing the kind of fortune any new invading and colonising exercise offers. The difference is that I am also descended from Ngarigu people. Barwick descends from settler-colonists who are of Indigenous Irish heritage. Our personal stories frame both our friendship and our research collaborations. We both do research, individually and as colleagues, to support Aboriginal communities to continue to perform their unique music and dance. We are now helping my own Ngarigu alpine people of the Snowy Mountains in south-eastern Australia to sing and dance on our Country, our land (Harris, Barwick and Troy 2022a).

19 Singing from the mountains: when things really go right

In her recent seminal work on ethics in linguistics, *Something's Gotta Change: Redefining Collaborative Linguistic Research*, Lesley Woods (2023), Ngiyampaa woman, my friend and fellow linguist, guided researchers in best practice in ethical, community-engaged collaborative research. She challenged researchers to move away from the extractive model that besets the academy where a researcher's personal ambitions overshadow the role of their community colleagues. In researching recent practice in linguistic research Woods has observed:

> many non-Indigenous linguists are working hard to find constructive solutions to help address the issues and concerns of Indigenous people around ethics in linguistic research. There is a genuine desire to see urgent reforms in the linguistic research framework, in ways that would give agency to Indigenous people and to develop genuinely ethical collaborative working relationships. (Woods 2023, 3)

For researchers who are truly engaged with communities in their work, community members are treated as colleagues, not as subjects, and research begins with questions asked by Aboriginal people. Many researchers now aim to support communities. Such researchers create outputs that include non-traditional works including community-focused resources, co-created performances, films, artworks and exhibitions. More people are also including their community colleagues as co-authors in traditional peer-reviewed works, monographs, papers and conference presentations.

This community collaborative approach underpins the research I have been undertaking with my own Ngarigu community with Barwick as my guide in ethnomusicology. We now have a song of our Country that we sing every year to call the snow to come again as the warm time of the year ends and the cold envelops the mountains. The outcomes for my community have been enriching and uplifting:

> The song is now being embraced by Ngarigu of the High Country who see it as an important continuing connection with ancestral practices that are focused on caring for Country. Bringing the song back into Ngarigu cultural practice has been a very moving experience. (Harris, Barwick, and Troy 2022a, 5)

Barwick and I share a deeper purpose in our collaborations; we are exploring our commonalities as people of diaspora displaced and dispossessed. I believe Barwick understands me and my community because her own people have also suffered through invasion and colonisation. As mentioned, my ancestors were not only Ngarigu; some were also from Europe, including Ireland. Many Irish came to

Australia as convict labour co-opted against their will for petty crimes that would barely rate a fine by modern legal standards, or as political prisoners. Barwick is also of this stock and our peoples, Aboriginal and Irish, forged a common heritage. They shared in the development of new culture in Australia, even in the development of the very language that became our national identifier, Australian English, also in the creation of a new language, New South Wales Pidgin, the ancestor of the creole languages now spoken by Aboriginal people (Troy 1991). Ngarigu people have had our music, our language and our cultural heritage adversely impacted by the British invasion and colonisation of our Country. Barwick's Irish Australian family were also divested of their heritage by the British colonial experiment. Are we either of us any better off? Ngarigu people losing our rich culture and now slowly finding our way back, and Irish Australians disembodied of their Irishness: are our experiences so very different? Pat O'Shane shared her thoughts on having both Aboriginal and Irish heritage: "The Irish people I come from were dispossessed, disempowered in the same way my mother's people were dispossessed and disempowered so I've got a fight on both sides, I don't mind, but I choose to fight here".[2]

My collaborations with Barwick and historians Ann McGrath and Laura Rademaker have inspired me to find a new way to write about cultural renewal that is more personal and grounded in my own experiences. (Harris, Barwick and Troy 2022a; McGrath, Rademaker and Troy 2023). Emotional history writing allows me to put myself into my writing (Troy 2023, 42).

> In doing research with me about my people and my Country, Linda came on the journey as my partner in research. Not as an "outsider" but as an "insider", as a friend who could share my grief over what has gone from Ngarigu culture, feeling this same loss of culture from her own people. Linda became an insider to me, a Countrywoman, as we worked to renew the practice of a song of my people and shared our common love for my Snowy Mountains, *Kunama Namadgi* in Ngarigu. Linda collaborated with me to push the boundaries of merging "hard science" with creative practice to bring the song back to my people. Together we applied the core practices of our several disciplines, particularly musicology, linguistics, anthropology, visual arts and history, to consider what might have been the performative practices of Ngarigu people. Having found some answers from these disciplines, we then took these findings a step further, by engaging in speculation and, using our imaginations, asked, "what if?": ". . . to propose creative re-interpretations of the Song's content, with the purpose of incorporating

---

2 O'Shane in Kehoe 2013, 0'18".

19 Singing from the mountains: when things really go right

it within a larger renewal of Ngarigu cultural, performative and linguistic practices. (Troy and Barwick 2020, 87)

I am now very excited about the possibilities of pushing the boundaries of lexicography, the study of words, using what I call "creative lexicography". This new practice is for me a way to breathe life and meaning into old texts that seem unanalysable when using my disciplinary skills alone. It gives me the freedom to find what I know to be plausible and then allows the texts to "speak" to me as I use my imagination and creativity to go beyond what science can tell me and gives me freedom to let my Country also speak to me as part of the process.

This innovative, experimental collaboration has benefited my Ngarigu mob, "mob" being the Aboriginal English word for "community". The research collaboration between Barwick and me, as well as with my mob and other researchers at the universities of Sydney, Melbourne, and California Riverside, and which importantly includes community-based Aboriginal researchers, has given back to my mob a song, a performance and a cultural connection with our snowy environment that is now a key pillar in sustaining us as a mob into the future. Annually we are planning our gathering in the mountains just as our ancestors planned their gatherings for tens of thousands of years. Research is helping us on our long journey of renewing Ngarigu language and cultural practices. Now working on more songs, we bring together science and creative practice to make new meanings and new performances from archival records, community memory and feelings for Country. We use the power of collaborative research as a tool for my community to engage with on our journey back to our traditions after the catastrophe of invasion and colonisation.

In a groundbreaking study of the renewal of song from his own country, the Wangaaypuwan and Wiradjuri Nations of central and western New South Wales, Jesse Hodgetts argued for the importance and need to support community collaborative research to renew Aboriginal song practices:

> Our languages and our songs are our voice. It is how we express ourselves and transfer knowledge. Tragically, Aboriginal people in NSW have significantly lost many languages and songs as a result of colonisation. Although there has been great effort to record and revive Aboriginal Language in NSW through the work of language champions and linguists . . . little has been done to revive the original music styles and characteristics of traditional Aboriginal song in NSW and the cultural knowledge and identity that they hold. (Hodgetts 2022, 3)

In performing our songs on our snowy Country at what is now our annual corroboree, my Ngarigu community is part of a growing movement to continue our performative culture and renew language and cultural practices. Coupled with the study by Hodgetts, I maintain:

> [Aboriginal Australians] are joining so many other Indigenous communities worldwide in this effort to renew language and culture after the suppression of their cultures and languages as a direct result of colonial oppression following the invasion of their lands by foreign powers. (Troy 2023, 40)

Each year since 2021 we, members of my community under the banner of our community organisation Ngarigo Nation Indigenous Corporation, have met at Jindabyne, Dalgety and Thredbo to perform "The Snow Song" to continue our corroboree. Hodgetts exhorted us to keep our corroboree going:

> there are many Aboriginal people who are still composing and performing songs in their language. Our Corroborees in NSW by various Aboriginal cultural groups are examples of continued unbroken traditional cultural practises as well as Language and song revitalisation of what was lost. (Hodgetts 2022, 3–4)

Song has great significance in Aboriginal communities. Grace Koch, writing about song as evidence of connection to Country in Aboriginal land claims and native title claims, highlighted the importance of the connection between song and knowledge of and connection to Country:

> [they] provide evidence of traditional practices that are longstanding . . . Some of these practises serve to maintain the health of the land . . . The wellbeing of estates is ensured by song and ceremony . . . Another way that people look after country is by performing rituals that ensure food and water supplies. (Koch 2013, 29)

For members of the Ngarigo Nation Indigenous Corporation and other Ngarigu from the mountains, the performance of corroboree on Country and calling out to Country to bring the snow each year is our way to continue this embodied practice of engaging human agency with the agency of the environment to ensure that the things that should happen on Country continue to happen. Without the snow, there is no melt and no alpine bogs, rivulets, cascades and rushing rivers, no water to flow into the great riverine system that ultimately feeds the Murray Darling Basin from our High Country, from up at the top, *Kunama Namadgi*. We will continue to perform the rituals that are our responsibility in caring for Country to ensure that it continues to freeze and to melt. For me, performing "The Snow Song" ensures every human and non-human aspect of the environment is healthy and has a future (Harris, Barwick and Troy 2022a, 3). Its appellation, "The Snow Song" arose because that is how Barwick and I have explained the

19 Singing from the mountains: when things really go right

song and its purpose, as a corroboree used by my people to sing out to Country, our ancestral lands, to bring the snow. It is spectacularly successful in having this effect and every time we sing it there are immediately media reports of huge falls of snow and more to come. Cold weather and snow in the south-east of Australia now prompt jovial questions to me from other Aboriginal and non-Aboriginal people alike about whether my mob are responsible for any cold snap.

I propose, again drawing on Barwick's scholarship, that innovating and adapting the performance of this song for the contemporary era is an authentic continuation of music performance that is part of a larger movement across Aboriginal communities throughout Australia. Music and performance in general have not been static across the tens of thousands of years my people have lived and performed in the snow Country. Now, as always, we draw on a "continuity of norms across deep time" (Barwick 2023, 112) revealed to us through our research, including research by performance as we "feel" the song on and off Country. Barwick explains how Aboriginal communities engage with a persistent formula for music while allowing for innovation and creativity:

> The cumulative effects of intergroup sharing, conscious intergroup variegation, combinatorial flexibility, and context-responsive musical innovation across thousands of generations of adaptive performance-based song transmission must lead us to acknowledge that present-day song practice is profoundly different from that of sixty-five thousand years ago. Yet the far-reaching repetition of core themes, narratives, and principles of formulation suggests that their persistence today maybe be indicative of continuity of norms across deep time. Indeed, in contemplating songs and singing practice in relation to deep time, we can begin to apprehend how the flexibility and adaptiveness of human inventiveness interlocks and is entangled with other forms of flexibility and adaptiveness that take place across different orders of timescale. (Barwick 2023, 112)

The renewal of performance of our songs connects my community with our practices over deep time through the "everywhen", a term for synchronicity in our Aboriginal "histories" proposed by Ann McGrath (McGrath, Rademaker and Troy 2023).

My research is also enriched through my collaborations with the Torwali of Swat, North Pakistan. The Torwali are also alpine, mountain people living in the valleys and high pastures of the Hindu Kush, part of the Himalayan range. I have found in this community kindred spirits, mountain people who are striving to preserve their traditions, their songs of the mountains, some of which also call out to the snow. I take comfort in knowing that we are not the only people in the world who have had our musical and performative traditions suppressed and that other people are taking their music into the future, embracing it on social media and sharing it where and when they are able to safely perform. In the personal experience of Mujahid Torwali, my colleague from the Torwali community, the Taliban insurgency of 2008–09 effectively suppressed singing, playing music or dancing publicly, as people feared what the Taliban would do to them; yet some still perform. As part of our Ngarigu song project, Mujahid Torwali has performed with us on Country, singing and dancing with my Elders and community members, sharing his own experiences of keeping performance strong against all odds (Torwali and Troy 2021).

The song of the women of the Monero

Lhotsky's publication "The Song of the Women of the Menero" is in many ways a mysterious text. It was based on a performance that he witnessed performed by women of my Ngarigu community on the banks of the Snowy River near Dalgety in what is now called the Monaro in south-eastern New South Wales. The score of Lhotsky's sheet music is complicated and it was a work created by Lhotsky assisted by his "musical gentlemen" friends who arranged it in parlour music style, favoured at the time, for popular consumption. It became a hybrid piece of music influenced by the musical gentlemen but also remaining true to what Lhotsky seems to have remembered of the performance and was able to reproduce:

> Given the lack of harmonic basis of most Australian Indigenous musics, we may conjecture that . . . not only the piano accompaniment, but also the fitting of the melody itself to the harmonic framework of the parlour music style through introduction of leading notes, passing notes, leaps within phrases and melismatic decorations, are likely, if not certain, additions by Lhotsky's "Musical Gentlemen". Other features, however, remain unidiomatic to the parlour music genre – perhaps due to Lhotsky's insistence on including features he had noted from the original performance. (Troy and Barwick 2020, 97)

It is worth noting Lhotsky was using staff notation for music that did not adhere to Western diatonic conventions, and furthermore, he would have been relatively unfamiliar with the structure of Aboriginal music, and to this he added European musical flourishes designed to appeal to musicians in Sydney, and elsewhere, who would buy the music. The lyrics are as Lhotsky remembered or possibly from notes he made on the spot, now missing. They follow the score and are in an Aboriginal language, most likely Ngarigu. He does not translate the song or offer any comments about its purpose or meaning beyond the title, which attributes it

19 Singing from the mountains: when things really go right

to female singers. At the end of the music there is an epithet that speaks to what Lhotsky saw as the demise of the community of the singers, not a translation of the lyrics (Troy and Barwick 2020).

Analysing the score and understanding and translating the text were inter-related exercises. Knowing the text gave sense to the rhythm and metre of the music. Barwick began by cleaning the music of all the obvious Europeanness and playing it on a synthesiser. She was surprised just how much like music of south-eastern Australia the score sounded, drawing on what is known about these traditions (Troy and Barwick 2020, 96). I still remember the moment I first heard this sound: the sound of a song of my people. A unique song in that it came directly from a period in the early 19th century when my people were still holding corroboree, still carrying out traditional practices halted by invasion of our Country by settler-colonists. I was transfixed and kept playing it, and the sound stuck in my mind. I can still hear that first sound. I always will; it has become part of me, a direct connection to my Ngarigu ancestors. We were confident that the sound was connected to the sounds of my people singing in the past. I was inspired to consider whether the meaning of the text, the lyrics Lhotsky had transcribed, could also be recovered as a record of an Aboriginal language and most specifically something relevant to the people of my Country, our language. I am not alone in my visceral response to hearing the music of my people for the first time. Rachel Perkins wrote about the poignant moment when she shared with her friend Margy Lynch, and her sisters, the sound of Arrente music of their community:

> [the sound of] their mother's voice – alone, high and sweet – stretched across the decades that had passed since her death, to touch them again. She sang the same song as *her* mother. "We are rich," Margy said and she and her sisters tried to hide the tears that flowed. I cried with them . . . (Perkins 2016)

My first place to look for information to help me analyse the text were documents produced by George Augustus Robinson (Robinson 2000). Robinson travelled through my Country in the 1840s and 1850s and documented languages from Victoria to southern New South Wales on the east coast. I have detailed elsewhere the process of analysing the text of the song (Troy and Barwick 2020, 93–96); however here I highlight the importance of the process of ruminating on items in the text and thinking about what people would be doing in late summer, early autumn in my Country when Lhotsky witnessed the song. I let Country guide me in my research. We are people of snow and ice and of the melt. We would be calling for the snow in late March as the autumn begins, because we know that, for our Country to thrive, we must have the snow. At that time of year, the moon has a frosty ring around it, and glows in the dark starry night. Under a full moon on a frosty night in late March, Lhotsky heard my ancestors sing; he sat with them and witnessed the women singing under this full moon, drumming on the possum skin in drums while men were accompanied with their own voices and percussion. Words in the text evoke the idea of snow; if the base form for snow is *ku-*, then other parts of the text suggest calling out. Robinson records *kabatá* "moon". The text began to reveal itself as maybe being a call out to the moon to bring the snow, again and again, bring it for us. A snow increase ceremony song? A call to Country to continue the cycles of freeze and melt that creates and continues the unique alpine biosphere of the Snowy Mountains. The rhythm of the music helped me consider what parts of the text belonged together, the music and the text together make meaning, different from spoken language; sung language in Aboriginal music does not require a single, unambivalent meaning.

Once Barwick and I decided that we had the pitch, rhythm, tone and words, the next step was for us to try out this song with our bodies and to do this together supporting each other to hear and feel this song again. As I flew down to meet Barwick, I was anticipating how it would be to sing this song with my own people. I was nervous because the sounds were very awkward for me; I was looking for guidance from Barwick and from Allan Marett, who could help with how men would have performed with the women, maybe using clapsticks. We also knew that there was probably drumming by the women on possum-skin drums. This was probably a sound that we could reproduce using pillows. First, we sat just singing, then we started singing and drumming. Then Marett accompanied us with clapsticks. We thought about how women perform at corroborees, drawing on Barwick's and Marett's many years of fieldwork attending Aboriginal performances. We decided to walk and dance and sing, to embody the song in our movements. Performing this song while walking around Linda's living room, swinging our hips and singing in this very Aboriginal dance style with Marett on clapsticks transformed the song from an archival document to part of my lived experience. Now I could imagine performing the song with my community. With this experience and knowledge came something that, for me, was giving me the freedom to express myself as a Ngarigu person through song and dance, through performance.

After the few hours we spent together, I flew back to Canberra and the song and the performance stayed with me in my body and mind. Arriving home, I couldn't wait to share it with my mother and my daughter. My mother very much embraced what I was doing and shared in my enthusiasm for this song of our Country and the possibility of bringing back into practice a song of our people. My daughter was less excited by this song, finding the sound unpleasant. My rendition of it didn't speak to her, but the agentive purpose of the song calling for snow did

19 Singing from the mountains: when things really go right

capture her attention, and she was very careful not to be dismissive. It was already beginning to mean something to her, and in her own way she was embracing the performative practices of our people. Musicologist Christopher Small wrote of how we are enculturated to tonal functional harmony and cannot perceive other music: "But although we cannot escape the conditioning which our culture imposes upon us we do not need to remain bewitched by it; the fish can learn to be aware of the water in which he swims" (Small 1996, 8).

So began the long journey of this song back into performance with my Ngarigu community of the High Country. We are the people of the highest area in Australia; we have the highest mountains of the highest Alps. There are other Ngarigu people who also have performative traditions, and who dance and perform, but these people are mostly from the southern area, lower down. They do come into our Country and perform, but this song is not part of their repertoire. This song is part of our High-Country Ngarigu repertoire, restored to us, and we will perform it every year to call the snow.

I am inspired to continue to explore further the range of historical records and community knowledge about my Country to consider how to creatively use the materials to help connect my community to Country through performance. It may even be that we can recover some of our songlines of the snow Country. The word *kunyimá* that Robinson translated as "snow" (Troy and Barwick 2020, 94) is similar to Cooma, a major centre in the Snowies and also part of the name for the top of the Snowies, Kunama Namadgi – known to my community as our name for what is now called Mount Kosciuszko. Cooma is at the beginning of the snowline and beyond Cooma, rising up to the high mountains, Jindabyne – which seems to have the form *djinda* "star" as its root. Jindabyne is where, at night, driving in it looks like you are reaching the stars. The Tinderry Range runs from the Snowy Mountains through to the "star" root. It could be the case that this is part of a snow and star Dreaming. I like to think that Cooma, where the snowline begins, rises up to the place where you first see the stars, and as you get closer, higher up into the mountains, the stars open up in a velvety sky so close that you could reach up and touch them (Troy 2023). "The Snow Song" might even be part of a songline about snow and stars, of the highest part of the Australian continent, about making snow, making stars and the stars being scattered from the mountains along the Tinderry Range towards the western slopes of New South Wales. Stories of stars and the sky and the connection to land stretch across Australia. Most famous is the Seven Sisters Dreaming story, the story of the sisters who fled chased by brothers from the west to the east, a story of the Milky Way. But this is now my further musing inspired by my collaborations with Linda Barwick and with my community as we explore our song traditions and continue to sing from the mountains.

References

Abraham, Otto and Erich M. von Hornbostel. 1909. Vorschläge für die transkription exotischer melodies. *Sammelbände der internationalen musikgesellschaft* 11: 11–25.

Adorno, Theodor W. 1945. A social critique of radio music. *Kenyon review* 7(2): 208–17.

AIATSIS. 2022. The AIATSIS journey. *AIATSIS*. Last updated 8 September 2022. https://aiatsis.gov.au/aiatsis-journey.

AIATSIS. 2002–2003. *Australian Institute of Aboriginal and Torres Strait Islander Studies annual report.* Canberra: AIATSIS.

Albrecht, Paul. 2002. *From mission to church, 1877–2002: Finke River Mission.* Hermannsburg, NT: Finke River Mission.

Ames, Eric. 2003. The sound of evolution. *Modernism/Modernity* 10(2): 297–325.

Appadurai, Arjun. 1994. Commodities and the politics of value. In Susan M. Pearce, ed. *Interpreting objects and collections*, 76–91. London: Routledge.

Apted, Meiki. 2010. Songs from the Inyjalarrku: The use of non-decipherable, non-translatable, non-interpretable language in a set of spirit songs from north-west Arnhem Land, Australia. *Journal of linguistics* 30(1): 93–103.

Apted, Meiki. 2008. Songs from the Inyjalarrku: An investigation of non-translatable spirit song language from north-western Arnhem Land. Honours thesis, University of Melbourne.

Arnott, Kate. 2013. Preserving Asia and the Pacific's cultural traditions [televised news report]. *Australia network news.* Australian Broadcasting Corporation. 28 October. https://www.abc.net.au/news/2013-10-24/an-preserving-asia-and-the-pacific27s-cultural-traditions/5042756.

ARIA. n.d. ARIA chart. https://www.aria.com.au/charts/.

Arora, Payal. 2006. Karaoke for social and cultural change. *Journal of information, communication and ethics in society* 4(3): 121–30.

Arrow, Michelle. 2017. Love is in the air? Love in Australian rock and pop music. In Hsu-Ming Teo, ed. *The popular culture of romantic love in Australia*, 285–318. Melbourne: Australian Scholarly Publishing.

Austlang. 2022. W41: Noongar/Nyoongar. *AIATSIS*. https://collection.aiatsis.gov.au/austlang/language/w41.

Ayonghe, Lum Suzanne and Alphonsius Ategha. 2018. The power of film translation in Cameroon: dubbing or subtitling? *International journal of English language and translation studies* 6(4): 40–8.

Ayre, Margaret and John Mackenzie. 2013. "Unwritten, unsaid, just known": The role of Indigenous knowledge(s) in water planning in Australia. *Local environment* 18(7): 753–768. https://doi.org/10.1080/13549839.2012.665864.

Bailes, Freya and Linda Barwick. 2011. Absolute tempo in multiple performances of Aboriginal songs: Analyzing recordings of Djanba 12 and Djanba 14. *Music Perception* 28(5): 473–90.

Bailes, Freya and Linda Barwick. 2008. Memory for tempo in oral music traditions: Evidence for absolute tempo in Aboriginal ceremonial song? *The 10th International Conference on Music Perception and Cognition* (ICMPC10), 25–29 August 2008, Sapporo, Japan.

Banivanua Mar, Tracey. 2015. Shadowing imperial networks: Indigenous mobility and Australia's Pacific past. *Australian historical studies* 46(3): 340–55.

Barkataki-Ruscheweyh. 2017. *Dancing to the state: Ethnic compulsions of the Tangsa in Assam*. Oxford: Oxford University Press.

Barnecutt, Vicky. 2021. True Echoes: Daniels Ethnographical Expedition to New Guinea, 1904. Blog post, 23 March. *Sound and vision blog*. https://blogs.bl.uk/sound-and-vision/2021/03/true-echoes-daniels-ethnographical-expedition-to-new-guinea-1904.html.

Barney, Katelyn, ed. 2023. *Musical collaboration between Indigenous and non-Indigenous people in Australia: Exchanges in the third space*. New York: Routledge.

Barney, Katelyn S. ed. 2014. *Collaborative ethnomusicology: New approaches to music research between Indigenous and non-Indigenous Australians*. Melbourne: Lyrebird Press.

Barney, Katelyn. 2007. Sending a message: How Indigenous Australian women use contemporary music recording technologies to provide a space for agency, viewpoints and agendas. *World of music* 49(1): 105–24.

Barney, Katelyn S. 2004. Repositioning music analysis: Preparatory thoughts for a case study of Indigenous Australian women's contemporary music. In Michael Ewans, John A. Phillips and Rosalind Halton, eds. *Music research:*

New directions for a new century, 156–65. Buckinghamshire: Cambridge Scholars Press.

Bartleet, Brydie-Leigh and Lukas Pairon. 2021. The social impact of music making. *Musicae scientiae* 25(3): 271–3.

Bartleet, Brydie-Leigh. 2016. The role of love in intercultural arts theory and practice. In Pamela Burnard, Elizabeth Mackinlay and Kimberly Powell, eds. *The Routledge international handbook of intercultural arts research*, 91–101. London: Routledge.

Bartók, Béla. 1981. *The Hungarian folk song*. Edited by Benjamin Suchoff, translated by M.D. Calvocoressi, with annotations by Zoltán Kodály. Albany, NY: State University of New York Press.

Barwick, Linda. 2023. Songs and the Deep Present. In Ann McGrath, Laura Rademaker and Jakelin Troy, eds. *Everywhen: Australia and the language of deep history*, 93–124. Sydney: New South Publishing.

Barwick, Linda. 2018. Performance as frame for pluriculturality. *The Australian Academy of the Humanities 49th Annual Symposium: "Clash of civilisations: Where are we now?"* Sydney: State Library of New South Wales, 16 November.

Barwick, Linda. 2017. Keepsakes and surrogates: Hijacking music technology at Wadeye (northwest Australia). In Thomas Hilder, Henry Stobart and Shzr Ee Tan, eds. *Music, indigeneity, digital media*, 156–75. New York: University of Rochester Press.

Barwick, Linda. 2012. Including music and the temporal arts in language documentation. In Nicholas Thieberger, ed. *The Oxford handbook of linguistic fieldwork*, 166–79. Oxford: Oxford University Press.

Barwick, Linda. 2011. Musical form and style in Murriny Patha *Djanba* songs at Wadeye (Northern Territory, Australia). In Michael Tenzer and John Roeder, eds. *Analytical and cross-cultural studies in world music*, 316–54. New York: Oxford University Press. https://doi.org/10.1093/acprof:oso/9780195384581.003.0009.

Barwick, Linda. 2009. Transcribe! Created by Seventh String Software. *Language documentation and conservation* 3(2): 236–40.

Barwick, Linda. 2005a. Networking digital data on endangered languages of the Asia Pacific region. *International journal of Indigenous research* 1(1): 11–16.

Barwick, Linda. 2005b. Marri Ngarr Lirrga songs: A musicological analysis of song pairs in performance. *Musicology Australia* 28(1): 1–25.

Barwick, Linda. 2005c. A musicologist's wishlist: Some issues, practices and practicalities in musical aspects of language documentation. *Language documentation and description* 3: 53–62.

Barwick, Linda. 2004. Turning it all upside down . . . imagining a distributed digital audiovisual archive. *Literary and linguistic computing* 19(3): 253–63.

Barwick, Linda. 2003. *Jadmi Junba: Public dance songs by Nyalgodi Scotty Martin* [audio CD and booklet]. Sydney: Undercover Music RRR135.

Barwick, Linda. 2002. Tempo bands, metre and rhythmic mode in Marri Ngarr "Church Lirrga" songs. *Australasian music research* 7: 67–83.

Barwick, Linda. 2000a. Recording and CD notes. In Yawulyu Mungamunga. *Dreaming songs of Warumungu women*. Tennant Creek: Festival Records and Papulu Apparr-kari Language and Culture Centre.

Barwick, Linda. 2000b. Song as an Indigenous art. In Sylvia Kleinert and Margo Neale, eds. *The Oxford companion to Aboriginal art and culture*, 328–35. Melbourne: Oxford University Press.

Barwick, Linda. 1999. *Preliminary report on song and language in the Goldfields region*. Kalgoorlie: Goldfields Land Council.

Barwick, Linda. 1995. Unison and "disagreement" in a mixed women's and men's performance from the Ellis Collection, Oodnadatta, 1966. In Linda Barwick, Allan Marett and Guy Tunstill, eds. *The essence of singing and the substance of song: Recent responses to the Aboriginal performing arts and other essays in honour of Catherine Ellis*, 95–105. Oceania Monograph 46. Sydney: Sydney University Press.

Barwick, Linda. 1992. Women as performers and agents of change in the Italian ballad tradition. In Margaret Baker, Giuseppe Bolognese, Antonio Comin and Desmond O'Connor, eds. *Riflessi e riflessioni: Italian reflections*, 189–202. Adelaide: Flinders University of South Australia.

Barwick, Linda. 1991a. Group project on Antikirinya women, 1966–68 expeditions: Secondary documentation. AIATSIS MS 3042. Canberra: Australian Institute of Aboriginal Studies.

Barwick, Linda. 1990. Central Australian women's ritual music: Knowing through analysis versus knowing through performance. *Yearbook for traditional music* 22: 60–79.

Barwick, Linda. 1989. Creative (ir)regularities: The intermeshing of text and melody in performance of Central Australian song. *Australian Aboriginal studies* 1989(1): 12–28.

Barwick, Linda. 1988–1989. Transcription as deflowering: Collection practices in Italy, pre-1939. *Musicology Australia* 11(1): 35–43.

Barwick, Linda. 1987. Vacillating voices: Representations of women in Italian popular song. *Literature and popular culture (Australian journal of cultural studies, special issue)*: 151–61.

References

Barwick, Linda. 1985. Critical perspectives on oral song in performance: The case of "Donna Lombarda". PhD thesis, Flinders University of South Australia, Adelaide.

Barwick, Linda, Bruce Birch and Nick Evans. 2007. Iwaidja Jurtbirrk songs: Bringing language and music together. *Australian Aboriginal studies* 2007(2): 6–34.

Barwick, Linda, Bruce Birch, Nicholas Evans, Murray Garde, Allan Marett, Isabel O'Keeffe and Ruth Singer. 2011–2015. The West Arnhem Land song project metadata database, http://elar.soas.ac.uk/deposit/0155.

Barwick, Linda, Bruce Birch and Joy Williams. 2005. *Jurtbirrk love songs of Northwestern Arnhem Land* [audio CD and booklet]. Batchelor: Batchelor Institute Press.

Barwick, Linda, Nicholas Evans, Murray Garde, Allan Marett and Isabel O'Keeffe. 2012. Western Arnhem Land Song Project data collection. https://elar.soas.ac.uk/Collection/MPI1013566.

Barwick, Linda, Jennifer Green and Petronella Vaarzon-Morel, eds. 2020. *Archival returns: Central Australia and beyond*. Sydney: Sydney University Press.

Barwick, Linda, Jennifer Green, Petronella Vaarzon-Morel and Katya Zissermann. 2019. Conundrums and consequences: Doing archival returns in Australia. In Linda Barwick, Jennifer Green and Petronella Vaarzon-Morel, eds. *Archival returns: Central Australia and beyond*, 1–27. *Language documentation and conservation special publication* 18. Honolulu and Sydney: University of Hawai'i Press and Sydney University Press. https://hdl.handle.net/10125/64640.

Barwick, Linda, Mary Laughren and Myfany Turpin. 2013. Sustaining women's Yawulyu/Awelye: Some practitioners' and learners' perspectives. *Musicology Australia* 35(2): 191–220.

Barwick, Linda and Allan Marett. 2011. Aural snapshots of musical life: The 1948 recordings. In Martin Thomas and Margo Neale, eds. *Exploring the legacy of the 1948 Arnhem Land Expedition,* 355–75. Canberra: ANU Press.

Barwick, Linda and Allan Marett. 2003. Aboriginal Traditions. In John Whiteoak and Aline Scott–Maxwell, eds. *Currency companion to music and dance in Australia*, 26–27. Sydney: Currency Press.

Barwick, Linda and Allan Marett. 1995. Introduction. In Linda Barwick, Allan Marett and Guy Tunstill, eds. *The essence of singing and the substance of song. Recent responses to the Aboriginal performing arts and other essays in honour of Catherine Ellis*, 1–10. Oceania Monograph 46. Sydney: University of Sydney.

Barwick, Linda, Allan Marett, Joe Blythe and Michael Walsh. 2007. Arriving, digging, performing, returning: An exercise in rich interpretation of a Djanba song text in the sound archive of the Wadeye Knowledge Centre, Northern Territory of Australia. *Research in anthropology and linguistics* 1: 6–34.

Barwick, Linda, Allan Marett and Ngarinyin Aboriginal Corporation. 1998–1999. Ceremonial and non-ceremonial music from the Kimberleys. AIATSIS BARWICK-MARETT-NGAR_01 (A016982-A016986; A017089-A017110).

Barwick, Linda, Allan Marett, Michael Walsh, Joe Blythe, Nick Reid and Lysbeth Ford. 2009. *Wadeye song database.* Sydney: University of Sydney.

Barwick, Linda, Allan Marett, Michael Walsh, Nicholas Reid and Lysbeth Ford. 2005. Communities of interest: Issues in establishing a digital resource on Murrinh-patha song at Wadeye (Port Keats), NT. *Literary and linguistic computing* 20(4): 383–97.

Barwick, Linda, Isabel O'Keeffe and Ruth Singer. 2013. Dilemmas in interpretation: Contemporary perspectives on Berndt's Goulburn Island song documentation. In John Stanton, ed. *Little paintings, Big stories. Gossip songs of Western Arnhem Land,* 46–71. Perth: Berndt Museum of Anthropology.

Barwick, Linda and Nick Thieberger. 2018. Unlocking the archives. In Nicholas Ostler, Vera Ferreira and Chris Mosely, eds. *FEL XXI Alcanena 2017: Communities in control*, 135–139. Hungerford, UK: Foundation for Endangered Languages.

Barwick, Linda and Nick Thieberger. 2006a. Cybraries in paradise: New technologies and ethnographic repositories. In Cushla Kapitzke and Bertram C. Bruce, eds. *Libr@ries: Changing information space and practice*, 133–49. Mahwah: Lawrence Erlbaum Associates.

Barwick, Linda and Nick Thieberger, eds. 2006b. *Sustainable data from digital fieldwork*. Sydney: Sydney University Press.

Barwick, Linda and Joseph Toltz. 2017. Quantifying the ineffable? The University of Sydney's 2014 guidelines for non-traditional research outputs. In Robert Burke and Andrys Onsman, eds. *Perspectives on artistic research in music,* 67–77. Lanham, MD: Lexington Books.

Barwick, Linda and Myfany Turpin. 2016. Central Australian women's traditional songs: Keeping Yawulyu/Awelye strong. In Huib Schippers and Catherine Grant, eds. *Sustainable futures for music cultures: An ecological perspective*, 111–44. New York: Oxford University Press.

Bayard, Samuel P. 1950. Prolegomena to a study of the principal melodic families of British-American folk-song. *Journal of American folklore* 63: 1–44.

Beagrie, Neil, and John Houghton. 2014. *The value and impact of data sharing and curation: A synthesis of three recent studies of UK research data centres*. Report. Bristol: Jisc. http://repository.jisc.ac.uk/5568/.

References

Beagrie, Neil and John Houghton. 2013. *The value and impact of the Archaeology Data Service: A study and methods for enhancing sustainability.* Salisbury, UK: Charles Beagrie Ltd.

Becker, Alton and Judith Becker. 1979. A grammar of the musical genre "Srepegan". *Journal of music theory* 23(1): 1–44.

Becker, Judith. 1986. Is Western art music superior? *Musical Quarterly* 72: 341–59.

Bell, Diane. 1988. Aboriginal women and the recognition of customary law in Australia. In B.W. Morse and G.R. Woodman, eds. *Indigenous law and the state*, 297–314. Berlin: De Gruyter Mouton.

Bell, Jeanie. 2013. Language attitudes and language revival/survival. *Journal of multilingual and multicultural development* 34(4): 399–410.

Bell, Joshua A., Kimberley Christen and Mark Turin. 2013. Introduction: After the return. *Museum anthropology review* 7(1–2): 1–21.

Bendrups, Dan. 2015. Sound recordings and cultural heritage: The Fonck Museum, the Felbermayer Collection, and its relevance to contemporary Easter Island culture. *International journal of heritage studies* 21(2): 166–76.

Bennett, Lou. 2023. Black fulla, White fulla: Can there be a truly balanced collaboration? In Katelyn Barney, ed. *Musical collaboration between Indigenous and non-Indigenous people in Australia: Exchanges in the third space*, 9–22. New York: Routledge.

Bennett, Lou. 2019. The need for truthing in language rematriation. Faculty of Fine Arts and Music, University of Melbourne. Blog post, 29 October. https://finearts-music.unimelb.edu.au/about-us/news/lou-bennett2.

Berez-Kroeker, Andrea L., Lauren Gawne, Barbara F. Kelly, Tyler Heston, Susan Kung, Gary Holton et al. 2018. Reproducible research in linguistics: A position statement on data citation and attribution in our field. *Linguistics* 56(1): 1–18.

Bernard, H. Russell. 1992. Preserving language diversity. *Human organization* 51(1): 82–9.

Berndt, Ronald Murray. 1976. *Love songs of Arnhem Land*. Melbourne: Nelson.

Berndt, Ronald Murray and Catherine Helen Berndt. 1951. *Sexual behaviour in western Arnhem Land*. New York: Viking Fund.

Bernède, Franck. 1997. Music and identity among Maharjan farmers: The Dhimay Senegu of Kathmandu. *European bulletin of Himalayan research* 12–13: 21–56.

Berson, Josh. 2014. The dialectal tribe and the doctrine of continuity. *Comparative Studies in society and history* 56(2): 381–418.

Biddle, Jennifer. 2019. Milpirri: Activating the at-risk. In D. Kahn, ed. *Energies in the arts*, 251–371. Cambridge, MA: MIT Press.

Bininj Kunwok Regional Language and Culture Centre. n.d. *Buninj Kunwok: kunwok dja mankaree kadberre – our language, our culture*. https://bininjkunwok.org.au.

Birch, Bruce and Archie Brown. 2006. *Nginji Mamurrng*. DVD. Minjilang, NT: Iwaidja Inyman.

Birch, Eugenie. 2016. A midterm report: Will Habitat III make a difference to the world's urban development? *Journal of the American Planning Association* 82(4): 398–411.

Bird, Douglas W., Rebecca Bliege Bird, Brian F. Codding and David W. Zeanah. 2019. Variability in the organization and size of hunter-gatherer groups: Foragers do not live in small-scale societies. *Journal of human evolution* 131: 96–108.

Bishop, Laura E. and Werner Goebl. 2018. Performers and an active audience: Movement in music production and perception. *Jahrbuch musikpsychologie* 28: 1–17.

Blacking, John. 1971. Deep and surface structures in Venda music. *Yearbook of the International Folk Music Council* 3: 91–108.

Blacking, John. 1976. *How musical is man?* London: Faber & Faber.

Blanatji, David, Tjoli Laiwangka and Tom Yorkdjanki. 1976. *Songs of Bamyili*. Mosman, NSW: Aboriginal Artists Agency.

Blum, Stephen. 1992. Analysis of musical style. In Helen Myers, ed. *Ethnomusicology – an introduction*, 165–218. New York: W.W. Norton.

Bohlman, Philip. 2011. Translating Herder translating: Cultural translation and the making of modernity. In Jane F. Fulcher, ed. *The Oxford handbook of the new cultural history of music*, 501–22. Oxford: Oxford University Press.

Bohlman, Philip V. 2003. Music and culture; historiographies of disjuncture, ethnographies of displacement. In Martin Clayton, Trevor Herbert and Richard Middleton, eds. *The cultural study of music: A critical introduction*, 28–40. London: Routledge.

Bohlman, Philip, and Carol Pegg. 2001. Ethnomusicology. *Grove music online. Oxford music online.* Oxford University Press.

Bolisani, E. and Bratianu, C. 2018. *Emergent knowledge strategies: Strategic thinking in knowledge management*. Cham: Springer.

Boretz, Benjamin. 1969. Meta-variations: Studies in the foundations of musical thought. *Perspectives of new music* 8(1): 1–74.

References

Borgerhoff Mulder, Monique, Samuel Bowles, Tom Hertz, Adrian Bell, Jan Beise, Greg Clark et al. 2009. Intergenerational wealth transmission and the dynamics of inequality in small-scale societies. *Science* 326(5953), 682–8.

Born, Georgina, and Andrew Barry. 2018. Music, mediation theories and actor-network theory. *Contemporary music review* 37(5–6), 443–87.

Boro, Krishna. 2017. A grammar of Hakhun Tangsa. PhD thesis, University of Oregon.

Bracknell, Clint. 2023. A third, brave space for Indigenous language. In Katelyn Barney, ed. *Musical collaboration between Indigenous and non-Indigenous people in Australia: Exchanges in the third space*, 23–42. New York: Routledge.

Bracknell, Clint. 2024. Songman? Considering virtuosity and Noongar song revitalisation. In Louise Devenish and Cat Hope, eds. *Contemporary musical virtuosities*, 39–55. London: Routledge.

Bracknell, Clint. 2020a. Rebuilding as research: Noongar song, language and ways of knowing. *Journal of Australian studies* 44(2): 210–23.

Bracknell, Clint. 2020b. The emotional business of Noongar song. *Journal of Australian studies* 44(2): 140–53.

Bracknell, Clint. 2019a. Connecting Indigenous song archives to kin, Country and language. *Journal of colonialism and colonial history* 20(2). https://doi.org/10.1353/cch.2019.0016.

Bracknell, Clint. 2019b. Identity, Language and Collaboration in Indigenous Music. In Lawrence Bamblett, Fred Myers and Tim Rowse, eds. *The difference identity makes: Indigenous cultural capital in Australian cultural fields*, 99–123. Canberra, ACT: Aboriginal Studies Press.

Bracknell, Clint. 2017a. Conceptualizing Noongar song. *Yearbook for traditional music* 49: 93–113.

Bracknell, Clint. 2017b. Maaya waab (play with sound): Song language and spoken language in the south-west of Western Australia. In Jim Wafer and Myfany Turpin, eds. *Recirculating songs: Revitalising the singing practices of Indigenous Australia*, 45–57. Canberra: Australian National University.

Bracknell, Clint. 2015a. Natj Waalanginy (what singing?): Nyungar song from the south-west of Western Australia. PhD thesis, University of Western Australia, Perth.

Bracknell, Clint. 2015b. "Say you're a Nyungarmusicologist": Indigenous research and endangered song. *Musicology Australia* 37(2): 199–217.

Bracknell, Clint and Linda Barwick. 2021. The fringe or the heart of things? Aboriginal and Torres Strait Islander musics in Australian music institutions. *Musicology Australia* 42(3): 70–84.

Bracknell, Clint, Brenda Gifford, Aaron Wyatt and Deborah Cheetham. 2019. What Indigenous music in tertiary institutions could be. Panel discussion. Monash Music and Performance, Monash University. https://vimeo.com/426115078.

Bracknell, Clint, Pierre Horwitz, Trevor Ryan and Jonathan W. Marshall. 2021. Performing kayepa dordok living waters in Noongar boodjar, south-western Australia. *River research and applications* 37(8): 404–11.

Bracknell, Clint, and Casey Kickett. 2017. Inside out: An Indigenous community radio response to incarceration in Western Australia. *ab-Original: Journal of Indigenous studies and First Nations' and First Peoples' cultures* 1(1): 81–98. https://doi.org/10.5325/aboriginal.1.1.0081.

Bracknell, Clint and Kim Scott. 2020. Ever-widening circles: Consolidating and enhancing Wirlomin Noongar archival material in the community. In Linda Barwick, Jennifer Green and Petronella Vaarzon-Morel, eds. *Archival returns: Central Australia and beyond*, 325–38. *Language documentation and conservation special publication* 18. Honolulu and Sydney: University of Hawai'i Press and Sydney University Press. https://hdl.handle.net/10125/64640.

Breen, Gavan. 2001. The wonders of Arandic phonology. In Jane Simpson, David Nash, Mary Laughren, Peter Austin and Barry Alpher, eds. *Forty years on: Ken Hale and Australian languages*, 45–69. Pacific Linguistics Series. Canberra: Australian National University.

Breen, Marcus, ed. 1987. *Missing in action*. Melbourne: Verbal Graphics.

Brenzinger, Matthias, Akira Yamamoto, Noriko Aikawa, Dmitri Koundiouba, Anahit Minasyan, Arienne Dwyer et al. 2003. *Language vitality and endangerment*. UNESCO Expert Meeting on Safeguarding Endangered Languages. https://unesdoc.unesco.org/ark:/48223/pf0000183699.

Britannica, The Editors of the Encyclopedia. n.d. Alfred Cort Haddon. *Encyclopedia Britannica*. https://www.britannica.com/biography/Alfred-Cort-Haddon.

Bronson, Bertrand. 1969. Toward the comparative analysis of British American folk tunes. *Journal of American folklore* 72(284): 165–91.

Bronson, Bertrand. 1959–72. *The traditional tunes of the Child Ballads*. Princeton: Princeton University Press.

Brown, Kevin. 2015. *Karaoke idols: Popular music and the performance of identity*. Chicago: Intellect Books.

Brown, Reuben. 2017. A different mode of exchange: The mamurrng ceremony of western Arnhem Land. In Don Niles, Kirsty Gillespie and Sally Treloyn, eds. *A distinctive voice in the Antipodes: Essays in honour of Stephen A. Wild*, 41–72. Canberra: Australian National University Press.

Brown, Reuben. 2016. Following footsteps: The Kun-Borrk/Manyardi song tradition and its role in western Arnhem Land society. PhD thesis, University of Sydney. https://ses.library.usyd.edu.au/handle/2123/15671.

Brown, Reuben and Nicholas Evans. 2017. Songs that keep ancestral languages alive: A Marrku songset from Western Arnhem Land. In Jim Wafer and Myfany Turpin, eds. *Recirculating songs: Revitalising the singing practices of Indigenous Australia*. 287–300. Canberra: Australian National University.

Brown, Reuben, David Manmurulu, Jenny Manmurulu, Isabel O'Keeffe and Ruth Singer. 2017. Maintaining song traditions and languages together at Warruwi (western Arnhem Land). In Jim Wafer and Myfany Turpin, eds. *Recirculating songs: Revitalising the singing practices of Indigenous Australia*, 268–286. Canberra: Australian National University.

Brown, Reuben, Rupert Manmurulu, David Manmurulu, Jenny Manmurulu and Isabel O'Keeffe. 2018. Dialogues with the archives: Arrarkpi responses to recordings as part of the living song tradition of manyardi. *Preservation, digital technology and culture* 47(3): 102–14.

Brown, Reuben and Sally Treloyn. 2017. Relational returns: Relationships and the repatriation of legacy song recordings in Australia. *University of Melbourne collections* 20: 50–61.

Budrikis, Amy and Clint Bracknell. 2022. Indigenous online creative responses to the COVID-19 pandemic lockdown in Western Australia. *Preservation, digital technology and culture* 51(2): 63–73.

Byrne, David. 2012. *How music works*. San Francisco: McSweeneys.

Cambridge Anthropological Expedition to Torres Strait, 1898. n.d. *True Echoes*. https://www.true-echoes.com/1898-torres-strait-and-new-guinea/.

Campbell, April, Margaret Carew, Jennifer Green and Ben Foley. 2021 [2013]. Arrernte. *Iltyem-iltyem – Australian Indigenous sign languages*. https://iltyemiltyem.com/search/?post_types=arrernte&_sft_category=actions.

Campbell, April, Clarrie Long, Jennifer Green and Margaret Carew. 2016. *Mer Angenty-warn alhem. travelling to Angenty Country*. Batchelor, NT: Batchelor Institute Press.

Campbell, Genevieve. 2023. *The old songs are always new: Singing traditions of the Tiwi Islands*. Sydney: Sydney University Press.

Campbell, Genevieve. 2017. Singing with the ancestors: Musical conversations with archived ethnographic recordings. In Jim Wafer and Myfany Turpin, eds. *Recirculating songs: Revitalising the singing practices of Indigenous Australia*, 301–17. Canberra: Asia-Pacific Linguistics, Australian National University.

Campbell, Genevieve. 2014. Song as artefact: The reclaiming of song recordings empowering Indigenous stakeholders – and the recordings themselves. In

Amanda Harris, ed. *Circulating cultures: Exchanges of Australian Indigenous music, dance and media*, 101–127. Canberra: ANU Press.

Campbell, Genevieve. 2013. Ngarukuruwala-we sing: The songs of the Tiwi Islands, Northern Australia. PhD thesis, University of Sydney.

Campbell, Genevieve. 2012. Ngariwanajirri, the Tiwi "Strong Kids Song": Using repatriated song recordings in a contemporary music project. *Yearbook for traditional music* 44: 1–23.

Campbell, Genevieve, Jacinta Tipungwuti, Amanda Harris and Matt Poll. 2022. Animating cultural heritage knowledge through songs: Museums, archives, consultation and Tiwi music. In Amanda Harris, Linda Barwick and Jakelin Troy, eds. *Music, dance and the archive*, 55–77. Sydney: Sydney University Press.

Castles, John. 2016. Tjungaringanyi: Aboriginal rock (1971–91). In Philip Hayward, ed. *Sound alliances: Indigenous peoples, cultural politics, and popular music in the Pacific*, 11–25. London: Bloomsbury Publishing.

Chambers, Anne, Keith S. Chambers, David R. Counts, Dorothy A. Counts, Suzanne Falgout, Nancy Guy et al. 2002. Returning ethnographic materials. In S.R. Jaarsma, ed. *Handle with care: Ownership and control of ethnographic materials*, 211–14. ASAO Monograph Series, no. 20. Pittsburgh: University of Pittsburgh Press.

Chanan, Michael. 1995. *Repeated takes: A short history of recording and its effects on music*. London and New York: Verso.

Chaudhuri, Shuba. 2021. Potentials and challenges of repatriation. *World of music* 10(1): 93–104.

Chiu, Chi-Yue, Michele J. Gelfand, Toshio Yamagishi, Garriy Shteynberg and Ching Wan. 2010. Intersubjective culture: The role of intersubjective perceptions in cross-cultural research. *Perspectives on psychological science* 5(4): 482–93. https://doi.org/10.1177/1745691610375562.

Christen, Kimberley. 2006. Tracking properness: Repackaging culture in a remote Australian town. *Cultural anthropology* 21(3): 416–46.

Christen, Kimberley. 2005. Gone digital: Aboriginal remix and the cultural commons. *International journal of cultural property* 12: 315–45.

Chun, William. 2004. Toronto Asian karaoke and karaoke bars. *Institute for Canadian music newsletter* 2(1): 7–9.

Clark, Ian D. (2006). Land succession and fission in nineteenth-century western Victoria: The case of Knenknenwurrung. *Australian journal of anthropology* 17(1), 1–14.

Clark, Tom. 2006. "I'm Scunthorpe 'til I die": Constructing and (re)negotiating identity through the terrace chant. *Soccer and society* 7(4), 494–507.

Clouter, Isobel. 2020. True Echoes project: collaboration – communication – continuation. Blog post, 14 December. *Sound and vision blog.* https://blogs.bl.uk/sound-and-vision/2020/12/introducing-true-echoes.html.

Clunies-Ross, Margaret. 1989. The Aesthetics and Politics of an Arnhem Land Ritual. *Drama Review* 33(4): 107–127. https://doi.org/10.2307/1145970.

Clunies Ross, Margaret, and Stephen A. Wild. 1987. Research into Aboriginal songs: The state of the art. In Margaret Clunies Ross, Tamsin Donaldson and Stephen A. Wild, eds. *Songs of Aboriginal Australia*, 1–13. Sydney: University of Sydney.

Cockington, James. 2001. *Long way to the top: Stories of Australian rock & roll.* Sydney: ABC Books for the Australian Broadcasting Corporation.

Cogan, Robert. 1987. Science, music values and the study of music: Mozart, Tibetan chant, Boulez. *Sonus* 7: 10–28.

Cogan, Robert. 1984. *New images of musical sound.* Cambridge, MA: Harvard University Press.

Cogan, Robert and Pozzi Escot. 1976. *Sonic design.* Englewood Cliffs: Prentice-Hall Inc.

Cooper, Rae, Amanda Coles and Sally Hanna-Osborne. 2017. *Skipping a beat: Assessing the state of gender equality in the Australian music industry.* Report for the Media Entertainment and Arts Alliance. Sydney: University of Sydney. https://ses.library.usyd.edu.au/handle/2123/21257.

Corn, Aaron. 2023. Theorising ganma: Yothu Yindi and third-space musical collaborations. In Katelyn Barney, ed. *Musical collaboration between Indigenous and non-Indigenous people in Australia: Exchanges in the third space*, 43–58. New York: Routledge.

Corn, Aaron. 2010. Land, song, constitution: Exploring expressions of ancestral agency, intercultural diplomacy and family legacy in the music of Yothu Yindi with Mandawuy Yunupiŋu. *Popular music* 29(1): 81–102.

Corn, Aaron. 2002. Burr-Gi Wargugu ngu-Ninya Rrawa: Expressions of ancestry and country in Songs by the Letterstick Band. *Musicology Australia* 25(1): 76–101.

Corn, Aaron. 1999. *Dreamtime wisdom – modern time vision: The Aboriginal acculturation of popular music in Arnhem Land, Australia.* Casuarina, NT: North Australia Research Unit, Australian National University.

Corn, Aaron with Naparrnga Gumbula. 2007. Budutthun ratja wiyinymirri: Formal flexibility in the Yolngu manikay tradition and the challenge of recording a complete repertoire. *Australian Aboriginal studies* 2007(2): 116–27.

Corti, Louise, Veerle Van den Eynden, Libby Bishop and Matthew Woollard. 2014. *Managing and sharing research data: A guide to good practice.* London: Sage Publications.

Cross, Ian. 2015. Music, speech and meaning in interaction. In Costantino Maeder and Mark Reybrouck, eds. *Music, analysis, experience: New perspectives in musical semiotics*, 19–30. Leuven, Belgium: Leuven University Press.

Cross, Ian. 2012. Cognitive science and the cultural nature of music. *Topics in cognitive science* 4(4): 668–77.

Cross, Ian. 2009. The evolutionary nature of musical meaning. *Musicae scientiae special issue* 2009–10: 179–200.

Cross, Ian. 2008. Musicality and the human capacity for culture. *Musicae scientiae* 12(1): 147–67.

Cross, Ian. 2007. Music and cognitive evolution. In R. Dunbar and L. Barrett, eds. *The Oxford handbook of evolutionary psychology*, 649–68. Oxford: Oxford University Press.

Cross, Ian. 2005. Music and meaning, ambiguity and evolution. In Dorothy Miell, Raymond MacDonald and David J. Hargreaves, eds. *Musical communication*, 27–43. Oxford: Oxford University Press.

Cross, Ian. 1999. Is music the most important thing we ever did? Music, development and evolution. In Suk Won Yi, ed. *Music, mind and science*, 10–39. Seoul, South Korea: Seoul National University Press.

Curran, Georgia. 2020a. *Sustaining Indigenous songs.* New York: Berghahn.

Curran, Georgia. 2019a. Incorporating archival cultural heritage materials into contemporary Warlpiri women's yawulyu spaces. In Linda Barwick, Jennifer Green and Petronella Vaarzon-Morel, eds. *Archival returns: Central Australia and beyond*, 91–110. *Language documentation and conservation special publication* 18. Honolulu and Sydney: University of Hawai'i Press and Sydney University Press. https://hdl.handle.net/10125/64640.

Curran, Georgia. 2019b. "Waiting for Jardiwanpa": History and mediation in Warlpiri fire ceremonies. *Oceania* 89(1): 20–35.

Curran, Georgia, Linda Barwick, Valerie Napaljarri Martin, Simon Japangardi Fisher and Nicolas Peterson. 2024. Vitality and change in Warlpiri songs and ceremonies. In Georgia Curran, Linda Barwick, Nicolas Peterson, Valerie Napaljarri Martin and Simon Japangardi Fisher, eds. *Vitality and change in Warlpiri songs*, 1–30. Sydney: Sydney University Press.

Curran, Georgia, Linda Barwick, Myfany Turpin, Fiona Walsh and Mary Laughren. 2019. Central Australian Aboriginal songs and biocultural knowledge: Evidence from women's ceremonies relating to edible seeds. *Journal of ethnobiology* 39(3): 354–70.

References

Curran, Georgia, Margaret Carew and Barbara Napanangka Martin. 2019. Representations of Indigenous cultural property in collaborative publishing projects: The Warlpiri women's Yawulyu songbooks. *Journal of intercultural studies* 40(1): 38–84.

Curran, Georgia, Simon Japangardi Fisher and Linda Barwick. 2018. Engaging with archived Warlpiri songs. In Nicholas Ostler, Vera Ferreira and Chris Mosely, eds. *FEL XXI Alcanena 2017: Communities in control: Learning tools and strategies for multilingual endangered language communities. Proceedings of FEL XXI Alcanena 2017*, 167–74. Hungerford, UK: Foundation for Endangered Languages.

Curran, Georgia and Enid Nangala Gallagher. 2023. *Yawulyu Mardukuja-patu-kurlangu:* Relational dynamics of Warlpiri women's song performance. *Journal of intercultural studies* 44(5): 716–33.

Curran, Georgia, Linda Barwick, Valerie Napaljarri Martin, Simon Japangardi Fisher and Nicolas Peterson, eds. 2024. *Vitality and change in Warlpiri songs.* Sydney: Sydney University Press.

Curran, Georgia, Valerie Napaljarri Martin, Simon Japangardi Fisher, Elizabeth Napaljarri Katakarinja, Linda Barwick, Theresa Napurrurla Ross and Mary Laughren. 2024. Archiving documentation of Warlpiri songs and ceremonies on-country at the Warlpiri Media Archive. In Georgia Curran, Linda Barwick, Valerie Napaljarri Martin, Simon Japangardi Fisher, Nicolas Peterson, eds. *Vitality and change in Warlpiri songs*, 31–58. Sydney: Sydney University Press.

Curran, Georgia, Barbara Napanangka Martin and Linda Barwick. 2024. Minamina yawulyu: Musical change from the 1970s through to the 2010s. In Georgia Curran, Linda Barwick, Valerie Napaljarri Martin, Simon Japangardi Fisher, Nicolas Peterson, eds. *Vitality and change in Warlpiri songs*, 107–144. Sydney: Sydney University Press.

Curran, Georgia and Calista Yeoh. 2021. "That is why I am telling this story": Musical analysis as insight into the transmission of knowledge and performance practice of a Wapurtarli song by Warlpiri women from Yuendumu, Central Australia. *Yearbook for traditional music* 53(December): 45–70.

Czepiel, Anna, Lauren K. Fink, Lea T. Fink, Melanie Wald-Fuhrmann, Martin Tröndle and Julia Merrill. 2021. Synchrony in the periphery: Inter-subject correlation of physiological responses during live music concerts. *Scientific Reports* 11(1): 22457.

Degai, Tatiana, David Koester, Jonathan D. Bobaljik and Chikako Ono. 2023. Kŋaloz'a'n Ujeret'i'n Ɖetełkila'n – keepers of the native hearth: The social life of the Itelmen language – documentation and revitalization. In John Ziker,

Vladimir Davydov and Jenanne Ferguson, eds. *The Siberian world*, 64–78. Oxfordshire: Routledge.

Deger, Jennifer. 2016. Thick photography. *Journal of material culture* 21(1): 111–32.

Denoon, Donald. 1990. Strong, Walter Mersh (1873–1946), *Australian dictionary of biography*. Canberra: Australian National University, https://adb.anu.edu.au/biography/strong-walter-mersh-8702/text15229.

Dessauer, Renata. 1928 (1967). *Das Zersingen. Ein Beitrag zur Psychologie des deutschen Volksliedes*. Nendel, Liechtenstein: Klaus Reprint Limited.

Diamond, Beverley. 2015. The doubleness of sound in Canada's Indian Residential Schools. In Victoria Lindsay Levine and Philip V. Bohlman, eds. *This thing called music: Essays in honor of Bruno Nettl*. 267–79. Lanham, MD: Rowman & Littlefield.

Diettrich, Brian. 2019. Returning voices: Repatriation as shared listening experiences. In Frank Gunderson, Robert C. Lancefield and Bret D. Woods, eds. *The Oxford handbook of musical repatriation*, 161–78. Oxford and New York: Oxford University Press.

Diettrich, Brian, Jane Freeman Moulin and Michael Hugh Webb. 2011. *Music in Pacific Island cultures: Experiencing music, expressing culture*. New York: Oxford University Press.

Dimer, Karl. 1989. *Elsewhere fine*. Kalgoorlie, WA: Karl Dimer.

Dixon, R.M.W. 1980. *The languages of Australia*. Cambridge: Cambridge University Press.

Dobson, Veronica. 2007. *Arelhe-kenhe merrethene: Arrernte traditional healing*. Alice Sprints, NT: IAD Press.

Douglas, Wilfred. 1965-1967. Sound recordings collected by Wilf Douglas. Canberra: AIATSIS Audiovisual Archive, tape recording. DOUGLAS_W01.

Drott, Eric A. 2018. Music as a technology of surveillance. *Journal of the Society for American Music* 12(3): 233–67.

Dunbar-Hall, Peter and Chris Gibson. 2004. *Deadly sounds, deadly places: Contemporary Aboriginal music in Australia*. Sydney: UNSW Press.

Dunbar-Hall, Peter and Chris Gibson. 2000. Singing about nations within nations: Geopolitics and identity in Australian Indigenous rock music. *Popular music and society* 24(2): 45–73.

Dussart, Françoise. 2000. *Politics of ritual in an Aboriginal settlement*. Washington, DC: Smithsonian Institution.

Dussart, Françoise. 1997. A body painting in translation. In H. Morphy and M. Banks, eds. *Rethinking visual anthropology*, 186–201. New Haven, CT: Yale University Press.

References

Eck, Kristina. 2022. Nepal in 2021: From bad to worse. *Asian survey* 62(1): 193–200.

Edmundson, Anna. 2022. Searching for origins: Archaeology and the government officers of Papua. In Hilary Howes, Tristen Jones and Matthew Spriggs, eds. *Uncovering Pacific pasts: Histories of archaeology in Oceania*, 325–39. Canberra: ANU Press.

Edmundson, Anna. 2019. For science, salvage, and state: Papua New Guinea's earliest colonial museums. *Journal of Pacific history* 54(1): 96–115.

Efi, Tui Atua Tupua Tamasese Taisi. 2005. Clutter in Indigenous knowledge, research and history: A Samoan perspective. *Social policy journal of New Zealand* 25: 61–9.

Elkin, A.P. 1970 [1938]. *The Australian Aborigines: How to understand them*, 3rd edn. Sydney: Angus & Robertson.

Ellingson, Ter. 1992. Transcription. In Ellen Myers, ed. *Ethnomusicology – an introduction*, 110–52. New York: W.W. Norton & Co.

Elliott, A. Raymond. 2020. A method comparison analysis examining the relationship between linguistic tone, melodic tune, and sung performances of children's songs in Chicahuaxtla Triqui: Findings and implications for documentary linguistics and indigenous language communities. *Language documentation and conservation* 14: 139–87.

Ellis, Catherine. 1997. Understanding the profound structural knowledge of central Australian performers from the perspective of T.G.H. Strehlow. In D. Hugo, ed. *Strehlow Research Centre occasional papers*, vol. 1, 57–78. Alice Springs, NT: Strehlow Research Centre Board.

Ellis, Catherine. 1995. Response: Whose truth. In Linda Barwick, Allan Marett and Guy Tunstill, eds. *The essence of singing and the substance of song: Recent responses to the Aboriginal performing arts and other essays in honour of Catherine Ellis*, 201–6. Oceania Monograph 46. Sydney: University of Sydney.

Ellis, Catherine J. 1994a. Powerful songs: Their placement in Aboriginal thought. In Catherine J. Ellis, ed. *Power-laden Aboriginal songs: Who should control the research?* Special issue of *World of music* 36(1): 3–20.

Ellis, Catherine J., ed. 1994b. *Power-laden Aboriginal songs: Who should control the research?* Special issue of *World of music* 36(1).

Ellis, Catherine J. 1985. *Aboriginal music: Education for living. Cross-cultural experiences from South Australia*. Brisbane: University of Queensland Press.

Ellis, Catherine J. 1984. Time consciousness of Aboriginal performers. In Jamie C. Kassler and Jill Stubington, eds. *Problems and solutions: Occasional essays in musicology, presented to Alice M. Moyle*, 149–85. Sydney: Hale & Iremonger.

Ellis, Catherine J. 1980. Aboriginal music and dance in southern Australia. In Stanley Sadie, ed. *New Grove dictionary of music and musicians*, 722–28. London: Macmillan.

Ellis, Catherine J. 1968. Rhythmic analysis of Aboriginal syllabic songs. *Miscellanea musicologica* 3: 21–49.

Ellis, Catherine and Linda Barwick. 1989a. Time consciousness of Indigenous Australians. In Gerald F. Messner, ed. *Introduction to the performing arts*, 1–27. Geelong: Deakin University.

Ellis, Catherine and Linda Barwick. 1989b. Antikirinya women's song knowledge 1963–1972: Its significance in Antikirinya culture. In Peggy Brock, ed. *Women, rites and sites: Aboriginal women's cultural knowledge,* 21–40. Sydney: Allen and Unwin.

Ellis, Catherine and Linda Barwick. 1988. Analytical data – texts, rhythms and explanations from Inma Ngintaka and related ceremonies under different names. Australian Institute of Aboriginal Studies. MS 2600.

Ellis, Catherine and Linda Barwick. 1987. Musical syntax and the problem of meaning in a Central Australian songline. *Musicology Australia* 10(1): 41–57.

Ellis, Catherine, Linda Barwick and Megan Morais. 1990. Overlapping time structures in a Central Australian women's ceremony. In Peter Austin, R.M.W. Dixon, Tom Dutton and Isobel White, eds. *Language and history: Essays in honour of Luise A. Hercus*, 101–36. C-116. Canberra: Pacific Linguistics, Australian National University.

Ellis, Catherine J., Arthur Ellis, Mona Tur and Antony McCardell. 1978. Classification of sounds in Pitjantjatjara-speaking areas. In Lester R. Hiatt, ed. *Australian Aboriginal concepts*, 68–80. Canberra: Australian Institute of Aboriginal Studies and Humanities Press.

England, Nicholas M. 1964. Symposium on transcription and analysis: A Hukwe song with musical bow. *Ethnomusicology* 8(3): 223–33.

Ericksen, Polly and Ellen Woodley with Georgina Cundill, Walter V. Reid, Luís Vicente, Ciara Raudsepp-Hearne. 2005. Using multiple knowledge systems: Benefits and challenges. *Ecosystems and human well-being* 4: 93–106.

Errington, Joseph. 2001. Colonial linguistics. *Annual review of anthropology* 30: 16–39.

Evans, Nicholas. 2021. Social cognition in Dalabon. In Danielle Barth and Nicholas Evans, eds. *Language documentation and conservation. Special publication no. 12. Social Cognition Parallax Interview Corpus (SCOPIC),* 22–84.

Evans, Nicholas. 2017a. Ngûrrahmalkwonawoniyan: Listening here. *Humanities Australia: Journal of the Australian Academy of the Humanities* 8: 34–44.

Evans, Nicholas. 2017b. Polysynthesis in Dalabon. In Michael Fortescue, Marianne Mithun and Nicholas Evans, eds. *The Oxford handbook of polysynthesis* 759–81. Oxford: Oxford University Press.

Evans, Nicholas. 2009. *Dying words: Endangered languages and what they have to tell us*. Malden, MA: Wiley-Blackwell.

Evans, Nicholas. 2003. *Bininj Gun-wok: A pan-dialectal grammar of Mayali, Kunwinjku and Kune*, 2 vols. Canberra: Pacific Linguistics, Australian National University.

Evans, Nicholas. 1992. Multiple semiotic systems, hyperpolysemy, and the reconstruction of semantic change in Australian languages. In Günter Kellerman and Michael D. Morrissey, eds. *Diachrony within synchrony: Language history and cognition*, 475–508. Frankfurt, Germany: Peter Lang.

Evans, Nicholas, Francesca Merlan and Maggie Tukumba. 2004. *A first dictionary of Dalabon (Ngalkbon)*. Maningrida, NT: Bawinanga Aboriginal Corporation.

Evans, Nicholas and David P. Wilkins. 2000. In the mind's ear: The semantic extensions of perception verbs in Australian languages. *Language* 76(3): 546–92.

Everist, Mark, ed. 1992. *Music before 1600: Models of music analysis*. Oxford: Blackwell Spring.

Falck, Robert and Timothy Rice, eds. 1982. *Cross-cultural perspectives on music (essays in memory of M. Kolinsky)*. Toronto: University of Toronto Press.

Feld, Steven. 2000. A sweet lullaby for "world music". *Public culture* 12(1): 145–71.

Feld, Steven. 1996. Pygmy POP: A geneology of schizophrenic mimesis. *Yearbook for traditional music* 28: 1–35.

Feld, Steven. 1992. Voices of the rainforest: politics of music. *Arena* 99(100): 164–77.

Feld, Steven. 1984. Sound structure as social structure. *Ethnomusicology* 28(3): 383–409.

Ford, Payi Linda, Linda Barwick and Allan Marett. 2014. Mirrwana and Wurrkama: Applying an Indigenous knowledge framework to collaborative research on ceremonies. In Katelyn Barney, ed. *Collaborative ethnomusicology: New approaches to music research between Indigenous and non-Indigenous Australians*, 43–62. Melbourne: Lyrebird Press.

Frith, Simon. 2007. *Taking popular music seriously: Selected essays*. Aldershot, UK: Ashgate.

Furlan, Alberto. 2005. Songs of continuity and change: The reproduction of Aboriginal culture through traditional and popular music. PhD thesis, University of Sydney.

Gaby, Alice and Lesley Woods. 2020. Toward linguistic justice for Indigenous people: A response to Charity Hudley, Mallinson, and Bucholtz. *Language* 96(4): 268–80.

Gallagher, Enid, Coral Napangardi, Peggy Nampijinpa Brown, Georgia Curran and Barbara Napanangka Martin. 2014. *Jardiwanpa yawulyu: Warlpiri women's songs from Yuendumu*. Batchelor, NT: Batchelor Institute Press.

Gallagher, Enid, Coral Napangardi, Dolly Nampijinpa Daniels, Judy Nampijinpa Granites, Lorraine Nungarrayi Granites, Lucky Nampijinpa Langton et al. 2017. *Yurntumu-Wardingki Juju-Ngaliya-Kurlangu Yawulyu: Warlpiri women's songs from Yuendumu*. Batchelor, NT: Batchelor Press.

Garde, Murray. 2005. The language of Kun-Borrk in western Arnhem Land. *Musicology Australia* 28(1): 59–89.

Garma Forum on Indigenous Performance Research. 2002. Garma Statement on Indigenous Music and Performance. https://msa.org.au/wp-content/uploads/2021/08/NRPIPA-Garma-Statement-2002.pdf.

Gellner, David N. and Rajendra Pradhan. 1995. Urban peasants: The Maharjan (Jyāpu) of Kathmandu and Lalitpur. In David N. Gellner and Declan Quigley, eds. *Contested hierarchies: A collaborative ethnography of caste among the Newars of the Kathmandu Valley, Nepal*, 158–85. Oxford: Oxford University Press.

Gibson, Jason. 2020. *Ceremony men: Making ethnography and the return of the Strehlow collection*. New York: SUNY Press.

Gibson, Jason, Shaun Angeles and Joel Liddle. 2019. Deciphering Arrernte archives: The intermingling of textual and living knowledge. In Linda Barwick, Jennifer Green and Petronella Vaarzon-Morel, eds. *Archival returns: Central Australia and beyond*, 29–45. *Language documentation and conservation special publication* 18. Honolulu and Sydney: University of Hawai'i Press and Sydney University Press. https://hdl.handle.net/10125/64640.

Gillespie, Kirsty. 2017. Protecting our shadow: Repatriating ancestral recordings to the Lihir Islands, Papua New Guinea. In Kirsty Gillespie, Sally Treloyn and Don Niles, eds. *A distinctive voice in the Antipodes: Essays in honour of Stephen A. Wild*, 355–74. Canberra: ANU Press.

Gillespie, Kirsty. 2010. *Steep slopes: Music and change in the Highlands of Papua New Guinea*. Canberra: ANU Press.

Gilliland, Anne J. 2017. Networking records in their diaspora: A reconceptualisation of "displaced records" in a postnational world. In James Lowry, ed. *Displaced archives*, 180–95. London: Routledge.

Ginsburg, Faye. 1995a. Mediating culture: Indigenous media, ethnographic film, and the production of identity. In Leslie Devereaux and Roger Hillman, eds. *Fields of vision: Essays in film studies, visual anthropology, and photography*, 256–91. Berkeley: University of California Press.

Ginsburg, Faye. 1995b. The parallax effect: The impact of Aboriginal media on ethnographic film. *Visual anthropology review* 11(2): 64–76.

Ginsburg, Faye. 1991. Indigenous media: Faustian contract or global village? *Cultural anthropology* 6(1): 92–112.

Gioia, Ted. 2015. *Love songs: The hidden history*. New York: Oxford University Press.

Giroux, Monique. 2021. Music research and the sound archive: A meditation on ethnomusicological engagement with collection-oriented research and re(p)(m)atriation. *Yearbook for traditional music* 53: 103–26.

Glass, Amee and Dorothy Hackett. 2003. *Ngaanyatjarra and Ngaatjatjarra to English dictionary*. Alice Springs, NT: IAD Press.

Goddard, Cliff. 1992. *Pitjantjatjara/Yankunytjatjara to English dictionary*. Alice Springs, NT: IAD Press.

Godt, Irving. 2005. Music: A practical definition. *Musical times*, 146(1890), 83–8.

Goody, Jack. 1987. *The interface between the written and the oral*. Cambridge, UK: Cambridge University Press.

Gordon Childe, Vere. 1956. *Society and knowledge*. London: George Allen & Unwin.

Goulding, Dorothy, Brian Steels and Craig McGarty, C. 2015. A cross-cultural research experience: Developing an appropriate methodology that respectfully incorporates both Indigenous and non-Indigenous knowledge systems. *Ethnic and racial studies* 39: 1–19.

Gourlay, Kenneth A. 1984. The non-universality of music and the universality of non-music. *World of music* 26(2): 25–36.

Government of Nepal. 2014. National Population and Housing Census 2011, social characteristics tables (caste/ethnicity, mother tongue and second language) Kathmandu: Central Bureau of Statistics. https://cbs.gov.np/wp-content/upLoads/2018/12/Volume05Part02.pdf.

Grandin, Ingemar. 1997. Raga Basanta. *European bulletin of Himalayan research* 12–13: 57–80.

Grandin, Ingemar. 1989. *Music and media in local life: Music practice in a Newar neighbourhood in Nepal*. Lingköping, Sweden: Lingköping University.

Grant, Catherine. 2015a. "They don't die, they're killed": The thorny rhetoric around music endangerment and music sustainability. *Sound matters: The SEM blog*, 15 April. https://soundmattersthesemblog.com/2015/04/15/they-dont-die-theyre-killed-the-thorny-rhetoric-around-music-endangerment-and-music-sustainability/.

Grant, Catherine. 2015b. Endangered musical heritage as a wicked problem. *International journal of heritage studies* 21(7): 629–41.

Grant, Catherine. 2014. *Music endangerment: How language maintenance can help*. New York: Oxford University Press.

Gray, Peter R.A. 2020. Aboriginal claimants: Adjusting legal procedures to accommodate linguistic and cultural issues in hearings in Aboriginal land rights claims in the Northern Territory of Australia. In Malcolm Coulthard, Alison May and Rui Sousa-Silva, eds. *The Routledge handbook of forensic linguistics*, 2nd edn, 329–43. Abingdon, UK: Routledge.

Gray, Peter R.A. 2000. *The Kenbi (Cox Peninsula) Land Claim No. 37: Report and recommendation of the former Aboriginal Land Commissioner, Justice Gray, to the Minister for Aboriginal and Torres Strait Islander Affairs and to the Administrator of the Northern Territory, Darwin, Northern Territory*. Office of the Aboriginal Land Commissioner. Canberra: Parliament of the Commonwealth of Australia.

Gray, Robin R.R. 2019. Repatriation and decolonization: Thoughts on ownership, access and control. In Frank Gunderson, Robert C. Lancefield and Bret D. Woods, eds. *The Oxford handbook of musical repatriation*, 723–38. Oxford and New York: Oxford University Press.

Green, Jennifer. 2014. *Drawn from the ground: Sound, sign and inscription in central Australian sand stories. Language culture and cognition*. Cambridge, UK: Cambridge University Press.

Green, Jennifer. 2010. *Central and Eastern Anmatyerr to English dictionary*. Alice Springs, NT: IAD Press.

Green, Jennifer. 2003. *Central Anmatyerr picture dictionary*. Alice Springs, NT: IAD Press.

Green, Jennifer, David Blackman and David Moore. 2019. *Alyawarr to English dictionary*, 2nd edn. Alice Springs, NT: IAD Press.

Green, Jennifer and Myfany Turpin. 2013. If you go down to the soak today: Symbolism and structure in an Arandic children's story. *Anthropological linguistics* 55(4): 358–94.

Greene, Paul. 2003a. Ordering a sacred terrain: Melodic pathways of Himalayan flute pilgrimage. *Ethnomusicology* 47(2): 205–227.

Greene, Paul. 2003b. Sounding the body in Buddhist Nepal. *World of music* 44(2): 93–114.

Gummow, Margaret. 1994. The power of the past in the present: Singers and songs from northern New South Wales. *World of music* 36(1): 42–51.

Gummow, Margaret. 1992. Aboriginal songs from the Bundjalung and Gidabal areas of south-eastern Australia. PhD thesis, University of Sydney. https://ses.library.usyd.edu.au/handle/2123/7249.

Gunderson, Frank D., Robert Lancefield and Bret D. Woods, eds. 2018. *The Oxford handbook of musical repatriation*. Oxford and New York: Oxford University Press.

Gutschow, Niels. 1982. *Stadtraum und Ritual der newarische Städte im Kathmandu-Tal*. Stuttgart, Germany: Kohlhammer.

Guy, Nancy. 2002. Trafficking in Taiwan Aboriginal voices. In Sjoerd R. Jaarsma, ed. *Handle with care: Ownership and control of ethnographic materials*, 195–209. Pittsburgh, PA: University of Pittsburgh Press.

Haddon, Alfred C. 1900. Studies in the anthropogeography of British New Guinea. *Geographical journal* 16(3): 265–91.

Haebich, Anna. 2008. *Spinning the dream: Assimilation in Australia 1950–1970*. Fremantle, WA: Fremantle Press.

Haebich, Anna. 2000. *Broken circles: Fragmenting Indigenous families 1800–2000*. Fremantle, WA: Fremantle Arts Centre Press.

Haebich, Anna and Jim Morrison. 2014. From karaoke to Noongaroke: A healing combination of past and present. *Griffith Review* 44: 1–8.

Hale, Kenneth. 1986. Notes on world view and semantic categories: Some Warlpiri examples. In P. Myusken and H.J. van Riemsdijk, eds. *Features and projections*, 233–54. Dordrecht, the Netherlands: Foris.

Hale, Kenneth. 1984. Remarks on creativity in Aboriginal verse. In Jamie C. Kassler and Jill Stubington, eds. *Problems and solutions: Occasional essays in musicology presented to Alice M. Moyle*, 254–62. Sydney: Hale & Iremonger.

Hanlon, David. 2003. Beyond the English method of tattooing: Decentering the practice of history in Oceania. *Contemporary Pacific* 15(1): 19–40.

Harris, Amanda. 2020. *Representing Australian Aboriginal music and dance 1930–1970*. New York: Bloomsbury Academic.

Harris, Amanda, Linda Barwick and Jakelin Troy. 2022a. Embodied culture and the limits of the archive. In Amanda Harris, Linda Barwick and Jakelin Troy, eds. *Music, dance and the archive*, 1–14. Sydney: Sydney University Press.

Harris, Amanda, Linda Barwick and Jakelin Troy, eds. 2022b. *Music, dance and the archive*. Sydney: Sydney University Press.

Harris, Amanda, Steven Gagau, Jodie Kell, Nick Thieberger and Nick Ward. 2019. Making meaning of historical Papua New Guinea recordings: Collaborations of speaker communities and the archive. *International journal of digital curation* 14(1): 136–49.

Harris, Robin P. 2017. *Storytelling in Siberia: the Olonkho Epic in a changing world*. Chicago: University of Illinois Press.

Hartley, Leslie P. 1953. *The Go-Between*. London: Penguin Books.

Haviland, John B. 2007. Master speakers, master gesturers: A string quartet master class. In Susan D. Duncan, Justine Cassell and Elena T. Levy, eds. *Gesture and the dynamic dimensions of language: Essays in honor of David McNeill*, 147–72. Special edition of *Gesture studies*.

Hawkins, Sarah. 2014. Situational influences on rhythmicity in speech, music, and their interaction. *Philosophical transactions of the Royal Society of London B: Biological sciences* 369(1658).

Hawkins, Sarah, Ian Cross and Richard Ogden. 2013. Communicative interaction in spontaneous music and speech. In Martin Orwin, Christine Howes and Ruth Kempson, eds. *Music, language and interaction*, 285–329. London: College Publications.

Hayes, Rebekah. 2021. True Echoes: Cambridge Expedition to the Torres Strait Islands, 1898. Blog post, 29 June. *True echoes*. https://blogs.bl.uk/sound-and-vision/2021/06/index.html.

Hayes-Bohme, Thomasina, Rowena Cooper, Jodie Cooper and Charlynna Roy. 2003. Love song. PARADISEC. https://catalog.paradisec.org.au/collections/JK1/items/LS001.

Hayward, Philip, ed. 1992. *From pop to punk to postmodernism: Popular music and Australian culture from the 1960s to the 1990s*. Sydney: Allen & Unwin.

He, Lulu, Jonathan C. Aitchison, Karen Hussey, Yongping Wei and Alex Lo. Accumulation of vulnerabilities in the aftermath of the 2015 Nepal earthquake: Household displacement, livelihood changes and recovery challenges. *International journal of disaster risk reduction* 31: 68–75. https://doi.org/10.1016/j.ijdrr.2018.04.017.

Heinitz, Wilhelm. 1921. Eine lexikalische Ordnung für die vergleichende Betrachtung von Melodien. *Archiv für musikwissenschaft* 3: 274–80.

Henderson, John and Veronica Dobson. 2020. *Eastern and Central Arrernte to English dictionary*, rev. edn. Alice Springs, NT: IAD Press.

Henley, Paul. 2020. *Beyond observation: A history of authorship in ethnographic film*. Manchester, UK: Manchester University Press.

Henrich, Joseph, Steven J. Heine and Ara Norenzayan. 2010. The weirdest people in the world? *Behavioral and brain sciences* 33(2–3): 61–83.

Henry, James. 2019. Dr Linda Barwick [interview]. *Who's your mob*. Podcast. https://soundcloud.com/whosyourmob/linda-barwick-mix.

Hercus, Luise. 1965–70. Songs, Mythology, Language Elicitation and Oral History. Audiotapes. AIATSIS Audiovisual Archive, HERCUS_L16.

Canberra, ACT: Australian Institute of Aboriginal and Torres Strait Islander Studies.

Hercus, Luise and Grace Koch. 1997. Old yet always new: Song traditions of southern central Australia. *Strehlow Research Centre occasional papers* 1: 83–106.

Hiatt, Lester and Betty Hiatt. 1966. *Songs from Arnhem Land*. Canberra: Australian Institute of Aboriginal Studies.

Hilder, Thomas R. 2015. *Sámi musical performance and the politics of indigeneity in northern Europe*. London: Rowman & Littlefield.

Hill, Barry. 2002. *Broken song: T.G.H. Strehlow and Aboriginal possession*. Sydney: Random House.

Hill, R.P. 1995. Blackfellas and whitefellas: Aboriginal land rights, the Mabo decision, and the meaning of land. *Human rights quarterly*, 17, 303–322.

Himmelmann, Nikolaus P. 1998. Documentary and descriptive linguistics. *Linguistics* 36: 161–95.

Hinkson, Melinda. 2002. New media projects at Yuendumu: Inter-cultural engagement and self-determination in an era of accelerated globalization. *Continuum: Journal of media and cultural studies* 16(2): 201–20.

Hirst, William, Jeremy K. Yamashiro and Alin Coman. 2018. Collective memory from a psychological perspective. *Trends in cognitive sciences*, 22(5), 438–451.

Hodgetts, Jesse. 2022. Guthi Girrmara "stirring up songs": Reawakening archived Wangaaypuwan and Wiradjuri songs to inform our culture, language and identity. PhD thesis, the Wollatuka Institute, University of Wollongong, NSW.

Hoffmann, Anette. 2021. Close listening: Approaches to research on colonial sound archives. In Michael Bull and Marcel Cobussen, eds. *The Bloomsbury handbook of sonic methodologies*, 529–42. New York: Bloomsbury Academic.

Holbrook, Morris B. 2000. The millennial consumer in the texts of our times: Experience and entertainment. *Journal of macromarketing* 20(2): 178–92.

Holton, Gary. 2012. Language archives: They're not just for linguists any more. In Frank Seifart, Geoffrey Haig, Nikolaus P. Himmelmann, Dagmar Jung, Anna Margetts and Paul Trilsbeek, eds. *Potentials of language documentation: Methods, analyses, and utilization*, 111–17. Honolulu: University of Hawai'i Press.

Homan, Shane and Tony Mitchell. 2008. *Sounds of then, sounds of now: Popular music in Australia*. Hobart: ACYS Publishing, University of Tasmania.

hooks, bell. 2000. *All about love: New visions*. London: Women's Press.

Hopkins, Pandora. 1966. The purposes of transcription. *Ethnomusicology* 10(3): 310–17.

Hornbostel, Erich M. von. 1912. Melodie und Skala. *Jahrbuch des musikbibliothek Peter für 1912* 19: 11–23.

Hou, Yingying, Bei Song, Yinying Hu, Yafeng Pan and Yi Hu. 2020. The averaged inter-brain coherence between the audience and a violinist predicts the popularity of violin performance. *NeuroImage* 211: 116655.

Howard, Keith. 2016. SamulNori: Sustaining an emerging Korean percussion tradition. In Huib Schippers and Catherine Grant, eds. *Sustainable futures for music cultures: An ecological perspective*, 239–70. New York: Oxford University Press.

Hunter, David. 1986. Music copyright in Britain to 1800. *Music and letters* 67(3): 269–282.

Hunter, Ruby. 2000. True lovers. Song. Bloodlines Music. https://open.spotify.com/track/7eIcU28NKj2gaVUFf8Umr9?si=04aaec7058de43ea.

Hutt, Michael, Mark Liechty and Stefanie Lotter, eds. 2021. *Epicentre to aftermath: Rebuilding and remembering in the wake of Nepal's earthquakes*. Cambridge, UK: Cambridge University Press.

IMC-UNESCO. 1952. *Notation of folk music*. Recommendations of the Committee of Experts. Convened by the International Archives of Folk Music, Geneva, 4–9 July 1949 and Paris, 12–15 December 1950.

Indigenous Hip Hop Projects. 2015. *NAAJA "Ripple Effect" Maningrida*. https://www.youtube.com/watch?v=eUgMo7cR0TQ.

Ingarden, Roman. 1961. Aesthetic experience and aesthetic object. *Philosophy and phenomenological research* 21(3): 289–313.

Ingram, Catherine. 2019. "Each in our own village": Creating sustainable interactions between custodian communities and archives. In Frank Gunderson, Robert C. Lancefield and Bret D. Woods, eds. *The Oxford handbook of musical repatriation*, 303–18. Oxford & New York: Oxford University Press.

Ingram, Catherine with Meifang Wu, Pinxian Wu, Xuegui Wu and Zhicheng Wu. 2011. Discussing fair use of minority music recordings from the mountains of southwestern China. In *Sustainable data from digital research: Humanities perspectives on digital scholarship*. Proceedings of the conference held at the University of Melbourne, 12–14 December 2011. http://hdl.handle.net/2123/7933.

Jairazbhoy, Nazir A. 1977a. Electronic aids to aural transcription. *Ethnomusicology* 21(2): 275–282.

Jairazbhoy, Nazir A. 1977b. The objective and subjective view in music transcription. *Ethnomusicology* 21(2): 263–74.

Jakobson, Roman. 1966. Grammatical parallelism and its Russian facet. *Language* 42(2): 399–429.

Jensen, K. 2016. Prosociality. *Current biology* 26(16): R748–R752.

Jolivétte, Andrew J. 2021. American Indian leadership: On Indigenous geographies of gender and thrivance. In Maggie Walter, Tahu Kukutai, Angela A. Gonzales and Robert Henry, eds. *The Oxford handbook of Indigenous sociology*. Online edn, Oxford Academic. https://academic.oup.com/edited-volume/37077/chapter/349583588.

Kaberry, Phyllis. 1939. *Aboriginal woman sacred and profane*. New York: Blakiston.

Kaiser, Thomas. 2008. The Songs of the Nagas. In Michael Oppitz, Thomas Kaiser and Alban von Stockhausen eds. *Naga identities: Changing local cultures in the northeast of India*, 233–51. Gand: Snoeck.

Karki, Jeevan, Steve Matthewman and Jesse Grayman. 2022. From goods to goats: Examining post-disaster livelihood recovery in the aftermath of the Nepal earthquake 2015. *Natural hazards* 114(3). https://doi.org/10.1007/s11069-022-05543-0.

Kartomi, Margaret. 1988. "Forty thousand years": Koori music and Australian music education. *Australian journal of music education* 1: 11–28.

Kauffmann, H. E. and M. Schneider. 1960. Lieder aus den Naga-Bergen (Assam) [Songs of the Naga Hills]. In *Les Coloques de Wégimont III – 1956, Ethnomusicologie II*, 187–295. Liège: Université de Liège.

Kehoe, Paula. 2013. *An Dubh ina Gheal: Assimilation* [film clip] https://www.youtube.com/watch?v=HWwoX34IZbk.

Kell, Jodie. 2022. True Echoes: Noise reduction on early sound recording. Blog post, 31 August. *Endangered language and cultures*. https://www.paradisec.org.au/blog/2022/08/true-echoes-noise-reduction-on-early-sound-recording.

Kell, Jodie and Steven Gagau (producers). 2023. PNG: Central Province music and dance. *Toksave – Culture talks: The PARADISEC podcast series*. Season 4, episode 14, 12 November. https://www.paradisec.org.au/toksave-podcast/.

Kell, Jodie and Cindy Jinmarabynana. 2022. Mermaids and cockle shells: Innovation and tradition in the "Diyama" song of Arnhem Land. In Amanda Harris, Linda Barwick and Jakelin Troy, eds. *Music, dance and the archive*, 157–83. Sydney: Sydney University Press.

Kell, Jodie, Rachel DjÍbbama Thomas, Rona Lawrence and Marita Wilton. 2020. Ngarra-Ngúddjeya Ngúrra-Mala: Expressions of identity in the songs of the Ripple Effect Band. *Musicology Australia* 42(2): 161–78.

Kelley, Jamey. 2016. Everyone's magical and everyone's important: karaoke community and identity in an American gay bar. *International journal of community music* 9(2): 135–55.

Kendon, Adam. 2013 [1988]. *Sign languages of Aboriginal Australia: Cultural, semiotic and communicative perspectives.* Cambridge: Cambridge University Press.

Keogh, Ray. 1990. Nurlu songs of the west Kimberleys. PhD thesis, University of Sydney. http://hdl.handle.net/2123/1318.

Keogh, Ray. 1995. Process models for the analysis of Nurlu songs from the western Kimberleys. In Linda Barwick, Allan Marett and Guy Tunstill, eds. *The essence of singing and the substance of song: Recent responses to the Aboriginal performing arts and other essays in honour of Catherine Ellis*, 39–52. Oceania Monograph vol. 46. Sydney: University of Sydney.

Kerman, Joseph. 1985. *Contemplating music.* Cambridge, MA: Harvard University Press.

Kerman, Joseph. 1980. How we got into analysis, and how to get out. *Critical inquiry* 7(2): 314–31.

Kila, Roge and Gulea Kila in conversation with Amanda Harris and Steven Gagau. 2020, Sydney Conservatorium of Music, 17 October. Archived at PARADISEC. https://dx.doi.org/10.26278/K553-JS43 and https://dx.doi.org/10.26278/PVMV-X262.

Knijnik, Jorge. 2018. Imagining a multicultural community in an everyday football carnival: Chants, identity and social resistance on Western Sydney terraces. *International review for the sociology of sport* 53(4): 471–89.

Knopoff, Steven. 2003. What is music analysis? Problems and prospects for understanding Aboriginal songs and performance. *Australian Aboriginal studies* 2003(1): 39–51.

Knopoff, Steven. 1992. Yuta Manikay: Juxtaposition of ancestral and contemporary elements in the performance of Yolngu clan songs. *Yearbook for traditional music* 24: 138–53.

Koch, Grace. 2019. "We want our voices back": Ethical dilemmas in the repatriation of recordings. In Frank Gunderson, Robert C. Lancefield and Bret D. Woods, eds. *The Oxford handbook of musical repatriation*, 195–214. Oxford and New York: Oxford University Press.

Koch, Grace. 2013. *We have the song, so we have the land: Song and ceremony as proof of ownership in Aboriginal and Torres Strait Islander land claims.* AIATSIS Discussion Paper, no. 33, July 2013. Canberra: AIATSIS Research Publications.

Kolinski, Mieczyslaw. 1982. Reiteration quotients: A cross-cultural comparison. *Ethnomusicology* 26(1): 85–90.

Korde, Shirish. 1985. Applications of contemporary notation to ethnomusicological analysis. *Studies in music* 19: 114–32.

Kral, Inge and Elizabeth Marrkilyi Ellis. 2020. *In the time of their lives: Communication and social interaction in the Western Desert of Australia*. Perth: UWA Publishing.

Kytö, Meri. 2011. "We are the rebellious voice of the terraces, we are Çarşı": Constructing a football supporter group through sound. *Soccer and society* 12(1): 77–93.

Lach, Robert. 1925. Das Konstruktionsprinzip der Wiederholung in Musik. *Sitzungs der akademie der wissenschaften.*

Lamb, Lara and Christopher Lee. 2023. *Repatriation, exchange, and colonial legacies in the Gulf of Papua: Moving pictures*. Cham, Switzerland: Springer International Publishing.

Lancefield, Robert C. [1998] 2019. Musical traces' retraceable paths: The repatriation of recorded sound. In Frank Gunderson, Robert C. Lancefield and Bret D. Woods, eds. *The Oxford handbook of musical repatriation*, 1–22. Oxford and New York: Oxford University Press.

Landau, Carolyn and Janet Topp Fargion. 2012. We're all archivists now: Towards a more equitable ethnomusicology. *Ethnomusicology forum* 12(2): 125–140.

Lander, Ned and Rachel Perkins. 1993. *Jardiwarnpa: A Warlbiri Fire Ceremony* (film). Sydney: Film Australia.

Langton, Marcia. 1993. *"Well, I heard it on the radio and I saw it on the television . . .": An essay for the Australia Film Commission on the politics and aesthetics of filmmaking by and about Aboriginal people and things*. Sydney: Australian Film Commission.

Language matters with Bob Holman. 2014. Film. Produced by David Grubin Productions Inc. and Pacific Islanders in Communications.

LaRue, Jan. 1970. *Guidelines for style analysis*. New York: W.W. Norton.

Latif, Nida, Adriano Barbosa, Eric Vatikiotis-Bateson, Monica Castelhano and Kevin Munhall. 2014. Movement coordination during conversation. *PLOS ONE* 9(8): e105036.

Laughren, Mary. 1988. Towards a lexical representation of Warlpiri verbs. In Wendy Wilkins, ed. *Thematic relations*, 215–242. San Diego, CA: Academic Press.

Laughren, Mary, Georgia Curran, Myfany Turpin and Nicolas Peterson. 2016. Women's Yawulyu songs as evidence of connections to and knowledge of land: The Jardiwanpa. In Peter K. Austin, Harold Koch and Jane Simpson, eds. *Language, land and song*, 419–450. London: EL Publishing.

Laughren, Mary, Kenneth Hale, Jeannie Egan Nungarrayi, Marlurrku Paddy Patrick Jangala, Robert Hoogenraad, David Nash and Jane Simpson. 2023. *Warlpiri to English encyclopedic dictionary*. Canberra: Aboriginal Studies Press.

Lee, Mitchell. 2018. Self and the city: Social identity and ritual at New York City Football Club. *Journal of contemporary ethnography* 47(3): 367–95.

Letterstick Band. 2004a. *Diyama*. Alice Springs: CAAMA.

Letterstick Band. 2004b. Gama Jin-ngardipa (Broken Love). Song. CAAMA music. https://open.spotify.com/track/79BpOqduw33Ko1aX9UKKIi?si=1268929e1c1241ed.

Levin, Theodore with Valentina Süzükei. 2006. *Where rivers and mountains sing: sound, music, and nomadism in Tuva and beyond*. Bloomington, Indiana: Indiana University Press.

Levy, Robert I. 1992. *Mesocosm: Hinduism and the organization of a traditional Newar city in Nepal*, 2nd edn. Delhi: Motilal Banarsidass.

Lewincamp, Barbara and Julie Faulkner. 2003. A keyhole to the collection: The AIATSIS Library Digitisation Pilot Program. *Australian library journal* 52(3): 239–245. https://doi.org/10.1080/00049670.2003.10721551.

Lewis, Tony. 2018. *Becoming a garamut player in Baluan, Papua New Guinea: Musical analysis as a pathway to learning*. London: Routledge. https://doi.org/10.4324/9781315406503.

Lhotsky, John. 1834. *A song of the women of the Menero tribe near the Australian Alps: Arranged with the assistance of several musical gentlemen for the voice and pianoforte, most humbly inscribed as the first specimen of Australian music to Her Most Gracious Majesty Adelaide, Queen of Great Britain and Hanover, by Dr J. Lhotsky, Colonist N.S. Wales*. Sydney.

Lomax, Alan. 1968. *Folk song style and culture: A staff report on cantometrics*. Washington, DC: American Association for the Advancement of Science.

Lum, Casey Man Kong. 1996. *In search of a voice: Karaoke and the construction of identity in Chinese America*. Mahwah: Laurence Erlbaum Associates, Inc.

Lundström, Håkan and Jan-Olof Svantesson. 2022. *In the borderland between song and speech: Vocal expressions in oral cultures*. Cheshire, UK: Lund University Press/Manchester University Press.

Luo, Changqing and Shihui Huang. 2022. Stridulatory sound production and acoustic signals of the longhorn beetle *Batocera lineolata* (Coleoptera: Cerambycidae). *Bioacoustics* 31(2): 148–59.

Lydon, Jane. 2010. Return: The photographic archive and technologies of Indigenous memory. *Photographies* 3(2): 173–87.

Mackinlay, Elizabeth. 1998. For our mother's song we sing: Yanyuwa women performers and composers. Unpublished PhD thesis, University of Adelaide.

Maddock, Kenneth. 1981. Warlpiri land tenure: A test case in legal anthropology. *Oceania* 52(2): 85–102.

Magowan, Fiona. 2007. *Melodies of mourning: Music and emotion in Northern Australia*. Oxford: James Currey Publishers.

Maharjan, Śrījana. 2014. *Bhajan mye munā saphū (Collection of devotional songs)*. Lalitpur, Nepal: author.

Majid, Asifa, ed. 2007. *Field manual* vol. 10. Nijmegen, Netherlands: Max Planck Institute for Psycholinguistics.

Malinowski, Bronislaw. 1923. The problem of meaning in primitive languages. In Charles Ogden and Ivor Richards, eds. *The meaning of meaning: A study of the influence of language upon thought and of the science of symbolism*, 296–336. London: Routledge.

Mānandhar, Triratna. 2015. *Hā̃de: dāphāyā mhasīkā va myeyā svaralipi [Introduction to dāphā and notation of songs]*. Kathmandu, Nepal: author.

Marett, Allan. 2010. Vanishing songs: How musical extinctions threaten the planet. *Ethnomusicology Forum* 19(2): 249–62.

Marett, Allan. 2005. *Songs, dreamings and ghosts: The Wangga of north Australia*. Middletown, CT: Wesleyan University Press.

Marett, Allan. 2001. Australia, Aboriginal Music, Northern Australia. *The New Grove dictionary of music and musicians*, 2nd edn, vol. 2, 193–202. London and New York: Macmillan.

Marett, Allan. 2000. Ghostly voices: Some observations on song-creation, ceremony and being in north western Australia. *Oceania* 71(1): 18–29.

Marett, Allan. 1998. Northern Australia. In Adrienne Kaeppler and J. Wainwright Love, eds. *Encyclopedia of world music, Oceania* 9: 418–27. New York: Garland Publishing.

Marett, Allan and Linda Barwick. 2007. Musical and linguistic perspectives on Aboriginal song. *Australian Aboriginal studies* 2007(2): 1–5.

Marett, Allan, and Linda Barwick. 2003. Endangered songs and endangered languages. In Joe Blythe and R. McKenna Brown, eds. *Maintaining the links: Language, identity and the land*, 144–51. UK: Foundation for Endangered Languages.

Marett, Allan and Linda Barwick. 1997. Songs from Belyuen, NT and the Kimberleys. AIATSIS MARETT-BARWICK_01 (A16946-A16981).

Marett, Allan and Linda Barwick. 1997–1999. Daly–Fitzmaurice region song and dance. AIATSIS MARETT-BARWICK_02 (A017038-A017088).

Marett, Allan and Linda Barwick. 1993. Liner notes for *Bunggridj–bunggridj: Wangga songs by Alan Maralung, Northern Australia* [audio CD]. Washington, DC: Smithsonian/Folkways Recordings. https://tinyurl.com/2xhr884f.

Marett, Allan, Linda Barwick, Nicholas Evans and Murray Garde. 2009. Bongolinj-bongolinj and its children: Collaborative research on the language, music and history of a songset from NW Arnhem Land. Seminar, Australian National University.

Marett, Allan, Linda Barwick and Lysbeth Ford. 2016. *Wangga CD Collection* [audio CDs and scholarly notes]. Sydney: Sydney University Press.

Marett, Allan, Linda Barwick and Lysbeth Ford. 2013. *For the sake of a song: Wangga songmen and their repertories.* Sydney: Sydney University Press.

Marett, Allan, Marcia Langton, Joseph Gumbula, Linda Barwick and Aaron Corn. 2006. The National Recording Project for Indigenous Performance in Australia: Year one in review. *The Australia Council – Backing Our Creativity: the National Education and the Arts Symposium 2005.* Sydney: Australia Council for the Arts, 12–14 September.

Marschall, Wolfgang. 2008. On the music of the Naga societies of Northeast India (and Burma). In Michael Oppitz, Thomas Kaiser, Alban von Stockhausen and Marion Wettstein, eds. *Naga identities,* 213–27. Ghent: Snoeck.

Matsui, Toru. 2001. The genesis of karaoke: How the combination of technology and music evolved. In Toru Matsui and S. Hosokawa, eds. *Karaoke around the world,* 31–44. New York: Taylor and Francis.

May, Stephen. 2013. Indigenous immersion education: International developments. *Journal of immersion and content-based language education* 1(1): 34–69.

McAllester, David P. 1954. Enemy way music: A study of social and esthetic values as seen in Navaho music. *Papers of the Peabody Museum of American Archaeology and Ethnology* 41(3). Reports of the Rimrock Project, Values Series no. 3. Cambridge, MA: Harvard University.

McCabe, Tim. 1994–1997. Cliff Humphries' recording of Noongar traditional songs, stories and words. Perth: State Library of Western Australia, tape recording [restricted].

McGrath, Ann, Laura Rademaker and Jakelin Troy, eds. 2023. *Everywhen: Australia and the language of deep history.* Lincoln, NE: University of Nebraska Press and the American Philosophical Society.

McGregor, Russell. 2009. Another nation: Aboriginal activism in the late 1960s and early 1970s. *Australian historical studies* 40(3): 343-60.

McPherson, Laura. 2018. The talking balafon of the Sambla: Grammatical principles and documentary implications. *Anthropological linguistics* 60(3): 255–94.

Megarrity, Lyndon. 2005. Indigenous education in colonial Papua New Guinea: Australian government policy (1945–1975). *History of education review* 34(2): 41–58.

Meier, John. 1906 (1976). *Kunstlieder im Volksmunde: Materialien und Untersuchungen.* Halle: Verlag Max Niemeyer.

Memmott, Paul, Erich Round, Daniel Rosendahl and Sean Ulm. 2016. Fission, fusion and syncretism: Linguistic and environmental changes amongst the Tangkic people of the southern Gulf of Carpentaria, northern Australia. In Jean-Christophe Verstraete and Diane Hafner, eds. *Land and language in Cape York Peninsula and the Gulf Country*, 105–36. Amsterdam: John Benjamins Publishing Company.

Merriam, Alan P. 1964. *The anthropology of music*. Evanston, IL: Northwestern University Press.

Meyer, Julien. 2011. Strategies to document the verbal content that is played on talking musical instruments: Methodologies on the edge of the music-language relation. Presentation at the 2nd International Conference on Language Documentation and Conservation (ICLDC) http://hdl.handle.net/10125/5253.

Michaels, Eric. 1994. *Bad Aboriginal art: Tradition, media and technological horizons*. Minneapolis: University of Minnesota Press.

Minyimak, David and others (composers/performers), Linda Barwick, Bruce Birch, Joy Williams and Sabine Hoeng. 2005. *Jurtbirrk love songs from North Western Arnhem Land*. Batchelor, NT: Batchelor Institute Press.

Monash University. 2022. *Wunungu Awara: Animating Indigenous knowledges*. https://www.monash.edu/arts/monash-indigenous-studies/wunungu-awara.

Montag, Christian, Haibo Yang and Jon D. Elhai. 2021. On the psychology of TikTok use: A first glimpse from empirical findings. *Frontiers in Public Health* 9: 641–73.

Moore, David. 2012. Alyawarr verb morphology. Master of Arts thesis, University of Western Australia, Perth.

Moore, Michael. 1972. The Seeger Melograph Model C. *Selected reports in ethnomusicology* 2(1): 3–13.

Morais, Megan, Lucy Nampijinpa Martin, Peggy Nampijinpa Martin, Marilyn Nampijinpa Martin, Helen Napurrurla Morton, Janet Nakamarra Long et al. In press. *Yawulyu Art and song in Warlpiri women's ceremony*. Canberra: Aboriginal Studies Press.

Morey, Stephen. 2019. The Tangsa-Nocte languages: An introduction. In Scott DeLancey and Linda Konnerth, eds. *Verb agreement in languages of the Eastern Himalayan region*, a special issue of *Himalayan linguistics* 18(1): 134–40.

Morey, Stephen and Jürgen Schöpf. 2019. The language of ritual in Tangsa – The Wihu Kuh Song. In Martin Gaenszle and Michael Witzel, eds. *Ritual speech in the Himalayas: Oral texts and their contents* (Harvard Oriental Series 93): 149–85. Cambridge, MA: Harvard University Press.

Morrison, Kyle J. 2022. Flow-state in Noongar performance. Master's thesis, Edith Cowan University, Perth.

Moyle, Alice. 14 November 1986. Letter to Ray Keogh. Held at AIATSIS, Canberra, MS3501/1/129/18.

Moyle, Alice. 1983. A note on early sound recordings in the AIAS archive. *Australian Aboriginal studies* 1983(2): 79–80.

Moyle, Richard. 2019. The banning of Samoa's repatriated Mau songs. In Frank Gunderson, Robert C. Lancefield and Bret D. Woods, eds. *The Oxford handbook of musical repatriation*, 491–502. Oxford and New York: Oxford University Press.

Moyse-Faurie, Claire. 2014. Du crayon au numérique: 35 ans d'enquêtes linguistiques en Kanaky. In V. Fillol and P.-Y. Le Meur, eds. *Terrains océaniens: Enjeux et méthodes L'enquête de terrain*, 24ème colloque, 139–58. Paris: Corail, L'Harmattan.

Murray, Neil. 2014. Cry when we're gone. In Ryan Christian, ed. *The best music writing under the Australian sun*, 181–194. Melbourne: Hardie Grant Books.

Myers, Fred. 1986. *Pintupi Country, Pintupi self: Sentiment, place and politics among Western Desert Aborigines*. Canberra: Australian Institute of Aboriginal Studies.

Myers, Helen. 2019. Ethnomusicology: III post-1945 developments. In *Grove music online. Oxford music online*. Oxford University Press.

Napurrurla, Fanny Walker, Linda Barwick and Mary Laughren, with contributions from Sarah Holmes Napangardi, Jessie Simpson Napangardi, Judith Robertson Napangardi and Theresa Ross Napurrurla. 2024. Expert domains of knowledge in Ngurlu *yawulyu* songs from Jipiranpa. In Georgia Curran, Linda Barwick et al., eds. *Vitality and change in Warlpiri songs*, 145–206. Sydney: Sydney University Press.

Nash, David. 1982. An etymological note on kurdungurlu. In J. Heath, F. Merlan and A.Rumsey, eds. *Languages of kinship in Aboriginal Australia*, 141–159. Oceania Linguistic Monographs no. 24. Sydney: Sydney University Press.

National Museum of Australia. 2017 Maino's Gift. Film. https://www.youtube.com/watch?v=uoOW_cm-MRo.

Nattiez, Jean-Jacques. 2007. *Profession musicologue*. Montréal: Les Presses de l'Université de Montréal.

Nattiez, Jean-Jacques. 1993. Simha Arom and the return of analysis to ethnomusicology *Music analysis* 12(2): 241–65.

Nattiez, Jean-Jacques. 1990. *Music and discourse: Toward a semiology of music*. Princeton, NJ: Princeton University Press.

Nettl, Bruno. 2005. *The Study of ethnomusicology: Thirty-one issues and concepts*. Urbana and Chicago: University of Illinois Press, 2005.

Nettl, Bruno. 1989. *Blackfoot musical thought*. Kent, OH: Kent State University Press.

Nettl, Bruno. 1964. *Theory and method in ethnomusicology*. New York: Free Press.

Nettl, Bruno. 1958a. Some linguistic approaches to musical analysis. *Journal of the International Folk Music Council* 10: 37–41.

Nettl, Bruno. 1958b. Transposition as a composition technique in folk and primitive music. *Ethnomusicology* 2(2): 56–66.

Nettl, Bruno with contributions by Carol M. Babiracki, Béla Foltin, Jr, Darioosh Shenassa and Amnon Shiloah. 1987. *The Radif of Persian music, studies of structure and cultural context*. Champaign, IL: Elephant & Cat.

Nettl, Bruno and Ronald Riddle. 1973. Taqsim Nahawand: A study of sixteen performances by Jihad Racy. *Yearbook of the International Folk Music Council* 5: 11–50, https://doi.org/10.2307/767493.

Neuenfeldt, Karl. 2001. Cultural politics and a music recording project: Producing Strike em! Contemporary voices from the Torres Strait. *Journal of intercultural studies* 22(2): 133–45.

Neuenfeldt, Karl. 2007. Notes on the engagement of Indigenous peoples with recording technology and techniques, the recording industry and researchers. *World of music* 49(1): 7–21.

Nicastro, Reno, Simone Stacey and Naomi Wenitong. 2002. Stop Callin' Me. *So fresh: The hits of summer 2003*. [CD] BMG Australia.

Niles, Don. 2018. Find, get, use: Lessons from the repatriation of early Papua New Guinea sound recordings. *Asian European music research* 1: 3–12.

Nketia, J. H. Kwabena. 1982. Interaction through music: The dynamics of music-making in African societies. *International social science journal* 34(4): 639–56.

O'Grady, Geoff N. 1984. The evolution of verbs of singing in Pama-Nyungan. In Jamie C. Kassler and Jill Stubington, eds. *Problems and solutions: Occasional essays in musicology, presented to Alice M. Moyle*, 382–84. Sydney: Hale & Iremonger.

O'Keeffe, Isabel Anne. 2016. Multilingual manyardi/kun-borrk: Manifestations of multilingualism in the classical song traditions of western Arnhem Land. PhD thesis, University of Sydney. http://hdl.handle.net/11343/122873.

O'Keeffe, Isabel. 2010. Kaddikkaddik Ka-Wokdjanganj "Kaddikkaddik spoke": Language and music of the Kun-Barlang Kaddikkaddik songs from western Arnhem Land. *Australian journal of linguistics* 30(1): 35–51.

O'Keeffe, Isabel. 2007. Sung and spoken: An analysis of two different versions of a Kun-barlang love song. *Australian Aboriginal studies* 2007(2): 45–62.

O'Keeffe, Isabel, Linda Barwick, Carolyn Coleman, David Manmurulu, Jenny Manmurulu, Janet Mardbinda et al. 2018. Multiple uses for old and new recordings: Perspectives from the multilingual community of Warruwi. In Nicholas Ostler, Vera Ferreira and Chris Mosely, eds. *FEL XXI Alcanena 2017: Communities in control*, 140–47. Hungerford, UK: Foundation for Endangered Languages.

O'Keeffe, Isabel, Ruth Singer and Caroline Coleman. 2020. The expression of emotions in Kunbarlang and its neighbours in the multilingual context of western and central Arnhem Land. *Pragmatics and cognition: Emotion, body and mind across a continent* 27(1): 83–138.

Odora-Hoppers, C. 2002. Indigenous knowledge and the integration of knowledge systems: Towards a conceptual and methodological framework. In C. Odora Hoppers, ed. *Indigenous knowledge and the integration of knowledge systems: Towards a philosophy of articulation*, 139–43. Claremont, South Africa: New Africa Books.

Office of the Aboriginal Land Commissioner. 1981. *Lander Warlpiri Anmatjirra land claim to Willowra pastoral lease report*. Canberra: Department of Aboriginal Affairs, Australia.

Ogden, Richard and Sarah Hawkins. 2015. Entrainment as a basis for co-ordinated actions in speech. *International Congress for Phonetic Sciences 2015*, Glasgow.

Ong, Jonathan Corpus. 2009. Watching the nation, singing the nation: London-based Filipino migrants' identity constructions in news and karaoke practices. *Communication, culture and critique* 2(2): 160–81.

Or, Elsie M. and Dustin M. Estrellado. 2023. Legacy language materials in the Ernesto Constantino Collection: Challenges and lessons for building a Philippine language archive. *Archive journal* 4 (1–2): 157–207.

Oram, Nigel D. 1979. Ahuia Ova (1877–1951). *Australian dictionary of biography*, National Centre of Biography, Australian National University. https://adb.anu.edu.au/biography/ahuia-ova-4980/text8269.

Oram, Nigel D. 1968. Culture change, economic development and migration among the Hula. *Oceania* 38(4): 243–75.

Oram, Nigel D. 1942–1994. Papers of Nigel Oram. National Library of Australia. https://nla.gov.au/nla.cat-vn1929512.

Ottosson, Åse. 2016. *Making Aboriginal men and music in central Australia*. London: Bloomsbury Academic.

Oxford English Dictionary. 2021. www.oed.com.

Palanchoke, Pushpa. 2021. Understanding dāphā: A sacred music tradition in Nepal. Presentation at the Music, spirituality and wellbeing conference, Boston University. https://youtu.be/v-lIzgOcPV0.

Pandey, Basu Dev, Mya Myat Ngwe Tun, Kishor Pandey, Shyam Prakash Dumre, Khin Mya Nwe, Yogendra Shah et al. 2022. How an outbreak of COVID-19 circulated widely in Nepal: A chronological analysis of the national response to an unprecedented pandemic. *Life* (Basel) 12(7): 1087. https://doi.org/10.3390/life12071087

Parish, S. 1994. *Moral knowing in a Hindu sacred city*. New York: Columbia University Press.

Parsons, Talcott, ed. 1951. *Toward a general theory of action*. London: Oxford University Press.

Pascasio, Luis. 2021. Diasporic performativity in the practice of karaoke. *Ethnic Studies Review* 44(3): 88–113.

Patrick, Steven Wanta Jampijinpa and Jennifer L. Biddle. 2018. Not just ceremony, not just dance, not just idea: Milpirri as hyperrealism, a key word discussion. *Visual anthropology review* 34(1): 27–35.

Pearce, Eiluned, Jacques Launay, Max van Duijn, Anna Rotkirch, Tamas David-Barrett and Robin Dunbar. 2016. Singing together or apart: The effect of competitive and cooperative singing on social bonding within and between sub-groups of a university fraternity. *Psychology of music* 44(6): 1255–73.

Perkins, Rachel. 2016. Songs to live by: The Arrernte Women's Project is preserving vital songs and culture. *The monthly*, July.

Peterson, Nicolas. 2008. Just humming: The consequences of the decline of learning contexts amongst the Warlpiri. In Jean Kommers and Eric Venbrux, eds. *Cultural styles of knowledge transmission: Essays in honour of Ad Borsboom*, 114–18. Amsterdam: Askant.

Pettan, Svanibor, and Jeff Todd Titon, eds. 2015. *The Oxford handbook of applied ethnomusicology*. Oxford and New York: Oxford University Press.

Phillips, Jessica. 2020. Curatorial preface. In Bábbarra Women's Centre, ed. *Jarracharra: Dry season wind*, 45–7. Catalogue accompanying the Jarracharra: Dry Season Wind exhibition at the Australian Embassy, Paris, October 2019 – January 2020.

Picken, Lawrence, with Rembrandt Wolpert, Allan J. Marett, Jonathan Condit, Elizabeth J. Markham and Yōko Mitani. 1981. *Music from the Tang court*, vol. 1. London: Oxford University Press.

Picken, Lawrence, with Rembrandt F. Wolpert, Allan J. Marett, Jonathan Condit, Elizabeth J. Markham, Yōko Mitani and Noël J. Nickson.1985. *Music from the Tang court*, vol. 2. Cambridge: Cambridge University Press.

Pietikäinen, Sari, Riikka Alanen, Hannele Dufva, Paula Kalaja, Sirpa Leppänen and Anne Pitkänen-Huhta. 2008. Languaging in Ultima Thule: multilingualism in the life of a Sami Boy. *International journal of multilingualism* 5(2): 79–99.

Piwowar, Heather A. 2011. Who shares? Who doesn't? Factors associated with openly archiving raw research data. *PLoS ONE* 6(7): e18657. https://doi.org/10.1371/journal.pone.0018657.

Poignant, Roslyn and Axel Poignant. 1996. *Encounter at Nagalarramba*. Canberra: National Library of Australia.

Poirier, Sylvia. 1996. *Les jardins du nomade: Cosmologie, territoire et personne dans le désert occidental australien.* Münster, Germany: Lit Verlag with CRNS (French National Centre for Scientific Research).

Post, Mark W. 2007. A Grammar of Galo. PhD thesis, La Trobe University.

Povinelli, Elizabeth A. 1993. *Labor's lot: The power, history and culture of Aboriginal action.* Chicago, IL: Chicago University Press.

Powers, Harold S. 1980. Language models and musical analysis. *Ethnomusicology*, 24(1): 1–60.

Rabinowitch, Tal-Chen, Ian Cross and Pamela Burnard. 2013. Long-term musical group interaction has a positive influence on empathy in children. *Psychology of music* 41(4): 484–98.

Radhakrishnan, Mahesh. 2019. Musicolinguistic approaches to the study of song. *Performance research* 24(1): 53–7.

Rahn, Jay. 1983. *A theory for all music: Problems and solutions in the analysis of non-Western forms.* Toronto: University of Toronto Press.

Ram, Kalpana. 2011. Being "rasikas": The affective pleasures of music and dance spectatorship and nationhood in Indian middle-class modernity. *Journal of the Royal Anthropological Institute* 17: S159–S175.

Ramnarine, Tina K. 2007. Musical performance in the diaspora: Introduction. *Ethnomusicology forum* 16(1): 1–17.

Ramnarine, Tina K. 2019. Dance, music and cultures of decolonisation in the Indian diaspora: Towards a pluralist reading. *South Asian diaspora* 11(2): 109–25.

Rampton, Ben. 2015. Conviviality and phatic communion? *Multilingual margins: A journal of multilingualism from the periphery* 2(1): 83–91.

Reed, Daniel B. 2019. Reflections on reconnections: When human and archival modes of memory meet. In Frank Gunderson, Robert C. Lancefield and Bret D. Woods, eds. *The Oxford handbook of musical repatriation*, 23–36. New York and Oxford: Oxford University Press.

Reed, Liz. 2002. Songs of Australian Indigenous women. *Australian historical studies* 33(119): 22–37.

Rex, Idena. 1992. Kylie: The making of a star. In Philip Hayward, ed. *From pop to punk to postmodernism: Popular music and Australian culture from the 1960s to the 1990s*, 149–60. Sydney: Allen & Unwin.

Rice, Timothy. 2013. *Ethnomusicology: A very short introduction.* Oxford: Oxford University Press.

Riemann, Hugo. 1893. *Vereinfachte Harmonielehre oder die Lehre von den tonalen Funktionen der Harmonie.* London: Augener.

Ripple Effect Band. 2023. *Loving and Caring* [song]. Self-released. https://open.spotify.com/track/4ju9eqqHYOrrPHi7s8KepA?si=f10a2070a2ec4b5a

Ripple Effect Band. 2018. *Wárrwarra.* Self-released. Spotify Australia. https://open.spotify.com/album/1cWG08mF0YpUvF9pSDZmy6?si=BrzgFYDCRGSTLt-yb9R9Gg. Also available as JK1-WA01 at https://catalog.paradisec.org.au/collections/JK1/items/WA01.

Robinson, George Augustus. 2000. *The papers of George Augustus Robinson, Chief Protector, Port Phillip Aboriginal Protectorate.* ed. Ian D. Clark. Ballarat: Heritage Matters.

Robledo, Juan Pablo, Sarah Hawkins, Carlos Cornejo, Ian Cross, Daniel Party and Esteban Hurtado. 2021. Musical improvisation enhances interpersonal coordination in subsequent conversation: Motor and speech evidence. *PLoS ONE* 16(4), e0250166.

Robledo Del Canto, J. P., Sarah Hawkins, Ian Cross and Richard Ogden. 2016. Pitch-interval analysis of periodic and aperiodic question+answer pairs. *Speech prosody 2016*: 1071–5.

Rose, Deborah Bird. 1996. *Nourishing terrains: Australian Aboriginal views of landscape and wilderness.* Canberra: Australian Heritage Commission.

Rosenblum, Daisy. 2021. Virtual visits: Indigenous language reclamation during a pandemic. *Globe and Mail* (Canada), 15 March. https://rsc-src.ca/en/voices/virtual-visits-indigenous-language-reclamation-during-pandemic

Ross, Alexander, Donald Pwerle and Terry Whitebeach. 2007. *The versatile man: the life and times of Don Ross, Kaytetye stockman.* Alice Springs, NT: IAD Press.

Rostron, Tara in conversation with Jodie Kell, 24 June 2022. Audio interview and transcript available as JK1-LS003-01 at http://catalog.paradisec.org.au/collections/JK1/items/LS003.

Rostron, Victor. 2021. *Marraradj* (Wildfire Manwurrk). Song. https://open.spotify.com/track/20AV1DvKp0aakU4PJ0B4Nm?si=f7fd80657c2c4321.

Rouget, Gilbert. 1980. *La musique et la transe. Esquisse d'une théorie générale des relations de la musique et de la possession.* Paris: Gallimard.

Rousseau, Jean-Jacques. 1998 [1767]. *Dictionnaire de musique.* Reprint. Genève, Switzerland: Minkoff.

Rumsey, Alan. 1994. On the transitivity of "say" constructions in Bunuba. *Australian journal of linguistics* 14(2): 137–53. https://doi.org/10.1080/07268609408599507.

Rumsey, Alan and Don Niles. 2011. *Sung tales from the Papua New Guinea Highlands: Studies in form, meaning, and sociocultural context*. Canberra: ANU Press. http://press.anu.edu.au?p=145421.

Ryan, Trevor. 2022. Keniny Kaadadijiny: Restoring and developing dance for Noongar Boodjar. Master's thesis, Edith Cowan University, Perth.

Śākya, Jogamān and Dharmaratna Śākya. 1997. *Dāphā bhajanayā rāg tathā gvārā myẽ va cālī myẽyā rūparekhā (Outline of the rāgs, gvārā songs and cālī songs of dāphā devotional singing)*. Lalitpur, Nepal: Hiraṇyavarṇa Mahāvihāra.

Śākya, Kirtimān and Śākya, Jogamān. 1988. *Jhīgu bājā jhīgu saṃskriti (dāphā bhajanayā gvārā saṃgraha) (Our music, our culture: A collection of gvārā of dāphā devotional singing)*. Lalitpur, Nepal: Hiraṇya Varṇa Mahāvihāra.

Sandhall, Roger and Nicolas Peterson. 1969. *A Walbiri Fire Ceremony, Ngatjakula* [motion picture]. Canberra: Australia Institute for Aboriginal Studies.

Sansom, Basi. 2001. Irruptions of the Dreamings in post-colonial Australia. *Oceania* 72(1): 1–32.

Scheff, Thomas J. 2011. *What's love got to do with it? Emotions and relationships in pop songs*. London: Routledge.

Schenker, Heinrich. 1994–1997. *The masterwork in music: A yearbook*. Edited by William Drabkin, translated by Ian Bent et al. Cambridge: Cambridge University Press.

Schippers, Huib and Catherine Grant. 2016. *Sustainable futures for music cultures: An ecological perspective*. Oxford: Oxford University Press.

Schneider, Marius. 1964. Kriterien zur Melodiegestalt. In Horst Heussner, ed. *Festschrift H. Engel*, 331–4. Kassel, Germany: Bärenreiter.

Schroeter, Ronald and Nick Thieberger. 2006. EOPAS, the EthnoER online representation of interlinear text. In Linda Barwick and Nick Thieberger, eds. *Sustainable data from digital fieldwork*, 99–124. Sydney: Sydney University Press.

Schubert, Peter. 1994. Authentic analysis. *Journal of musicology* 12(1): 3–18.

Schuiling, Floris. 2019. Notation cultures: Towards an ethnomusicology of notation. *Journal of the Royal Musical Association* 144(2): 429–58.

Schwab, Jerry. 2006. *Final report to the Warlpiri Education and Training Trust Advisory Committee: Options for education and training*. Canberra: ANU.

Seeger, Anthony. 2004. Traditional music ownership in a commodified world. In Simon Frith and Lee Marshall, eds. *Music and copyright*, 157–70. Edinburgh: Edinburgh University Press.

Seeger, Anthony. 2019. Archives, repatriation, and the challenges ahead. In Frank Gunderson, Robert C. Lancefield and Bret D. Woods, eds. *The Oxford handbook of musical repatriation*, 145–60. Oxford and New York: Oxford University Press.

Seeger, Anthony. 1987. *Why Suyá sing: A musical anthropology of an Amazonian people*. Cambridge: Cambridge University Press.

Seeger, Anthony. 1986. Oratory is spoken, myth is told, and song is sung, but they are all music to my ears. In Joel Sherzer and Greg Urban, eds. *Native South American discourse*, 59–82. Berlin: Mouton-de Gruyter.

Seeger, Charles. 1958. Prescriptive and descriptive music-writing. *Musical quarterly* 44(2): 184–95.

Seligman, C.G. 1910. *The Melanesians of British New Guinea*. Cambridge: Cambridge University Press.

Senft, Gunther. 2009. Phatic communion. In Gunther Senft, Jan-Ola Östman and Jef Verschueren, eds. *Culture and language use*, 226–33. Amsterdam: John Benjamins.

Senft, Gunther. 2018. Theory meets practice – H. Paul Grice's maxims of quality and manner and the Trobriand Islanders' language use. In Alessandro Capone, Marco Carapezza and Franco Lo Piparo, eds. *Further advances in pragmatics and philosophy: Part 1 from theory to practice*, 203–20. Cham, Switzerland: Springer International Publishing.

Senior, A. Kate, Janet Helmer and Richard Chenhall. 2017. "As long as he's coming home to me": Vulnerability, jealousy and violence in young people's relationships in remote, rural and regional Australia. *Health Sociology Review* 26(2): 204–18.

Shayan, Shakila, Ozge Ozturk and Mark A. Sicoli. 2011. The thickness of pitch: Crossmodal metaphors in Farsi, Turkish, and Zapotec. *Senses and Society* 6(1): 96–105. https://doi.org/10.2752/174589311X12893982233911.

Shelemay, Kay Kaufmann, ed. 1990. *Cross-cultural musical analysis. Vol. V. The Garland Library of readings in ethnomusicology*. New York and London: Garland Publishing.

Si, Aung. 2016. *The traditional ecological knowledge of the Solega: A linguistic perspective*. Cham, Switzerland: Springer International Publishing.

Sievers, Beau, Larry Polansky, Michael Casey and Thalia Wheatley. 2013. Music and movement share a dynamic structure that supports universal expressions of emotion. *Proceedings of the National Academy of Sciences* 110(1): 70–5.

Singer, Ruth and Salome Harris. 2016. What practices and ideologies support small-scale multilingualism? A case study of Warruwi community, northern Australia. *International journal of the sociology of language* 241: 163–208.

Sleeper, Morgan and Griselda Reyes Basurto. 2022. Musicolinguistic documentation: Tone and tune in Tlahuapa Tù'un Sàví songs. *Language documentation and conservation* 16: 168–208.

Slobin, Mark. 2011. *Folk music: A very short introduction*. Oxford: Oxford University Press.

Sloggett, Robyn, and Lyndon Ormond-Parker. 2013. Crashes along the superhighway: The information continuum. In Lyndon Ormond-Parker, Aaron Corn, Cressida Fforde, Kazuko Obata and Sandy O'Sullivan, eds. *Information technology and Indigenous communities*, 227–46. Canberra: AIATSIS Research Publications.

Small, Christopher. 1996. *Music, society, education*. Hanover, NH: University Press of New England.

Smith, Linda Tuhiwai. 1999. *Decolonizing methodologies: Research and Indigenous peoples*. London: Zed Books.

Smith, Graeme and Judith Brett. 1998. Nation, authenticity and social difference in Australian popular music: Folk, country, multicultural. *Journal of Australian studies* 58: 3–17.

Solly, Meilan. 2019. Around 2,000 artifacts have been saved from the ruins of Brazil's National Museum Fire. Smithsonian Magazine, 15 February. https://www.smithsonianmag.com/smart-news/around-2000-artifacts-have-been-saved-ruins-brazils-national-museum-fire-180971510.

Sorce Keller, Marcello. 2021. Why should we listen to the music we do not like . . . and put our lives on the line. In Juliane Brandes, Moritz Heffter, Sarah Platte and Meinrad Walter, eds. *Klang und bedeutung: Diskurse über musik zur emeritierung von Joseh Williman*, 433–44. Hildesheim, Germany: Georg Olms Verlag.

Sorce Keller, Marcello. 2012. *What makes music European – looking beyond sound*. Lanham, MD: Scarecrow Press.

Sorce Keller, Marcello. 2010. Was ist Musik? Einige Gründe dafür, warum wir die "Musik" nicht mehr als "Musik" bezeichnen sollten. *Schweizer jahrbuch für musikwissenschaft* 30: 11–26.

Sorce Keller, Marcello. 2001. Why do we misunderstand today the music of all times and places, and why do we enjoy doing so. In Barbara Haggh, ed. *Essays on music and culture in honor of Herbert Kellman*, 567–74. Paris-Tours: Minerve.

Sorce Keller, Marcello. 1990. "Gesunkenes Kulturgut" and Neapolitan songs: Verdi, Donizetti and the folk and popular traditions. In A. Pompilio, ed. *Proceedings of the International Musicological Society*, 401–5. Turin, Italy: EDT.

Sorce Keller, Marcello. 1984. The problem of classification in folksong research: A short history. *Folklore* 95(1): 100–4.

Sowa, Remigiusz, Anna Sowa and Richard Widdess. 2021. Film: *Gūlā: music for a sacred time*. Director: Remigiusz Sowa. Producer: Anna Sowa. Chouette Films. https://vimeo.com/chouettefilms/review/463037781/527fdc7cd7.

Sparling, Heather, Peter MacIntyre and Susan Baker. 2022. Motivating traditional musicians to learn a heritage language in Gaelic Nova Scotia. *Ethnomusicology* 66(1): 157–81.

Sperber, Dan, and Deidre Wilson. 1986. *Relevance: Communication and cognition*. Oxford: Blackwell.

Spitzer, Nicholas R., Roger D. Abrahams, Robert Cantwell, Gerald L. Davis, Archie Green, Jim Griffith et al. 2007. Cultural conversation: Metaphors and methods in public folklore. In Robert Baron and Nick Spitzer, eds. *Public folklore*, 77–104. Jackson, MS: University Press of Mississippi.

Stanner, W.E.H. 1989 [1963/1966]. *On Aboriginal religion*. Oceania Monograph no. 36. Sydney: Oceania Publications.

Stock, Jonathan. 1993. The application of Schenkerian analysis to ethnomusicology: Problems and possibilities. *Music analysis* 12(2): 215–240.

Stockhausen, Karlheinz. 1957. . . . wie die Zeit vergeht . . . *Die Reihe* 3: 13–42.

Stokes, M. (2004). Music and the global order. *Annual review of anthropology* 33(1): 47–72.

Strehlow, T.G.H. 1971. *Songs of Central Australia*. Sydney: Angus & Robertson.

Strelein, Lisa, 2013. Native Title bodies corporate in the Torres Strait: Finding a place in the governance of a region. In Toni Bauman, Lisa M. Strelein and Jessica K. Weir, eds. *Living with Native Title: The experiences of registered Native Title corporations*, 65–111. Canberra: AIATSIS Research Publications.

Stubington, Jill. 2007. *Singing the land: The power of performance in Aboriginal life*. Sydney: Currency House Inc.

Stubington, Jill, and Peter Dunbar-Hall. 1994. Yothu Yindi's "Treaty": Ganma in music. *Popular Music* 13(3): 243–59.

Stubington, Jill. 1978. *Yolngu Manikay: Modern performances of Australian Aboriginal clan songs*. Melbourne: Monash University.

Suppan, Wolfgang, Wiegand Stief and Hartmut Braun, eds. 1976–83. *Melodietypen des deutschen volksliedes*, 4 vols. Tutzing, Germany.

Sutton, Peter. 1987. Mystery and change. In Margaret Clunies Ross, Tamsin Donaldson and Stephen Wild, eds. *Songs of Aboriginal Australia*, 77–96. Sydney: Oceania Publications.

Swain, Tony. 1993. *A place for strangers: Towards a history of Australian Aboriginal being*. Cambridge: Cambridge University Press.

Swarbrick, D., D. Bosnyak, S.R. Livingstone, J. Bansal, S. Marsh-Rollo, M.H. Woolhouse et al. 2019. How live music moves us: Head movement differences in audiences to live versus recorded music. *Frontiers in psychology* 9: 2682.

Szabolcsi, Bence. 1943. Five-tone scale and civilization. *Acta Musicologica* 15(1–4): 24–34.

Tamisari, Franca. 1998. Body, vision and movement: In the footprints of the ancestors. *Oceania* 68(4): 249–70.

Tamminen, Jakke, Kathleen Rastle, Jess Darby, Rebecca Lucas and Victoria J. Williamson. 2017. The impact of music on learning and consolidation of novel words. *Memory* 25(1): 107–21.

Tāmrakār, Govinda. 2017. *Śrī śrī Siddhinarasiṃha Malla Rājājuyā pragyātagu 32 pu mye* (32 celebrated songs of King Siddhinarasiṃha Malla). Lalitpur, Nepal: author.

Tāmrakār, Govinda. 2002. *Dāphā bhajanyā mye munā* (Collection of dāphā songs). Lalitpur, Nepal: author.

Tarr, Bronwyn, Jacques Launay and Robin Dunbar. 2016. Silent disco: Dancing in synchrony leads to elevated pain thresholds and social closeness. *Evolution and human behavior* 37(5): 343–9.

Tasman, Maxwell Walma Japanangka and Carmel O'Shannessy. 2020. *Kajawarnu-jangka "From the bush"*. NT: PAW Media and Canberra: ANU.

Tatz, Colin. 1999. Genocide in Australia. *Journal of genocide research* 1(3): 315–52.

Taylor, Hollis. 2008. Decoding the song of the pied butcherbird: An initial survey. *Transcultural music review* 12: 1–30.

Temu, Deveni 2003. Nurturing cultural identity. *Meanjin* 62(3): 144–152.

Temu, Deveni. 1981. Extending school library and community information services to a scattered population: Papua New Guinea. *IFLA Journal* 7(3): 232–41. https://doi.org/10.1177/034003528100700305.

Temu, Deveni, Prue Ahrens and Sioana Faupula. 2009. Stories of the sea: Travellers across the Pacific. *National Museum of Australia*, 16 September. https://www.nma.gov.au/audio/vaka-moana-series/transcripts/stories-of-the-sea-travellers.

Temu, Deveni in conversation with Amanda Harris and Steven Gagau, 2 June 2022, Australian National University, Canberra. Archived as part of TCT1–11 at PARADISEC. https://dx.doi.org/10.26278/HMTN-FF43.

Tenopir, Carol, Suzie Allard, Kimberly Douglass, Arsev Umur Aydinoglu, Lei Wu, Eleanor Read et al. 2011. Data sharing by scientists: Practices and perceptions. *PLoS ONE* 6(6): e21101. https://doi.org/10.1371/journal.pone.0021101.

Teo, Hsu-Ming. 2017a. Introduction: The popular culture of romantic love in Australia. In Hsu-Ming Teo, ed. *The popular culture of romantic love in Australia*, 1–38. Melbourne: Australian Scholarly Publishing.

Teo, Hsu-Ming, ed. 2017b. *The popular culture of romantic love in Australia*. Melbourne: Australian Scholarly Publishing.

Thieberger Nick. 2020. Technology in support of languages of the Pacific: Neo-colonial or post-colonial? *Asian-European music research journal* 5–3: 17–24. https://doi.org/10.30819/aemr.5-3.

Thieberger, Nick. 2017. LD&C possibilities for the next decade. *Language documentation and conservation* 11: 1–4.

Thieberger, Nick. 2004. Documentation in practice: Developing a linked media corpus of South Efate. *Language documentation and description* 2: 169–178. https://doi.org/10.25894/ldd298.

Thieberger, Nick and Linda Barwick. 2012. Keeping records of language diversity in Melanesia: The Pacific and Regional Archive for Digital Sources in Endangered Cultures (PARADISEC). In Nicholas Evans and Marian Klamer, eds. *Melanesian languages on the edge of Asia: Challenges for the 21st century*, 239–53. Honolulu: University of Hawai'i Press.

Thieberger, Nick, Amanda Harris and Linda Barwick. 2015. PARADISEC: Its history and future. In Amanda Harris, Nick Thieberger and Linda Barwick, eds. *Research, records and responsibility: Ten years of PARADISEC*, 1–15. Sydney: Sydney University Press.

Thieberger, Nick and Michel Jacobson. 2010. Sharing data in small and endangered languages: Cataloging and metadata, formats and encodings. In Lenore Grenoble and Louanna Furbee, eds. *Language Documentation: Practice and values*, 147–58. Amsterdam: Benjamins.

Thomas, Rachel. 2023. "Waláya". Self-released by Ripple Effect Band. Australia. https://www.youtube.com/channel/UCs0UygrnqKj6FrAkFejKGew. Also available as JK1-W002 at https://catalog.paradisec.org.au/collections/JK1/items/W002.

Thompson, David and Michael Connolly. 2006. Clapsticks and karaoke: The melting pot of Indigenous identity. *Pacifica* 19(3): 344–55.

Thorner, Sabra, Linda Rive, John Dallwitz and Janet Inyika. 2019. Never giving up: Negotiation, culture-making, and the infinity of the archive. In Linda Barwick, Jennifer Green and Petronella Vaarzon-Morel, eds. *Archival returns: Central Australia and beyond*, 263–84. *Language documentation and conservation special publication* 18. Honolulu and Sydney: University of Hawai'i Press and Sydney University Press. https://hdl.handle.net/10125/64640.

Thornton, Thomas, Mary Rudolph, William Geiger and Amy Starbard. 2019. A song remembered in place: Tlingit composer Mary Sheakley (Loo) and Huna Tlingits in Glacier Bay National Park, Alaska. *Journal of ethnobiology* 39(3): 392–408.

Thorpe, Kirsten, Shannon Faulkhead and Lauren Booker. 2020. Transforming the archive: Returning and connecting Indigenous repatriation records. In Cressida Fforde, C. Timothy McKeown and Honor Keeler, eds. *The Routledge companion to Indigenous repatriation: Return, reconcile, renew*, 822–34. Abingdon, UK: Routledge.

Tiersot, Julien. 1889. *Musiques pittoresques: Promenades musicales a l'Exposition de 1889*. Paris: Librairie Fischbacher.

Tindale, Norman. 1968. Discussion with Murray Newman. AIATSIS Audiovisual Archive, tape recording. TINDALE_N08. Canberra.

Tindale, Norman. 1966–1968. Site information, songs, cultural discussions from south-west WA. AIATSIS Audiovisual Archive, tape recording. TINDALE_N07. Canberra.

Titon, Jeff Todd. 2020. Music and sustainability: An ecological viewpoint. In *Toward a sound ecology: New and selected essays*, 152–70. Bloomington: Indiana University Press.

Titon, Jeff Todd. 2009. Music and sustainability: An ecological viewpoint. *World of music* 51(1 "Music and Sustainability"): 119–37.

Titon, Jeff Todd. 2016. Sustainability, resilience, and adaptive management for applied ethnomusicology. In Svanibor Pettan and Jeff Todd Titon, eds. *The Oxford handbook of applied ethnomusicology*. New York: Oxford University Press.

Toner, Peter G. 2007. The gestation of cross-cultural music research and the birth of ethnomusicology. *Humanities research* 14(1): 85–110.

Torres Strait Regional Authority. 2016. *Land and sea management strategy for Torres Strait 2016–2036*. Report prepared by the Land and Sea Management Unit, Torres Strait Regional Authority. https://www.tsra.gov.au/__data/assets/pdf_file/0019/11782/TSRA-Land-and-Sea-Strategy-2016-2036-FINAL-WEB-VERSION.pdf

Torres Strait Regional Authority. n.d. Culture art and heritage: Program overview. *TSRA*. https://www.tsra.gov.au/the-tsra/programmes/culture-arts-and-heritage.

Torwali, Mujahid and Troy, Jakelin. 2021. Saving Torwali music and dance: Community led performance and "public" archiving. *Preservation, digital technology and culture* 50(3–4): 151–63.

Treloyn, Sally. 2022. Intergenerational knowledges: Change and continuity in music transmission and ethnomusicological praxis. *Music research annual* 3: 1–27.

Treloyn, Sally. 2017. Singing with a distinctive voice: Comparative musical analysis and the central Australian musical style in the Kimberley. In Kirsty Gillespie, Sally Treloyn and Don Niles, eds. *A distinctive voice in the antipodes: Essays in honour of Stephen A. Wild*, 147–69. Canberra: ANU Press.

Treloyn, Sally. 2016. Music in culture, music as culture, music interculturally: Reflections on the development and challenges of ethnomusicological research in Australia. *Voices: A world forum for music therapy* 16(2).

Treloyn, Sally. 2007. Flesh with country: Juxtaposition and minimal contrast in the construction and melodic treatment of jadmi song texts. *Australian Aboriginal studies* 2007(2): 90–9.

Treloyn, Sally. 2006. Songs that pull: Jadmi junba from the Kimberley region of northwest Australia. PhD thesis, University of Sydney.

Treloyn, Sally. 2003. Scotty Martin's Jadmi Junba: A song series from the Kimberley region of northwest Australia. *Oceania* 73: 208–20.

Treloyn, Sally, and Rona Goonginda Charles. 2021. Music endangerment, repatriation and intercultural collaboration in an Australian discomfort zone. In Beverley Diamond and Salwa El-Shawan Castelo-Branco, eds. *Transforming ethnomusicology*, vol. II: *Political, social and ecological issues*. Online edn, Oxford Academic. https://doi.org/10.1093/oso/9780197517550.003.0009.

Treloyn, Sally, Rona Goognida Charles and Sherika Nulgit. 2013. Repatriation of song materials to support intergenerational transmission of knowledge about language in the Kimberley region of northwest Australia. In Mary Jane Norris, ed. *Endangered languages beyond boundaries: Proceedings of the 17th Foundation for Endangered Languages*, 18–24. Ottawa: Foundation for Endangered Languages.

Treloyn, Sally and Andrew Morumburri Dowding. 2017. Thabi returns: The use of digital resources to recirculate and revitalise Thabi songs in the western Pilbara. In Jim Wafer and Myfany Turpin, eds. *Recirculating songs: Revitalising the singing practices of Indigenous Australia*, 58–68. Canberra: Asia-Pacific Linguistics.

Treloyn, Sally and Andrea Emberly. 2013. Sustaining traditions: Ethno-musicological collections, access and sustainability in Australia. *Musicology Australia* 35(2): 159–77.

Treloyn, Sally, Matthew Dembal Martin and Rona Goognida Charles. 2016. Cultural precedents of the repatriation of legacy song records to communities of origin. *Australian Aboriginal studies* 2016(2): 94–103.

Treloyn, Sally, Matthew Dembal Martin and Rona Googninda Charles. 2019. Moving songs: Repatriating audiovisual recordings of Aboriginal Australian dance and song (Kimberley Region, northwestern Australia). In Frank Gunderson, Robert C. Lancefield and Bret D. Woods, eds. *The Oxford handbook of musical repatriation*, 591–606. Oxford and New York: Oxford University Press.

Troutman, John William. 2016. *Kīkā Kila: How the Hawaiian steel guitar changed the sound of modern music*. Chapel Hill, NC: University of North Carolina Press.

Troy, Jakelin. 2023. Standing on the ground and writing on the sky: An Indigenous exploration of place, time and histories. In Ann McGrath, Laura Rademaker and Jakelin Troy, eds. *Everywhen: Australia and the language of deep history*, 37–56. Lincoln: University of Nebraska Press and the American Philosophical Society.

Troy, Jakelin. 2020. Walking, sketching and dogs: Autoethnography in the time of fire and Rona. In Sydney University Alumni, staff and students. *Earth cries: A climate change anthology*, 34–8. Sydney: Sydney University Press.

Troy, Jakelin. 2019[1993]. *The Sydney language*. Canberra: Aboriginal Studies Press.

Troy, Jakelin. 1991. "Der mary this is fine cuntry is there is in the wourld": Irish-English and Irish in late eighteenth and nineteenth century Australia. In John B. O'Brien and Pauric Travers, eds. *The Irish emigrant experience in Australia*, 148–80. Dublin: Poolbeg.

Troy, Jakelin and Linda Barwick. 2020. Claiming the "Song of the women of the Menero tribe". *Musicology Australia* 43(2): 85–107. http://doi.org/10.1080/08145857.2020.1945254.

Tschacher, Wolfgang, Steven Greenwood, Sekhar Ramakrishnan, Martin Tröndle, Melanie Wald-Fuhrmann, Christoph Seibert et al. 2021. Physiological synchrony in audiences of live concerts. *Psychology of aesthetics, creativity, and the arts* 17(2).

Tuck, Eve, and Rubén Gaztambide-Fernández. 2013. Curriculum, replacement, and settler futurity. *Journal of curriculum theorising* 29(1): 72–89.

Turino, Thomas. 2008. *Music as social life: The politics of participation*. London: University of Chicago Press.

Turner, Victor. 1969. *The ritual process: Structure and anti-structure*. Chicago: Aldine Publishing.

Turpin, Myfany. 2018. Traditional Aboriginal songs: From digital files to living culture. *Australasian sound archive* 42: 27–43.

Turpin, Myfany. 2017a. Finding Arrernte songs. In Jim Wafer and Myfany Turpin, eds. *Recirculating songs: Revitalising the singing practices of Indigenous Australia*, 90–102. Hamilton, NSW : Hunter Press.

Turpin, Myfany. 2017b. Parallelism in Arandic song-poetry. *Oral tradition* 31(2): 535–60.

Turpin, Myfany. 2015. Alyawarr women's song-poetry of central Australia. *Australian Aboriginal studies* 2015(1): 66–96.

Turpin, Myfany. 2013. Semantic extension in Kaytetye flora and fauna terms. *Australian journal of linguistics* 33(4): 488–518.

Turpin, Myfany. 2007. Artfully hidden: Text and rhythm in a central Australian Aboriginal song series. *Musicology Australia* 29: 93–108.

Turpin, Myfany. 2005. Form and meaning of Akwelye: A Kaytetye women's song series from central Australia. PhD thesis, University of Sydney.

Turpin, Myfany, April Pengart Campbell, Catherine Ingram, Meifang Wu, Meifang, Pinxian Wu et al. 2017. *Songs of home: Anmatyerr and Kam singing traditions*. Batchelor, NT: Batchelor Institute Press.

Turpin, Myfany and Nigel Fabb. 2017. Brilliance as cognitive complexity in Aboriginal Australia. *Oceania* 87(2): 209–30.

Turpin, Myfany and Jennifer Green. 2018. Rapikwenty: "A loner in the ashes" and other songs for sleeping. *Studia metrica et poetica* 5(1): 52–80.

Turpin, Myfany and Lana Henderson. 2015. Tools for analyzing verbal art in the field. *Language documentation and conservation* 9: 89–109.

Turpin, Myfany and Mary Laughren. 2013. Edge effects in Warlpiri Yawulyu songs: Resyllabification, epenthesis and final vowel modification. *Australian journal of linguistics* 33(4): 399–425.

Turpin, Myfany and Felicity Meakins. 2019. *Songs from the stations: Wajarra as sung by Ronnie Wavehill Wirrpnga, Topsy Dodd Ngarnjal and Dandy Danbayarri at Kalkaringi*. Sydney: Sydney University Press.

Turpin, Myfany and Alison Ross. 2013. *Antarrengeny Awely. Alyawarr women's traditional songs of Antarrengeny country*. Batchelor, NT: Batchelor Institute Press.

Turpin, Myfany and Alison Ross. 2012. *Kaytetye to English dictionary*. Alice Springs, NT: IAD Press.

Turpin, Myfany, and Alison Ross. 2004. *Awelye Akwelye: Kaytetye women's songs from Arnerre, central Australia*. Tennant Creek: Papulu Apparr-kari Language and Culture Centre.

Turpin, Myfany and Alison Ross. 2003. *Growing up Kaytetye*. Stories by Tommy Kngwarraye Thompson. Alice Springs, NT: IAD Press.

Turpin, Myfany, Alison Ross, Veronica Dobson and Margaret Kemarr Turner. 2013. The spotted nightjar calls when dingo pups are born: Ecological and social indicators in central Australia. *Journal of ethnobiology* 33(1): 7–32.

Turpin, Myfany and Tonya Stebbins. 2010. The language of song: Some recent approaches in description and analysis. *Australian journal of linguistics* 30(1): 1–17.

Turpin, Myfany, Calista Yeoh and Clint Bracknell. 2020. Wanji-wanji: The past and future of an Aboriginal travelling song. *Musicology Australia* 42(2): 123–47.

Tuttle, Jan-Olof and Håkan Lundström. 2022. Athabascan vocal genres in Interior Alaska. In Håkan Lundström and Jan-Olof Svantesson, eds. *In the borderland between song and speech vocal expressions in oral cultures*, 123–88. Lund, Sweden: Lund University Press/Manchester University Press.

Tuzin, Donald F. 1992. The Melanesian archive. In Sydel Silverman and Nancy J. Parezo, eds. *Preserving the anthropological record*, 23–34. New York: Wenner-Gren Foundation for Anthropological Research.

United Nations, Office of the High Commissioner for Human Rights. 2022. Australia violated Torres Strait Islanders' rights to enjoy culture and family life, UN Committee finds. Press release, 23 September. *United Nations Office of the High Commissioner for Human Rights*. https://www.ohchr.org/en/press-releases/2022/09/australia-violated-torres-strait-islanders-rights-enjoy-culture-and-family.

Vaarzon-Morel, Petronella. 2021. The silence of the donkeys: Sensorial entanglements between people and animals at Willowra and beyond. *Australian journal of anthropology* 32(S1): 114–31.

Vaarzon-Morel, Petronella, Linda Barwick and Jennifer Green. 2021. Sharing and storing digital cultural records in central Australian Indigenous communities. *New media and society* 23(4): 692–714.

Valiquette, Hilaire. 1993. *A basic Kukatja to English dictionary*. Wirrimanu (Balgo) WA: Luurnpa Catholic School.

Vallier, John. 2012. Archives, sound recording and moving image. *Grove music online*. https://www.oxfordmusiconline.com/grovemusic/view/10.1093/gmo/9781561592630.001.0001/omo-9781561592630-e-1002227217.

van Ham, Peter and Aglaja Stirn. 2004. *Naga – Songs from the Mist*. Frankfurt: Stirn and van Ham Archives. CD and booklet of 22 pages.

Van Heekeren, Deborah. 2017. Searching for fish names with the Vula'a of Papua New Guinea. *History and anthropology* 28(5): 605–29.

Van Heekeren, Deborah. 2012. *The shark warrior of Alewai: A phenomenology of Melanesian identity*. Wantage, UK: Sean Kingston.

Van Heekeren, Deborah. 2011. Singing it "local": The appropriation of Christianity in the Vula'a villages of Papua New Guinea. *Asia Pacific journal of anthropology* 12(1): 44–59.

Van Puyvelde, Martine, Gerrit Loots, Lobcke Gillisjans, Nathalie Pattyn and Carmen Quintana. 2015. A cross-cultural comparison of tonal synchrony and pitch imitation in the vocal dialogs of Belgian Flemish-speaking and Mexican Spanish-speaking mother–infant dyads. *Infant behavior and development* 40: 41–53.

Vatsyayan, Kapila. 1987. *Traditions of Indian folk dance*, 2nd enlarged and rev. ed. New Delhi: Clarion Books.

Vaughan, Jill. 2018. "We talk in saltwater words": Dimensionalisation of dialectal variation in multilingual Arnhem Land. *Language and communication* 62: 119–32.

Vaughan, Jill. 2018. Meet the remote Indigenous community where a few thousand people use 15 different languages. *The Conversation*, 5 December. https://theconversation.com/meet-the-remote-indigenous-community-where-a-few-thousand-people-use-15-different-languages.

Villepastour, Amanda. 2014. Talking tones and singing speech among the Yorùbá of southwest Nigeria. *Jahrbuch des Phonogrammarchivs der Österreichischen Akademie der Wissenschaften*, 44: 29–47. Göttingen, Germany: Cuvillier Verlag.

Vitebsky, Piers. 1993. *Dialogues with the dead: The discussion of mortality among the Sora of eastern India*. Cambridge: Cambridge University Press.

von Brandenstein, Carl Georg. 1971–1976. Songs and narratives from Western Australia and New South Wales. AIATSIS Audiovisual Archive, tape recording. VON-BRANDENSTEIN_C05. Canberra.

von Brandenstein, Carl Georg. 1967–1970. Sound recordings collected by Carl Von Brandenstein. AIATSIS Audiovisual Archive, tape recording. VON-BRANDENSTEIN_C04. Canberra.

von Sturmer, John. 1989. Aborigines, representation, necrophilia. *Art and text* 32: 127–39.

von Sturmer, John. 1987. Aboriginal singing and notions of power. In Margaret Clunies Ross, Tamsin Donaldson and Stephen Aubrey Wild, eds. *Songs of Aboriginal Australia,* 63–76. Sydney: University of Sydney.

Vuoskoski, Jonna K., Eric F. Clarke and Tia DeNora. 2016. Music listening evokes implicit affiliation. *Psychology of music* 45(4): 584–99.

Wachsmann, K.P. 1971. Universal perspectives in music. *Ethnomusicology* 15(3): 381–84.

Wafer, James and Myfany Turpin, eds. 2017. *Recirculating songs: Revitalising the singing practices of Indigenous Australia*. Canberra: Pacific Linguistics.

Wallam, Angus, Suzanne Kelly and Norma MacDonald. 2004. *Corroboree*. Perth: Cygnet Books.

Walsh, Michael. 2010. A polytropical approach to the "Floating Pelican" song: An exercise in rich interpretation of a Murriny Patha (Northern Australia) song. *Australian journal of linguistics* 30(1): 117–30.

Walsh, Michael. 2007. Australian Aboriginal song language: So many questions, so little to work with. *Australian Aboriginal studies* 2007(2): 128–44.

Walsh, Michael, Linda Barwick and Allan Marett. 2011. Archiving language and song in Wadeye: Future access to song knowledge. *2nd International Conference on Language Documentation and Conservation (ICLDC)*. Honolulu: University of Hawai'i.

Warlpiri women from Yuendumu. 2017. *Yurntumu-wardingki juju-ngaliya-kurlangu yawulyu: Warlpiri women's songs from Yuendumu* (with accompanying DVD). Batchelor, NT: Batchelor Institute Press.

Watkins, Lee, Elijah Madiba and Boudina McConnachie. 2021. Rethinking the decolonial moment through collaborative practices at the International Library of African Music (ILAM), South Africa. *Ethnomusicology forum* 30(1): 20–39.

Webb, Michael. 2015. Heart, spirit and understanding: Protestant hymnody as an agent of transformation in Melanesia, 1840s–1940s. *Journal of Pacific history* 50(3): 275–303.

Weber, Ernst and Yehudah L. Werner. 1977. Vocalisations of two snake-lizards (Reptilia: Sauria: Pygopodidae). *Herpetologica* 33(3): 353–63.

Wegner, Gert-Matthias. 2023. *Drumming in Bhaktapur: Music of the Newar people of Nepal*. Heidelberg, Germany: Documenta Nepalica.

Wegner, Gert-Matthias. 2009. Music in urban space: Newar Buddhist processional music in the Kathmandu Valley. In Richard K. Wolf, ed. *Theorizing the local: Music, practice, and experience in South Asia and beyond*, 113–40. New York: Oxford University Press.

Wegner, Gert-Matthias. 1986. *The dhimaybājā of Bhaktapur*. Wiesbaden, Germany: Franz Steiner.

Wei, Xiaoshi. 2018. Archiving the nation: History and current practices of sound archives in China. PhD thesis, Indiana University.

Were, Graeme. 2015. Digital heritage in a Melanesian context: Authenticity, integrity and ancestrality from the other side of the digital divide. *International Journal of heritage studies* 21(2): 153–65.

West, LaMont. 1963. *Arnhem Land popular classics*. Wattle D-5, Wattle Ethnic Series No. 3. New York, LP disc recording.

White-Radhakrishnan, Georgia Curran and Arian Pearson. 2021. The value of music. *Music!Dance!Culture!* podcast, Episode 1, Part 1. Australia: Spotify and Apple Podcasts. Curated by Mahesh White-Radhakrishnan and Georgia Curran.

Widdess, Richard. 2013. *Dāphā: Sacred singing in a South Asian city. Music, performance and meaning in Bhaktapur, Nepal.* London: Ashgate.

Widdess, Richard. 2019. Time changes: Heterometric music in South Asia. In C. Hasty and R. Wolf, eds. *Thought and play in musical rhythm: Asian, African, and Euro-American perspectives*, 273–313. Oxford: Oxford University Press.

Widdess, Richard and Nutandhar Sharma. 2024. Singing histories: A comparative survey of devotional singing groups (dāphā) in the Kathmandu Valley, Nepal (Data repository). *OSF*. April 21. https://osf.io/6tv72/?view_only=11a30687d1a64e2ea300365886eb314e.

Wiessner, Polly W. 2014. Embers of society: Firelight talk among the Ju/'hoansi Bushmen. *Proceedings of the National Academy of Sciences* 111(39): 14027–35.

Wild, Stephen A. 2006. Ethnomusicology down under: A distinctive voice in the Antipodes? *Ethnomusicology* 50(2): 345–52.

Wild, Stephen. 1984. Warlbiri music and culture: Meaning in a central Australia song series. In Jamie C. Kassler and Jill Stubington, eds. *Problems and solutions: Occasional essays in musicology presented to Alice M. Moyle*, 186–203. Sydney: Hale & Iremonger.

Wilson, Shawn. 2008. *Research is ceremony: Indigenous research methods.* Black Point, NS: Fernwood Pub.

Wiora, Walter. 1957. *Europäische Volksmusik und abendländische Tonkunst.* Kassel: Hinnenthal.

Wolfe, Paula. 2020. "A Studio of One's Own" (Wolfe 2012): Self-production, music technology and gender. In Paula Wolfe, ed. *Women in the studio: Creativity, control and gender in popular music sound production*, 93–123. London: Routledge.

Woods, Lesley. 2023. *Something's gotta change: Redefining collaborative linguistic research.* Canberra: ANU Press.

Woolhouse, Matthew, Dan Tidhar and Ian Cross. 2016. Effects on interpersonal memory of dancing in time with others. *Frontiers in psychology* 7.

Wooltorton, Sandra. 1986. Interviews with Cliff Humphries and Hazel Winmar for the Noongar Language and Culture Centre. AIATSIS Audiovisual Archive, tape recording. Canberra.

Wright, Wayne. 2007. Heritage language programs in the era of English-only and No Child Left Behind. *Heritage language journal* 5(1): 1–26.

Xun, Zhou, and Francesca Tarocco. 2007. *Karaoke: The global phenomenon.* London: Reaktion Books.

Yasser, Joseph. 1932 [1975]. *A theory of evolving tonality.* New York: Da Capo Press.

Zuckermann, Ghil'ad. 2020. *Revivalistics: From the genesis of Israeli to language reclamation in Australia and beyond.* New York: Oxford University Press.

www.ingramcontent.com/pod-product-compliance
Lightning Source LLC
Chambersburg PA
CBHW061127010526
44116CB00023B/2990